D1823487

After Brexit

Nazaré da Costa Cabral
José Renato Gonçalves
Nuno Cunha Rodrigues
Editors

After Brexit

Consequences for the European Union

Editors
Nazaré da Costa Cabral
CIDEEFF - School of Law, Univ of Lisbon
University of Lisbon
Lisbon, Portugal

Nuno Cunha Rodrigues
CIDEEFF, University of Lisbon School of
Law - Faculdade de Direito da Universidade
de Lisboa
Alameda da Universidade - Cidade
Universitária
Lisbon, Portugal

José Renato Gonçalves
CIDEEFF, University of Lisbon School of
Law - Faculdade de Direito da Universidade
de Lisboa
Alameda da Universidade - Cidade
Universitária
Lisbon, Portugal

ISBN 978-3-319-66669-3   ISBN 978-3-319-66670-9   (eBook)
https://doi.org/10.1007/978-3-319-66670-9

Library of Congress Control Number: 2017955290

© The Editor(s) (if applicable) and The Author(s) 2017
This work is subject to copyright. All rights are solely and exclusively licensed by the Publisher, whether the whole or part of the material is concerned, specifically the rights of translation, reprinting, reuse of illustrations, recitation, broadcasting, reproduction on microfilms or in any other physical way, and transmission or information storage and retrieval, electronic adaptation, computer software, or by similar or dissimilar methodology now known or hereafter developed.
The use of general descriptive names, registered names, trademarks, service marks, etc. in this publication does not imply, even in the absence of a specific statement, that such names are exempt from the relevant protective laws and regulations and therefore free for general use.
The publisher, the authors and the editors are safe to assume that the advice and information in this book are believed to be true and accurate at the date of publication. Neither the publisher nor the authors or the editors give a warranty, express or implied, with respect to the material contained herein or for any errors or omissions that may have been made. The publisher remains neutral with regard to jurisdictional claims in published maps and institutional affiliations.

Cover Illustration: Andrei Korzhyts / Alamy Stock Photo

Printed on acid-free paper

This Palgrave Macmillan imprint is published by Springer Nature
The registered company is Springer International Publishing AG
The registered company address is: Gewerbestrasse 11, 6330 Cham, Switzerland

Acknowledgments

The editors are grateful to the leading scholars and experts in European affairs that have contributed to the chapters of this book.

Contents

Contributors

Mark Baimbridge is a Senior Lecturer in Economics at the University of Bradford, UK. His main research area is the political economy of European integration focusing on monetary union and the UK-EU relationship. He has published over 40 articles in journals, while his 16 books include: *The Impact of the Euro* (Macmillan, 2000); *Economic and Monetary Union in Europe* (Edward Elgar, 2003); *Current Economic Issues in EU Integration* (Palgrave, 2004); *Implications of the Euro* (Routledge, 2006); *Britain, the Euro and Beyond* (Ashgate, 2008); *The Political Economy of the European Social Model* (Routledge, 2012); *Crisis in the Eurozone* (Palgrave, 2015). During the late 1980s and early 1990s he worked with various think tanks to co-author a series of publications that initiated the critical examination of Britain's membership of the EU, the ideas of which are now central to the current debate.

Samo Bardutzky studied law in Ljubljana and Greifswald. In 2013, he obtained his doctorate from the Faculty of Law of the University of Ljubljana, where he taught Constitutional Law and European Constitutional Law and coordinated a legal clinic for refugees and foreigners. After passing the Slovenian state exam in 2009, he was a legal advisor to the Ministry of Justice of Slovenia. In 2012/2013, he was a Fulbright Research Scholar at the University of Michigan. Since 2013, he works as a Postdoctoral Research Associate at the University of Kent within an ERC-funded project on the role and future of national constitutions in European and global governance. He was also a Teaching Fellow at SOAS, University of London, School of Law, and Visiting Researcher at the

Walter Hallstein Institute for European Constitutional Law at the Humboldt University of Berlin.

Ansgar Belke is a Full Professor of Macroeconomics and Director of the Institute of Business and Economic Studies (IBES) at the University of Duisburg-Essen. Since 2012 he is a (ad personam) Jean Monnet Professor. Moreover, he is a member of the Adjunct Faculty Ruhr Graduate School in Economics (RGS Econ) and visiting professor at the Europa-Institut at Saarland University, Saarbrucken, and the Hertie School of Governance, Berlin. Ansgar Belke was a visiting researcher at the IMF in Washington, DC, CentER Tilburg, CEPS Brussels, IfW Kiel, DIW Berlin and OeNB Vienna. Furthermore, he was Research Director for International Macroeconomics at the German Institute for Economic Research (DIW), Berlin, and now is Research Professor at the Centre for European Policy Studies (CEPS), Brussels. He is President of the European Economics and Finance Society (EEFS) and a member of the "Monetary Expert Panel" of the European Parliament, the Scientific Advisory Council of IAW Tubingen, the Councils of "Arbeitskreis Europäische Integration" (AEI), the "Institut für Europäische Politik" (IEP), the Executive Committee of the International Atlantic Economic Society (IAES) and the Scientific Committee of the International Network for Economic Research (INFER). He is also a Research Fellow of IZA Bonn and CELSI (Bratislava), member of the professional central bank watchers group "ECB Observer", member of the Bureau of European Policy Analysis (BEPA) Visitors Programme of the European Commission, external consultant of DG ECFIN of the European Commission, external consultant of the European Union Committee of the House of Lords (UK) and he successfully conducted research projects on behalf of the German Federal Ministries of Finance and of Labour and Social Affairs. He serves as editor-in-chief of *Credit and Capital Markets—Kredit und Kapital* and *Konjunkturpolitik—Applied Economics Quarterly* and as co-editor of *International Journal of Financial Studies, Empirica, International Economics and Economic Policy, Journal of Economic Studies, Vierteljahreshefte für Wirtschaftsforschung, Aestimatio—The International IEB Journal of Finance, E-conomics* (Kiel Institute for the World Economy), as editor of the book series *Financial and Monetary Policy Studies*, Springer, and as co-editor of the book series *Quantitative Ökonomie*, Eul Verlag. He has published widely in international refereed journals and other outlets and has regular appearances in the printed press and in national as well as international TV broadcasts. He is ranked on the 11th place of the research ranking of the Handelsblatt which incorporates 3600 German-speaking economists. In the worldwide ranking of the largest bibliographic database in economics, IDEAS, he is among the top 1%. He spoke as keynote lecturer at a wide array of conferences, among them in 2010, the "Jeddah Economic Forum", Jeddah/Saudi Arabia; the "Global Economic Forum", Istanbul/Turkey; and the international conference "Policies for Growth and Financial Stability beyond the Crisis – The Scope for Global Cooperation", Mumbai/India; in 2012 the "Asan Plenum" and "The Economist Bellwether Series Conference", both in Seoul/South Korea; in 2014 the "Greek Government Roundtable" in Athens/Greece; and in 2014 as Plenary Speaker of the ECOMOD Conference in Bali/Bank of Indonesia. His main areas of interest are in the fields of international macroeconomics, monetary economics, European integration and applied econometrics.

Annette Bongardt is currently a Visiting Senior Fellow in Political Economy at the European Institute of the London School of Economics and Political Science, London. She has been a Senior and SCR Member at St Antony's College, Oxford University, and a Visiting Fellow at the Robert Schuman Centre for Advanced Studies of the European University Institute (EUI) in Florence. She has been long-standing Professor and Head of European Studies at the Portuguese National Institute for Public Administration and Associate Professor at UFP in Portugal. After receiving her PhD in Economics from the EUI in 1990, she was a Schuman Fellow of the European Commission at CEPS, Assistant Professor (eq.) at the Rotterdam School of Management and Senior Research Fellow at ICER (Turin). She was also a Visiting Professor at the Universities of Aveiro, Pisa, Roma (II) and Victoria, BC, Canada, and Católica, Lisbon, among others, as well as Academic Visitor and consultant of the European Commission.

António Barreto Menezes Cordeiro holds a licentiate degree in Law (2008), from the University of Lisbon, a LLM (2009), from King's College London, and a PhD (2014), from the University of Lisbon. He has worked in varying capacities in other universities, specifically in Germany, Spain, Italy and Brazil. A registered lawyer since 2008 and jurisconsult since 2013. He practiced law at *Cuatrecasas*—Lisbon's Office (2008–2011). He has acted as counsel and arbitrator in national and international arbitrations, since 2014. He has been Professor, since 2013, of the University of Lisbon, where he has taught Civil Law, Securities Law, Banking Law, *Company Law* and Comparative Law, and of the European University (*Laureate Group*), since, 2015, where he has taught Civil Law. He has more than 30 publications, including *Da simulação no Direito civil* (sham transactions), 2014; *Do trust no Direito civil* (trust in civil law), 2014; *Direito dos valores mobiliários*, Vol. I, (securities law), 2015; and *Manual de Direito dos* *valores mobiliários* (securities law for students), 2016. He has sat on the editorial committee of the *Revista de Direito das Sociedades* (*Companies Law Review*), since 2014, and is a founding member of the *Revista de Direito Civil* (*Civil Law Review*), 2014. He is Vice-President of the *Instituto de Direito do Consumo* (Consumer Law Institute), since 2016, and of the *Instituto de Direito Brasileiro* (Brazilian Law Institute), since 2016.

Nazaré da Costa Cabral holds a license degree (1994), a Masters (1998) and a PhD (2007) in law, from Lisbon Law School (Faculdade de Direito, Universidade de Lisboa), and she holds a license degree in economics (2015), from Nova SBE—School of Business and Economics (Universidade Nova de Lisboa). Nazaré is an Associate Professor, in Lisbon Law School, and a principal researcher of the Center for European, Economic, Fiscal and Tax Law Research (CIDEFF) of the same University (Group IV on "Crises, Public Policies, Fiscal Policy and the Euro"). Nazaré is Vice-President of the journal *Revista de Finanças Públicas e Direito Fiscal* (*Public Finances and Tax Law Journal*), published by IDEFF and Almedina Editors. She is also a member of the Executive and Editorial Board of the journal *Concorrência & Regulação* (*Competition & Regulation*), published by the Portuguese Competition Authority, IDEFF and Almedina, and a member of the Editorial Board of the journal *Economia & Segurança Social* (*Economics & Social Security*), published by Diário de Bordo Editores. Nazaré is author of several books, articles and working papers, and her research areas are mainly on Public Finances, Public Budgeting and Social Security. Currently (since 2015), she is a national expert at FreSsco ("Network of Experts on Intra-EU Mobility—Free Movement of Workers and Social Security Coordination"), and between 2015 and 2016 she was also a national expert at the EU project, led by CEPS (Centre for European Policy Studies) to the European Commission, entitled "National feasibility assessment of the different European unemployment benefit scheme options".

R. Deniz Agaoglu is a senior Vice-President in the Enterprise Improvement practice at AlixPartners in London. She helps companies gain competitive advantage by delivering complex strategic transformations and operational enhancements. She has 14 years of experience advising mainly financial services and PE clients across the UK, EMEA and Turkey to reduce cost, drive value and improve performance. Throughout her career, Deniz worked at both leading global consultancies and major banks, including Deutsche Bank's Group Strategy & Consulting unit, EY's EMEIA Financial Services Advisory team based in London, and at PwC Consulting in Istanbul, working on numerous strategic, transaction-related and operational improvement projects predominantly in banking, insurance and asset/wealth management sectors. Deniz is a certified post-merger integration, carve-out and project management practitioner. She holds an MBA degree from London Business School.

Ana Paula Dourado obtained her PhD in law, a Master's degree in Law and her undergraduate in law from the Faculty of Law, University of Lisbon. She is a Professor of Tax Law and International and European Tax Law at the University of Lisbon. She has been a Visiting Professor at the University of Vienna from 2010 until 2011; University of Florida since 2010; Global Law School, Catholic University of Lisbon since 2009; University of Lausanne since 2012; and International Tax Centre, University of Leiden since 2007. She is a founding member of Group for Research on European and International Taxation (GREIT). She has drafted and negotiated the tax reforms in Portuguese-speaking countries as an expert in the legal department of the International Monetary Fund (2003–present). She was a member of the Centre for Tax Studies at the Portuguese Ministry of Finance and a delegate for Portugal in the working groups for direct tax harmonization at the European Community and in the working group for tax avoidance and evasion at the OECD. She edited several books by IBFD on international and European Tax Law and has published several articles and book chapters in International and European tax law and comparative tax law; she is a correspondent for EC Tax Law, H&I and several other tax law journals; she is a member of the editorial board of Intertax, Rev. de Finanças Públicas e Direito Financeiro and the Executive Board of the EATLP. Among others, a few of her publications include *Is this a pipe? Validity of a Tax Reform for a Developing Country, Tax, Law and Development* (Brauner/Stewart, eds.), Elgar, 2013; *Exchange of Information and Validity of Global Standards in Tax Law: Abstractionism and Expressionism or Where the Truth Lies*, EUI Working Paper RSCAS 2013/11; *A Single Principle of Abuse in EC Law: A Methodological Approach to Rejecting a Different Concept of Abuse in Personal Taxation, A General Principle of Abuse in European Law* (eds. de la Feria/Vogenauer), Hart, 2011. Her areas of expertise include tax law, international and European tax law. She is the Principal Researcher of the research group on Tax Governance: International Standards, Patriotisms and Exiles, and a member of the research group on Crisis, Public Policies, Taxation Policies and the Euro. Her published papers can be found at: http://www.cideeff.pt/who-we-are/Profa-Doutora-Ana-Paula-Dourado/15/?zID=6.

Michael Emerson is a graduate in politics, philosophy and economics from Balliol College, Oxford University. After some years at the OECD in Paris, he joined the European Commission in 1973, where until 1990 he worked as an economist on macroeconomic affairs and as economic adviser to the President. In 1991 he was appointed as the EU's first Ambassador to the USSR (subsequently Russia). Returning from Russia in 1996 Emerson joined the London School of Economics as Senior Research Fellow and from 1998 at the Centre for European Policy Studies (CEPS) in Brussels. Emerson has published extensively on European affairs and external relations. He has worked intensely on the Brexit question over the last two years, alongside a research project on the three new Association Agreements and DCFTAs of the EU with Georgia, Moldova and Ukraine.

Federico Fabbrini is a Full Professor of European Law at the School of Law & Government. He holds a PhD in Law from the European University Institute (2012) and interned as a clerk for Justice Sabino Cassese at the Italian Constitutional Court (2010–2011). He was an Associate Professor of European & International Law at iCourts (the Center of Excellence for International Courts) at the Faculty of Law of the University of Copenhagen, in Denmark, and Assistant Professor of European & Comparative Constitutional Law at Tilburg Law School, in the Netherlands, where he was awarded tenure. Federico Fabbrini has published articles in Common Market Law Review, European Law Review, Columbia Journal of European Law, European Constitutional Law Review, Oxford Yearbook of European Law, Cambridge Yearbook of European Legal Studies, Berkeley Journal of International Law and Harvard Human Rights Journal. He is the author of two monographs with Oxford University Press, *Fundamental Rights Europe: Challenges and Transformations in Comparative Perspective* (2014, the published version of his PhD thesis at the EUI), and *Economic Governance in Europe: Comparative Paradoxes and Constitutional Challenges* (2016). Moreover, he has co-edited five other volumes with Hart Publishing and Elgar Publishing and edited two Special Journal Issues. He is currently authoring a textbook on EU law together with Marta Cartabia and Joseph H.H. Weiler.

José Renato Gonçalves holds a license degree, a Masters and a PhD in Law (Law and Economics Sciences) from the University of Lisbon School of Law (Faculdade de Direito da Universidade de Lisboa), where he is professor. His teaching and research activities focus on European Union Law, Economic and Monetary Union, Financial and Monetary Regulation and Supervision,

International Economic Law, Development Studies, Public Finance, Access to Information and Personal Data Protection. Currently, he is the president of the Pedagogical Council of the University of Lisbon School of Law, deputy director of the board of the Centre for Research in European, Economic, Financial and Tax Law (CIDEEFF) and member of the board of the European Institute (Instituto Europeu) of the University of Lisbon School of Law and of the editorial board of the quarterly *Competition and Regulation Journal* (*Revista de Concorrência e Regulação*). As an integrated member of CIDEEFF, he has contributed mostly to the research groups (II) Globalization, Economic Integration and Development, and (IV) Crises, Public Policies, Fiscal Policies and the Euro. He was a visiting professor of postgraduate courses in several scientific institutes and universities, including Eduardo Mondlane University School of Law, in Maputo, Mozambique, and Agostinho Neto University School of Law, in Luanda, Angola. He is author of some books and articles on EU Law and Economics, particularly in European Monetary Union, on International Economic Law, on Economic, Financial and Monetary Regulation and Supervision, on Public Finance and on Access to Official Information and Personal Data Protection.

Yves Jorens is a professor of European social law and social criminal law at the Faculty of Law, Ghent University (Belgium) and director of studies. After nearly 20 years of research in the specific area of EU coordination of social security for migrant workers, he is acknowledged as one of the main international experts in this field. Throughout the years, he has participated in or directed numerous projects in the field of international employment and European social law. Since now more than ten years he is a project director of the network on social security for migrant workers and free movement (former trESS, now FreSsco), a unique project set up by the European Commission, DG Employment, Social Affairs and Social Inclusion. This Project informs the EC about the application and implementation of EU Regulations 883/2004 and 987/2009 on social security for migrant workers in the Member States. He has written several articles and books on European social (security) law issues, international employment, international social fraud and European health care. Professor Jorens has a solid track record in managing large-scale (research and training) networks. Professor Jorens is currently also a director of *IRIS*, the International Research Institute on Social Fraud, a knowledge center that gathers relevant information of regional, national and international interest regarding social fraud in the broadest sense of the word.

Marco Lamandini was born in Bologna, the 3rd of July 1966. Since 2001 he is a Full Professor (Chair) of Commercial Law at the University of Bologna, where he teaches at the School of Economics, Management and Statistics classes on: (a) European Capital Markets' Regulation, (b) Financial Law, (c) International and European Company Law, (d) European and Comparative Antitrust Law. He is affiliated to the Department of Sociology and Economic Law (SDEI) of the University of Bologna, with offices in Via San Giacomo 3, 40126 Bologna (+39 051 2099973; www.sde.unibo.it). He is the author or co-author of several law books and over 100 articles in the field of Company, Banking, Securities and Antitrust Law (see section "publications"). He is a regular speaker at national and international conferences in his field of expertise. In 2015 he was awarded, together with his co-authors David Ramos Munoz and Javier Solana, a research grant by the European Central Bank for the preparation of a study under the 2015 ECB Legal Research program. The study was presented at the ECB International Conference of 1–2 September 2015, was published by the Bank of Italy in its series of Legal Research Studies (Quaderno di Ricerca Giuridica no. 79/2015) and originated two additional and further developed articles, forthcoming in the ECB Legal Working Papers. He is a cofounder and codirector of "RDS—Rivista di diritto societario interno, internazionale, comparato e comunitario" and a member of the editorial board of "ECL—European Company Law Review" and "Le Società". He is a member of the Academic Board of ECMI—the European Capital Market Institute, based in Brussels. He is a member of EuBAR—a research group established by the University of Luxembourg to conduct a thorough review of sanctions in the European Banking Union and a member of the Luxembourg MPI (Max Planck Institute) research group on boards of appeals and quasi-judicial review in the EU law.

Karel Lannoo has been the (PRIVATE) Chief executive of CEPS since 2000, one of the leading independent European think tanks. He has published some books and numerous articles in newspapers, specialized magazines and journals on general European public policy, and specific financial regulation and supervision matters. Latest book: *The Great Financial Plumbing: From Northern Rock to Banking Union*, Rowman & Littlefield, 2015. Karel Lannoo holds a baccalaureate in philosophy (1984) and an MA in modern history (1985) from the University of Leuven, Belgium, and obtained a postgraduate in European Studies (Centre d'Etudes européennes, CEE) from the University of Nancy, France (1986). Before joining CEPS, he worked for STUC (students' cultural centre), did a stage in the EU Commission (spokesmen's service), was employed by an Italian agro-food company (Ferruzzi) and a professional association and was also active as freelance journalist.

David Ramos Muñoz (Badajoz, 1979) is a Senior Lecturer (Profesor Ayudante Doctor) of Commercial Law at the Universidad Carlos III de Madrid. He has been a fellow, among others, at the Real Colegio de España en Bolonia (2007–2009), the London School of Economics (2010). His research has benefited from different grants, among others, the Colegio de España grant (2007) or the José Castillejo programme (2010). His publications include the book *The Law of Transnational Securitiz*ation (Oxford University Press, 2010) and a number of articles, including "In Praise of Small Things: Securitization and Governance Structure" *Capital Markets Law Journal* Vol. 5, No. 4 (October 2010); "SEC v Goldman Sachs and the new wave of (asset-backed) securities litigation. What are the arguments? What is at stake?" *Law and Financial Markets Review* Volume 4, No. 4, (July 2010) pp. 413–420; or "Living on the Edge: Securitization Supervision and Characterization Problems", *European Company Law Review* (October 2009), 6 (5), pg. 217–227. Ramos Muñoz teaches Commercial Law and since 2005/2006 is the coach of the Willem C V is International Commercial Arbitration Moot team of Universidad Carlos III. He is also a coordinator of the Moot Madrid (http://www.mootmadrid.es/). David Ramos is fluent in English and Italian and has an intermediate command of French. He lives in Madrid with his wife and two children.

Ioanna Ntampoudi is a political sociologist, trained at Lancaster University (BA Hons Sociology—First) and the University of Strathclyde (MSc Political Research—Distinction). Ioanna holds a PhD in Social Psychology and European Politics from Aston University. Her doctoral research focused on Greek citizens' national and European identities during the Euro crisis and explored the Greek debt crisis through a collective identity perspective. Ioanna's research interests include European Union politics, political identities, the theorization of identity crises, the politics of immigration and qualitative and participatory research methods.

Pompeo Della Posta is a tenured (associate) professor at the University of Pisa. He holds an MA in Economics (University of Warwick, UK) and a PhD in Economics (European University Institute, Italy). He also studied as a visiting student in Princeton University (USA) and Stanford University (USA) and was awarded a Fulbright Scholarship, a Scholarship of the Ente Einaudi, and a MontePaschi Scholarship. As a scholar he has been visiting and giving courses and seminars in various universities and research institutions across the world, including Yokohama National University (Japan), IMF Tokyo (Japan), George Washington University (Washington, DC, USA), CIRANO Research Center (Montreal, Canada), Johns Hopkins SAIS center (Bologna center, Italy),

Stanford University (Florence Center, Italy), University of Victoria (Canada), Beijing Normal University (China), Delhi School of Economics (New Delhi, India), Durham University (UK). He has published in international journals (included the *Journal of Policy Modeling*, *Open Economies Review*, *Global Economy Journal*) and edited several books for publishers like Palgrave Macmillan. He has been acting as referee for several international journals, and since 2011 he has been a member of the Board of Directors of the International Trade and Finance Association (years 2011–2015). He has been teaching courses at all levels, including Masters in Economics and Finance, PhD in Economics, Masters in Business Administration, and presented papers and given seminars at a large number of conferences and meetings across the world. His main research interests relate to International Monetary Economics and Finance, Fiscal policies and fiscal and monetary policy coordination, European Economic and Monetary Union, Economic and financial globalization.

Scheherazade Rehman is the GW Deans Professorial Fellow of International Finance, GW Director of the European Union Research Center and Professor of International Affairs (Elliott School of International Affairs) at The George Washington University. Dr. Rehman is currently the Director of the GW World Executive MBA with Cyber-Security (WEMBA). She was the former Chair of the GW University Faculty Senate. She is a Senior Research Fulbright Scholar and an expert on global financial markets, financial crises management, global risk assessment and the Eurozone. Prior to GWU she served as a foreign exchange and money market trader in the Middle East. She has advised OPIC, USAID, US State Department, World Bank, IMF and various central banks/finance ministries. Dr. Rehman regularly guests on various national and international televised programs and radio on financial matters on PBS Newshour, BBC World News, CNBC, Al Jazeera, NPR, Reuters, C-Span Washington Journal, Colbert Report, Voice of America, CCTV, among others, and has appeared several times before the US Congress and regularly at the Brookings Institute to discuss the current European financial crisis. Dr. Rehman has written over 80 scholarly articles, book chapters, conference papers, and published 7 books, including *The Path To European Economic and Monetary Union*, *Financial Crisis Management in Regional Blocs*, *The Quest For Exchange Rate Stability in the Next Millennium* and the latest (co-authored) titled *Corruption and Its Manifestation in the Persian Gulf* (2010). Dr. Rehman blogs weekly for the US News & World Report for "World Report" and occasionally for the Huffington Post.

Nuno Cunha Rodrigues is a Professor at the Faculty of Law, University of Lisbon. He earned his PhD in legal and economic sciences, his master's degree, and completed his graduation in law from the Faculty of Law, University of Lisbon. He is also Vice-President of the European Institute and of IDEFF and was a Visiting Professor at the Law School of Louvain-la-Neuve (Belgium), Salgaocar Law School (Goa—India), International Law Institute (New Delhi—India), Eduardo Mondlane University (Maputo—Mozambique), Fundação Getúlio Vargas (São Paolo—Brazil), Catholic University (Lisbon). He has published several articles and books, namely, in his area of expertise which lies with EU Law, Economic Law, Competition Law, Public Procurement and Public Finance. He joined the research group on Globalization, Economic Integration and Development: European and Lusophone Perspectives and the group on Crisis, Public Policies, Taxation Policies and the Euro as a member. Nuno Cunha Rodrigues was granted with a "Jean Monnet module", by the European Commission, in the field of International and European Public Procurement (2015–2018).

Claudio Scardovi is a teaching professor at Bocconi University in Milan and at Imperial College in London in the fields of restructuring and turnaround, risk management, capital markets, financial systems and real estate. He has 15 books published to date as well as 200 articles and position papers. As a Managing Director (MD) at AlixPartners LLP, Claudio currently helps EMEA and global-level clients by leading projects for global financial institutions groups, helping them restructure, transform, grow and innovate. He has been advising, dealing with and investing in Financial Institutions Groups for the last 20 years and as Managing Director for the last 15. He has an extensive experience in strategic and industrial consulting, as former MD and Country Head for Oliver Wyman, with specific track record in Growth/Strategic and Restructuring Plans, Value Based and Risk Management. He has also been MD and Country Head of FIG for Lehman Brothers and Nomura, focusing on M&A, Active Capital Management and Principal Investing. Claudio is also a member of the strategic advisors group of the World Economic Forum.

Pauline Schnapper is a Professor of British Studies at the University of Paris Sorbonne Nouvelle. She is author of several articles and books on this issue, including (with David Baker) the recent publication *Britain and the Crisis in the European Union*, Palgrave 2015.

Grega Strban is a Professor of Social Security Law at the Faculty of Law, University of Ljubljana. He completed postgraduate specialization course of the EU law at the University of Cambridge (*with distinction*), master course on European social security at the University of Leuven (*magna* cum *laude*), and defended doctoral thesis at the University of Ljubljana. He performed research at Max Planck Institute for Social Law and Social Policy in Munich, at first as *Stipendiat* of the Institute and later as a Humboldt Fellow. He is also an external correspondent of the same Institute. Prof Strban is Vice-Dean of the Faculty of Law, University of Ljubljana, President of the Slovenian Association for Labour Law and Social Security and as such member of the Executive Committee of the International Society for Labour and Social Security Law, Geneva. He is also Vice-President of the European Institute of Social Security, Leuven, and a member of Judicial Council of Slovenia. Prof Strban is active in several Slovenian and international projects (among them he leads the research group of the Ljubljana Faculty of Law and acts as scientific manager of EU project FreSsco). He is author of many publications and a member of several editorial boards. He was awarded Best Young Lawyer in Slovenia (2001) and received Roger Dillemans Award for Excellence in Social Security, KU Leuven (2004).

Francisco Torres is a Visiting Senior Fellow in European Political Economy at the LSE and Visiting Professor of European Political Economy at Católica Lisbon School of Business and Economics. He is also a PEFM Research Associate at St Antony's College, Oxford University, and EU Steering Committee Member of ECPR. Before moving to Oxford and London in 2012, where he teaches European (and International) Political Economy, he also taught at the universities of Victoria, Canada, Rome (Tor Vergata), Bolzano and Aveiro (Associate Professor, 5 years), and at the Catholic University, both at the Economics Department and at the European Studies Institute, of which he was Director and Research Coordinator. He was a Visiting Fellow at the EUI, Florence, the ESC, Oxford University, and the first Robert Schuman Fellow of the European Commission at CEPS, Brussels. He holds a PhD in European Political Economy (UCP), an MSc in Economics (UNL, Lisbon) and a "licenciatura" also in Economics (UCP). He also studied Economics at the EUI (PhD programme) and holds an MA in International Affairs from the Johns Hopkins University.

Philip B. Whyman is a Director of the Lancashire Institute for Economic and Business Research at the University of Central Lancashire, UK. He has published 46 papers in learned journals and is the author/editor of 17 books including: *Sweden and the 'Third Way': A Macroeconomic Evaluation* (Ashgate, 2003),

Third Way Economics: Theory and Evaluation (Palgrave, 2006), *Implications of the Euro: A Critical Perspective from the Left* (Routledge, 2006), *The Political Economy of the European Social Model* (Routledge, 2012), *Crisis in the Eurozone: Causes, Dilemmas and Solutions* (Palgrave, 2015). He is active in various professional bodies and undertakes research and consultancy for government, corporations and charitable bodies, advising on various aspects of economic policy and European integration.

List of Figures

List of Tables

1

Introduction

Nazaré da Costa Cabral, José Renato Gonçalves, and Nuno Cunha Rodrigues

1.1 General Observations

In the past decade, Europe has been hit by important problematic events that have challenged European Union (EU) institutions and its legal framework in a new way, unimagined before. The 2007–2008 financial crisis (followed by the sovereign debt and Euro crises) and the more recent refugee crisis have confronted the EU with its limitations in important framework aspects, such as its economic-monetary and external affairs pillars. The EU was challenged to show its economic capacity and political availability to cope with shocks of a different nature, but the response given was not out of shortcomings and insufficiencies. These crises have made clear that the Economic and Monetary Union's (EMU) construction was not as solid as one might have thought, and this was so first and foremost because it was not founded on truthful political integration. On the other hand, these recent and severe crises have confronted Europe (and not only the EU) with its economic and social fragilities in a

N. da Costa Cabral (✉) • J.R. Gonçalves • N.C. Rodrigues
Lisbon University School of Law, Lisbon, Portugal

© The Author(s) 2017
N. da Costa Cabral et al. (eds.), *After Brexit*,
https://doi.org/10.1007/978-3-319-66670-9_1

1

globalized world and also with its progressive political and geo-strategic weakening, at least when compared with other developed or developing regional blocks. Consequently, Europe as a space capable of economic progress and social development and cohesion is now at stake.

The Brexit decision, in the 23 June 2016 referendum, can hence be seen as a consequence of all these fundamental contradictions and insufficiencies, and it has raised more questions than answers about what will be (and should be) the future of the European integration project. The process now seems irreversible: Theresa May, Prime Minister of the United Kingdom (UK), on 29 March 2017, formally triggered Article 50 of the Treaty on European Union (TEU). Previously, in February 2017, the UK had stated, in the document entitled 'The United Kingdom's exit from and new partnership with the European Union', the departing terms of exit that should be at the centre of the negotiation process with the European institutions. The more recent signals, either resulting from current UK political circumstances or relative to the on-going negotiation between UK leaders and the representatives of the EU, have already made clear that the nature of Brexit ('hard' or 'soft') is for now imprecise and that the process will be long and difficult.

As for the EU, it has certainly perceived the danger of disintegration that Brexit could/can imply, also acknowledging the need to engage in profound and urgent reform measures, regarding both its economic and monetary arm and its political and geo-strategic role. In fact Brexit, along with other disruptive changes in the international panorama—such as the unprecedented driving forces pushing the EU's relationship with the new United States (USA) administration—can be seen as an opportunity to substantially and effectively reform the EU.

As an important illustration of this movement, recall the launching, in March 2017, by European Commission President Juncker, of the 'White Paper on the Future of Europe', where five possible scenarios for reform of the remaining EU27 have been brought up for discussion, all involving—as mentioned there—pros and cons: (i) 'Carrying on scenario', involving a positive agenda of reinforcement of the status quo, both on economic and political grounds, in particular, the EU27 managing to positively shape the global agenda in a number of fields such as climate change, financial stability and sustainable development; (ii) 'Nothing but the single market', which in fact means a step backwards in the process of integration, since the EU would now basically have as its main driver the internal market, while at the same time, this could imply an increase in internal disagreements on the approach to international trade; migration and some foreign policy issues would increasingly be left to bilateral cooperation and humanitarian and development aid dealt with on national grounds; the EU as a whole would cease being represented in a number of international fora as it would fail to agree on a common position on issues of relevance to global partners such as climate change, fighting tax evasion, harnessing globalization and promoting international trade; (iii) 'Those who want more do more', in fact, the approach of a 'two-speed Europe', a scenario where the EU27 proceeds as today, but where certain Member States wish to go further together in specific policy areas such as defence, internal security, taxation and social issues; (iv) 'Doing less more efficiently', where the EU27 would focus on specific areas and notably step up its work in fields such as innovation (including further cooperation on space, high-tech clusters and the completion of regional energy hubs), trade, security, migration, the management of borders and defence; (v) 'Doing much more together', which indeed means a step ahead in the integration process, in fact, cooperation between all Member States would go further than ever before in all domains and decisions would be agreed faster at the European level and more rapidly enforced; furthermore, the euro area would be strengthened (e.g. much greater coordination on fiscal, social and taxation matters, as well as European supervision of financial services).

Bearing all this in mind, the present volume intends to identify the short- to medium-term economic, financial and social consequences of Brexit, but also to discuss—in a longer-term and broader perspective—what will be its consequences on the design of the EU and the path of integration that can be followed from now on.

The raison d'être of the book is therefore widely justified. The crucial challenge is to address the major areas that can be affected by Brexit, bearing in mind—to avoid dispersion and to guarantee analytic cohesion—the fundamental legal framework of the EU, and particularly the European Treaties' basic, foundational principles of free movement (of goods, capital, services and people).

For this reason, two major types of Brexit effects can be disentangled: firstly, *general effects on the European integration process*, in which the authors will investigate in which way Brexit can work as a factor of integration or, on the contrary, a factor of disintegration for the EU ('more or less Europe'), without ignoring constitutional and contractual implications that might arise and which will certainly be at the centre of the political discussion during the exit negotiation process; secondly, *sectorial effects* that, on the other hand, can be separated into two dimensions (bearing in mind the aforementioned basic principles of free movement): the first dimension is to assess the effects of Brexit considering the free movement of goods and people, and here the discussion will embrace problematic aspects such as trade, (im)migration, social rights and social security; the second dimension considers the free movement of capital and will highlight the effects on the financial markets, not only for the UK—as usually mentioned—but for the whole EU.

The book is an interdisciplinary work involving economic, political-philosophical and legal perspectives, although in a logical sequence of items previously selected to ensure its global coherence and non-redundancy. The contributors have different nationalities and are affiliated to prominent academic or sectorial institutions, which also ensures diversified perspectives and opinions about the current impasse and transition moment being experienced in Europe, and above all the high quality of the respective analysis.

Finally, it is worth mentioning that this volume is the epilogue to one of the research projects carried out by Group IV ('Crisis, Public Policies, Fiscal Policy and the Euro') of the Centre for Research in European, Economic, Financial and Tax Law (CIDEEFF) of the University of Lisbon, to which the editors are affiliated. The intensive and noteworthy work of the CIDEEFF's work since its inception (articles published in international peer-reviewed journals, books and conferences) already certifies it as a leading hub in Portuguese academia regarding European affairs, both in their legal and economic dimensions.

1.2   The Structure of the Book

In Part I—dealing with Brexit's general effects (notably on the future of the European integration process)—Pompeo Della Posta and Scheherazade Rehman, in chapter entitled "Brexit: Origins and Future Perspectives"

(Chap. 2), go back in time, investigating the deepest and former origins of Brexit, identifying it with the globalization process as it has evolved since the late 1970s. Notwithstanding this, in the authors' opinion, the triggering moment was the 2007–2008 crisis, since it definitively changed the perception of the effects of that process. In a similar perspective, José Renato Gonçalves, in his chapter "Brexit and the EU in the context of Globalization" (Chap. 3), presents a general outlook of the main implications of Brexit, taking into consideration the economic and political position of the EU in a globalized world.

The following two chapters—from Nuno Cunha Rodrigues ("Brexit and the Future of the EU: Move Back or Move Forward?" Chap. 4) and Pauline Schnapper ("Brexit and the Risk of European Disintegration", Chap. 5)—address the effects of Brexit in the European integration process, discussing if Brexit can be seen as an opportunity to go further and deeper in that process or if, on the contrary, this might mean moving back to the beginning (to the primordial economic community), and ultimately a first step to an irretrievable disintegration.

Brexit, which has already provided a new argument for discussing the EU's future nature (as the aforementioned 'White Paper on the Future of Europe' proves), will also provide a new platform for tension between centripetal forces (more centralization of powers within the European institutions regarding the main policies) and centrifugal forces (decentralization of powers in the Member States). The most extreme opposite results of this confrontation can, on the one hand, offer the option of a political federalist model and, on the other hand, the recovery of a sovereign-nationalist-type model.

However, most of all, as stressed by Annette Bongardt and Francisco Torres, in their chapter "A Qualitative Change in the Process of European Integration" (Chap. 6), the UK's exit from the EU marks a qualitative change in the nature of EU membership. In the authors' opinion, Brexit has illustrated the need to discuss what the model of society is that European citizens prefer, also showing that the redefinition of the EU model requires a more homogeneous club in terms of preferences. For this reason, Brexit may be seen as a positive development in the integration process, since it has opened the door for discontent Member States and other outliers to leave the club, reinforcing the idea that as Member

States, they need to contribute to the common good and be committed to shared values.

What is more, the effects of Brexit should be questioned on constitutional and legal grounds. Federico Fabbrini, in chapter "Brexit and the Reform of Economic and Monetary Union" (Chap. 7), examines in particular the implications of Brexit in the field of EMU, summarizing the main proposals that have been made to reform the EMU and analysing the legal mechanisms available to this end, particularly EU legislation, amendments to intergovernmental treaties concluded outside EU law and amendments to the EU treaties.

An important and ultimately legal issue that must not be ignored particularly within the on-going exit negotiation process is the legal and contractual implications that might arise for the future. The issue is not entirely new in the EU where a similar assessment had to be made in other circumstances and particularly when the euro came into force: the issue at that time was about the implications for legal and contractual claims and obligations that had been initially defined in national currencies. The problem with Brexit is different, firstly because the UK has kept its own currency and now formal redenomination will not occur. However, different sorts of consequences regarding running contracts and other commitments should not be ignored. This precaution is considered in chapter by António Barreto Menezes Cordeiro, "Brexit as an Exceptional Change of Circumstances?" (Chap. 8), where the author approaches this matter in the light of the well-known civil law principle, *exceptional change of circumstances.*

Parts II and III are related to Brexit's sectorial effects: in the former, consequences related to trade and free movement of goods and citizens are considered; in the latter, effects regarding free movement of capital and the financial markets. Part II is introduced by the chapters from Michael Emerson ("Which Model for Brexit?", Chap. 9) and from Mark Baimbridge and Philip B. Whyman ("Economic Implications of Alternative Trade Relationships: Post-Brexit Options for the UK", Chap. 10), where the possible trade models relating to the UK and the EU are considered—the choice amongst those options will also mean a choice between hard and soft Brexit, and this will influence future trade and the economic position of both the EU and the UK in a globalized economy.

The three following chapters address one of the core issues that the Brexit process has involved and which was certainly one of the main driving forces of the June 2016 Referendum result—free movement of workers, (im)migration and social security. In the first of the chapters, Samo Bardutzky discusses "The Position of EU Citizens in the UK and of the UK Citizens in the EU27 Post-Brexit: Between Law and Political Constitutionalism" (Chap. 11); then, in the second chapter, Ioanna Ntampoudi addresses "Post-Brexit Models and Migration Policies: Possible Citizenship and Welfare Implications for EU Nationals in the UK" (Chap. 12); finally, Yves Jorens and Grega Strban raise and discuss the question concerning "New Forms of Social Security for Persons Moving Between the EU and the UK" (Chap. 13).

Part III proceeds with the assessment of sectorial effects, now considering the free movement of capital and Brexit's consequences for financial markets. In the first chapter, "Free Movement of Capital and Brexit" (Chap. 14), Ana Paula Dourado addresses another major implication of Brexit on the free movement of capital, that which derives from direct and indirect taxation. Assuming an extreme Brexit scenario, the author starts by mentioning that the UK can be handled as the USA or Brazil, for example. In the bilateral relationship between the UK and the EU Member States, there will be no legal obligations for the UK deriving from either primary or secondary law, whereas the EU Member States are still forbidden to restrict capital movements from and to the UK. The CFC (Controlled Foreign Company) Rule in the Anti-Tax Avoidance Directive, the EU standard on exchange of information, EU Good Governance Clauses and their application in the Brexit extreme scenario are also discussed. Marco Lamandini and David Ramos Muñoz, in chapter "Free Movement of Capital: Could the CJEU Smooth Brexit?" (Chap. 15), start by considering whether and how free movement of capital will continue to apply to companies still established in the UK after Brexit.

Following this, Ansgar Belke addresses Brexit's "Policy Uncertainty and Spillovers into International Financial Markets" (Chap. 16), arguing that it has the potential to damage the real economy in both the UK and other European countries, in particular the so-called 'GIIPS' economies: Greece, Ireland, Italy, Portugal and Spain. Finally, Karel Lannoo, in chapter "EU Financial Markets After Brexit" (Chap. 17), analyses the panorama for financial services provision in the following years, whereas Claudio Scardovi and Rabia Deniz Agaoglu discuss "How Brexit May Affect Banks' Business Models and the Financial System in the UK and the EU: Opportunity to Revitalize the Existing Banking Structures" (Chap. 18).In the authors' opinion, despite the immediate costs borne by the City, Brexit can be an opportunity for the modernisation of financial services and for the improvement of banking models both in the UK and in the EU.

Part I

Brexit's General Effects: The Future of the European Integration Process

2

Brexit: Origins and Future Perspectives

Pompeo Della Posta and Scheherazade S. Rehman

2.1   Introduction

This chapter discusses the origins and the likely economic and political implications of Brexit and "Trumpism" for the future of globalization.

The choice of the UK to exit the European Union during the June 23, 2016 referendum, which is now commonly referred to as Brexit, must be understood jointly with the ascension of Donald Trump to the US presidency. Both seem to originate (albeit, the many differences) from a deep dissatisfaction with globalization.

The world has seen three waves of globalization to date. The first wave of globalization began in the 1870s with the "Belle Époque"[1] up until World War I (WWI), with the second wave beginning after World War

P. Della Posta (✉)
Dipartimento di Economia e Management, Università di Pisa, Pisa, Italy

S.S. Rehman
School of Business, International Business Department, The George Washington University, Washington DC, USA

© The Author(s) 2017
N. da Costa Cabral et al. (eds.), *After Brexit*,
https://doi.org/10.1007/978-3-319-66670-9_2

II (WWII). The third wave of globalization began in 1979/80 with the election of Margaret Thatcher and Ronald Reagan.

During this third wave, globalization evolved exponentially in all its dimensions of goods, services, capital and labor, and the backlash against it was felt almost at the onset building momentum until the turn of the millennium. It was the 2007/08 global financial and economic crisis and what followed that fast-tracked this hostile response against globalization to an all-time high. This was in large part due to the historic disruption of the flow of liquidity into the USA and partly into the UK and unchecked growing income gaps in the West. Modern Western economic ailments, such as long-term unemployment, underemployment, stagnant wages, income inequality and fears of immigration are the underpinnings of the growing dissatisfaction with the status quo of the post-WWII order.

This chapter further stipulates that the third wave of globalization may have run its course and that we are entering a fourth wave beginning in 2016/17 with Brexit and the Trump presidency. Once again the UK and the USA have shifted the paradigm on globalization. More importantly, this fourth wave of globalization marks the beginning of a period of reversal of some key aspects of globalization. In fact, one can see a pull-back on both regionalism and multilateralism—the hallmarks of the post-World War order and globalization, respectively, together with growing restrictions on immigration and labor mobility. This is apparent in Trump's protectionist "America first" motto, in the exit of the UK from the European Union, and in the renewed talks of a possible US-UK and other bilateral trade negotiations that could ignite other bilateral arrangements circumventing the World Trade Organization (WTO).

2.2   May and Trump Versus Thatcher and Reagan

As underscored above, Brexit is connected to the rise of the Trump US presidency (see also Lagrain, 2016). This is not the first time that momentous global shifts have taken place in the aftermath of the USA and UK changing directions in tandem. This occurred in the past after the elections of Margaret Thatcher, in May 1979, and that of Ronald Reagan in January 1980. This time it is UK conservative politician Theresa May (who replaced David Cameron, the Tory who lost the Brexit referendum) and US Republican candidate, Donald Trump. The similarities are noteworthy as in both cases two conservative center-right politicians won the elections, in both cases a woman marked the change in the UK and an actor/showman (and businessman in this case) did it in the USA. Additionally, in both cases the change occurred first in the UK and immediately later in the USA. But above all, in both cases those elections can be interpreted as having marked in the past and marking now the beginning of a new economic and political global era. Our task here is not to discuss the many similarities and differences between these two historical events as the events are too recent, but rather to identify their common roots and to discuss the global economic and political implications of the latest ones.

The third phase of economic globalization started in 1979/80. It was characterized by markets liberalization (especially those of goods, services, and capital), and accompanied by the abandonment of the Keynesian policies that emerged as a response to the 1929 great crisis.

The events of the second half of 2016 (Brexit and "Trumpism") seem to mark its true symbolic end, although there is a case to be made that the 2007/08 global financial crisis was the actual beginning of the end of the third wave of globalization as it began a partial revision and restructuring of the globalization of financial markets.[2] More importantly, these events seem to mark the beginning of a period of reversal of some key aspects of globalization. In fact, one can see a pullback on both multilateralism and regionalism as well. This is apparent in Trump's "America first" motto, in the exit of the UK from the European Union, and in the renewed talks of a possible US-UK bilateral trade deal, that seems to have ignited talks of other bilateral arrangements circumventing the WTO. One thing is certain, though, that the implications of the victory of the "Leavers" in the UK (albeit significantly weakened in the wake of snap elections on June 8, 2017, which left PM May's government crippled) and of the "protesters of globalization" in the USA disprove the validity of the famous Margaret Thatcher's TINA (there-is-no-alternative) paradigm. Hence a new political and economic era. But why are we witnessing a global or at least regional widespread backlash against globalization? Is there any coherent and credible economic evidence linking the current economic and political problems in the West to the consequences of globalization? Is this just a phase resulting from irrational feelings fueled by populist rhetoric or from what is now defined as the "post-truth[3]"? Populist political aspects, sociocultural trends, economic realities and fears of terrorism, among others, all played a significant role in exacerbating the fear of globalization. This chapter will focus on primarily the economic conditions that lead to the results of the British referendum and Trump's election. We conclude that the current state of globalization goes well beyond the economic sphere.

In order to answer the questions above and to discuss the current situation, we need to refer to the past three to four decades, which have been characterized by the liberalization of capital movements and the explosion of financial derivatives, beyond the deregulation, liberalization and privatization of markets in general. But the same period is also characterized by extraordinary technological developments related to information technology (IT) sectors, and in particular the development of the Internet (and subsequently the mobility of the Internet, cloud, big data and social media). The implications of such advances mingle themselves with those of globalization, so it is not always easy to detect who are the true culprits for the modern West economic ailments, such as long-term unemployment, underemployment and stagnant wages for the lower middle class and poor and income inequality.

The beginning of the third wave of globalization also coincides with the 1978 resurrection of China on the global economic scene, following Deng Xiao Ping's "open door policy", thus thrusting China back into the role of a major global player that it used to occupy centuries ago. India abandoned its protectionist import-substitution policies in 1991, and also started playing an increasingly important role in the world economy.

This is the period[4] in which neoliberal and monetarist policies are applied almost uniformly and uncritically. Economics was dominated by the theory of rational expectations that stated unequivocally the superiority of markets over the state. It was in this period where monetary and fiscal (demand side) policies, which represented the essence of Keynesian economics, were abandoned to make room for structural policies of market liberalization and privatization, essentially aiming at favoring growth by focusing on the supply side of the economy. The so-called Washington consensus based on, among other things, the prescription of a balanced fiscal budget and the need for monetary policy to concentrate exclusively on price stability was prescribed by the multilateral institutions such as the IMF and (to a lesser extent) the World Bank as a conditionality to be accepted by any country seeking financial support.[5]

The interests of the middle class did not seem to be negatively impacted by such financial and economic reforms, nor by the developments in liberalized trade and foreign investments trends. In fact, financial liberalization seemed rather to benefit the middle class as they enjoyed larger amounts of liquidity and more credit from abroad (generating a huge current account deficit in the USA) coupled with the availability of a larger variety of quality goods at lower prices. Moreover, the technological advancements in the USA and European countries determined reasonably low unemployment rates, resulting from the product innovations that only later on, with the maturing of the product life cycle, would be passed on to developing countries. This resulted in an environment in which the USA was importing goods and services from abroad with little or no limits, the financing of these imports being provided by the same exporting countries. In the EU the result was an accelerated push towards integration as it grew in membership size and GDP.

Yet as we turn the corner of 2017, the post-WWII Western institution, political and economic order, which heralded globalization for the past three to four decades, is being willfully disrupted by populist demands in the West. It is for this reason that this chapter focuses on the impact of the third wave of globalization from 1979/80 to 2016/17 in an attempt to understand this new world which can barely keep up with the mind-boggling pace of technology and innovation and is awash with fear as it enters into a forth wave of globalization (2016/17-unknown).

2.3 The Roots of Brexit and "Trumpism"

From the first signals against the third wave of globalization to the global financial and economic crisis of 2007/08

At the very beginning of the 1980s, complaints had already emerged about the negative effects of globalization on the blue collar workers in developed countries. They lamented losing their unskilled jobs because of (unfair, according to some interpretations) competition from emerging markets, or from the delocalization of domestic companies. The direct competition from immigrants came late in this wave of globalization. As a result, sporadic protectionist measures began to be applied, such as the "voluntarily" export restrictions adopted by Japanese firms to restrict their car exports to the USA. Such measures led to heated discussions whether free trade was still being pursued (Krugman 1987). This, however, did not alarm anyone as these episodic protectionist measures were interpreted as reasonable ways to manage and avoid major disruptions within the global economic and trading system (Rodrik 2016b).

Meanwhile, the European 1987 Single European Act served as the building block of the creation of a single market of goods, services, labor and capital that was realized in 1992. In 1994 the USA responded with the adoption of NAFTA—the free trade area agreement between the USA, Canada and Mexico—that, however, ruled out the free movement of the factors of production. In both cases, the regional blocs further ripened discontent among US and British citizens amidst an explosion of globalization. In the USA, the delocalization of companies beyond the Mexican border started creating resentment for the jobs taken away from the USA, in addition to the flow of illegal immigrants entering the country. In the UK, the free movement of people (in spite of the many exemptions that the UK managed to obtain), over the years brought many Europeans into the thriving UK job market, and this in turn fueled a growing uneasiness in the British population. While Brexit was a result of immigration concerns in the aftermath of the 2007/08 global financial crisis and the Syrian crisis, paradoxically, the Brexit referendums "Leave" votes came from areas with the lowest immigration rate, while the vote to "Remain" came from major metropolitan areas, such as London, where incidentally the large majority of immigration is concentrated.

At the end of the 1990s, Western economies' low and middle class workers began to experience a change of perspectives regarding globalization. There was a growing chorus of dissatisfaction and a significantly increased negative image of globalization began to emerge. These turned into the street protests that occurred at the WTO meeting in Seattle in 1999 and culminated with the riots of Genoa in July 2001 at the G8

Summit. The latter marked the height of a worldwide anti-globalization movement.

The protests were global in nature. In less developed and emerging markets, the process of globalization was perceived as being at least biased in favor of the developed countries. As a matter of fact, it was observed that the latter were enforcing growth recipes, including environmental protection and labor laws, that they themselves did not follow during the initial phases of their own economic development.[6] Protests, however, originated also in developed countries, with blue collar workers still complaining about the "unfair" competition from less developed and emerging markets, and the cultural élites complaining against the environmental and social implications of globalization that was shifting from the North/West to the South/East. Additionally, in every developed nation were the small but growing marginal and radical groups often associated with loud and sometimes violent forms of protests.[7]

The change of perspective that took place at the turn of the millennium can be associated with some significant events. The Millennium Development Goals were devised in the year 2000 by the United Nations, in order to address most of the concerns raised by the street protests and—although to a much lower extent—by public opinion in general. Issues of poverty and (to a lesser extent) inequality[8] acquired prominence and received greater attention. The WTO initiated the so-called Doha Round of negotiations that began in 2001 with the objective of creating "social inclusion and reduction of poverty" between the developed and underdeveloped world.[9]

This was all occurring during a rapidly changing economic global landscape emerging with the admission of China in the WTO in 2001 followed by the accession of Russia in 2012 and coupled with an even faster changing political landscape by the 9/11 terrorist attacks in the USA.

These events undoubtedly also mark the beginning of a change during which the hegemony of America and the EU are under discussion. The acronym BRICS gained more and more popularity, implying a growing role of those countries (Brazil, Russia, India, China and South-Africa) in the world scene and developing countries acquired gradually more strength and improved their bargaining position which now represents over 50 percent of the world economic might. It is not by chance that the Doha

Round has never been concluded, in spite of the fact that it began in 2001, precisely in order to provide developing/emerging countries with more opportunities for development. The stalled Doha Round in retrospect was signaling the rise of emerging markets. Additionally, reaching global agreements with the BRICS began to become more difficult as they flexed their muscles.[10]

Although around the turn of the millennium the protests were limited to only a minority of players, at some point the pace of delocalization, immigration, imports of goods and services was perceived more vehemently to result in a loss of unskilled jobs in developed countries. It should be noted that in actual fact OECD data on FDIs do not show significant changes in the net outward FDIs in the USA, for example, having remained below or close to 1 percent of the US GDP over the last decade. Needless to say, the onset of the 2007/08 financial and economic global crisis played the role of an accelerant in planting the seeds of discontent with globalization and ultimately cumulating in Brexit and the Trump presidency.

Financial liberalization was the true novelty of the third phase of globalization. The majority of people from developed countries did not find it problematic as it initially benefitted them until the 2007/08 global financial crisis erupted. This was the critical juncture of the third wave of globalization as the financial sector could no longer provide Western consumers liquidity to live beyond their means. This cumulated a problem in two of the dimensions of globalization, namely the goods market and the labor market. It was this that added fuel to an already large anti-globalization movement and negative perceptions of globalization spread to larger parts of the population.

The massive loss of wealth across the middle classes in the USA and EU due to the 2007/08 financial crisis, growing income disparity and diminishing economic and trade positions *vis-à-vis* the BRICS and other emerging markets all completed into the perfect storm and the backlash against globalization began in earnest in the West. Thus Brexit or Donald Trump's pronouncements of "buy American", "hire American" and "America first" should not have been surprising. It should be noted that unlike the UK's pro-globalization and pro-business stance, the USA is pro-business, but protectionist.[11] Needless to say, the current US stance of picking and choosing when to be pro-globalization or protectionist has been perceived as "free riding behavior". There is a growing risk of retaliation by partner countries through the legal imposition of constraints on the imports from the USA and through the spontaneous populist reactions. There is reason to pay caution to this as it is similar to the environment of the 1930s that prepared the ground for WWII. In the economic literature, this is well known as a simple application of the prisoner's dilemma[12] that leads to a Pareto[13] inferior solution in which all players are losers.

Moreover, it should be noted that the strong and safe haven US dollar, with its 30–40 percent appreciation in the post-2008 global financial crises era, has played a very significant role in putting pressure on low-skilled jobs as a strong dollar makes US exports more expensive and imports cheaper. The only reliable solution to counter this is by making US goods cheaper by moving production to low cost locales. Hence, trade retaliation to slow down foreign production of US goods by imposing import tariffs of even up to 20 percent would not persuade companies into "Made in America" programs.[14]

Reasons for protests on immigration, globalization-driven unemployment, technological developments, inequality, and inter-regional agreements

Unskilled workers from developed countries have been caught off guard by accelerated globalization, technological advances and innovation, possibly immigration and the severity of the long-lasting impact of the financial crisis, together with the lack of policies to absorb or at least soften the impact of globalization on them.

Technology certainly played a quite relevant role and it promises to displace more jobs in the future, for example, through the effects of the sharing economy, made possible by IT. Among the many other examples, one can list Fintech companies, Uber-like business models and the automation of the banking and travel industries. The more recent Artificial Intelligence (AI) resurrection threatens jobs that are repetitive, do not need creative thinking and tend to be low skilled.

Data projections[15] have shown that the low-skilled jobs are more at risk in the future than high-skilled jobs in terms of being automated. Approximately 70 percent of low-skilled jobs are in danger of being automated in 20 years versus 46 percent of middle-skilled and 8 percent of high-skilled jobs.

Economists, however, have stressed that the key Western competitiveness, in particular the US one, depends on the quality of jobs—high skilled and high wages. This may explain the lower attention reserved to the loss of low-skilled and low-wage jobs, although it can hardly explain the lack of attention towards the workers losing those jobs.[16]

It seems even possible to argue that while globalization has some alternatives, the third wave of globalization shows with clarity that slowing the technology drive is not one of those options. There has been a dramatic increase over the recent years in the installation of industrial robots worldwide. In 1995, the International Federation of Robots estimated that worldwide industrial robot installations hovered about 50,000, in 2013 it rose above 175,000, and projected that approximately 1.3 million new industrial robots would be installed worldwide between 2015 and 2018[17]. This may vindicate Margaret Thatcher's belief that while the TINA (there-is-no-alternative) paradigm may apply to technology, it is less applicable to globalization.

Needless to say, the perception that immigrant trends may be changing the structure and values of societies is a very complex subject area, on which there are many opposing views. In spite of immigration, delocalization and unskilled labor-saving technological developments, though, neither unemployment nor the rate of GDP growth seems to have suffered. In the USA the unemployment rate has been quite low and below 5 percent since September 2015, and similar data apply to the UK, as will be discussed below. The EU high unemployment has also remained quite steady, hovering between 8 percent and 10 percent for over a decade. Hence the impact of immigration is difficult to discern on overall unemployment.

A very different story, however, arises when considering poverty, quality of life (health and life expectancy) and income inequality. The data reported by Stiglitz (2016) tells us that income has been stagnating in the USA for the last 30 years. For everybody except the top 10 percent, the median real income for workers is lower than 42 years ago, and that real wages of the poorest people are at the level of 60 years ago. This is most assuredly a true and real cause of discontent among the middle- and lower middle class and poor.

Angus Deaton (2015) provides evidence of a reduction of life expectancy for parts of the white American population, and Branko Milanovic (2016) shows how over the last decades, the top 1 percent of the world population and the middle class of developing countries improved their situation, at the expenses of the bottom and middle class of advanced countries. The relevance of income and wealth inequality is also proved by the large amount of publications that have come out recently on the theme by, among others, Bourguignon (2015), Piketty (2014) and Atkinson (2015), not to mention Oxfam (2016). These studies are now showing us some base truths of the rise of discontent against globalization, government and the "system", hence the seeds of the Brexit and "Trumpism".

Brexit and the Trump presidency also have to do with the recent attempts to sign inter-regional and international agreements. Regional agreements are much easier to sign than multilateral ones, the latter being based on the most-favored-country nation WTO rules. This is one of the main reasons why during the decade of lack of progress on the Doha Round, regional agreements proliferated. Regional integration and bilateral agreements (the "spaghetti bowl" as coined by Bhagwati 2004) began to prevail in order to overcome the difficulties of multilateralism. Countries that tend to sign regional agreements are similar and their economic integration usually relates to intra-industry trade rather than inter-industry trade.

Recently, however, there have been several attempts to sign inter-regional agreements that integrate different economic areas among themselves. The Transatlantic Trade and Investment Partnership (TTIP), the Trans-Pacific Partnership (TPP), the EU-Canada Comprehensive Economic and Trade Agreement (CETA) are recent examples of inter-regional agreements. These types of arrangements have raised concerns among developed country populations, especially in the USA and the EU. They attempt to transform separate regional agreements into multilateral ones, by enlarging gradually the economic integration towards the WTO rules of the most-favored-nation type, but in trying to do that, the same difficulties experienced by multilateral agreements have arisen.

The curious thing is that TTIP found objections both in Europe for a widespread range of reasons, such as GMOs to milder sanitary regulations, and in the USA for fear of job loss. Other inter-regional agreements have similar concerns at varying levels. In early 2017, the USA unceremoniously discarded TPP as one of the first acts of the Trump presidency and in all probability has departed from multilateral approaches to trade agreements for the foreseeable future in favor of bilateral negotiations.

2.4   Brexit's Economic and Political Rationale and Consequences

Generally in the West it is now commonly accepted that globalization and accompanying technological advances have played a large role in the widening gap of income distribution. Essentially, labor has lost at the expense of capital, with profits increasing their share of the income pie. Economic sectors more exposed to global competition have been impoverished, thereby creating a wide income divergence. As mentioned above, little or no measures have been taken in favor of the so-called losers of globalization, which has exacerbated the average worker's problems.

Shift in UK exports of goods away from the EU reflects a change in the sources of economic growth, with Asia, in particular, gaining primacy. To some extent, other EU member states have also shifted their goods exports away from the intra-Europe market, but the effect has been most pronounced in the UK (Gros 2016). Germany, in spite of strong immigration, maintains a very low unemployment rate, since its comparative advantage has been in technologically advanced products that, in fact, found a quite significant market in developing countries, with a specialization that took advantage of globalization. The UK, instead, specialized more in financial services. The expansion of the financial services industry—which creates few but very highly paid jobs—has contributed to rising income inequality, which has been more prominent in the UK than elsewhere in the EU. And inequality helped fuel the widespread frustration with globalization and the so-called "establishment" élites. Clearly the 2008 and subsequent 2010 financial market downturn added nuclear fuel to this frustration as the UK economy went into a tailspin and is still struggling to recover from. Thus in spite of the overall percentage of immigrants in the UK being the same as in Germany, and in spite of the UK unemployment rate being below 5 percent, the anti-immigration sentiment prevailed and helped to carry the Brexit campaign to victory. The fact that the UK now relies more heavily on access to world markets than on access to the EU's internal market surely contributed to the Brexit vote, as it lessened the sacrifice that the UK would have to make to regain control over "hot-button" issues like immigration.

The general belief that the UK could secure privileged access to world markets through bilateral arrangements on its own rather than as part of the EU also helped.

The fact still remains that the EU has lost its second-largest economic power and the UK has lost its largest trading partner (EU). Approximately 50 percent of all the UK trade is still with the EU. Over the years, EU membership has provided the UK with cheaper goods and services and a greatly enhanced platform for UK exports. There is no doubt that Brexit will lower UK-EU trade due to higher tariffs and non-tariff barriers (NTBs). While the UK will benefit in that it would not be making net contributions to the EU budget, in the long run it could lose out on additional integration savings. In the end Brexit will actually result in a loss of GDP and productivity for the UK and all EU countries, at least in the medium term. While the UK may in the long term benefit from bilateral deals and less regulation (EU), it currently boosts as one of the least regulated product and services market in the OECD. Additional unknowns will be the UK future credit rating, UK stock market volatility, future exchange rate of the pound sterling which has hit a recent low of $1.1841/£, and other short-term financial stability and economic risks. Brexit has generally been seen as great folly by the markets and Continental Europeans.

While it was initially hoped that Brexit would mean a revised relationship with the EU single market, this hope was laid to rest on January 19, 2017.[18] At the Davos World Economic Forum Annual Summit, UK PM May announced a hard exit. She ended the speculation to a protracted negotiation within the single market framework (where Britain already has exemptions that are advantageous, that is, in labor law regulations or in the Schengen agreement). PM May had just cause to end Britain's EU single market membership as it restricts the UK's ability to negotiate bilateral deals, i.e. with the likes of the USA, China, India, Persian Gulf States, Australia and New Zealand. It should, however, be noted that the membership in the EU's Customs Union[19] is a more critical component once the UK is out of the EU Single Market since that deals directly with cross-border preferential tariffs. Thus PM May exited the EU with little fanfare, although it should be pointed out that one large downside is that the UK will have less global gravitas in such dealings without the EU. PM

May hopes, however, to transform to a new "Global Britain" that would leave the EU in its entirety in its attempt to become a hub for foreign investment. She foreshadows a bold vision for the UK in a 12-step plan which essentially entails turning the UK as a corporate tax haven, remedying the backlash against globalization, regaining control over its borders (immigrant issues), ending EU courts' jurisdiction in the UK and furthering British influence on the global stage.

Much of PM May's plan for a hard exit and a new beginning for the UK outside the EU fell apart when she misjudged the support for and fears of a post-Brexit world and called for snap elections on June 8, 2017, to consolidate her power. The snap elections led to a near fatal blow to PM May and left her with a hung parliament and no clear victory. The dramatic erosion of her power base also eroded all her major goals—including plans for a hard Brexit. She has had to do a sharp U-turn on her hard Brexit strategy, and this has now cemented the reality of a soft Brexit.

The ideological differences that have always carried an undertone in all EU policy deliberations have now been laid bare and visible to the naked eye. The war is on two fronts. First, a more widespread divide among its member states on continuing to push along step-by-step EU integration despite ongoing Eurozone economic malaise and lack of job recovery resulting from the 2007/08 global financial crisis and the 2010/12 Eurozone debt crisis, while austerity measures continue to exact a huge human toll. The Eurozone's unemployment rate stood at 9.8 percent at the beginning of 2017 (more than double the USA) with approximately 1 in 4 unemployed being youths under 25. The results have been sluggish growth, inability to create new jobs, migrant backlash, widening income disparities with a lost generation and a lost decade that has led to dissatisfaction with élite governance which in Europe is more directly sharply aimed at the EU institutions and integration as opposed to national governments.

Second, between the UK's long-standing Anglo Saxon ideological stance on labor, capitalism and free markets and Continental Europe's more social market approach which historically mandates a tight and highly regulated labor market structure relative to the UK and USA. The latter is usually believed to have played a role in creating decades of long-term unemployment, structural youth unemployment, high taxes and low productivity to labor wages ratio in most of continental Europe (Germany being the largest exception). It should be noted, however, that in the aftermath of the 2010 Eurozone crisis, many EU countries' labor markets were forced to liberalize as, for example, Italy. This resulted, though, in increased social problems, such as a higher resentment among the population in an environment of weak economic growth and persistent high unemployment. The process of European integration so far had followed the direction that all regional integration processes take, namely, intra-industry trade, given that there are no clear comparative advantages among countries that are approximately at the same level of industrialization. This is essentially why European integration, on the one hand, can claim that no industries have disappeared but, at the same time, these industries remain woefully less productive with higher wages as a norm as opposed to their US or Asian counterparts and have been struggling to compete due to decades of EU protection and/or subsidies. There are of course exceptions to the rule such as Germany as a whole and northern regions of the EU, where wages have increased with productivity, or the southern regions, where wages were low in absolute terms, but still too high compared to labor productivity.

While the general global consensus is that the US recovery is slow—but also tangible and real—the Eurozone recovery is limping along, and the major emerging markets will continue to have good growth albeit slower than in past decades. The fact is that economic data is not representing the realities or perceived realities on the ground for the common worker, and that is adding confusion to an already charged environment of facts and "alternative facts". Blaming populism for economic fear mongering might suggest implicitly that if one were to look beyond the rhetoric, economic recovery is occurring in the West. This is not the whole story. In the post-2008 world, there is a real gap between the actual economic data (i.e. the unemployment rate, the GDP growth, or the growth of the GDP per capita) and economic reality. For example, the USA's current 4.7 percent unemployment (Dec 2017) is by all standards good news, except that it does not take into account the millions of workers in forced part-time jobs or the underemployed who are counted as employed. Moreover, the unemployment issue in the West, in particular the USA, is not just about more jobs but rather the quality of jobs (more high-skilled jobs).

Furthermore, the growing gaps of income inequality have not been stemmed despite economic growth data showing that the West is recovering albeit slowly.

PM May perhaps has found some, although probably temporary, high ground for her vision for jettisoning the UK boldly out of the EU when US President Trump extended a hand and suggested a bilateral UK-US trade agreement. Even if a US-UK bilateral trade discussion replaces TTIP discussions, it will be difficult and it will take a long time to come to fruition. Another "Trumpism" is the unknown status of the UK's "special relationship" with the USA. While PM May portrayed the January 2017 visit to the USA as fruitful, it is unclear how much support she has inside the UK for a Trump presidency that is increasingly baffling, distressing and alienating the majority of the world. PM May will not be able to control the British public's outspoken criticism of Trump, for example, for the so-called Muslim Ban or the soft stance on Russia. Such criticism could easily upset the overly sensitive US President, especially if British public outcry derails an officially planned Trump visit to the UK. This could quickly sour relations between the USA and the UK. Thus, as the world charters an unknown course in this new era of uncertainty, markets will have heightened sensitivity and volatility, making trade deals harder to broker. Furthermore, at play are other fundamental differences that divide the UK and the USA. For example, the UK seeks to further its international goals and global leadership agenda while "Trumpism" calls for a retreat from multilateralism; the UK advocates free trade while Trump advocates protectionism albeit both leaders are pro-business. More importantly, Trump's beliefs and actions are in direct contradiction to those of the UK in key strategic arenas, such as NATO's role and importance, climate protection and Russian containment. The only common ground between the USA and the UK is Brexit, in that both see it as a good thing; but even on this issue half of the UK believes Brexit is a catastrophe. Thus it would seem that for the most part the UK is more in line with the EU's thinking on almost all matters rather than the USA. Immigration remains a mixed subject as we move forward from the French and towards the German national elections that are perhaps the most significant since WWII. While right-wing populists were gaining ground in Europe last year, the 2017 "Trumpism" factor seemed to have put a wind beneath their wings and victory seems more probable in spring 2017. Many believed that what was risky seemed to have gotten riskier. This, however, did not play out as expected. In fact, the French voted in a centrist Emmanuel Macron who dealt a humiliating blow to the traditional parties. The French embraced an untested centrist party in the wake of the right-wing populism threatening to take over Europe, thus effectively repelling the far-right challenge of Marie Le Pen's national front at an all-time high of French right-wing nationalism and populism. A month after the Presidential election, Macron won a landslide victory in the French legislative elections ending French party politics as we know it. For the first time in 50 years, more than half of the French voters abstained. Between the low turnout and a very strong performance of Macron's party, the 39-year-old French president is in a strong position to intact his pro-business reforms, including a battle with the French labor unions. Macron has a tough battle ahead of him as his is the first government since 1958 that includes both the extreme left and right. Many believe that the true gauge of the presence of right-wing populist will occur during the German elections in September 2017.

There are many reasons for the current European populism. First among equals is the 2008 and subsequent 2010 financial crisis that still plagues Europe as is evident with the ECB unlimited bond buying program for Southern Europe (mainly Italy and Spain), its version of QE and continued near zero percent interest rates. The subsequent austerity measures that were widening the already large income disparity and rampant joblessness added significant amount of fuel to ignite not only right-wing but also left-wing populism in Europe. It should be noted that the US right-wing and the European version of right-wing parties have ideological differences, but they share two key principles: eradication of the liberal order and of the "establishment". If the immigration and terrorism is added to this mix, it is nothing short of a highly charged and combustible mixture that will play out in the 2017 European election and referendum landscape. Adding to the mixture are escalating public fears to new heights of the threat of job loss due to technology with the specter of Artificial Intelligence (AI) ready to burst into a workforce that has already perceived itself to be hammered by 30 years of delocalization due to globalization. The more recent Artificial Intelligence (AI) resurrection will increase productivity but will put further pressure on low-skilled jobs. Europe's inability to remain competitive in wages, innovation and productivity versus the USA and more recently South East Asian and South Asian emerging markets has set the perfect breeding ground for populist movements in France's Marie Le Pen (NF) to Germany's Frauke Petry (AfD). Despite Macron's landslide victory and Le Pen's humiliating Presidential defeat, the Internet and social networks have provided these charismatic right-wing populist leaders direct access to the people while debunking conventional sources of news, hence "alternative facts" and "fake news".

Perhaps Britain's future is best captured by the phrase "Britain is Caught Between Trump and a Hard Place"[20] which lays bare PM May's new "geopolitical reality now: caught between a retrograde American administration with which it no longer shares a world view and a frustrated Europe it is trying to divorce" (Raynes 2016), with a questionable mandate to move forward on the EU divorce in the aftermath of the snap election. If this was all, democratic West may survive, but the perception of Brexit and "Trumpism" and the accompanied loss of Italy's PM Matteo Renzi's referendum and subsequent resignation have given the world the impression of an EU that is seemingly moving dangerously far right for many until recently. A pleasant surprise during the summer of 2017 in all major EU elections to date has proven otherwise. Italy will in all probability not follow a right-wing agenda and will follow a path similar to France but a more populist one much like the USA. There is a general sentiment that when the USA swings left or right, there is always a confidence that a correction towards the middle will occur at some point. European history has proven that shifts to the right in Europe are much longer-lasting with devastating consequences not just for itself but the world. In a surprising turn of events recently, Europe is resisting its right-wing tendencies under the weighty circumstances, and the UK has read the tea leaves wrong. Centrist French President Macron's victory plays a possible pivotal juncture in history in retrospect. Moreover, Britain, as like all other large European countries, lacks gravitas without the EU in the modern world of the USA, Russia, India and China (URIC).[21] Thus its departure not only hurts Britain itself, but Europe as a whole, as the knife-edge balancing of the far right on the Continent is not guaranteed a good outcome yet. Thus possibly impacting the whole world as it has done twice before—now specially since the post-WWII American watch-dog has turned to the right itself and pursuing a return to isolationism (albeit pro-business but protectionist) with weaning interest in the world plights if there is no self-interest. Brexit's timing could not be worse especially with the weakened mandate of the current government that is barely legitimate in the eyes of its own public; we all have cause to worry. Now the élites of the world pin their hope on Germany with Merkel to steer the EU on a safer course. Germany, ultimately, may have its turn to sure up the world's belief in democratic free markets.

2.5   Concluding Remarks

Psychological factors, populism, post-truth, alternative facts or the fear of a cultural invasion of foreigners and terrorism is preparing Trumpist USA and the right-wielding Europe for a clash of civilizations between the West and the East along religious lines.

We knew that the protests were coming from blue collars, who were seeing their jobs taken away both by delocalization or imports from foreign companies and from immigrants from less developed countries. However, now even the middle class feels challenged and resents the (true or perceived) economic/social/cultural costs and losses that the openness of international trade, capital mobility and labor flows may be inflicting on their local communities. This middle class reaction may well be proved by the fact that unemployment afflicts workers with secondary education, much more than in the past than those with primary education. And in the end all the referendums and elections are proving this correct. The modern Western economic ailments of long-term unemployment, underemployment, stagnant wages, and income inequality are the underpinnings of this growing dissatisfaction with the status quo of the post-World War II order.

It is already abundantly clear that the Brexit and "Trumpism" are causing global disruptions, but the question to ask is if this is only the first stages of a new era of disruption or destruction well beyond a fourth wave of globalization? The era of strong men seems to be emerging and people are embracing it from Turkey to the USA, India to the Philippines to name a recent few. One thing is clear: there are many more shock and awe events to come as the old World War II order is being challenged. Perhaps the most dangerous to the world is if history repeats itself on the European continent as it swings to the right,[22] only now the USA is swinging right with them and the UK is standing alone.

Notes

1. The first phase of globalization can be identified with the period coinciding approximately with the "Belle Époque", otherwise known as the "Beautiful Era or the Golden Age" (and that corresponds approximately with the US "gilded age") from the beginning of the 1870—with the opening of the Suez Canal and coinciding also with the coming of age of the French Third Republic—until WW1. This was a period characterized by peace, prosperity, optimism coupled with scientific/technological and cultural advancements in Europe where literature, music, theater, and visual art thrived. After the interlude of the two world wars, the second phase of globalization began from 1945 through the economic recovery and the high growth rates of the 1960s, to the instability of the 1970s (Della Posta 2009, 2017).
2. But this time difference may just reflect the usual distance that it takes between the occurrence of significant economic events and the political response to them, as it has been the case already in the 1929 Great Depression, followed by the new deal only a few years later, and of the 1973 oil crisis, followed by the neoliberal political revolution only a few years later (Kaletski 2017).
3. Post-truth is commonly referred to as that situation in which emotional or not verified beliefs prevail over objective facts.
4. At least until the end of the 1990s.
5. Only recently the role of neoliberalism in shaping those policies has been discussed critically by Ostry et al. (2016).
6. A critical review of the process of globalization over the last two centuries is provided by Nayyar (2007).
7. Several well established and respected economists agreed with some of those complaints, including Rodrik (1997, 1999, 2000, 2007) and Stiglitz (2002, 2005). The critical aspects of the process of economic

globalization were also analyzed by Della Posta (2009), European Commission (2002) and Oxfam (2002). Bhagwati (2004) instead is among the most convinced supporters of the benefits of economic globalization, especially when considering trade in goods and services. The role of economic theory relative to globalization was clarified by Krugman and Obstfeld: "If the market failures are not too bad to start with, a commitment to free trade might in the end be a better policy than opening the Pandora's box of a more flexible approach. This is, however, a judgment about politics rather than economics. We need to realize that economic theory does *not* provide a dogmatic defense of free trade, something that it is often accused of doing" (Krugman and Obstfeld 2008, p. 229). As argued by Rodrik (2016a), the fear that acknowledging some problems with globalization would have opened the way to populist critics, made most economists always support the case of internationally free markets, thereby undermining the credibility of the profession. This fits perfectly with what Zingales (2015) also wrote about the fact that too often economists have seemed to flank even bad financial institutions, again, just because not doing it would have meant to risk giving arguments to the anti-globalizers.

8. The reduction of inequality across or within countries was not included among the Millennium Development Goals.

9. The Doha Round has not been concluded successfully yet, also because of the resistance by developed countries to accept the reduction of the protection granted mainly to agriculture and manufactures.

10. It should be noted that the average tariff rates had already been reduced substantially and it is difficult now to reach an agreement in the remaining most contentious sectors, like agriculture and services, that had not been covered under the previous Uruguay Round.

11. This is far from new. When the USA had an economy still characterized by comparative advantages in agriculture, the "infant" industry claimed protection, and somebody like the US President Abraham Lincoln (1861–1865) was making declarations like this, in response to the British economists who were arguing against the imposition of American import tariffs: "I don't know much about the tariff, but I do know if I buy a coat in America, I have a coat, and America has the money" (reported by Oxfam 2002, p. 59).

12. This idea was originally designed in 1950 by Merrill Flood and Melvin Dresher of the RAND Corporation and later Albert Tucker formalized into a "game" using prison terminologies and renamed it the "prisoner's dilemma" (Poundstone 1992).

13. Vilfredo Pareto (1848–1923).

14. A large part of the American population is not persuaded either (Blinder, 2016).
15. Shinal, John (2014).
16. The assistance to workers losing their jobs is usually seen as potentially distortionary, since it might remove their incentives to actively look for a new job. It can be questioned, however, whether a structural and widespread loss of unskilled jobs—with fewer and fewer alternative possibilities of employment, as it has been happening in the past and is expected to happen in the future—may require a different approach.
17. Aeppel, Timoth (2015)
18. Brexit may still have a positive impact on the process of European integration (Torres and Bongardt, 2016). The effects of Brexit on the EU is also discussed by De Grauwe (2016) and Pisani-Ferry et al. (2016)
19. A customs union is a free trade area with a common external tariff.
20. Coined by Thomas Raines, Research Fellow and Program Manager, Europe Programme, Chatham House, in his Nov 16, 2016 article "Britain is Caught between Trump and a Hard Place".
21. Coined by Scheherazade Rehman, Director EU Research Center and Professor of International Finance/Business, The George Washington University, 2017. URIC @ copyright Scheherazade Sabina Rehman @ January 2017.
22. All across Europe there is a resurrection of right-wing and/or populist parties, for example, UK Independence Party, Norway's Progress Party, Finland's Finns Party, Denmark's Danish Peoples Party, Netherlands, Party of Freedom, Belgium's Vlaams Belang, Poland's Law and Justice, Switzerland's Swiss People's Party, Austria's Freedom Party of Austria, Slovakia's Slovak National Party, Hungary's Fidesz, Jobbick, and, with more populist connotations, Italy's Lega Nord and 5 Stars movement.

References

Aeppel, Timothy. 2015. What Clever Robots Mean for Jobs. *WSJ*, February 24.

Atkinson, Anthony. 2015. *Inequality: What Can Be Done?* Cambridge, MA: Harvard University Press.

Bhagwati, J. 2004. *In Defence of Globalisation*. Oxford: Oxford University Press.

Blinder, A. 2016. The American Public Against Trump. *Project Syndicate*, December 28. Available at the web address: https://www.project-syndicate.org/commentary/trump-economic-positions-unpopular-by-alan-s--blinder-2016-12.

Bourguignon, Francois. 2015. *The Globalization of Inequality*. Trans. Thomas Scott-Railton. Princeton: Princeton University Press.

De Grauwe, Paul. 2016. What Future for the EU After Brexit? *Forum The Post-Brexit European Union, Intereconomics* 51 (5): 248, September/October.

Deaton, Angus. 2015. *The Great Escape: Health, Wealth, and the Origins of Inequality*. Princeton: Princeton University Press.

Della Posta, Pompeo. 2009. Asymmetric Globalization: Theoretical Principles and Practical Behaviour Guiding Markets Liberalization. In *Globalization, Development and Integration: A European Perspective*, ed. Pompeo Della Posta, Milica Uvalic, and Amy Verdun, 19–33. Houndmills: Palgrave Macmillan.

———. 2017. *The Economics of Globalization* (mimeo).

European Commission. 2002. *Responses to the Challenges of Globalization. A Study on the International Monetary and Financial System and on Financing for Development*, European Economy, Special Report Number 1.

Gros, Daniel. 2016. The Economics of Brexit: It's Not About the Internal Market. *CEPS Commentary*, September 22. https://www.ceps.eu/publications/economics-brexit-it%E2%80%99s-not-about-internal-market.

Kaletsy, Anatole. 2017. *Trumping Capitalism?*, January 20, Project Syndicate – The world's opinion page. Available at: https://www.project-syndicate.org/onpoint/trumping-capitalism-by-anatole-kaletsky-2017-01?barrier=accessreg.

Krugman, P. 1987. Is Free Trade Passé? *The Journal of Economic Perspectives* 1 (2): 131–144.

Krugman, P., and M. Obstfeld. 2008. *International Economics: Theory and Policy*. 8th ed. Boston: Addison-Wesley.

Lagrain, Philippe. 2016. *Brexit Into Trumpland*. January 19. Available at the web page: https://www.project-syndicate.org/commentary/theresa-may-hard-brexit-by-philippe-legrain-2017-01.

Milanovic, Branko. 2016. *Global Inequality, A New Approach for the Age of Globalization*. Cambridge, MA: Harvard University Press.

Nayyar, Deepak. 2007. Globalisation, History and Development: A Tale of Two Centuries. *Cambridge Journal of Economics* 30: 137–159.

Ostry, Jonathan D., Prakash Loungani, and Davide Furceri. 2016. Neoliberalism: Oversold? *IMF Finance and Development* 53 (2, June): 38–41.

Oxfam. 2002. *Rigged Rules and Double Standards: Trade, Globalization and the Fight Against Poverty*. Oxford: Oxfam.

Oxfam. 2016. *An Economy for the 1% – How Privilege and Power in the Economy Drive Extreme Inequality and How this Can be Stopped*. Available at the web address: https://www.oxfam.org/sites/www.oxfam.org/files/file_attachments/bp210-economy-one-percent-tax-havens-180116-en_0.pdf.

Piketty, Thomas. 2014. *Capital in the XXI Century*. Cambridge, MA: Harvard University Press.

Pisani-Ferry, Jean, Norbert Rottgen, Andre' Sapir, Paul Tucker, and Guntram B. Wolfe. 2016. *Europe After Brexit: A Proposal for A Continental Partnership*. Brussels: Bruegel Institute.

Poundstone, William. 1992. *Prisoner's Dilemma*. New York: Anchor Books.

Raines, Thomas. 2016. *Britain Is Caught Between Trump and a Hard Place*. London: Chatham House.

Rodrik, Dani. 1997. *Has Globalization Gone Too Far?* New York: Institute for International Economics.

Rodrik, D. 1999. Globalisation and Labour, or: If Globalisation Is a Bowl of Cherries, Why Are there So Many Glum Faces Around the Table? In *Market Integration, Regionalism and the Global Economy*, ed. R. Baldwin, D. Cohen, et al. Cambridge: Cambridge University Press.

Rodrik, Dani. 2000. How Far Will International Economic Integration Go? *Journal of Economic Perspectives* 14 (1, Winter): 177–186.

———. 2007. *One Economics Many Recipes: Globalization, Institutions and Economic Growth*. Princeton: Princeton University Press.

———. 2016a. *Straight Talk on Trade, Project Syndicate*. November 15, Available at the web address: https://www.project-syndicate.org/commentary/trump-win-economists-responsible-by-dani-rodrik-2016-11.

———. 2016b. *No Time for Trade Fundamentalism, Project Syndicate*. October 14, Available at the web address: https://www.project-syndicate.org/commentary/protectionism-for-global-openness-by-dani-rodrik-2016–10 (some protection in the 1980s saved from closures).

Shinal, John. 2014. Future Economy: Many Will Lose Jobs To Computers. *USA Today*, May.

Stiglitz, Joseph E. 2002. *Globalization and Its Discontents*. New York: W.W. Norton.

Stiglitz, Joseph. 2005. The Overselling of Globalization. In *Globalization: What's New*, ed. M. Epstein. New York: Columbia University Press.

———. 2016. *Globalisation and Its New Discontents*, Project Syndicate. August 5.

Torres, Francisco, and Annette Bongardt. 2016. The Political Economy of Brexit: Why Making It Easier to Leave the Club Could Improve the EU. *Intereconomics* 51 (4): 214–219.

World Bank Group. 2016. *Taking on Inequality – Poverty and Shared Prosperity 2016*. International Bank for Reconstruction and Development/The World Bank.

Zingales, Luigi. 2015. *Does Finance Benefit Society?* Presidential Address of the 2015 American Financial Association, January.

3

Brexit and the European Union in the Context of Globalization

José Renato Gonçalves

1. Several circumstances were and are still core to the numerous international economic integration processes undertaken over the last few decades, particularly since the end of World War II, first and paradigmatically on the European continent and then in several other parts of the world.[1]

The reasons behind the need for international political and economic cooperation in an increasingly interdependent world are evident, namely, because everyone can now acquire goods produced in almost all points of the earth. Since the problems are no longer restricted to national borders, the solutions require combined measures by several States or the engagement or even the creation of new international bodies. The attention of researchers into the economic and political integration between countries has focused on the reasons and bases of this innovative process and the implications it carries, including the imposition of substantial, intense and apparently "definitive" restraints on States' sovereignty, which has for a long time been restricted by the expansion and exigency of international

J.R. Gonçalves (✉)
CIDEEFF, Lisbon University School of Law - Faculdade de Direito da Universidade de Lisboa, Alameda da Universidade - Cidade Universitária, Lisbon, Portugal

© The Author(s) 2017
N. da Costa Cabral et al. (eds.), *After Brexit*,
https://doi.org/10.1007/978-3-319-66670-9_3

relations, based above all on interstate cooperation, but States have never been as badly hit as in the recent situations of international economic "integration".

2. State sovereignty has never been considered an absolute reality and is understood within the context of recognition and relations between several sovereign entities, which make up a whole, to wit, the international community. The notion of sovereignty is therefore compatible with the States' legal binding to fulfil international duties. Accordingly, when it is stated that States enjoy total freedom to choose their economic and social regime, under any attempt by other States to interfere, according to article 2(1) of the Charter of Economic Rights and Duties of States, of 1974, this does not mean denying the evident and indispensable coexistence, on equal terms, of each sovereign State in relation to other States, likewise sovereign entities.[2]

As such, the United Nations Declaration on Principles of International Law concerning Friendly Relations and Co-operation among States [General Assembly Resolution 2625 (XXV)], of 24 October 1970, expressly recognizes that all States are equally sovereign: they have the same rights and duties and are members of the international community, regardless of their economic, social, political or other differences. This means that "each State has the right freely to choose and develop its political, social, economic and cultural systems" [e)], and that "[each State] has the duty to comply fully and in good faith with its international obligations and to live in peace with other States" [f)].

This traditional framework that explains the relations between sovereign States was not questioned by the successive and increasingly frequent economic relations based on international cooperation, generally driven by the reciprocal benefits of such relations, which are susceptible of being exploited by all players, public or private, legal persons or private individuals, particularly those that are most directly involved in these international relations, producers and consumers, exporters and importers, whose number has grown exponentially as international trade has grown also and become mainstream. This is the same as saying the increasing economic interdependence among the various countries, which led to the possible consumption by any one person, regardless of where they are on the planet, of any good produced anywhere else in the world, near or far, given his or her preference and choice.

The acts of political and economic cooperation among States to harmonize rules have generally reduced the barriers on international trade—by lowering customs duties; forbidding certain discriminatory practices against foreign products, services and producers or suppliers; demanding transparency of procedures; promoting good governance; and committing to the fight against corruption and other criminal behaviour. As a result, economic interdependence grew owing to the gradual globalization of exchanges, a centuries-old process that began in the fifteenth and sixteenth centuries with the Portuguese and the Spanish, and later developed by the Dutch and the British, until at least the end of the nineteenth century and beginning of the twentieth century, when, on the eve of World War I, the level of economic openness towards the outside was extraordinarily high, and did not just include the international trade of goods but also financial markets, based precisely in the City of London, as well as the free circulation of people, with an unprecedented number of migrants, even from different continents (mostly from Europe to America).

3. The informal international economic integration process that was carried out on a worldwide scale in the period prior to World War I was not based on minimally solid institutional pillars, but rather, essentially, on the will and tolerance of States, particularly the ones with greater economic relevance, in the sense that they not only allowed but also protected, unilaterally yet effectively on the political and legal levels, the aspirations of the players engaged in the international economic relations.[3]

The obvious institutional and legal weakness of the international economic order at the end of the nineteenth and start of the twentieth century made its collapse easier, when faced with the difficulties exposed by the growing mistrust towards foreigners, which worsened in the following years. Accordingly, this would only conform to nationalist and protectionist economic measures, inevitably intensified as the armed conflict initiated and escalated as of 1914.

Nationalist and protectionist policies predominated in several countries in the world up to the end of World War II in 1945. Their basic instruments were strict import and export quotas; the prohibition of international trade of certain goods with several countries deemed adversary or enemies; extremely high customs duties, rigid constraints on international financing and the circulation of capital, as well as of payments, plus the respective operations, were subject to casuistic clearing decisions grounded above all on political criteria, alongside other quantitative restrictions on imports and exports among various States, by all sorts of more or less declared or underlying confrontations, due to the growth in uncertainty and mistrust in international relations.

When the prejudicial economic consequences of nationalistic and protectionist political positions and measures (typical of explicit or latent armed conflict) were acknowledged, several negotiation processes were kick-started with the aim of finding new ways of international economic relations that could be in force following the end of war. These ways were not as based on nationalism and protectionism as during the inter-war period, but rather on the openness towards the outside and the non-discrimination of foreigners and among foreigners, or of goods according to their origin, to try to foster the creation of wealth with more predictable and long-lasting foundations, that would ultimately benefit all peoples, in a cosmopolitan perspective rather than just having some peoples against the others.

4. The new international economic order that began to be designed at the end of World War II was to be put in place as quickly as possible after the end of the conflict, as agreed at the Bretton Woods conference in New Hampshire, United States of America, in the summer of 1944. The establishment of an International Monetary System and an International Monetary Fund (IMF) was agreed on at this conference. The organization would be tasked with managing the monetary order, with the main goal of allowing, facilitating and ensuring international payments, required for international trade. It was later decided to set up a new international trade order, albeit in a relatively precarious and provisional manner at first, through an executive agreement, without solid and long-lasting institutional support, through the approval of the General Agreement on Tariffs and Trade (GATT) in 1947, that would only be gradually consolidated on a mostly factual basis given the failure in the negotiations at the Havana Conference in 1948, which envisaged the creation of an International Trade Organization and the entry into force of the Havana Charter (whose Part IV was the GATT), but which, nonetheless, would not be approved by the States.

With the purpose of setting up a new international economic order guided by non-discrimination towards the origin of goods or nationality of producers, the General Agreement did not yield immediate major impact effects on a global scale. This was above all due to its many weaknesses:

> With regard to its legal founding—an *executive agreement* rather than an international treaty, as proposed at the Havana Conference with regard to the "Havana Charter);
>
> As to the lack of a minimally consistent and stable institutional basis—the envisaged International Trade Organization, which was established in the Havana Charter, was never actually created;
>
> As to the restriction of its geographic scope—although it included the most significant states economically at the time, it did not cover several countries that decisively expanded their respective international economic clout in the following decades and up to now;
>
> Also with regard to its material scope—limited to goods.[4]

5. The new economic order was heavily criticized right from the very start, due to full or partial disagreement with its fundamental principles or simply the way in which these would be enforced, given the national specifications, which were often different to those principles, many times deemed prejudicial owing to the low level of the countries' development, without sufficient capabilities or motivation to face up to the added challenges of more openness to the outside and immediate subjection to international competition.

The first upfront rejection of the new world order was by the socialist-driven countries, whose economies were guided by the principle of central management, contrary to the market and to the freedoms of economic and entrepreneurial initiative, as well as owing to profit, characteristic of the capitalist economies. The Union of Soviet Socialist Republics (USSR) and several other countries under its direct influence coherently rejected the GATT.

A sort of "iron curtain" (a term Churchill made famous) had descended on Europe, from North to South, dividing it in two for a long time—East and West. The Eastern economic conception, inspired in the Mercantilism and Nationalism trends typical of closed economies, lasted and influenced other alternative conceptions to the prevailing economic regime, accepted in countries under Soviet influence and other socialist countries in several parts of the globe, from Latin America to Africa and Asia.[5]

Another reaction criticizing the international economic order came from less-developed countries, or developing countries, which then formed the "Non-Aligned Movement". In general, they understood that the major goal of development could only exceptionally be followed in a context of decreasing national barriers to trade, with good growth perspectives for industrialized countries only, whose income and wealth would tend to grow at very high levels, difficult to reach by less-developed countries due to their greater relative weaknesses.

This political position garnered a notable media and diplomatic impact and several decisive results, including the first major revision of the GATT, in which non-reciprocity and a more favourable treatment to less-developed countries were preferred, that is, in economic relations between the "Northern" and "Southern" hemisphere countries.

This more favourable treatment to developing countries in Western Europe and North America was reflected in the cooperation and development assistance agreements signed in the following years and up to now,[6] envisaging a heightened reduction or even elimination of customs on the import of goods, leading, in the end, to the recognition of a true and special status for less-developed and developing countries in the framework of the WTO agreements.

Other criticism was made to the prevailing international economic order, or certain parts of it, as asymmetric functioning of the international monetary system, high environmental risks owing to growth, worsening of international inequalities, increasing the number of those "discontents" with this "globalization".

6. Alongside the consecutive strengthening of international economic cooperation, a reflection of the perceptions favourable to its deepening due to the benefits it brought, according to the classical and neoclassical explanations of international trade given by David Ricardo in his theory of "comparative advantages",[7] a new means of relations between countries arose with great might: the international "economic integration". These countries were independent yet close, not just from the geographical point of view, but also in terms of their cultural, political, economic and

legal realms. Several means of international economic integration were known, but they would only grow and characterize the structure of a large part of the world economy after World War II.

The "Customs Union" was at the start of the process that led to the German unification in the nineteenth century, with priors since 1818 and consolidation in 1833, leading up to the creation of the German Empire in 1871. The free trade area was also known; and it is unnecessary to mention the separate phenomenon of national economic integration, within the State territory, which in principle comes before the eventual participation in an international economic integration agreement.[8]

A free trade area presumes freedom of circulation of goods among the participating territories of States or autonomous customs territories, without compromise as to the unification of customs duties applied by the various partners that make up the free trade zone in the economic relations with "third countries". This allows situations of "trade diversion" to make the most of lower customs duties levied by some States in the union. Among the many examples of free trade areas, we can find the European Free Trade Association (EFTA), created by the United Kingdom in 1960, under the Stockholm Treaty,[9] and, more recently, the North American Free Trade Agreement (NAFTA), set up by Canada, the United States and Mexico on 1 January 1994.[10]

7. In addition to the freedom of circulation of goods among the territories of the States or the autonomous customs territories that make it up, obviously without the possibility of imposing or levying any customs duties upon entry or exit of the goods from these territories, the customs union requires the adoption of a Common Customs Tariff for the whole union, both for the import and export of goods. From a perspective of customs duties and other rules on imports and exports, the setting is as though the territories of the various countries that are part of the customs union form one single unit throughout which no customs duties or other measures to restrict the circulation of goods are allowed. The requirement of customs duties or other import or export measures is only for the entry or exit of goods to and from "third countries" that are not part of the customs union.

Unlike what happens in a free trade area, where different customs duties can be levied by the various member States in their relations with third countries, the Common Customs Tariff renders any situations of "diversion of trade" useless. Besides the historical example of the German *Zollverein,* it suffices to note the undoubtedly most paradigmatic of all customs unions (as it became the template for many customs and economic unions created since the 1950s in all corners of the globe, from the Americas to Africa and Asia and Oceania): the European Economic Community (EEC), which currently corresponds to the European Union.[11]

8. As for international economic integration, it is worth distinguishing between its main classifications. Among those most frequently used,[12] we find, regarding the economic scope covered, (*i*) sectoral or "vertical" integration, which involves only one sector or certain sectors of activity (this is the case with the ECSC—European Coal and Steel Community), and (*ii*) general or "horizontal" integration, which encompasses all the economic sectors of the participating countries (cases with the EEC-EC-EU, NAFTA, Mercosul), and, according to Tinbergen (1965), (*iii*) "negative" or passive integration and (*iv*) "positive" or active integration, depending on whether the focus is essentially the elimination of means of discrimination and restriction on trans-border circulation of goods with the aim of trade liberalization ("negative" integration), or, more so than that, changes to instruments and institutions, or the creation of others, with a view to promoting the efficient functioning of markets. This runs alongside other goals, economic and social or wider ("positive" integration), or the opposition, by Lawrence (1996), between (*v*) shallow integration and (*vi*) deep integration, trying to show the differentiated joining of developing countries in relation to the established international trade system.

Given the level of international economic integration, how deep it is, it is usual to distinguish the process using the following categories (with differing variants):

- (*i*)   Free trade area (e.g., the EFTA);
- (*ii*)   Customs union (e.g., the German *Zollverein*);
- (*iii*) Common market ["single market", "internal market"—the formulas successively used by the European Economic Community (EEC), the European Community or European Communities (EC) and the European Union (UE), as the subsequent ones];
- (*iv*)   Economic union (to a certain extent, and with successive progress, e.g., the European Economic Community, the European Communities and the European Union);

- (*v*)   Monetary union (or else economic and monetary union, as the European Economic and Monetary Union - EMU - of the European Union, including the Euro);
- (*vi*) Tax union (to some extent, e.g., the European Community/ Communities and the European Union);
- (*vii*) Fiscal union (or else fiscal and tax union)(to a minor extent, e.g., the European Community/Communities and the European Union);
- (*viii*) Political union (Union of States)(with some traces, e.g., the European Union).

Although customary, it is not thorough to refer to "phases" or "steps" in international economic integration because nothing imposes one or another sequence for approximation or standardization of national economic regimes, with or without a time lag between them, although there may be strict interconnections between the various categories or ways listed above, which justify that the adoption of one of them (for instance monetary union) is preceded by other, or parallel to them. Some States may decide to create a political union at a certain point, coinciding or not with other integration scales. The German reunification following the fall of the Berlin Wall is elucidative of this.

9. As for the compatibility of the diverse means of economic integration with the principles of the international economic order in force, it is worth noting that the GATT and the WTO's cornerstones are non-discrimination, which is seen in their clauses of Most Favored Nation (MFN) (Article I of the GATT) and of National Treatment on internal taxation and regulation (Article III). As a rule, all members of the WTO have the right to being treated as Most Favored Nation by all remaining members.

One of the exceptions to the Most Favored Nation clause concerns less-developed countries, while the other respects to the situations of international economic integration—especially customs unions and free trade areas—but only if the agreement establishing this, or the provisional agreement that envisages its respective creation, does not contain provisions on customs duties and other trade regulations to be applied in the territories of WTO members that are not part of the union or area to be set up, which are as a whole higher or more restrictive than the prior general incidence of the trade duties and regulations applicable in the territories that decided to set up the customs union or free trade area and, if it's a provisional agreement, of being a programme for the establishment of the customs union or free trade area in a reasonable timeframe (cf. Article XXIV-4 and seq. of the GATT).

Since the general rule of the WTO is non-discrimination, any advantage granted by one member to another is automatically extended to all other members. With the exception of the advantages granted to adjacent countries to facilitate frontier traffic [Article XXIV-3-*a*)], and, above all, the more favourable treatment granted by developed members to less-developed members, of which they "do not expect reciprocity" with regard to the commitments undertaken (Article XXXVI-8 of Part IV—Trade and Development, introduced in 1965), the situations of "closer integration between the economies" of the participating countries in order to "increase the freedom of trade", "through voluntary agreements", are also allowed.[13]

10. The regional economic blocs, with their many configurations beyond the traditionally recognized ways, including the possible decision of integrating labour markets, make the respective assessment under the WTO law more complex (cf., for instance, Articles V and V-A of the GATS—General Agreement on Trade in Services).[14]

In any case, it is commonly acknowledged that the international economic integration agreements and organizations may contribute, and have effectively contributed, to the gradual consolidation of an international order that is more favourable to exchanges, characterized by the freedom of entering and trading goods produced abroad, as well as foreign service providers or those set up in the territory of other States, without discrimination between them and also with regard to national goods, producers and services.

Assuming the customs duties or other measures to restrict the circulation of goods and production factors between the parties of a regional economic bloc and third countries are not exacerbated, the greater economic openness within the bloc will contribute towards greater global economic liberalization, despite being restricted to that geographical scope and sectors covered, with the specificities agreed. Notwithstanding, the consistent and persistent evolution towards increasingly greater international economic integration over the last few decades, with rare moments and areas of exception, is not enough to rule out the chance of international economic disintegration—which for a long time seemed completely at bay, and more theoretical than practical, but it never disappeared, as the Brexit referendum abruptly showed beyond doubt in June 2016.

Within the scope of the less stringent economic cooperation, we can accept, at least implicitly, a clear trend towards a persistent evolution heading to a gradual adoption of the main principles of the international order in force, based on the GATT and the WTO. The dissenting positions to the international trade system seemed to be almost always understood as exceptional or transitory, regardless of the severity of some of their manifestations. The rejection of conventional solutions based on the founding principles of the international economic order was frequently underestimated, either due to its limited number, or to its alleged minor and temporary economic impact on an international scale—a sort of recurrent intervals in a long line of trends, surely subject to breaks, "hesitations" or "indecisions", but not a true change in direction or course.

11. But the crises that have arisen over the last few decades, sometimes quite serious, and other specific harmful effects that are frequently linked with the structure of the current international economic order, particularly those relating to the persistence and worsening of economic and social inequalities, as well as the issue of sustainability of high growth rates and their respective environmental impact, have increased uncertainty and doubt as to the future.

There has been no shortage of repeated proposals for a new international economic order, guided not predominantly by economic goals, rather more encompassing purposes—social, political, cultural, environmental—that are highly difficult to assess in all their scope using quantitative criteria only, requiring a weighting of methods and criteria and the inclusion of varied qualitative aspects.[15]

The enormous relevance of all these "new" issues of international coexistence imposes a judicious reflection in the light of the concepts of social market economy and democratic rule of law: they matter and the greater or lesser economic and social progresses in the countries cannot be overlooked. This is whether the growth is "high", "balanced" and "sustainable", measured in absolute or relative terms with identified goals, socially fair, without excluding productivity and competitiveness indicators, dependent on several "endogenous" and "exogenous" factors, "economic" and "non-economic", among which those relating to corporate modernization and other mechanisms for the functioning of the economy as a whole in an advanced society, opened to the world and all innovations and respective use.

International economic cooperation and integration are therefore still commonly understood as one of the most powerful and effective instruments for the expansion and harnessing of economic advantages by those who desire it, which doesn't mean that it is an egalitarian or fair way of sharing those advantages, whether between the countries or the people within each country—because in fact it isn't—, with the aim of using economies of scale and agglomeration, technological spillover relating to intangible goods, management and marketing skills, in addition to the international experience, capable of contributing to an increase in productivity in companies and sectors, as sustained generally by the international economics and economic growth and development theorists.[16]

12. The participation of practically all the countries of the world in international trade has grown continuously since the current economic order was adopted following World War II.

Between 1950 and 2007, international trade has grown on average and in real terms more than 6% per year, albeit in geographically differentiated ways—much greater growth in countries with a capitalist economy, specifically given the active policies of industrialization and replacement of imports adopted by countries from the "socialist bloc", as well as the countries from the "less-developed or developing bloc", up to the gradual adoption by these two "blocs" of the prevailing economic system, market based. Economic growth has also substantially increased, both in absolute terms—3.8% on annual average of GDP, between 1950 and 2007—, as per capita terms—2% on annual average of GDP—in all countries of the world, with noticeable differences along the periods: the annual growth in GDP was much greater from 1950 to 1973 (5.1% per year) than from 1974 to 2007 (2.9% per year), including in per capita terms (respectively, 3.1% and 1.1%).[17]

At the same time, the level of regional specialization of industrial production has decreased (according to data compiled by Krugman): the level of regional specialization decreased from around 0.7 in 1860 to 0.6 in 1880, it increased to 0.75 in 1900 and came close to 0.9 from 1914 to 1939, to then lower continuously to just over 0.8 in 1947, to around 0.65 in 1958, around 0.55 in 1967, around 0.5 in 1977 and around 0.45 in 1987... Always without prejudice to the local, national and regional specificities (differentiated levels of development, very distinctive economic structures, as well as diverse economic and political regimes, differing growth rates, either converging or diverging, own cultures), and even more decisive, without prejudice to the more or less "fair" results of the evolution seen.[18]

The historic trend of growing international economic cooperation and integration (or, simply, "globalization"), which we have already noted, does not exclude areas where the phenomenon did not propagate or where it propagated only restrictively, or "hesitation" or "indecision" intervals, or even the idea of changing course, for the most various reasons and with differing intensity and duration: in the period between the World Wars, in the 1970s and start of the 1980s with the oil crises, and more recently still with other international economic and financial crises, with varying severity and intensity, long or short in time, in the 1990s and start of the millennium, in several countries of the world, as well as at the end of the first decade of this century, with the major global economic and financial crisis of 2008–2009, triggered by the so-called "sub-prime" crisis in the United States in 2007–2008, the repercussions of which quickly became global or near-global, due to the mentioned growing interdependence of several economies, at levels that were undoubtedly greater than in the past.

From a strict economic perspective at least, the greater internationalization of most of the world's countries and the ensuing more intense international interdependence, albeit mostly based on legal instruments of (mere) international cooperation, already substantially reflects a sort of economic integration, certainly still with a fragmented and largely informal nature, as it is carried out through the repetition of numerous acts and relations of millions of subjects and operators, without being fully translated into integration agreements, although impeding the standardization at a global scale of economic regimes, without distancing convergence of criteria and solutions. These are sometimes done through tenuous and unnoticeable ways, without prejudice to the names and other specificities remaining different owing to the national legislations, on which States maintain, without doubt, full sovereignty, which does not waive those in charge from thoroughly weighting all the implications of the choices made.

13. In the international economic integration process, the diversity inherent to the various States has been gradually replaced in several aspects and scales by a new legal and economic reality with growing common traces,

whether from a material perspective, as institutional and procedurally-wise. The standard and typical national diversities, with a few coinciding policies, or not coinciding at all, have led in certain fields to identical solutions, increasingly shared by groups of States when faced with certain challenges that are henceforth dealt with in common, through "bloc" policies and measures. These have possible variants, but only insofar as they do not jeopardize the action of the whole, normally from a stable institutional basis, legally binding, long-lasting and not just dependent on the interpretation of those currently in power—or else there is a risk of casuistry, being transitory, non-consolidation, contrary to the spirit of international integration.[19]

This is therefore characterized by the trend of permanence and convergence of institutional solutions in the regional bloc, but not the irreversibility of the process, because the States are the active subjects and are still the owners of these processes in which they freely accept to participate, under the terms they see fit to bind themselves to, at the most through international treaties, due to the predictable constant weighting of national values and interests. Accordingly, the committed involvement in international integration experiences and processes, for longer or shorter periods, and in highly diversified fields, does not prevent positions of greater or lesser acceptance, or rejection, when faced with projects that have higher or deeper thresholds of integration in a union that has already been formed, which may eventually lead to a full union of States, nor future positions contrary to those adopted beforehand, that may or not result in an eventual disintegration process, as happened with the United Kingdom in the European Union and then with Brexit.

Despite the impressive historic evolution over the last few decades, in international political and economic cooperation the diversity among the various States of the world continues to prevail. The areas for joint action continue limited and are generally insufficient to jeopardize the States' individually. As sovereign entities, these continue to fully exercise their powers, that is, they have normally the last word as to the definition of internal economic rules—so long as they don't breach the State's external obligations.

On the contrary, in international economic integration the bonding and unifying ties for the restricted set of participating States, even when limited to a field or certain fields of policies, sectors or activities—since they are not exceptional, casuistic or merely transitory—tend to become more encompassing or at least to last over time and consolidate, materially and institutionally, in one or more economic or social fields. In principle these are connected, with implications on the exercise of the State's sovereign powers, representing a full, near full or at least highly substantial proximity and unity of points of view and solutions in essential economic or social areas (for example the free circulation of goods and capitals, freedom of establishment, monetary policy...).

14. The endogenous and exogenous causes of the European integration process are frequently distinguished.[20] Among the endogenous causes we can mention, firstly, the concern with ensuring peace in the continent and, afterwards, the goal of fostering economic and social prosperity for its peoples. Among the exogenous reasons for integration, we can refer the dangers emerging from the Cold War, which opposed the two superpowers, the United States and the Soviet Union, and, indirectly, the countries included in their respective spheres of influence, Western and Eastern, on either side of the "iron curtain".

These concerns remained for a long time, albeit in understandably distinctive terms, variable in time depending on the countries and peoples that decided to join the European Communities from the 1950s, when the following were created: European Coal and Steel Community (ECSC) in 1952 and the European Economic Community (EEC) and the European Atomic Energy Community (EAEC or Euratom) in 1958, up to the present day, with the European Union (EU), which succeeded the European (Economic) Community and includes 28 member States (or 27 member States, excluding the United Kingdom, after the conclusion of Brexit, according to the article 50 of the Treaty on European Union).

As the years went by, fear of armed conflict, one of the major threats at the start of the European integration process gradually diminished until a while back. This was mostly after the fall of the Berlin Wall in 1989, and consequently also due to the end of the so-called "iron curtain" and Cold War between the major political, economic, and military blocs, which divided not just Europe but also a large part of the world at the time.[21]

Diversely, the goal of economic and social progress of the peoples remained highly relevant for the countries with weaker economic and social indicators, whether before the time of joining the regional European economic bloc, whether while these indicators were distant from the average of the group.[22] Similarly, the objective of consolidation of political democracy and in general the rule of law was not, and still it is not today recognized in an identical manner in the various EU Member States, especially in recent years and worryingly so in some of the new Member States from former Eastern Europe.

In any case, the national sovereign decision by a State to participate, continue to participate or cease to participate in a "regional economic bloc" or economic union, as the case of the European Union, does not have to fundamentally depend on a detailed cost/benefit analysis of the integration process at present and likewise in the future. Yet, as it is well known, past gains do not guarantee gains in the present and even less so in the future. Anyhow, even if the cost/benefit balance of the integration process is not just clearly positive for a country as it is possible or "easy" to calculate or estimate, nothing prevents that country from choosing to abandon the Union at a certain moment in history, unavoidably a (very) difficult one.

The mere protection by the State of its exercise of determined sovereign powers, which are restricted by integrating a union, under the terms of which those powers are exercised through a common institution, may lead to a decision to withdraw from the organization. Even if the economic balance between costs and benefits of remaining a member of the union is widely positive. Even if the economic and social costs, or those of another nature are very high, or too painstaking to bear, in the medium or long term, with probable harmful effects in several fields (for instance, loss of direct access to developed specialized and large scale markets on a global world, relocation of companies in specific sectors from national territory to other parts of the globe, with consequent loss of income, jobs and public revenue).

Even so, a member State of a union can always choose to consciously exit the partnership, for instance, with the goal of being able to decide on the respective future rules for the organization and functioning of its economy and society, namely, imposing certain limits on the entry into national soil of foreigners, to safeguard the security of its citizens, or simply to stop bearing the cost of hefty sums allocated to the Union's budget, choosing instead to apply those resources to modernizing national structures (education, health, transportation, etc.).

A different matter is determining if the ends that led to the decision to withdraw can be effectively pursued by the country out of the European Union and if the costs necessary to reach the intended goals are not (a lot) higher than the previous ones, stemming from participating in the bloc. More worrying though is if most of the studies drawn up by experts to identify and calculate the costs and benefits of participating in the Union conclude without any doubt that the price of exiting is clearly higher than the price of staying, and, even so, the country chooses to exit.

15. The volume of international trade has grown several dozen-fold since World War II and the flows of foreign investment have also increased, yet today we continue to experience a situation of "semi-globalization" (Ghemawat), because several aspects continue to reflect strong resistance from people and countries to international economic cooperation and integration, that is, to the growing interdependence between the various world economies, the same being applied to globalization. For example, according to some estimates, internet traffic between different countries has not yet reached 2% of the total traffic.[23]

In effect, the States' protectionist concerns are not relics from the past, they have been felt again and are gaining more clout and huge concrete projection, particularly at times of greater difficulty, uncertainty, fear and, in general, severe economic and social crisis, yet not necessarily crises that affect equally all, but mainly some groups in societies that are recurrently and worryingly social and economically fragmented. It could be worth observing that, according to several studies,[24] more than half the *Fortune 500* companies and about half of the companies with the fastest growth in the United States were generated at times of recession or when the markets were at a low, and that, apparently, the companies created at times of recession are better prepared to face up the challenges of expansion and adversity.

The gradual establishment of a regime close to liberalized trade at a truly global scale became possible mostly through the deepening of the phenomena of international economic cooperation and integration. This was as much at a regional or continental scale, as at a universal or quasi-universal scale, to a large extend due to the clear surpassing of bilateralism and its replacement with multilateralism, materialized by the GATT and more recently the WTO agreements, which were conducive to the current economic "globalization" level and trend, likewise reflected in several other fields, a sort of overview that characterizes the persistent and incredibly strong trend of the growing economic interdependence among all or almost all the countries in the world and their respective crucial institutions, whether political or legal, economic or social and cultural.

16. There has undoubtedly been a world economy since the fifteenth–seventeenth centuries, which in the meantime very gradually settled and strengthened, without nonetheless having to overcome numerous and quite often difficult setbacks, until reaching a state of substantial structuring, nowadays, around a series of specific international organizations that were created following World War II.

There are glimpses of economic globalization in many works, such as Adam Smith's *The Wealth of Nations,* where the advantages of having international trade without barriers are heightened, so that the advantages of the division and specialization of labour can be fully exploited. About a century later, Karl Marx also referred to a universal market for trade and finance. More recently, in different fields of knowledge, several authors have drawn on theories of globalization. Teilhard de Chardin, for instance, imagined a society where everyone would communicate among one another, and Marshall McLuhan forecast the creation of a "global village" owing to progress made and the dissemination and access by all audio-visual means.

Globalization is effectively much more than a simple increase or development of the "internationalization" of the national economies. It presumes a veritable qualitative leap, way beyond the mere expansion of international trade and means of cooperation, with a view to, namely, the reduction and suppression of customs barriers and the growing integration among the various countries. Without prejudice to the persistence of several discontinuities and breaks, trade is already carried out or can be carried out virtually, almost borderless, in practically the whole planet. And, since it is justified to mention economic globalization, one can also talk about political, legal, social, cultural, ecological globalization.

No matter how important the major regional economic blocs are—ranging from the European Union to NAFTA (North American Free Trade Agreement), from Mercosul/Mercosur to APEC (Asia-Pacific Economic Cooperation)—in the future most trading will probably be done at a global scale, that is "above" or "beside" those or other major regional economic blocs, especially until the negotiations on the larger trans-pacific and transatlantic partnerships are resumed and the agreements enter into force [Trans-Pacific Partnership (TPP) and Transatlantic Trade and Investment Partnership (TTIP)], in spite of the relevance that other partnerships may take on, such as the Comprehensive Economic and Trade Agreement (CETA) between Canada and the European Union.[25] Trade inside the major three world geographical zones (American, Euro-African and Asian-Pacific) accounts for about half of all international trade in the world, while the remaining half is done indiscriminately between all the countries, under global institutions such as the WTO, the IMF and the UNCTAD,[26] in accordance with the provisions they define.

Time of globalization is characterized by (*i*) economic transactions carried out in real time, thanks to the advances in information technology and telecommunications systems, particularly e-mail and the internet; (*ii*) permanent stock markets that operate almost continuously (there is a 20-hour difference between the opening of the Sidney market and the closing of San Francisco); (*iii*) worldwide financial and monetary markets, including of derivatives (options, futures); (*iv*) the use of the same language (English). Given a new (quasi-) global system, with challenges at a planetary scale, with problems and risks also (quasi-) global (sustainability, environmental protection, security, inequality, lack of preparation by some countries and many people, etc.), truly (quasi-) global institutions are essential, that are capable of satisfactorily responding to the new demands. Therein lies the importance of a better coordination between the several world leading organizations, at a "global" scale, inevitably involving the United Nations.

17. Economic globalization has created many "discontents" (to use the expression made famous by Stiglitz 2002), insofar as, just as predicted, the evolution of the (quasi-) global international economy nowadays would benefit more some countries or peoples, admissibly the richer ones, with bigger losses to the poorer, the most part of humanity, living in "less-developed" or "developing countries".

Among the problems repeatedly underlined by chief critics of the actual phenomenon of globalization are: (*i*) excessive volatility of financial markets, not only in emerging countries, due to insufficient regulation and oversight; (*ii*) marginalization of developing countries, submerged in the poverty, which required a policy to eradicate the problem[27]; (*iii*) insecurity in the labour markets owing to the effect of liberalization, public budget cuts and the erosion of the social or welfare State, which instead of allowing a fairer distribution of available resources among the poorer and the richer tends to benefit the wealth of the latter; and (*iv*) lack of capability by some governments to make important decisions in an increasingly globalized world.

All of this can contribute to solve the controversy that has arisen, which also extends itself to the issue of knowing whether it is preferable to have a world economic liberalization agreement or to firstly achieve regional agreements for economic liberalization and integration. The assessment of the anti-globalization movement or movements is highly complex, just as is the very phenomenon of globalization, with all its respective restraints and effects. It requires extremely attentive consideration as to both the reliability and the relevance and weight of the several aspects to be pondered or which should prevail, to avoid distortions based on partial, insufficient or erroneous data.

One cannot overlook the fact that several countries in the world, some large in scale, were included in the "developing" group half a century ago, and yet they managed to become true economic powers, because they were able to suitably make the most of the advantages of greater openness, in the context of increasing international economic cooperation or quasi-integration, conducive to the present "globalization", while other countries favourable to protectionism and industrial policies bore the costs of refusing economic openness, particularly in some sectors more vulnerable to intense international competition, not seldom at a global scale.

This does not mean that the rules of the game do not tend to favour more advanced countries or not, as they are in the core of the prevailing international economic system in force. In any case, the centrality of the more advanced countries, just as with all the prior evolution stages of the international economy, won't certainly hold "forever". The gravitational fields of the world economy are constantly shifting, although generally in a gradual and quite often in an almost unnoticeable way.

18. It is in this general and highly complex framework of "globalization", a result of the growing international economic cooperation and integration at a universal scale that we must analyse the United Kingdom's decision to exit the European Union in June 2016.

If on the one hand it is surprising in a general context of a trend towards globalization, where countries that choose to not take part risk missing out on opportunities, including taking part in decision-making processes, on the other hand it finds its reasoning in both the upfront and repeated disagreement with the requirements of the European unification project's advances, as they question specific and crucial aspects of national sovereignty (for example, in the field of financial regulation from Brussels, eventually hindering the City of London, conditioning the immigration policy, regarding the amount of national contribution to the European Union budget compared to other Member States...) and, also, perhaps, the circumstance that "globalization" probably won't depend, at least decisively, on the phenomenon of economic regionalism.

The current massive relevance of the international economic integration experiences, particularly in Europe and in the European Union, with a huge impact on the configuration and definition of the actual international economic order's rules, as well as the differences in legal regimes among the member States and those that take part in international economic integration organizations against all other countries in the world, under the WTO law, all contribute to inexorably increase economic and political uncertainty and risks as to the maximum exploitation of the opportunities to generate wealth and expanding competitiveness offered by the status of belonging to the EU. Comparable advantages for the UK outside of the EU will depend on thousands of bilateral agreements with identical content, which will only be feasible after successive negotiations in matters that are typically very difficult and complex.

On the European Union side, problems won't be lesser or easier to solve. The decision to withdraw arises surely by default of the widespread and deep trend that has prevailed until now, of growing economic and political cooperation and integration on an international or "quasi-universal" scale, the globalization, despite the recurring hesitations, breaks and setbacks, but at a time when the disgruntled and discontent with the general sense of the evolution witnessed do not just strengthen their voice, but rather their perspectives against globalization, or at least their somewhat resistance to it have given them votes and mandates in elections. This is, to a large extent, because not everyone has benefited (and or think that has not benefited) in a balanced and fair way with the economic growth rates of our times, in the era of globalization, whether inside or outside the EU.

The general impact of the United Kingdom's exiting the European construction project is no less worrying: this is the first time a member State withdraw from the EU. In the past, the number of members increased consecutively because the act of joining represented prosperity, democracy and human rights, it stood for a real improvement in people's living conditions, as history showed. The pioneering exit of the United Kingdom from the EU put all or at least an important part of it in question. Additionally, the United Kingdom cannot be considered a member State just like any other, because of its unique history and everything it stands for in the political, geographical, military, cultural, social and economic fields.

It appears for now that everything is still out in the open, mostly due to the enormous complexity and inevitably hard effects of the several issues Brexit raised, which will lead to sensitive judgements and choosing concrete solutions deemed most appropriate, on one hand, for the European Union and European citizens, and, on the other hand, for the United Kingdom and British citizens, depending on enduring and arduous negotiations and subsequent political closing decisions, which are impossible to anticipate at the onset, since the positions and interests on the table are to a large scope divergent. Yet only those decisions and solutions will be able to dictate the near and especially the far future of the United Kingdom, including the City, and of the European Union, that is the future of British and European citizens, as well as of the next shapes of international economic cooperation and integration (i.e., globalization), or, on the contrary, disintegration.

Notes

1. The text refers chiefly to the international economic integration process that occurred on the European continent following World War II, with the creation of three European Communities (ECSC, EEC and EAEC), which later led to the current European Union (succeeding the EEC and remaining to this day, such as the EAEC; the ECSC lasted for 50 years, from 1952 to 2002, under the terms of the respective founding Treaty). In Europe, in addition to the mentioned integration process, by far the most important and the object of numerous replicas throughout several continents, it is worth recalling the immediate predecessors,

based fundamentally on international cooperation, with and around the Organization for European Economic Co-Operation (OEEC), including the European Payments Union (EPU) and the European Monetary Agreement (EMA), inspired and funded by the United States, through its Marshall Plan, as well as other later experiences in cooperation and integration, whether in the Western part with the European Free Trade Association (EFTA), founded in 1960 by initiative and influence of the United Kingdom, whether in the Eastern part, with the COMECON (Council for Mutual Economic Assistance), founded in 1949 and which lasted until 1991, under the initiative and guidance of the Soviet Union, encompassing the countries in its sphere or bloc of influence (mostly as a reaction to the Marshall Plan and subsequent creation of the OEEC).

2. There are numerous general studies on states' economic sovereignty. Among others, we can refer to Herdegen (2013, 53 ss), Qureshi and Ziegler (2011, 47 ss), Carreau and Juillard (2010, 23 ss), Lowenfeld (2008, 3 ss), Hoekman and Kostecki (2001, 9 ss) and Jackson (1997, 79 ss).

3. Cf. Graff et al. (2014, Part I, 23–152), Tamames and Huerta (2010, Parts 1–2), Knox et al. (2003).

4. As today, the 1947 GATT's purpose was the international trade of goods, with exceptions that were increased as it was applied and where "self-limitations" on exchanges were accepted and several exceptions claimed, many with doubtful conformity as to the multilateralism in force, up to the change of the *Uruguay Round*, with the approval of the agreements that set up the World Trade Organization (WTO) on 1 January 1995. Cf. Herdegen (2013), Qureshi and Ziegler (2011), Carreau and Juillard (2010), Tamames and Huerta (2010), Lowenfeld (2008), Mota (2005), Hoekman and Kostecki (2001), Jackson (1997).

5. In the Soviet Union, Eastern Europe and China, whose economies were planned by the state at central level, state-owned companies followed the government decisions on the production and distribution of goods. In these countries, international trade was of lesser relevance than in countries with a market economy, but they also resorted to international economic cooperation, namely, within the framework of the CMEA, or COMECON— Council for Mutual Economic Assistance, created in 1949 upon initiative of the Soviet Union, and which remained in place until 1991, involving the Eastern European countries and communist countries from other parts of the world that were under the Soviet Union's political and economic influence. Initially this was a replica of the US Marshall Plan for European

reconstruction, which gave rise to the Organization for European Economic Co-operation (OEEC), which preceded the European integration process that developed from then to date, whose cornerstones were the three European Communities created in the 1950s (in 1951, by the Treaty of Paris, and in 1957, by the Treaties of Rome) in Western Europe, which led to the current European Union, as well as the Organization for Economic Co-operation and Development (OECD), in 1961.

6. The European Union (EU, at the time the European Communities) promoted from the onset active cooperation for development. The 1957 Treaty of Rome envisaged the creation of a European Development Fund to support Member States' overseas territories and colonies, which meanwhile became independent. This policy expanded later and included a greater number of African, Latin American and Asian countries, in addition to neighbouring European regions. In 2000, the Cotonu Agreement was signed between the European Union and the African, Caribbean and Pacific countries (ACP), to last for 20 years, with the goal of combining efforts to eradicate poverty and help recipient countries integrate in the world economy. The European Union is also present in other areas of the world through complementary financial instruments, such as the Development Cooperation Instrument and the European Neighbourhood and Partnership Instrument, in the context of the United Nations (UN) Millennium Development Goals, with the aim of reducing poverty by 2015. Seventeen (17) new Sustainable Development Goals to be reached by 2030 replaced the eight (8) Millennium Development Goals, where among other goals we have the eradication of poverty and hunger, as well as quality health and education for all human beings.

7. David Ricardo (1817, 135) argued the theory of "comparative advantages", using as reference the explanation offered by Adam Smith (1776) on "absolute advantages", putting in crisis the prior vision of Mercantilism, which had dominated from 1500 until up to around 1750. The developments of Ricardo's theory are still at the core of the International Economics discussion. Cf. Krugman et al. (2012, 24–47).

8. Economic integration tends to occur at a restrictive and "local" scale at first, and only then does it become larger geographically and materially, until it gains a "national" dimension, by a decisive boost by the State. Without prejudice to the various specificities. Effective integration, that is, not just economic and social but also political and cultural, depends on multiple circumstances, and, namely, the geographical extension and continuity of the territory and the nature and effective exercise of political power. Depending on the fields of integration and the specificities of

the State, some attained it long before others. Some countries continue to apply restrictive commercial measures within their territory that are identical to those required at external borders.

9. The EFTA (European Free Trade Association) was set up under the Stockholm Treaty in 1960. Its signatories, in addition to the United Kingdom, were Austria, Denmark, Norway, Portugal, Sweden and Switzerland. Iceland joined in 1961, Finland in 1986 and Liechtenstein in 1991, while Denmark and the United Kingdom exited EFTA in 1972, Portugal in 1985, and Austria, Finland and Sweden in 1994, in all cases to join the European Communities, nowadays the European Union. The Treaty of Porto (Oporto) of 1992 preview the establishment on 1 January 1994 of the European Economic Area (EEA), between the European Communities/European Union and the EFTA member States, with exceptions. According to the agreement, the European Union Law dispositions on the Single or Internal Market, mainly the four European economic freedoms (free movement of goods, capital, persons and services, including the fredom of establishment), as well as the European competion law, are mandatory. Consequently, as of 2016, the European Union internal market law is applied to 31 States: the 28 EU member States and three EFTA members: Iceland, Liechtenstein and Norway; it is also partially applied to Switzerland in fulfilment of the bilateral agreements celebrated with the EU.

10. The North American Free Trade Area (NAFTA), set up by Canada, Mexico and the United States of America on 1 January 1994 followed immediately from the Canada-USA Free Trade Agreement, which entered in force on 1 January 1989.

11. Article 9(1) of the 1957 Treaty of Rome, which set up the EEC (TCEE), established that [the Community] "shall be based upon a customs union which shall cover all trade in goods and which shall involve the prohibition between Member States of customs duties on imports and exports and of all charges having equivalent effect, and the adoption of a common customs tariff in their relations with third countries". This wording of the original Treaty of Rome matches the one we still find today in article 28(1) of the Treaty on the Functioning of the European Union (TFEU), the new name of the 1957 Treaty that set up the European Economic Community (EEC), renamed in 1992 (in the Treaty of the European Union or Treaty of Maastricht) as Treaty of the European Community (EC) and, lastly, in 2007 (in the Treaty of Lisbon), as Treaty on the Functioning of the European Union (TFEU).

12. International or "regional" economic integration, in the sense of being developed at interstate level among sovereign States but not at a universal scale is different to (*i*) internal or national economic integration, which operates within the territory of each sovereign State, that is, with a more restrictive geographical scope than that set up between more than one State, depending on the size of the national territory; it is also different to (*ii*) "global" or "universal" economic integration, which is global in scale and theoretically involves (at least nowadays or in the days we can forecast), all the countries and territorial points of the Earth, which, in that imaginary framework, would form a single world economic bloc, without any discrimination or internal barriers on trade based on the origin of the goods or the nationality of the producers of those goods or service providers, when national borders had to be crossed... The current international economic order, run by the WTO, can be seen as an attempt towards gradual global economic integration. Cf. Viner (1950), Tinbergen (1956), Balassa (1961), Mansfield and Milner (1997), Yamamoto (1999), Knox et al. (2003), Pitta e Cunha (2004), Stiglitz (2006), Renato Gonçalves (2010, 2016), Porto (2016), Paz Ferreira (2016).

13. Article XXIV-4 of the GATT establishes that "the purpose of a customs union or of a free trade area should be to facilitate trade between the constituent territories and not to raise barriers to the trade of other contracting parties [*retius* of other Member (States)] with such territories".

14. Article V-A of the GATS establishes that the Agreement "shall not prevent any of its Members from being a party to an agreement establishing full integration (...) of the labour markets between or among the parties to such agreement, provided that such agreement: (a) exempts citizens of parties to the agreement from requirements concerning residency and work permits; (b) is notified to the Council for Trade in Services", and a note is then added to say that "Typically, such [full labour market] integration provides citizens of the parties concerned with a right of free entry to the employment markets of the parties and includes measures concerning conditions of pay, other conditions of employment and social benefits".

15. There are many studies on the critiques, both general and specific, to the prevailing international economic order following World War II and particularly in the last few decades. In addition to the ones already mentioned, cf. E. Paz Ferreira (2004), Held and Kaya (eds.) (2007), Tamames

and Huerta (2010) and, specifically on the international monetary and financial system, Eichengreen (2007).

16. Among the various currents of International Economics that have delved into the subject, it is worth mentioning the contribution made by Paul Krugman (1991a, b, 2008) with the so-called New Economic Geography. Cf. also Knox et al. (2003).

17. Cf. WTO (2008, Part II).

18. Cf. WTO (2008, Part II), Krugman (2008), Eichengreen (2008), Gillingham (2003).

19. The general bibliography on economic regionalism is also highly vast: Porto (2016), Eichengreen (2008), Pitta e Cunha (2004), Gillingham (2003), Knox et al. (2003), Tang (2000), Yamamoto (1999), Mansfield and Milner (eds.) (1997), Storper (1997), Lawrence (1996).

20. We continue to refer here mainly to the international economic integration process that occurred on the European continent following World War II, with the creation of the European Communities which later led to the present European Union.

21. From the security and defence perspective, the situation has changed deeply in the last few years, more recently with the occupation of Crimea and other Eastern Ukrainian lands, and ensuing Russian annexation of that peninsula in 2014. At a first instance, Russia officially denied this occupation and later, with the unilateral declaration of the "reunification" of Crimea with Russia, following a referendum that was deemed illegal by a United Nations General Assembly Resolution. Only nine countries in the world recognized this annexation: Zimbabwe, Venezuela, Syria, Nicaragua, Sudan, Belarus, Armenia, North Korea and Bolivia.

22. On the subject, cf. J. Renato Gonçalves (2010, 2016), Eichengreen (2008), Gillingham (2003), Tang (ed.) (2000).

23. Ghemawat (2011) offers several examples of "resistance" to the phenomenon of globalization: the letters sent by post cross-border represent about 1% of all letters, the length of international phone calls represents around 2%, internet traffic between countries is lower than 2%, the patents held by OECD countries that involved international cooperation in research correspond to about 7.5%, university students that study abroad are about 2% of the total, the intensity of international trade measured by products and services exported from one country to another, in terms of GDP percentage in 2009 was about 23% and foreign direct investment that crosses borders in the proportion of gross fixed capital formation

corresponds to 10% of the total, on average over the last few years. There are obviously major differences between countries and beyond this, the data put forward correspond to global averages. In any case, it seems certain that the phenomenon of globalization does not reach the scale that is often currently mentioned.

24. Cf. *The Economist* (February 26th 2015).
25. After seven years of negotiations, the Trans-Pacific Partnership (TPP), which combined Australia, Brunei, Canada, Chile, Japan, Malaysia, Mexico, New Zealand, Peru, Singapore, the United States of America (up to 23 January 2017) and Vietnam was signed in 2016, but its effectiveness was completely compromised when the United States drew out of the agreement by decision of the new President, Donald Trump. As for the Transatlantic Trade and Investment Partnership (TTIP) between the United States and the European Union, negotiations should continue until at least 2019–2020. The Comprehensive Economic and Trade Agreement (CETA) between Canada and the European Union was signed on 30 October 2016 and later approved by the competent parliaments, starting with the European Parliament on 15 February 2017.
26. The United Nations Conference on Trade and Development (UNCTAD) is a permanent intergovernmental body established by the United Nations General Assembly in 1964.
27. Cf. Galbraith (1994), Sen (1999), Stiglitz (2002, 2006), Ferreira (2004).

References

Balassa, B. 1961. *The Theory of Economic Integration*. Westport: Greenwood Press.

Carreau, D., and P. Juillard. 2010. *Droit International Économique*. 4th ed. Paris: Dalloz.

Cunha, P. Pitta e. 2004. *Integração Económica*. Coimbra: Almedina.

Eichengreen, B. 2007. *Global Imbalances and the Lessons of Bretton Woods*. Cambridge, MA: The MIT Press.

———. 2008. *The European Economy Since 1945*. Princeton: Princeton University Press.

Ferreira, E. Paz. 2004. *Valores e Interesses: Desenvolvimento Económico e Política Comunitária de Cooperação*. Coimbra: Almedina.

————, ed. 2016. *União Europeia: Reforma ou Declínio*. Lisboa: Vega.

Galbraith, J. 1994. *A Journey Through Economic Time*. New York: Mariner.

Ghemawat, P. 2011. *World 3.0. Global Prosper It and How to Achieve It*. Boston: Harvard Business Review Press.

Gillingham, J. 2003. *European Integration, 1950–2003: Superstate or New Market Economy?* Cambridge: Cambridge University Press.

Gonçalves, J. Renato. 2010. *O Euro e o Futuro de Portugal e da União Europeia – The Euro and the Future of Portugal and the European Union*. Lisboa/Coimbra: Wolters Kluwer/Coimbra Editora.

————. 2016. Trinta anos de Portugal 'na Europa': Nem sempre a caminho da prosperidade e da coesão — Thirty years of Portugal 'in Europe': Not always on the road to prosperity and cohesion. In E. Paz Ferreira, ed. 2016. *União Europeia. Reforma ou Declínio*, 191–207.

Graff, M., A. Kenwood, and A. Lougheed. 2014. *The Growth of the International Economy 1820–2000: An Introductory Text*. 5th ed. London: Routledge.

Held, D., and A. Kaya, eds. 2007. *Global Inequality. Patterns and Explanations*. Cambridge: Polity.

Herdegen, M. 2013. *Principles of International Economic Law*. Oxford: Oxford University Press.

Hoekman, B., and M. Kostecki. 2001. *The Political Economy of the World Trading System: The WTO and Beyond*. 2nd ed. Oxford: Oxford University Press.

Jackson, J. 1997. *The World Trading System*. 2nd ed. Cambridge, MA: The MIT Press.

Knox, P., J. Agnew, and L. McCarthy. 2003. *The Geography of the World Economy: An Introduction to Economic Geography*. 4th ed. London: Arnold.

Krugman, P. 1991a. *Geography and Trade*. Cambridge, MA: The MIT Press.

————. 1991b. Increasing Returns and Economic Geography. *Journal of Political Economy* 99: 483–499.

————. 2008. The Increasing Returns Revolution in Trade and Geography. *American Economic Review* 99 (3): 561–571.

Krugman, P., M. Obstfeld, and M. Melitz. 2012. *International Economics: Theory and Policy*. 9th ed. Boston: Addison-Wesley.

Lawrence, R. 1996. *Regionalism, Multilateralism, and Deeper Integration*. Washington, DC: Brookings Institution.

Lowenfeld, A. 2008. *International Economic Law*. 2nd ed. Oxford: Oxford University Press.

Mansfield, E., and H. Milner, eds. 1997. *The Political Economy of Regionalism: New Directions in World Politics*. New York: Columbia University Press.

Mota, P. Infante. 2005. *O Sistema GATT/OMC: Introdução Histórica e Princípios Fundamentais*. Coimbra: Almedina.

Porto, Manuel. 2016. *Teoria da Integração e Políticas da União Europeia*. 5th ed. Coimbra: Almedina.

Qureshi, A., and A. Ziegler. 2011. *International Economic Law*. 3rd ed. London: Sweet & Maxwell.

Ricardo, D. 1817. *On the Principles of Political Economy and Taxation*. Cambridge: Cambridge University Press, 1951.

Sen, A. 1999. *Development as Freedom*. Oxford: Oxford University Press.

Smith, A. 1776–1789. *The Wealth of Nations*. London: Methuen, ed. C. Edwin Cannan, 1904.

Stiglitz, J. 2002. *Globalization and Its Discontents*. New York: W. Norton.

———. 2006. *Making Globalization Work*. New York: W. Norton.

Storper, M. 1997. *The Regional World: Territorial Development in a Global Economy*. New York: The Guilford Press.

Tamames, R., and B. Huerta. 2010. *Estructura Económica Internacional*. 21th ed. Madrid: Alianza Editorial.

Tang, H., ed. 2000. *Winners and Losers of EU Integration: Policy Issues for Central and Eastern Europe*. Washington, DC: World Bank.

Tinbergen, J. 1956. *International Economic Integration*. Amsterdam: Elsevier.

Viner, J. 1950. *The Customs Union Issue*. New York: Carnegie Endowment for International Peace.

WTO. 2008. *World Trade Report 2008: Trade in a Globalizing World*. Geneva: WTO.

Yamamoto, Y., ed. 1999. *Globalism, Regionalism & Nationalism: Asia in Search of Its Role in the 21st Century*. Oxford/Malden: Blackwell.

4

Brexit and the Future of the EU: Move Back or Move Forward?

4.1 Introduction

The issues raised by *Brexit* have been on the agenda since the first disintegration movements emerged in the United Kingdom.

In the Member States, particularly in the southern countries, tension points had multiplied and intensified with austerity and the euro crisis.

At the epicentre of the reactions was the incompleteness of the European model, where the asymmetries caused by the absence of a minimum federalization of fiscal rules, the shallowness of the political status of the Union and the reduced transparency of *governance* and *accountability* were looming. Southern countries seemed to be subject to strict scrutiny, while other Member States were spared with justifications for arbitrary times (*La France c'est toujours la France!*) or devaluing the legal

---

Member of CIDEEFF – School of Law, University of Lisbon, Alameda da Universidade, Lisbon, Portugal. Professor at the School of Law of the University of Lisbon (www.fd.ulisboa.pt). Coordinator of a Jean Monnet module in International and European Public Procurement. Vice-President of the European Institute of the Law School of Lisbon. nunorodrigues@fd.ulisboa.pt

N. Cunha Rodrigues (✉)
Law School of Lisbon, Lisbon, Portugal

© The Author(s) 2017
N. da Costa Cabral et al. (eds.), *After Brexit*,
https://doi.org/10.1007/978-3-319-66670-9_4

65

consequences of maintaining trade balance *surpluses* (as in the case of Germany).[1]

The announcement of the referendum in the United Kingdom began as a political move by David Cameron to discipline his party concerning what appeared to be the advantages of being part of the EU.

But then the fractures in the political community and in civil society became evident. Moreover, the historical reservations that the United Kingdom had traditionally had to many aspects of the EU were known.

Indeed, several *opting-out* clauses enabled this Member State to remain on the sidelines of major developments of the Union, some of a technical nature and therefore less known—like the British rebate, also known as the British check—others, more accessible to the public, such as the *opting-out* clauses of the Eurozone or the *Schengen* agreement. In any case, the United Kingdom has been traditionally seen as being close to Euro-scepticism, hostile to certain aspects of the structure and functioning of the Communities and the Union, including those resulting from the loss of national sovereignty, the necessary financial contribution and the complex European bureaucracy.

It can, in a sense, be said that relations between this Member State and the European Union are continuously characterized by a level that, rather than *circumstantial*, was *existential*.

Nevertheless, the outcome of the referendum was surprising.

This is also why the value of *Brexit* (which joined separatist reactions within the United Kingdom) exploded. It has become the recurring theme of political commentary and individual opinions.

The outcome of the last general elections held in the United Kingdom on 8 June 2017, by surprise, added drama to the debate and introduced a significant number of variables that are triggering the number and multiplicity of forecasts.

This has increased the volume of available information but also has increased the noise and the difficulty of carrying out an integrated analysis of the issues.

On the other hand, the acceleration of the process of the separation of the United Kingdom from the European Union has been dominated by empirical perspectives which have political, sociological or statistical value but lack theorization.

The state of the art and the vertigo of the events are, therefore, responsible for facts being predominantly treated as news, with no systemic concerns.

For all these reasons, this chapter aims to carry out a more legal and political analysis of relevant issues raised by *Brexit* and the impact they may have, in the future, on both sides of the English Channel referring, where appropriate, to the network to which they are connected.

The aim is not to undertake a deep study of the issue, but rather to establish causal relationships and observe the political and legal implications of *Brexit* more closely.

This method does not intend to ignore the influence that individual or collective agents may have at any given moment or context, with ideas, aspirations, memories and creativity, and even their capacity to change causal relationships that seemed, until then, to be operative.[2] We must therefore take into account the fluctuations in thought and political action in the United Kingdom and within the European Union that gained ground up to the elections held in June 2017 in the United Kingdom.

In fact, with the outcome of the general elections held in June 2017, while the European Union made its discourse more flexible and some Member States proclaimed "that the door was still open", public opinion in the United Kingdom was divided between a *hard Brexit* and a *soft Brexit*. This trend worsened with the political solution adopted by the conservatives to obtain a parliamentary majority.

The impact that post-*Brexit* will have on the future of the European Union should also be considered. In fact, the European Union has always been going through a process of enlargement. For the first time, with *Brexit*, the European Union will see its number of Member States reduced.

We may find ourselves at a tipping point.

Regardless of the consequences that *Brexit* will have on relations between the European Union and the United Kingdom, this momentum seems to be crucial for the European Union to reflect on the past and, indeed, on the future it seeks for itself.

Brexit may sound like the ringing of an alarm that will allow us to relaunch the European Union project, leading to the conclusion that *Brexit* can represent an opportunity to revive, relegitimize and deepen the process of the construction of the European Union.

4.2   The Constitutional Significance of *Brexit*

Brexit implies, first of all, a constitutional transformation in the shape and balance of the European Union.[3]

For this reason, the consequent legal and political operations will involve difficulties which the Treaties themselves do not provide means to dissipate them. They are predominantly of an economic and geostrategic nature and are explained, first and foremost, by the genesis of the European Communities.

As it is known, the watermark of the Communities was the aspirations of the European peoples and constituted a reply to the Council of Europe. This involved the provisioning and sharing of production assets such as coal, steel and atomic energy and, above all, peace, social cohesion and development.

The (late and reserved) accession of the United Kingdom to the EU imported the acceptance of the *acquis communautaire* which was already significant at that time.

Over time, and particularly following recent events in sensitive areas of the world, notably Ukraine, Turkey and Syria, and the multiple tensions in Africa, Asia and South America, the situation of the United Kingdom, as a Member State, was moving towards paroxysm.

The economy has been in crisis in most Member States and the Union's policies have begun to address factors of instability arising in other areas, especially peace, security, refugee status and migration.

For example, the importance of the United Kingdom as a nuclear power and the involvement of NATO in Eastern Europe and Turkey may, with *Brexit*, require the review of defence mechanisms and the security of the European Union itself.

This means that *Brexit* is, to a certain extent, the culmination of a breaking process produced by changing geostrategic conditions, through the accumulation of disintegration factors, by the weakening of the *governance* capacity and *accountability* of policymakers and by the fractures which have occurred in the cohesion of the EU and the majority of Member States.

The changes require a review of the EU's own internal decision-making processes, not only as a result of the referendum but also as a window of opportunity for Member States who are unhappy with the outcome of the Lisbon Treaty.

What *Brexit* thus means is the need to find a new political and legal framework which defines future models of cooperation and, in some areas, of integration with the United Kingdom.

And yet, the negotiations rest on a delicate historical background.

The history of relations between the United Kingdom and the Communities or the European Union is full of episodes in which Member States agreed to what could be called "à la carte" options for the United Kingdom.

This condescension reflected Europe's interest in the United Kingdom's accession.

Now, this interest may work in the opposite direction.

The EU is not expected to be prepared to accept the segmentation of the negotiations in the unilateral interest of the United Kingdom.[4]

On the other hand, the European Union has acquired an important role as an actor on the international scene, taking value from its bilateral relations. A substantial change in the balance resulting from this role would have constitutional consequences, first and foremost as a consequence of the creation of a polarity (the United Kingdom) influencing world geostrategy.

Therefore, it is expected that the geostrategic and security and defence spheres will be autonomous.

It is no longer likely that there will be a negotiation which will mean the segmentation of economic freedoms, particularly the freedoms of movement of goods and people.

If this is the negotiating position of the United Kingdom, especially in relation to the free movement of people, the issues that have been at the centre of the concerns that lead to the referendum could become the Gordian knot.

The negotiation process will understandably develop in two phases:

In the first, the parties will exacerbate their differences and the points of conflict.

In the second, they will embark on a path of commitment and rapprochement that will avoid rupture. The reticence which the United Kingdom continues to express in the formula "it is better not to have an agreement than to have a bad agreement" is only a way of announcing those negotiating phases for, unless there are factors that revolutionize pre-existing geostrategic conditions, an exit without prior agreement would represent a Europe dominated by the Franco-German axis. This would necessarily produce centralizing effects and would turn the United Kingdom into a country in search of new partners.

Trump's inconstancy and the idiosyncrasy of Russia's and China's foreign policies do not augur an easy task in this area.

Through the importance of identity, the constitutional dimension of *Brexit* also includes European citizenship and the European social model that will be mentioned below.

4.3   European Citizenship

The institution, by the Treaty of Maastricht, of European citizenship was an important milestone in the evolution of the Union's constitutional dimension representing a mitigating element of the preponderance the Economic and Monetary Union had represented in the approval of that treaty.

This importance was due not only to its holistic and symbolic significance but, above all, to establish rights and open channels for expanding the status of nationals of other Member States and their families.

Euro-scepticism was translated, in this matter, by reactions that mixed diverse feelings. Citizenship was seen by some as an "empty shell", an "ambivalence in favour of the market citizen", a "confusion", a "cynical exercise" or "an unidentified political object".[5]

It was generally said that the legitimacy of Union decisions would continue to be based on nationality and not on citizenship.

It should be noted that, from the outset, the divisions involved, on the one hand, legal issues and, on the other, issues of identity and belonging.

Both raised reservations in the British legal community, reflecting the proverbial dialectic between Anglo-Saxon and continental cultures.[6]

As a result of the case law of the Court of Justice, citizenship has become, in large measure, a decisive instrument for resolving issues of non-discrimination and, in general, protection of fundamental rights.

Very little has been mentioned about this aspect but it may represent an important *item* in the negotiations, especially with regard to citizens of Member States resident in the United Kingdom. It is also an important issue regarding the intentions of young UK nationals who, as seen in the recent general elections, do not seem to want to give up the *Erasmus* spirit and their sense of belonging to the European Union.

4.4   Economic Integration

Access to a market of more than 500 million consumers will certainly be at the heart of UK business affairs.

We have already seen, however, that this claim can hardly be separated from the freedom of movement of workers.

Moreover, there is a clear connection between the various economic freedoms which include the right of establishment and the inherent issue of the transfer of workers.

A negotiation based on the atomization of choices which could set aside, for example, the right of establishment, could push back the marketing models used by both parties.

Statistics show that trade between the United Kingdom and the European Union accounts for about half of the former's total trade. The failure of negotiations would mean a return to the rules of the World Trade Organization. In a "pessimistic" scenario with larger increases in trade costs, *Brexit* will lower income in the United Kingdom by 2.6% (£1,700 per household).[7]

But other Member States would also suffer with the United Kingdom's exit, particularly those maintaining a high level of trade with this Member State.

Looking for alternatives, some are increasingly taking refuge in a similar scenario to the European Economic Area, with particular reference to Norway.

However, it should be noted that the contexts are different. The political and social fractures and the opinion trends in the United Kingdom are not comparable to those which characterize the situation in Norway.

On the other hand, accession to the European Economic Area would not significantly alter the nature of things. It is sufficient to note that, on a *per capita* basis, Norway's financial contribution to the European Union reaches 83% of the United Kingdom's[8] contribution and that the obligations that the country entered into with the European Union give an artificial character to the perception of the advantages and disadvantages.

Norway is subject to most of the obligations of the Member States of the European Union, but does not have the same powers.

In the United Kingdom, the referendum registered a majority representing only 52% of voters.

In these circumstances, if the United Kingdom does not reverse the outcome of the referendum (which seems unlikely) it will be very difficult for political actors and public opinion to accept a new model, such as Norway, where the losses would become apparent.

The campaign that supported the exit was based on *slogans* that made voters think that the EU is a failed project and that integration, even with reservations that the country has always demanded, was causing, at the end, a considerable deficit for the country.

The instability provoked by the referendum and the debates it has induced have brought a more detailed, though not always objective, knowledge to the general public concerning the situation that would produce more informed choices.

Voters would be more aware of the areas in which the country would be left out but they would be confronted with the implications of a new statute in which obligations had no counterparts, especially with regard to *governance* and powers involving institutional or legal conformation, particularly in matters of legislative and judicial competence.

4.5   Mobility of Workers

The free movement of persons was not raised as a first priority negotiating objective for the UK Government, in *Brexit*, as if it were a side issue.

However, this has a historical background with almost civilizational dimensions.

This was not born with the European Treaties since it was, and is, already present in various other treaties approved at the international level.[9]

The Treaties and secondary law have given this freedom a unique importance. With the progressive advancement of protection, the freedom of movement of persons has acquired a content that its initial vocation did not allow it to foresee: the right to move and reside is unconditional for nationals of Member States who carry out an economic activity in another Member State; the residence of nationals seeking employment in another Member State may be submited to time limits which the Member States, however, have to determine on reasonable terms; those who are "inactive" must only demonstrate that they have sufficient income and sickness insurance; students benefit from a scheme similar to the latter.[10]

The extension and deepening of protection regimes have often been motivated or inspired by the case law of the Court of Justice.

This is an important fact, as it is well known that, on the question of sovereignty, the Union's jurisdictional powers form an important element of the reluctance of the British.

In the freedom of movement of persons, the problem of the movement of workers is of particular importance. But freedom is valid not only for its economic value but also for the social effects of mobility in terms of European identity and cohesion. A side view which, in a very specific sector, shows the virtues of mobility is the *Erasmus* programme. In cultural and scientific circles and in the world of work today, the crucial role of the programme regarding interculturalism, vocational training and technical and scientific innovation has been unanimously acknowledged.[11]

The United Kingdom's exit from the EU would result in an erosion of these values and the impact it would have on a sector of the population which is decisive for the future is unpredictable.

Furthermore, migration was one of the most sensitive aspects of the debates that preceded the referendum.

These generally showed an unjustified assimilation of causes and effects, with reference to the Commonwealth countries and the European Union.

It turns out that they are different realities.

Net annual immigration to the United Kingdom from the rest of the European Union has more than doubled between 2012 and 2015, reaching 183,000 people this past year.[12]

A change in this trend will have consequences for the identity and social cohesion of the residents, without possibly favouring integration mechanisms. Furthermore, the fall in emigration from the United Kingdom to other Member States will have considerable effects in the European Union, in areas ranging from culture to European trade models and practices, where the uses (and use of the English language) had penetrated on a large scale.

4.6   Financial Markets

The repercussions of *Brexit* will also hit capital movements, with an emphasis on investment.

The situation of the *City* as a financial centre has been especially emphasized.

The opportunity to relocate and perhaps decentralize financial markets within the Union would change pre-existing balances and would be used to review the regulatory mechanisms within the Union, with likely and significant losses for the United Kingdom.

The movement of capital is an economic freedom which, over time, has largely escaped regulation.

With globalization and exposure to the outside world, risks (with the exponential rise in crime and market distortion activities, such as money laundering, fraud, tax evasion and exchange rate turmoil) have increased in the same exact proportion in which control mechanisms have lost effectiveness.

The United Kingdom's position, the tradition of economic agents, the knowledge of the peculiarities of this market and the country's connections with the United States of North America and the countries of the Commonwealth gave it a centrality that will be tested with *Brexit*.

It is a landscape full of challenges, risks and opportunities.

The *City* exerts a seduction on third country markets which is based on an eco-system that combines talent, efficiency and resources. However, the perception of the financial centre as a gateway into the European Union contributes substantially to this attraction.[13]

Brexit will surely change the operating logic of the market.

The idea of *equivalence* suggested by some authors, in the sense that the European Commission could accept a financial control carried out by third countries, subject to the condition that the regulation and supervision of these countries were equivalent to those of the Union hopelessly contains risks of uncertainty and precariousness.

The *equivalency* criterion has been applied in various fields of European Union Law, with emphasis on the protection of fundamental rights. But even here, it calls for a harmonization of principles that is geared towards jurisdictional intervention. In the hands of the community authorities, the application of the *equity* criterion would keep these characteristics, leading to slow procedures that are averse to the speed required by financial market operations.

The United Kingdom is known for its ability to assess risks.

But it cannot be excluded that certain financial centres in Member States want to seize the opportunity and put pressure on policymakers.

This point did not seem to belong to the hard core of the negotiations but will probably be a major factor in the balance of gains and losses.

4.7   The European Social Model

The European social model has not lost any relevance in the European reality. On the contrary, it was boosted by the Europe 2020 strategy, which is about delivering smart, sustainable and inclusive growth.

The economic crisis and the upheavals that occurred in the financial and budgetary systems reverberated heavily on essential aspects of the *model,* due to the abruptness of the transition from one phase of encouraging public investment to another of fiscal restraint, and due to the reversal of expectations driven by austerity.

The sustainability of the model emerged as an inescapable topic that was gaining practical consistency with the explosion of public debt, the persistence of banking system problems and the refugee crisis.

The idea of a *European social model* has, however, become a point of reference and has acquired identifying features. Europe has become an area of economic prosperity and social justice unparalleled in other latitudes.

The increase in the costs of social protection and the spread of objectives to other areas, such as the environment and consumption, have intensified the challenges. It became difficult to integrate variables in an environment of falling employability and the need to respond to new issues such as social security in the face of increased life expectancy.

The effects were felt in budget forecasts and in the establishment, in civil society, of feelings of instability, doubt and contingency.

For its part, the choice of public policies remained a prisoner of the measures adopted by the European Union, especially the European Central Bank. Whatever the commitment that each of the Member States expressed regarding the *European social model*, overcoming that difficult internal crisis has given greater visibility to certain issues which, in the United Kingdom, were recurrent.

The losses of sovereignty and the inefficiency and lack of legitimacy of the Brussels bureaucracy have been used as justifications for the absence or failure of national policies.

Brexit was developed in this breeding ground and that has to be taken into account in the negotiations. Indeed, it will not be easy because there is a growing argument saying that it is paradoxical that the protests are made at the door of the Government of the United Kingdom and that the political decision makers are camped in Brussels.

Signs of recovery of economic growth in most Member States (and not so much in the United Kingdom) are likely to reverse certain factors but, in essence, the idea will persist that the crisis has exposed the need for paradigm shifts and that the structure and functioning of the European Union must be rethought.

The success of Macron's speech is explained by the feeling that has spread in French society regarding this point.

4.8   The *Euratom* Problem

In the *White Paper* in which the UK government invoked Article 50 of the TFEU it is clearly said that *Brexit* will include the *Euratom*.[14]

This consequence has generally been ignored or undervalued.

However, in the context of the European reality, the nuclear industry has an undeniable strategic importance. In light of this, the United Kingdom has stated that it will seek alternative agreements with a view to pursuing cooperation for protection, security and trade with Europe.

The difficulties lie in the sensitivity of the issues but also in the eventual change of agents.

At stake are key instruments, such as the *Euratom* Agency which centralizes and controls the supply of nuclear materials, the European Commission which develops research programmes in the field of nuclear energy and the Security Directory which ensures that nuclear materials are not diverted from their statutory (non-proliferation) use.

Brexit will necessarily entail reciprocal losses and require the adoption of arrangements in a complex area where costs are high (for the period 2014–2020, the European Union budgeted €2.7 billion to finance only 45% of the construction of International Thermonuclear Experimental Reactor)[15] and there is a need to concentrate decision-making processes and clear control instruments.

4.9   The *Praxis* of International Trade

With the accession of the United Kingdom, the jurisdictional method increasingly has associated the continental (*civil law*) tradition to the Anglo-American (*common law*) *tradition.*

Not only because of the importance given to precedence which was already a rule in the decision-making process of the Court of Justice, but also by the strengthening of the capacity to integrate principles and practices of international trade.

It is not the English language which will be threatened by *Brexit,* as a communication and legal interpretation tool.

The United Kingdom's presence brought to the Union the bundle of international relations and business experience.

This aspect has not received much emphasis although it represents a potential loss factor for the European Union.

The preparation of treaties between the EU and third countries[16] will also suffer from the United Kingdom's exit, given the multilateral nature of the relations of this Member State as a result of its historical presence in the culture and economy of different countries of different continents, such as the countries that make up the *Commonwealth*.

Finally, it should be noted that the approval of the *Brexit* agreement must necessarily involve all EU Member States and their parliaments which will be called upon to ratify the agreement.

This view has moreover been recently borne out by the Court of Justice in its Opinion 2/2015, in which it clearly acknowledged, in connection with the trade agreement between the European Union and Singapore, that the free trade agreement with Singapore cannot, in its current form, be concluded by the EU alone, because some of the provisions envisaged fall within competences shared between the EU and the Member States. It follows that the free trade agreement with Singapore can, as it stands, be concluded only by the EU and the Member States acting together.[17]

Keeping this understanding under the *Brexit* agreement means that a parliament in a Member State may block the approval of this agreement, similar to what happened in the past when the Wallonia parliament, in Belgium, passed a resolution against CETA, in October 2016.

4.10   Conclusions

Through its constitutional and identity repercussions, *Brexit* requires negotiations involving the examination of partial issues but primarily the overall analysis of the effects of the exit on the organization and functioning of the European Union and the effectiveness of the *acquis communautaire* relating to economic freedoms.

In particular, account should be taken of the rights of nationals of Member States resident in the United Kingdom and of the impact on the various markets, mainly financial markets.

Brexit poses, therefore, a challenge and an also opportunity for the European Union to review its structure and its decision-making and reassess, in particular, the issues raised by the single currency which have produced and continue to produce unsustainable asymmetric economic effects.

This is the background that emerged in the document issued by the European Commission entitled "White paper on the future of Europe:

Avenues for unity for the EU at 27" which presents five different scenarios for the future of the EU.[18]

The negotiation process requires a prospective method that considers the paradigm shift, in particular in the field of social protection. In this respect, it is crucial to consider the *European social model* as a constitutional prerequisite in order to guarantee the cohesion and sense of belonging in European society.

Notes

1. See Regulation (EU) no. 1176/2011 which details the procedure to detect and correct macroeconomic imbalances and Regulation (EU) no. 1174/2011 which lays down an enforcement mechanism. This mechanism culminates with financial sanctions for euro area countries which do not comply with the Macroeconomic Imbalance Procedure (MIP) recommendations made at EU level to remedy their excessive imbalance.

   Concerning the Economic and Monetary Union, see NUNO CUNHA RODRIGUES and JOSÉ RENATO GONCALVES, *The European Union and the banking Economic and Monetary Union: the puzzle is yet to be completed,* in NAZARÉ DA COSTA CABRAL; JOSÉ RENATO GONÇALVES and NUNO CUNHA RODRIGUES, *The Euro and the crisis—perspectives for the Eurozone as a monetary and budgetary union,* Springer, 2017, pp. 271–288.

2. See PEDRO MAGALHÃES, *"The 'Science' in Political Science"* in AP Ribeiro (ed.), *The Urgency of Theory,* Carcanet Press, Manchester, 2007, p. 214.

3. Analysing Brexit from a global perspective, see MASSIMO LA TORRE, *El Brexit and her misery del global constitutionalism,* in El Cronista del Social Democratic State y Derecho, n. 64, 2016, pp. 4–11.

4. In a certain way, it could be said that the project of European integration was not sustainable with the inclusion of the United Kingdom. In this sense, see ANNETTE BONGARDT and FRANCISCO TORRES, *Brexit: a European perspective,* Brotéria, Lisbon, number 182, 2016, pp. 451–470, available at http://broteria.pt/revista-broteria/artigos/139-maiojunho-2016-brexit-uma-perspectiva-europeia (last accessed on 20 June 2017).

5. See J.N. CUNHA RODRIGUES, *A propos European Citizenship: the Right to move and reside freely*, in Constitutionalizing the US judicial system, Hart Publishing, 2012, pp. 201–213.

6. See PHILIP LARKIN, *The Limits to European Social Citizenship in the United Kingdom*, in Modern Law Review, vol. 68, 2005, pp. 435–447.

7. See SWATI DHINGRA, GIANMARCO OTTAVIANO, THOMAS SAMPSON and JOHN VAN REENEN, *The consequences of Brexit for UK trade and living standards*, CEP BREXIT ANALYSIS number 2, London School of Economics, p. 2, available at http://cep.lse.ac.uk/pubs/download/brexit02.pdf (last accessed on 20 June 2017).

8. See SWATI DHINGRA, GIANMARCO OTTAVIANO, THOMAS SAMPSON and JOHN VAN REENEN, *The consequences of Brexit for UK trade and living standards*, CEP BREXIT ANALYSIS number 2, London School of Economics, p. 4, available at http://cep.lse.ac.uk/pubs/download/brexit02.pdf (last accessed on 20 June 2017).

9. The Universal Declaration of Human Rights of 1948 proclaims this in Article 13, paragraphs 1 and 2. The International Covenant on Civil and Political Rights of 1966 makes reference to this in detail. The Council of Europe attached particular importance to it in the European Convention on Human Rights of 13 December 1955 and on Protocol no. 4 of 16 September 1963 and in the European Agreement on Regulations governing the Movement of Persons between Member States of the Council of Europe of 13 December 1957.

10. See Articles 6 and 7 of the Directive 2004/38/EC of the European Parliament and of the Council of 29 April 2004 on the right of citizens of the Union and their family members to move and reside freely within the territory of the Member States.

11. Reflections of *Brexit* in social representations are absorbed faster by young people and have a considerable symbolic and contagious coefficient. Several media reported that between June 2016 and March 2017, British universities registered a fall of 9% in student enrolment from other member countries of the European Union.

12. See the report made by Capital Economics for Woodford Investment Management, *The Economic Impact of 'Brexit'*, February 2016, available at https://woodfordfunds.com/economic-impact-brexit-report/ (last accessed on 20 June 2017).

13. See GEORGES SITBON, Brexit: *quel impact pour l'union et son marché financier?*, 27 Novembre 2016, available at https://fr.linkedin.com/pulse/brexit-quel-impact-pour-lunion-et-son-march%C3%A9-financier-georges-sitbon (last accessed on 20 June 2017).

14. See point 8.30. of the Policy paper "The United Kingdom's exit from, and new partnership with, the European Union", available at https://www.gov.uk/government/publications/the-united-kingdoms-exit-from-and-new-partnership-with-the-european-union-white-paper/the-united-kingdoms-exit-from-and-new-partnership-with-the-european-union--2 (last accessed on 20 June 2017).

15. See ENRICO NANO and SIMONE TAGLIAPIETRA, *Brexit goes nuclear: The consequences of leaving Euratom,* available at http://bruegel.org/2017/02/brexit-goes-nuclear-the-consequences-of-leaving-euratom/ (last accessed on 20 June 2017).

16. Concerning the new EU Trade and Investment strategy, see NUNO CUNHA RODRIGUES, *The use of public procurement as a non-tariff barrier: relations between the EU and the BRICS in the context of the new EU trade and Investment Strategy,* in Public Procurement Law Review, 2017, number 3, pp. 135–149.

17. The ECJ added that it is in respect of only two aspects of the agreement that the EU is not endowed with exclusive competence, namely in the field of non-direct foreign investment ("portfolio" investments made without any intention to influence the management and control of an undertaking) and the regime governing dispute settlement between investors and States. See Opinion 2/15, of 16 May 2017.

18. See European Commission COM (2017) 2025 of 1 March 2017. Available at http://europa.eu/rapid/press-release_IP-17-385_en.htm (last accessed on 20 June 2017).

References

Bongardt, Annette, and Francisco Torres. 2016. *Brexit: A European Perspective.* Brotéria, Lisbon, 182: 451–470. Available at http://broteria.pt/revista-broteria/artigos/139-maiojunho-2016-brexit-uma-perspectiva-europeia. Last accessed 20 June 2017.

Dhingra, Swati, Gianmarco Ottaviano, Thomas Sampson, and John van Reenen. *The Consequences of Brexit for UK Trade and Living Standards*, CEP BREXIT ANALYSIS number 2, London School of Economics, 2. Available at http://cep.lse.ac.uk/pubs/download/brexit02.pdf. Last accessed 20 June 2017.

La Torre, Massimo. 2016. El Brexit and Her Misery del Global Constitutionalism, in El Cronista del Social Democratic State y Derecho, n. 64, pp. 4–11.

Larkin, Philip. 2005. The Limits to European Social Citizenship in the United Kingdom. *Modern Law Review* 68: 435–447.

Magalhães, Pedro. 2007. The 'Science' in Political Science. In *The Urgency of Theory*, ed. A.P. Ribeiro, 214. Manchester: Carcanet Press.

Nano, Enrico, and Simone Tagliapietra. *Brexit Goes Nuclear: The Consequences of Leaving Euratom*. Available at http://bruegel.org/2017/02/brexit-goes-nuclear-the-consequences-of-leaving-euratom/. Last accessed 20 June 2017.

Rodrigues, J.N. Cunha. 2012. A Propos European Citizenship: The Right to Move and Reside Freely. In *Constitutionalizing the US Judicial System*, 201–213. Oxford: Hart Publishing.

Rodrigues, Nuno Cunha. 2017. The Use of Public Procurement as a Non-Tariff Barrier: Relations Between the EU and the BRICS in the Context of the New EU Trade and Investment Strategy. *Public Procurement Law Review* 3: 135–149.

Rodrigues, Nuno Cunha, and José Renato Gonçalves. 2017. The European Union and the Banking Economic and Monetary Union: The Puzzle Is Yet to Be Completed. In *The Euro and the Crisis – Perspectives for the Eurozone as a Monetary and Budgetary Union*, ed. Nazaré da Costa Cabral, José Renato Gonçalves, and Nuno Cunha Rodrigues, 271–288. Cham: Springer.

Sitbon, Georges. 2016. *Brexit: quel impact pour l'union et son marché financier?*, 27 Novembre. Available at https://fr.linkedin.com/pulse/brexit-quel-impact-pour-lunion-et-son-march%C3%A9-financier-georges-sitbon. Last accessed 20 June 2017.

5

Brexit and the Risk of European Disintegration

Pauline Schnapper

On 23 June 2016 a slim majority (51.9%) of the British voters who turned out to vote in the referendum on whether to stay in the European Union (EU) decided the leave the EU, breaking a 40-year course of enlargement from the original six members of the European Economic Community (EEC) to the present 28 members. For the first time, except for the limited case of Greenland which chose to leave the EEC in 1985 when it gained autonomy from Denmark, a member state has democratically chosen to divorce from the Union and reclaim 'full sovereignty', as the *Brexiters* put it. This unprecedented move in the EU, affecting one of its bigger member states, raises a number of questions both about the British polity and about the future of the European project, which has been confronted with an equally unprecedented number of crises since the late 2000s. They started with the financial crisis in 2007–2008, followed by the Eurozone sovereign debt crisis in 2010–2011. Wars in the Middle-East led to a refugee crisis in 2015 which was a challenge for countries such as Greece, Italy, Germany or Austria and increased tensions

P. Schnapper (✉)
Université de la Sorbonne Nouvelle-Paris 3, Paris, France

© The Author(s) 2017
N. da Costa Cabral et al. (eds.), *After Brexit*,
https://doi.org/10.1007/978-3-319-66670-9_5

between member states. In the background to these challenges, and fuelled by them, lay the deeper and unresolved question of the growing disconnect between European citizens and their institutions, reflected in the rise of populist anti-EU political parties across the continent.

It is too early to assess the long-term impact of Brexit, which will not occur until 2019, on the future of European integration. But a number of questions on the impact of the vote can already be addressed. Is it the start of process of disintegration of the European Union, by which the Brexit vote creates a precedent attracting other votes in other countries? Or are we witnessing a hollowing out of the EU independently of Brexit? Or instead can we hope that the Brexit vote will act as wake up call for Europeans and democrats on the continent?

In order to try and answer these questions, the first section of this chapter will look at the specifically domestic factors explaining the referendum vote in the UK. Then I will show that it cannot be completely separated from a wider legitimacy crisis affecting the EU as a whole, which is well documented in the academic literature. In a third section, I will describe the reactions of other EU governments and institutions to the British vote, both before and after 23 June 2016. In a fourth section, I will look at the different options faced by the EU-27 when dealing with the May government. Finally, I will examine the risks that Brexit poses for the unity of the EU in the coming years.

5.1 A Domestic Issue

The result of the EU referendum in the UK cannot be understood if a number of domestic factors are not factored in, which are a reminder of British exceptionalism in the European Union. Britain only joined the then EEC in 1973, 17 years after it was created and after two applications by a Conservative then Labour government were vetoed by French president Charles de Gaulle in 1963 and 1967. The decisions to apply for membership were never taken as a result of a full acceptance of the political dimension of European integration, but rather as a result of a utilitarian calculation that the UK would be better off economically as a member of the single market and customs union than outside. The lack of commitment of the

British elites, for whom membership was a stopgap solution at a time of relative economic decline, explains why Britain remained an 'awkward partner' for decades (George 1998; Young 1998; Baker and Schnapper 2015). There was never an emotional attachment to the idea of Europe, as consistently shown by barometer opinion polls: the percentage of British respondents saying that they felt European and the percentage of respondents thinking that membership of the EU was a good thing was always lower than the EC/EU average (Baker and Schnapper 2015: 85–89).

Euroscepticism, now embedded in the EU as a whole (Usherwood and Startin 2013), started as a specifically British phenomenon in the early 1990s, after the signing of the Maastricht treaty (Baker et al. 1994; Alexandre-Collier 2002). It exposed strong divisions between and within mainstream political parties, which had already been in view in the 1960s and 1970s but became much more acute, and politically problematic, within the Conservative Party in the 1990s and 2000s. John Major's premiership (1990–1997) was particularly affected by these divisions. The United Kingdom Independence Party was created in that period to campaign for withdrawal from the European Union and, after a slow start, became increasingly an electoral threat for the Conservative party, winning more and more votes in European and general elections, though no MP until 2014 because of the first-past-the-post electoral system (Ford and Goodwin 2014).

When David Cameron became leader of the Conservative party in 2005, he pledged to 'stop banging about Europe' at the following party conference and hoped to keep the issue out of the table. But he gave in to Eurosceptic pressure by pledging to take Conservative members out of the European Parliament's European People's Party (EPP), deemed too federalist, and rejected the Lisbon treaty signed by Gordon Brown in 2007, promising 'not to let matters rest' when it was ratified by the Labour majority in the Westminster Parliament. Once he became Prime Minister in 2010, he introduced a European Union bill in Parliament, which reasserted the sovereignty of Westminster and made a referendum compulsory in case of any new transfer of sovereignty to the European Union. At that point he refused to contemplate an in/out referendum in his country, which a sizeable minority of his own backbenchers supported. But by January 2013, he had changed his mind under pressure from hard Eurosceptics in his party, the press and UKIP and had promised a referendum before the end of 2017 in his Bloomberg speech. By May 2015, when he won the general election, the referendum was inevitable.

The referendum therefore took place in a context of increasing discontent towards Europe in the UK, reinforced by the Eurozone crisis (which entrenched the idea that the whole euro project was doomed) and the refugee crisis, even though it did not directly affect Britain, which is not part of the Schengen agreement (Baker and Schnapper 2015). The referendum was also deeply affected, as the campaign showed, by the decision taken by the Blair government in 2004 to lift any restriction to the free circulation of citizens from the new member states who joined the EU. This led to the immigration of over one million Poles and other East Europeans in the UK (to a total of over 3.3 million EU citizens living in the UK in 2016), which became increasingly contentious in the British political debate from 2005 onwards. Immigration proved to be the most successful argument of the Leave campaign in the referendum, especially when Nigel Farage sponsored a poster showing a line of refugees in the Balkans with the slogan 'Breaking Point – The EU has failed us'. Andrew Cooper, a pollster, attributed to it the loss of 5 percentage points to the Remain campaign (Shipman 2016: 20). More generally, the Leave campaign focussed on the theme of 'taking back control', which included reclaiming control of British borders and of the sovereignty of Westminster over British laws (Bennett 2016). It was able to tap into a widespread feeling that EU institutions were too powerful and imposed costs and regulation which the British public was opposed to and that it was not accountable in the way national politicians were to their own parliament.

The third domestic issue which played a part, though not directly, in the referendum result had to do with the economic and social policies adopted since 2010 in the UK in response to the economic crisis. Spending cuts, especially affecting benefits, had a lasting impact on many working-class families who also faced wage stagnation and unaffordable housing in many parts of the country. This explains, at least partly, why the economic argument in favour of staying in the EU had little traction with sections of the public for whom leaving could have a negative impact on the City or abstract figures like the GDP, but could not make things worse than they already were for them, or so they felt.

So four domestic factors—traditional misgivings about European integration, a historical attachment to the idea of parliamentary sovereignty, however mythical in reality, immigration policy under New Labour and the spending cuts adopted by the coalition government between 2010 and 2015—explain to a large extent the result of the referendum. Leave voters were predominantly those affected by immigration and austerity: the less educated, less well-off older English population outside London were the section of the population most likely to vote for Brexit.

5.2   Scepticism as a European Pattern

Although domestic factors explain to a large extent the result of the British referendum, it cannot be separated from wider developments at play across the European Union, to which the UK is not immune. Euroscepticism, or the rejection of the European project, is now a widespread phenomenon in Europe, reflected in opinion polls and the success of anti-European populist parties in elections to the European Parliament, and indeed their achieving power in both Hungary and Poland. The aquiescence of European citizens to the process of European integration in the 1950s and 1960s, which Lindberg and Scheingold (1970) called 'permissive consensus' has given way to what Hoogue and Marks (2009) have called a 'constraining dissensus'. This has been happening as a result of the politicization of European issues across the EU, which has led to a widespread contestation of, if not the project as a whole, at least many of the policies and perceived inadequacies of the EU institutions. In 2007, only 34% of respondents in the Eurobarometer poll thought that their voices counted in the EU, and only 22% in Britain (Eurobarometer 2007: 100). This may explain why turnout in European elections has been consistently going downwards since 1979, from an average of over 60% to just over 40% in 2014.[1]

The rise of populist anti-European parties throughout the continent has been the most obvious manifestation of the voters' discontent. The first parties which made electoral gains were the Lega Nord in Italy, the FPÖ in Austria and the Front National in France in the late 1980s–early 1990s. Since then, they have been joined by an array of parties from the north to the south of the continent and from east to west, including Belgium, the

Netherlands, Sweden, Denmark, Greece or Hungary. Anti-EU members of the European parliament now comprise about a quarter of the total number of MEPs following the 2014 elections. They challenge the principles on which the EU has been built: shared sovereignty, liberalism, pluralism, solidarity, equality and respect for minorities. Ominously, parties sharing some or all of these views are now in power in Hungary (Fidesz) and Poland (PiS).

Although these developments predate 2008, they have been amplified by the economic then eurozone crisis, which fuelled popular discontent in several ways. First it showed that the EU could not shield the European population from global economic turbulence, and that indeed it could even make it worse. Second, it exposed the flaws in the conception of the euro, identified by Joseph Stiglitz (2016), which had proven unable to reduce divergence in competitiveness and deficits between Northern and Southern countries. As a result, tensions between member states, especially Germany and Greece, grew and the EU became increasingly unpopular in Mediterranean countries (Baker and Schnaper 2015: Chap. 5). In the UK, the EU-wide crisis was interpreted as evidence that the European Union was not a successful economic bloc but a declining bureaucratic and inefficient system. The refugee crisis of 2015 added to these tensions, with a new East-West dimension to it when Eastern European countries, especially Hungary and Poland, refused to leave their borders open and to accept a quota of refugees, as the European Commission had suggested. It also raised the question of the effectiveness of the Schengen area system, with many member states re-introducing controls at their national borders.

Beyond these separate crises, commentators have pointed more generally to an identity crisis for the EU, which is no longer seen as legitimate. Part of the general public consider it as unable to provide security and prosperity to its citizens, undermining national sovereignty and as having failed to build a common identity. Scholars have distinguished between an input (with citizen participation) and output legitimacy, where the EU's output legitimacy is no longer sufficient to satisfy voters, to which Vivien Schmidt added 'throughput' legitimacy, concerned with processes (Schmidt 2006). She sums up the conundrum in which the EU finds itself when it generates 'policy without politics', whereas politics takes place at the national level but has largely been deprived of policy outputs, 'politics without policy'.

One of the ways in which member states attempted to reconnect voters with the European project was to resort more frequently to the use of referendums, as a way to reintroduce direct democracy in a process which seemed too aloof and technocratic. At first, referendums were used as bargaining tools for national governments to gain concessions in their negotiations with the EU. Then they became, as Matt Qvortrup puts it, means to 'gain legitimacy, leverage, and to pass the political buck all at the same time' (Qvortrup 2016). Over 40 referendums on European issues have been organized since 2000, four times as much as in the previous decade. But, starting in 1992 with the rejection of the Maastricht treaty by Danish voters, a string of referendums about EU treaties have led to negative outcomes. It was followed by the failed ratification of the Nice treaty in Ireland in 2001 (although it was reversed in a second one, after assurances were given to the electorate over the contested issues of defence and abortion), then Danish and Swedish voters rejected the euro in 2000 and 2003. The European constitutional treaty was rejected in France and the Netherlands in 2005, the Lisbon treaty in Ireland again in 2008 (with again a second positive one after the EU agreed to maintain one EU commissioner per country). Denmark voted against an opt-in in Home and Justice Affairs in 2015 and finally Dutch voters rejected the association agreement with Ukraine in 2016. All these results point to a level of dissatisfaction with anything smacking of 'Europe' on the continent even before the British referendum. One may even wonder if direct democracy, the process meant to address the disconnection with voters, did not actually reinforce it by giving voters opportunities to express overall dissatisfaction and widespread anger at the political system.

The British referendum therefore came at a time when the European project as a whole was threatened. It was an illustration of the extent of the crisis Europe was facing and had the potential to make it worse. As an anonymous German policy-maker, quoted in the *Financial Times*, put it: 'The European house is burning down and Britain wants to waste time rearranging the furniture' (1 February 2016). The fact that the EU was already facing multiple crises also meant that the consequences of a Brexit were potentially very serious.

5.3   The EU's Reaction to the Referendum

The first reaction of EU member states to Cameron's pledge to organize an in/out referendum was one of puzzlement, for which there were two main reasons. First, the UK already benefitted from the best of both worlds, with full membership of the Union and its single market but also opt-outs on the single currency, the Schengen agreement and opt-ins for cooperation in home and justice affairs. It meant that London kept a mostly intergovernmental approach to EU affairs, where it enjoyed the benefits of cooperation in a number of fields, including security, defence and foreign policy, while having less constraints than if it had been a member of the Eurozone, for instance.

Another paradoxical development making Britain's detachment difficult to comprehend was that the European Union had become increasingly 'British' in the last few years. The traditional preferences of successive British governments—an emphasis on the single market, support for enlargement, intergovernmentalism as opposed to further integration— were de facto adopted at the EU level from the early 2000s. The European Commission adopted a programme to complete the single market and reduce regulation, which fitted exactly with what consecutive British governments had argued for years. The 2004 round of enlargement to 10 new members, mostly in East and Central Europe was also in line with the British vision of enlarging rather than deepening the EU. Finally, post-Maastricht, the EU had been engaged in 'integration without supranationalism' with the European Council, as opposed to supranational institutions like the Commission, occupying central stage in what was called 'new intergovernmentalism' (Bickerton et al. 2015).

None of the other European governments, nor interestingly their publics, wished for a Brexit. A poll published in Spring 2016 showed that 75% of the German, Dutch or Spanish respondents thought it would be a bad idea for Europe. Even in France, traditionally seen as more hostile to the UK, a majority of 62% of voters thought it was not a good idea for the UK to withdraw from the EU (Pew 2016). All EU heads of government supported keeping the UK in the EU.

So, seen from the outside, organizing a referendum on whether to stay in the EU was certainly unwise, especially in the context described in the previous section. But since the decision had been taken by the British government, Britain's European partners had two concerns. Before the referendum took place on 23 June 2016, they did not wish to do or say anything that would increase the risk of a negative vote in the UK. Chancellor Merkel, in particular, sent positive signals that she would try to accommodate British concerns during the negotiation, particularly concerning migrants' access to social rights, provided the principle of freedom of circulation was not undermined. She also approved of Cameron's diagnosis about the weaknesses of the European economies as set out in his Bloomberg speech.[2] Other leaders, like French President François Hollande and Commission president Jean-Claude Juncker, refrained from intervening in the referendum campaign, which they feared would be counter-productive, except to warn about the possible consequences of Brexit.[3]

Once the referendum had taken place, the concern of European leaders became to limit the damage to the rest of the Union and contain a possible contagion effect to other countries where Euroscepticism had been on the rise. Their fear was that, emboldened by Brexit, other anti-European political forces across the continent would put pressure on their governments to organise similar ballots in their countries. If the British referendum proved to be a successful precedent, it would be the start of a dangerous process of unravelling for the rest of the European Union. This explains why French, German, Italian and other European leaders insisted that there would be no special treatment for the UK once the negotiations on article 50 of the Lisbon treaty, setting the divorce process, started and that there could be no undermining of the four freedoms of circulation if the British government wished to remain in the European single market. François Hollande was keen to repeat that there had to be a price to pay for leaving the EU while Chancellor Merkel insisted that the UK could not 'cherry-pick' aspects of the single market without contributing to the budget and respecting the free circulation of people.[4] Theresa May had hoped to find an ally in Germany because of the trade links between the two countries and their shared economic vision, but it soon became clear that for the government in Berlin maintaining the unity of the EU-27 would be more important than accommodating the wishes of the British government, even if it was to the relative detriment of German exporters. Other traditional allies of the UK in the EU, such as the Netherlands or

Poland, sent similar signals—the latter because they would not accept restrictions to free circulation and wanted to protect the rights of their citizens living in Britain.[5]

The first few months after the referendum therefore showed a quite remarkable display of unity among the EU-27 in the way they faced the prospect of Brexit, in an effort to prevent further strains on an already weakened European project. Interestingly, this was not only true at the government level but also at the public opinion one. An IFOP survey conducted for the Robert Schuman Foundation in five EU countries (France, Germany, Spain, Italy and Poland) in November 2016 showed that European respondents' concerns about Brexit had abated since June: except for Poland, where 55% thought Brexit was 'very serious' for the EU, only 20 to 30% of respondents in other countries saw Brexit as an existential threat. A majority (except in Italy) also felt that the consequences for the British economy would be negative, which does not testify to a momentum for leaving the EU outside of the UK. Similarly, a majority of respondents expressed their fears, not their hope (except for populist party voters) about a possible domino effect following the UK's choice to leave the EU (Schuman Foundation 2017).

So it looked as if, in the short term at least, the Brexit vote had not led to a surge in europhobia (as opposed to Euroscepticism, which remains widespread) among EU-27 voters.

Another possible explanation for this relative strength of European opinion is that the first stages of the Brexit process in the Autumn 2016 proved extremely tortuous and confused in the UK, with the May government taking several months to set up the institutions and civil servants in charge of 'exiting the EU' as well as to agree on an official position for the coming negotiation with the EU, thereby possibly creating a deterrent effect for other countries in the EU.

5.4   The Difficult Process of Leaving the EU

Leaving the European Union is unprecedented, which means that it is very difficult to assess both the process itself and its outcome, as well as its consequences for the future of European integration. It took several months before the British government made public that it intended to activate article 50 of the Lisbon treaty by the end of March 2017. This starts a two-year period during which the UK negotiates both the terms of its parting and, supposedly, its new relationship with the EU. This is a short period for a very complex negotiation, which is supposed to end in 2019, before the next European elections, especially as the different actors (member states, the Commission, the European Parliament) will have different agendas and priorities. There might be time only for a transition agreement about the terms of the divorce before an agreement can be discussed, in particular on a future trade deal.

The British government's priorities in these exit negotiations were unclear for several months. Strains between the Brexiters and Remainers in government were apparent as well as a level of uncertainty about the plan for Brexit, illustrated by the abrupt resignation in early January 2017 of the UK ambassador to the EU, Sir Ivan Rodgers, who had been dismissed by Brexiters for warning that negotiations could take years. Commentators pointed to a choice between a 'soft Brexit', where association with the EU would remain strong, allowing access to the single market and the customs union even if it meant contributing to the budget and allowing free circulation (as in the case of Norway) and a 'hard Brexit' which would prioritise the control of borders, even if it meant cutting all links to the single market, in the hope of signing a trade deal with the EU in the future, in the same way as any other third country. Other important issues, such as the future of cooperation in defence and foreign policy, home and justice affairs or the rights of EU citizens in the UK (and British citizens in the EU) were less salient in the British public debate.

Theresa May (2016) insisted in her Autumn Conservative conference speech on voters' concerns about immigration ('we are not leaving the European Union only to give up control of immigration all over again'), which already pointed towards a 'hard Brexit'. This was confirmed in the speech she gave in January 2017 where she hailed a future 'Global Britain' in control of its own laws and of the number of people coming in. She made clear Britain would not stay in the single market:

What I am proposing cannot mean membership of the Single Market. European leaders have said many times that membership means accepting the "four freedoms" of goods, capital, services and people. And being out of the EU but a member of the Single Market would mean complying with the EU's rules and regulations that implement those freedoms, without having a vote on what those rules and regulations are. It would mean accepting a role for the European Court of Justice that would see it still having direct legal authority in our country. It would to all intents and purposes mean not leaving the EU at all… So we do not seek membership of the Single Market. Instead we seek the greatest possible access to it through a new, comprehensive, bold and ambitious Free Trade Agreement (May 2017).

The Prime Minister was compelled by a judgement of the Supreme Court to introduce a bill in Parliament authorising the government to activate article 50 of the Lisbon treaty. In the accompanying white paper, the government confirmed these choices, mentioning 'tariff-free trade in goods that is as frictionless as possible between the UK and the EU Member States' and a 'new customs agreement' (HM Government 2017). The government hoped to negotiate sectoral trade agreements with the EU, what they called 'access' to rather than membership of the single market. A Repeal Bill would be introduced in Westminster in 2017 to repatriate all EU legislation to the UK before each ministerial department chooses which pieces to keep and which ones to abolish.

An already complex negotiating stance became even less clear when Theresa May unexpectedly decided to call a new general election on 8 June 2017 in the hope of strengthening her majority and silencing both the Remain side and the Hard Brexiters in her own party. Her gamble failed spectacularly when she lost the small majority she had held instead, leaving her as leader of a minority government. As a result, previously silent Remainers or supporters of a 'soft' Brexit, (meaning staying in the customs union and possibly the single market), were heard again, especially the Chancellor of the Exchequer, Philip Hammond, who insisted on the priority to protect jobs in Britain. As negotiations started with the EU-27, the government was weakened and its objectives still somewhat a mystery.

There was no evidence either that May's negotiating stance could be acceptable to other member-states, who were faced with a dilemma— should they be 'tough' on the British to avoid any risk of contagion or should they be as accommodating as possible in order to limit the risks of economic disruption? Their priority was to keep the integrity of the single market and accepting that a country outside the EU could trade freely with the single market without having to implement all its rules or be subjected to the European Court of Justice was likely to be unacceptable as it would undermine the single market and possibly encourage others to leave the EU. As the Maltese Prime Minister, rotating president of the EU in the first semester of 2017, put it: 'We are saying two things: that we want a fair deal, but that fair deal needs to be inferior to membership. Honestly, I cannot see a situation where someone gets out of a club and then expects that the new relationship is even better than being a member'.[6]

The two sides in the negotiation were not equal either: 45% of UK exports go to the EU and 7 of its top 10 trading partners are in the EU. Instead, the UK accounts for only 4 or 5% of all other EU countries' imports and 6–7% of their exports.[7] This means that the British government was not in the strongest position to negotiate a favourable deal. Its main assets were its large contribution to the EU budget and its strategic and military weight, which other member states will be keen to harness to the continent.

All in all, it is unlikely that the terms of the divorce and an agreement on the future relationship between the UK and the EU could be achieved in two years—or actually rather 18 months, as time will be needed to get the agreement of the European Parliament. EU institutions will be busy negotiating Brexit while at the same time trying to prevent the further weakening of the EU project and facing continuing and new challenges such as a new unpredictable US administration.

5.5   The European Union at a Crossroads

The election of Donald Trump as president of the United States has added an unexpected difficulty to the European Union. The principles on which he was elected run counter to European values of multilateralism, open trade, common security or respect for minorities. Close to Nigel Farage, the leader of UKIP, Trump explicitly embraced Brexit, calling it a 'great thing' in an interview with Michael Gove for *The Times* (16 January 2017). In the same interview he criticised the EU, which he saw as a 'vehicle for

Germany' and added: 'I believe others will leave. I do think keeping it together is not gonna be as easy as a lot of people think'. This was an unprecedented attack for an American president, breaking with a tradition of over 60 years of bi-partisan support for European integration, at a time when the EU was already weakened. Ominously, several populist parties in Europe hailed the election of Donald Trump and his hostile stance towards refugees and (Muslim) migrants brought him support from several Central European governments in Poland, Hungary and Slovakia.[8]

Although the EU showed a high degree of resilience in the immediate aftermath of the Brexit vote, questions remain about the mid- to long-term future of the European project and its underlying weaknesses. If the Brexit vote has not destroyed it, centrifugal forces ranging from internal divisions and lack of solidarity to the rise of 'illiberalism' and populism continue to pose an existential challenge to the Union. Whether the EU-27 will be able to successfully confront them remains an open question.

In the Bratislava (September 2016) and Malta (January 2017) European Councils, EU-27 leaders pledged to strengthen European defence, made more urgent by Trump's equivocal message about NATO being 'obsolete" and the protection of European borders, two relatively consensual fields which are also two main voters' concerns. Whether these objectives can be implemented and whether the EU can take other initiatives to strengthen its output and reconnect with voters also depend on the results of the different national elections across the EU in 2017. As it turned out, Geert Wilders's relative lacklustre performance in the Dutch elections, Emmanuel Macron's victory against Marine Le Pen in the French presidential election and Chancellor Merkel's popularity in Germany showed that the populist wave could be confronted and potentially stopped.

Even if populist forces are contained, it is unlikely in any case that there will be a revision of the treaties in the near future. There is no appetite in European capitals for another round of protracted negotiations in parallel to the Brexit ones, and fear of referendums is now widespread, although Chancellor Merkel sent positive signals concerning the need to strengthen the eurozone following the election of the new French president. Finally, ideas of a multi-speed Europe have resurfaced at the Malta summit, supported by the German government but opposed by countries like Poland which fear being isolated in Europe.

5.6 Conclusion

The vote on Brexit was the result of a mixture of domestic, European and international factors. One of its main consequences has been to add a further level of uncertainty and disruption to an already embattled European Union. While opinion polls in the rest of the member states show that the vote has not, in the short term, led to an increase in anti-EU feeling and the fear of immediate contagion to other countries seems to have been overblown, Brexit remains a huge challenge for the EU as it will require complex and difficult negotiations for years, though this complexity seems to have had a deterrent effect in other EU countries.

It is too early to say whether the British referendum will represent a further step towards disintegration or whether, on the contrary, it—together with the Trump challenge—will serve as a wake-up call for citizens and leaders who have taken the peace and stability afforded by the EU for decades for granted. The first indications are that European public opinion has not turned even further against the EU and that its political leaders are keen to strengthen its structures. It must be hoped that governments do not muddle through in the EU, unwilling to contemplate major reforms for fear of fuelling more discontent or exposing the divisions between member states, and that they are able to put forward plans for the future of Europe which can appeal to a majority of voters.

Notes

1. http://www.ukpolitical.info/european-parliament-election-turnout. htm.
2. Quoted in the *Financial Times*, 4 October 2015.
3. "'Deserters will not be welcome back', Juncker warns UK voters", *Financial Times*, 20 May 2016.
4. "UK must pay price for Brexit, says François Hollande", *The Guardian*, 7 October 2016; "Angela Merkel: Theresa May cannot 'cherry pick' Brexit terms", *The Independent*, 6 December 2016.
5. "UK will pay huge price for prioritising migration curbs, says Dutch PM", *The Guardian*, 19 January 2017.

6. Quoted in "No special favours for UK in Brexit deal, says Maltese Prime Minister", *The Guardian*, 29 January 2017.
7. http://visual.ons.gov.uk/uk-perspectives-2016-trade-with-the-eu-and-beyond/.
8. 'Hungary's Prime Minister Viktor Orban praises Donald Trump's 'America First' nationalism', *The Independent*, 23 January 2017, http://www.independent.co.uk/news/world/europe/donald-trump-nationalist-hungary-pm-viktor-orban-praise-america-first-a7542361.html.

References

Alexandre-Collier, Agnes. 2002. *La Grande-Bretagne eurosceptique?* Lille: Editions du Temps.

Baker, David, and Pauline Schnapper. 2015. *Britain and the Crisis of the European Union*. Basingstoke: Palgrave Macmillan.

Baker, David, Andrew Gamble, and Steve Ludlam. 1994. The Parliamentary Siege of Maastricht 1993: Conservative Divisions and British Ratification. *Parliamentary Affairs* 47 (1): 37–60.

Bennett, Owen. 2016. *The Brexit Club: The Inside Story of the Leave Campaign's Shock Victory*. London: Biteback Publishing.

Bickerton, Christopher J., Dermot Hodson, and Puetter Uwe. 2015. *The New Intergovernmentalism: States and Supranational Actors in the Post-Maastricht Era*. Oxford: Oxford University Press.

Eurobarometer 67. 2007. *Public Opinion in the European Union*. Available at http://ec.europa.eu/public_opinion/archives/eb/eb67/eb67_en.pdf. Accessed 12 Jan 2017.

Fondation Robert Schuman. 2017. Les Européens et les conséquences du Brexit. *Question d'Europe* n° 416, January 9.

Ford, Richard, and Matthew Goodwin. 2014. *Revolt on the Right: Explaining Support for the Radical Right in Britain*. London: Routledge.

George, Stephen. 1998. *An Awkward Partner: Britain in the European Community*. Oxford: Oxford University Press.

HM Government. 2017. *The United Kingdom's Exit from and New Partnership with the European Union*. Cm 9417, February. Available at https://www.gov.uk/government/uploads/system/uploads/attachment_data/file/588948/The_United_Kingdoms_exit_from_and_partnership_with_the_EU_Web.pdf.

Hooghe, Liesbet, and Gary Marks. 2009. A Postfunctionalist Theory of European Integration: From Permissive Consensus to Constraining Dissenssus. *British Journal of Political Science* 39 (1): 1–23.

Lindberg, Leon, and Stuart Scheingold. 1970. *Europe's Would-Be Polity: Patterns of Change in the European Community*. Englewood Cliffs: Prentice Hall.

May, Theresa. 2016. *Speech to the Conservative Party Conference*. Birmingham. http://press.conservatives.com/. October 2.

———. 2017. *Speech on Brexit*. London. https://www.politicshome.com/news/europe/eu-policy-agenda/brexit/news/82451/read-theresa-mays-full-speech-outlining-britains-12.

Pew Research Center. 2016. *Europeans Overwhelmingly Agree that UK Departure Would Hurt the EU*. http://www.pewglobal.org/2016/06/07/euroskepticism-beyond-brexit/pm_2016-06-07_brexit-07/. June 6.

Qvortrup, Matt 2016. Europe Has a Referendum Addiction. *Foreign Policy*, June 21. http://foreignpolicy.com/2016/06/21/europes-referendum-mania-brexit/.

Schmidt, Vivien A. 2006. *Democracy in Europe*. Oxford: Oxford University Press.

Shipman, Tim. 2016. *All Out War: The Full Story of How Brexit Sank Britain's Political Class*. London: HarperCollins.

Stiglitz, Joseph. 2016. *The Euro and Its Threat to the Future of Europe*. London: Penguin.

Usherwood, Simon, and Nick Startin. 2013. Euroscepticism as a Persistent Problem. *Journal of Common Market Studies* 51 (1): 1–16.

Young, Hugo. 1998. *This Blessed Plot: Britain and Europe from Churchill to Blair*. Basingstoke: Macmillan.

6

A Qualitative Change in the Process of European Integration

Annette Bongardt and Francisco Torres

The views here summarised were part of our 2017 winter and spring term presentations in various classes and seminars at the LSE (including the LSE's Brexit lecture series), King's College London and Católica Lisbon SBE, in seminars at the ESC, St Antony's, Oxford University, the National Defence Institute, Lisbon, and the University of Düsseldorf and in classes at Nova SBE and INA. We are grateful to the many students and to colleagues for helpful discussions and insights, especially to Paul De Grauwe, Brigid Laffan, Waltraud Schelkle, Gijs De Vries, Michiel van Hulten, José Tavares, Teresa Lloyd Braga, Lorenzo Codogno, Kevin Featherstone, Simona Talani, Kalypso Nicolaïdis, Charles Enoch, Russell Kincaid, Jorge Braga de Macedo, Stefan Thierse, Hartwig Hummel and Benedicta Marzinotto and to the many people who kindly commented on our regular posts on the LSE, "The UK in a Changing Europe" and the Oekonomenstimme pages.

A. Bongardt (✉)
European Institute, London School of Economics and Political Science, London, UK

National Institute for Public Administration, Lisbon, Portugal

F. Torres
European Institute, London School of Economics and Political Science, London, UK

PEFM, St. Antony's College, Oxford University, Oxford, UK

Católica Lisbon School of Business and Economics, Lisbon, Portugal

© The Author(s) 2017
N. da Costa Cabral et al. (eds.), *After Brexit*,
https://doi.org/10.1007/978-3-319-66670-9_6

6.1   Introduction: Why Brexit Means British Exit from the European Union

Following up on the result of its in-out referendum on membership of the European Union (EU) of 23 June 2016 that had yielded a majority for Leave, the United Kingdom (UK) invoked Article 50 TEU—an exit clause introduced by the Lisbon Treaty, which allows EU members to voluntarily leave the Union—on 29 March 2017.[1] Fundamentally, the UK opted for exit from the EU club rather than for voice and loyalty.[2] By doing so the country created facts (it will leave the EU) but also defined its perspective on the present and future relationship with the Union: as non-cooperative, with the wish to be no longer part of the European integration process.

Henceforth the challenge boils down to disentangling and severing the UK's manifold ties with the highly integrated Union, whose level of economic integration had risen further to an Economic and Monetary Union (EMU) under the Maastricht Treaty, from the initial customs union with a common market under the founding Rome Treaty. With its notification to the EU the UK had set the clock ticking for achieving an orderly withdrawal from the Union within the two-year time limit established for exit negotiations. Prime Minister May's decision to call snap elections on 8 June 2017 did little else but to delay the beginning of the negotiations and to shorten the available time by some three months.

The EU27 have given their chief negotiator, former commissioner Michel Barnier, an agenda and public and detailed guidelines for negotiating the UK's withdrawal from the EU. On the UK's part in contrast, negotiation objectives have remained nebulous even after the start of withdrawal negotiations, apart from repeated commitments to "Brexit means Brexit" coupled with expectations that the UK could simultaneously "have its cake and eat it" with regard to a future relationship. Much ado might also be owed to negotiating posturing. In the opening session UK negotiators came round to fall in line with the EU's sequential approach (nothing else was on offer) that makes talks on the post-exit relationship dependent on sufficient progress on withdrawal. Still, and somewhat contradictorily, UK negotiators announced that they were seeking a (not further defined) new, deep and special partnership with the European Union (objective enshrined in the Queen's speech 2017). Still, should it not be possible to reach agreement on how to unwind more than 40 years of UK–EU relations and consecutively on the future bilateral relationship, the UK would find itself out of the EU on 30 March 2019 with a third country status and, by default, fall back to trading with the EU on World Trade Organization (WTO) terms.[3]

This chapter is interested in the likely impact on and consequences of a British exit from the EU (Brexit) for the EU. It argues that Brexit has already led to a qualitative change of EU membership, which is positive for the club's sustainability. It cautions against the dangers for the Union and the future of EU integration that lie in giving in to demands for a post-Brexit bespoke agreement by the UK (and eventually other countries whose preferences diverge too much from the preferences of the Union), if it meant putting members at a disadvantage, as that would weaken cohesion and thereby undermine the very foundations of the Union.

The remainder of the chapter is organised as follows. Section 6.2 recalls that it was a fully democratic process that led the UK to leave the EU. Section 6.3 explains why the UK needs to leave the EU before it can aim at a preferential trade agreement with the Union. Section 6.4 confronts Brexit perspectives from the standpoint of the EU (common interest) with the UK's (national interest), evaluating the available options for a post-Brexit trade relationship and explaining why Brexit means a hard Brexit and why soft Brexit bespoke agreement can be interpreted as an attempt to free ride on club benefits post Brexit. Section 6.5 examines the qualitative change in the nature of EU membership that has resulted from Brexit and its positive implications for European integration. Section 6.6 argues that a strong political core built around EMU is a precondition for making possible differentiated overlapping integration with countries that do not wish to participate fully in the EU club. Section 6.7 concludes with respect to future perspectives.

6.2   The UK Voted and Decided to Leave the EU Altogether

6.2.1   The UK's Democratic Process to Leave the EU and the Single Market

The UK took the decision to leave the EU, which went through an unequivocally democratic process.[4] This process comprises the following decisions:

1. The European Union Referendum Act 2015, which was passed by 544–53 votes in its second reading in the Commons and was approved by the House of Lords;

   – Following agreement by both Houses on the text of the Bill it received Royal Assent on 17 December 2015 and became an Act of Parliament (law);

2. The outcome of the June 2016 consultative in-out referendum was clearly in favour of Brexit: 52% to 48% of the vote;
3. The decision to leave the EU was subsequently taken in parliament by an overwhelming majority of MPs at the end of March 2017;

   – Even an amendment to the Article 50 bill by the House of Lords, proposing that the government should commit to staying in the single market, was defeated by 299 votes to 136—even the Labour party did not support it on the grounds that it would mean acting "as if the referendum hadn't happened". The Labour leader and leader of the opposition said: "I am asking all our MPs not to block Article 50 and make sure it goes through next week". The Article 50 bill was given Royal Assent by the monarch;

4. The UK government, with overwhelming support from parliament, invoked Article 50on 29 March 2017, notifying the EU of its intention to leave the Union;
5. In the UK general elections of 8 June 2017 (also dubbed the Brexit elections) more than 84% of the vote went to parties (Conservatives, Labour and UKIP), which on their party electoral platforms pledged to respect the referendum result and the decision of parliament to trigger Brexit;
6. Negotiations for an orderly withdrawal of the UK from the EU are under way since 19 June 2017;
7. The Queen's speech of 21 June 2017 (programme of the incoming government), stating that ministers are committed to working with parliament on the country's future outside the European Union, was approved in parliament.

   – An attempt to approve an amendment to the Queen's speech, which called for the government to abandon the idea that "no deal is better than a bad deal" in3 the Brexit talks and to negotiate for the UK to remain in the single market and the customs union (also referred to as soft Brexit), was defeated by a very large margin in parliament.[5] Clearly, like the Conservatives', Labour's official stance is not in favour of staying in the single market or the customs union. For the two big parties Brexit means Brexit, that is, leaving the EU altogether.

Despite attempts to reverse the democratic decision of the referendum to leave the EU (by appeals to the Supreme Court and to the House of Lords), the UK Parliament and the popular vote in the general elections of 8 June 2017 have overwhelmingly reconfirmed the decision to leave.

By invoking Article 50 the UK not only decided to leave the EU, it also created legal facts, which condition and narrow down its further options. It does not really matter what type of agreement the UK thought possible to achieve after settling the divorce terms and leaving. There is no menu to choose from, as whatever option there might be in theory needs to find the favour of and be agreed by the remaining 27 member states.

6.2.2   A Closer Look at the 2017 ("Brexit") General Elections and Lessons for the EU

Looking at the outcome of the 8 June general elections one can only conclude that the UK Parliament got another strong and clear popular mandate for delivering Brexit. More than 84% of the vote was on a clear Brexit platform (Conservatives, Labour, UKIP), promising to respect the Brexit referendum result. Most MPs were elected on a Brexit or even hard Brexit platform.[6] The vote for Brexit came to imply a hard Brexit.[7]

In that sense, the UK prime minister, Theresa May, achieved her aims—the anticipated elections re-confirmed both the referendum and the Article 50 notification bill (voted for by a large majority in both houses). There is also a significant change in so far as MPs this time ran on their party's manifestos while they had not been candidates on such a platform in the previous elections in 2015, that is, before the June 2016 referendum. Of course, there can be no denial that Theresa May miscalculated her bet to call snap elections to substantially increase the number of Conservative MPs and thereby her grip on the Tory party. May and almost everybody else (even in the Labour party) underestimated Jeremy Corbyn's success in the election campaign. Yet it is puzzling that many analyses of the election results have focused on the Labour party's electoral success (although the party obtained 56 fewer seats than the Conservatives) and on May's failed gamble, deriving implications for Brexit that we think are ill founded upon a closer look.

As a matter of fact, under Theresa May the Tories' vote share actually increased by 5.5%, that is, from 36.9% to 42.4%. Putting the result into perspective, it equals Margaret Thatcher's achievement (albeit twice) in the 1980s and has not been matched either by any of the other European leaders in recent legislative elections, not even by Angela Merkel in Germany. Whereas the current UK prime minister may have failed to increase the number of Tory MPs, she clearly won the popular vote, as 42.4% of the UK electorate supported her hard Brexit stance including the idea of "better no deal than a bad deal" (the so-called cliff edge scenario) with the EU. The elections also meant that Jeremy Corbyn's clearly pro-Brexit stance in the Labour party won.[8] Corbyn's position in the previous parliament in favour of triggering Article 50 was confirmed and his leadership was reinforced. Conversely, the internal opposition (defenders of a so-called soft Brexit, who constantly challenged his leadership) was weakened. Labour does not further discuss what type of Brexit it wants but it is clear in avoiding any mention of staying in the single market even if that was possible—in fact, it only pledges "tariff free access to the EU market", which can be read as a free trade agreement.

On the other hand, the share of the vote of the parties that were against Brexit decreased. The Scottish National Party (SNP), opposing Brexit, went significantly down, from 4.7% to 3.1% of the vote and lost 13 MPs to the Tories running on Theresa May's hard Brexit platform. The Liberal Democrats (Lib Dems), who had aimed at getting the vote of part of the referendum's 48% remain vote, also went down to 7.4% of the vote. Their pledge to hold a second EU referendum did not resonate with voters.[9]

The election results have shown that the UK electorate backed the parties whose platform was explicitly (Conservatives, UKIP) or implicitly (Labour) for a hard Brexit (roughly 84% of the vote) and withdrew support from the parties that opposed Brexit or had pledged a so-called soft Brexit (SNP, Lib Dems and other smaller parties, among them the pro-Brexit Democratic Unionist Party that supports the government, and which got together roughly only 16% of the vote).

It stands out that the leave decision and the outcome of the Brexit elections are in line with Eurobarometer findings, according to which UK respondents identify little with the European Union.[10]

That notwithstanding, many anti-Brexit (not necessarily pro-European as we argue below) observers circle in on May's failed gamble to gain more parliamentary seats to interpret the election results as popular support for a softer Brexit or even for remain. These interpretations have once again proved wrong and attempts to overwrite the democratic decision to leave have been frustrated, as the two major parties in parliament made no concessions for a so-called soft Brexit (which they know is an impossibility, as Brexit means to leave the EU and all of its institutions) after the election.[11]

6.3   Brexit: Withdrawal from the EU

After all those political and legal decisions to leave the EU, confirmed by various overwhelming majorities in parliament, Brexit has become de facto an irreversible process, for two orders of reasons:

1. From a UK perspective, a reversal of the process would make a mockery of democracy and of its domestic institutions (the Queen, the House of Commons, the House of Lords, the government, the diplomatic service, etc.), which have repeatedly pledged to leave the EU. It would be a self-inflicted humiliation and bound to cause a huge loss of credibility and negotiating capacity vis-à-vis the EU and also the international community. On the other hand, a U-turn on leaving the EU would be rightly seen as a betrayal of the will of the people, most likely with dire political consequences for the country. Furthermore, the UK would face an internal permanent opposition to and non-acceptance of EU membership.[12]
2. From an EU perspective, if the decision to leave were not to be respected, any UK government would again be hostage to Eurosceptic political fractions that would rightly feel betrayed, making the Union in turn (even more than in the past) hostage to the UK's particular national

interests. The continuation and aggravation of the non-constructive attitude from within the club would impede the EU's normal functioning and obstruct its problem-solving capacity, leading to discontentment and populism across Europe and to the possible demise of the EU.[13] This scenario is obviously not acceptable for the EU. On the other hand, the EU cannot allow countries to use Article 50 as a strategic bargaining tool to impose their preferences on the other EU members.[14]

In sum, and in spite of some naïve or circumstantial declarations on "doors remaining open" for the UK that were pronounced by some European politicians and EU officials, possibly forgetting that such a decision can only be taken by unanimity of the EU27, a U-turn on Brexit does not seem possible or desirable.[15]

That is not to say that the EU, following its principles, should not welcome all European countries that want to contribute to the project of an ever-closer union and that are committed to playing by the rules in line with shared values and principles. It means that the UK should be always welcome to (re-)apply for membership of the EU or the European Economic Area (EEA), provided that it is willing to comply with the well-defined obligations and commitments that those memberships imply. However, the UK has to complete its withdrawal from the EU first before a reapplication can even be considered. Any other outcome would mean giving in to UK special interests, without any consideration for what has been negotiated among all EU countries over the years and in the common interest.

The same can be said for the future relationship between the UK and the EU. The EU cannot permit that the UK "has its cake and eats it, too". That is, set on leaving the Union the UK cannot be allowed to "cherry-pick" in the single market or on any EU policies and be granted privileges that are reserved for membership. For the EU it is not a question of wanting to punish the UK for leaving. The issue goes deeper and is more complex, as the EU is not an intergovernmental organisation but a deep economic and political integration project. Any country that leaves the club has to face the consequences from doing so, most obviously losing the associated benefits.

The UK had already come to claim a special status inside the EU, on top of its many accumulated derogations, opt-outs and special privileges.

The UK's "enhanced special status" that the EU leaders granted Prime Minister Cameron in February 2016, for him to support the remain option in the UK's referendum, turned out to be a dangerous precedent, damaging the EU's credibility. Together with the UK's permanent opposition from within, the situation had already become untenable, inflicting a heavy toll on the EU's good functioning and holding up the political integration project.[16] As we argued in a previous paper (Bongardt and Torres 2016b), in the end it was divergent (insurmountable) preferences over the nature and shape of the economic union that put the UK on a collision course with the EU's integration objectives (Economic and Monetary Union).

Within the EU club the UK had developed into its least integrated member. The situation would have been aggravated further if the "Remain" camp had won the referendum and the UK special settlement deal gone ahead with even more exemptions (among which from ever-closer union and brakes on the evolution of the single market). The result would have been a very different EU club, with an erosion of EU institutions and action capacity, and a EU consequently unable to deliver results to its citizens, which would only contribute to even stronger anti-EU rhetoric both in the UK and in the other 27 EU member states. Thankfully then for most other EU member states that had acted unwisely (not to say undemocratically by conceding the UK pre-referendum settlement), the Brexit vote made those very problematic and self-harming EU concessions invalid. Otherwise, after the UK's long-standing battle to revert the process of European integration towards a more apolitical free trade zone, which culminated in that unfortunate pre-referendum settlement, UK permanence in the EU would have hindered the other member states' efforts to move ahead and deal with the real contemporary challenges facing the EU.

6.4   The UK's Short-Term National Interests Versus the EU Common Good

In our view, the discussion about Brexit in the UK is excessively focused on the national interest, which explains that no attention is paid in political and public discussions to the fact that the EU is there to defend the common good of the Union and the interest of the remaining 27 EU member states (each with its own concerns with regard to Brexit, like Ireland or Spain). Rather, the UK's perspective resumes to getting the most out of Brexit ("make Brexit a success for the UK"). Conversely, the EU's interest is how to best pursue with and make a success of the European integration project.[17]

When the UK triggered Article 50 this meant that the country was to leave the EU altogether. Neither partial membership of the EU nor cherry-picking in political domains is on offer. For that reason the present negotiation is about disentangling the UK from the EU, not about any deal making. The terms of the UK's participation in the EU were negotiated before it joined the European Community (EC) in 1973 and further fleshed out over time by means of numerous treaty revisions and intergovernmental deals (one may want to recall that those involve all member states and were agreed by unanimity). What is currently being discussed before the UK leaves the EU are hence the divorce terms (settlement of bills, etc.) to sever the created existing ties.

It is the UK government that represents the country in the negotiation—it got a mandate from parliament to freely negotiate Brexit when parliament approved the Article 50 bill and invoked it—and that seeks to agree the terms of the separation with the EU (encountering on the EU side clear negotiating guidelines from the EU27, limited to withdrawal negotiations). Still, as to help smoothen the UK's transition from a EU insider to a EU outsider, the Union has accepted to already start talking about a possible future agreement at a later point in the withdrawal negotiations provided that the talks on the divorce settlement are sufficiently advanced and go well. Of course, any trade or other bilateral agreement can only come into existence once the UK has left the EU (by definition the EU cannot strike international agreements with member states).[18] And surely, with regard to an international agreement it is not only the UK's preferences that count but so do the ones of the EU and its member states. In fact, it is the EU that is in a stronger bargaining position in light of the significant difference in relative size.[19]

Once (if) the terms of separation are agreed and implemented, the UK might want to keep a closer trading relation with the EU than the one it would have by default. Multilateral WTO terms fall short of giving full market access and mean that trade is subject to tariffs, but leave the UK free to seek preferential trade deals.

6.4.1 Available Options for a Post-Brexit Trade Relationship

All alternative options come with trade-offs between sovereignty and economic benefits, apart from depending on EU approval. Economic benefits are related to the scope and conditions of single market access and the incidence of customs barriers (issues that are for instance important for the UK's large financial sector or to not disrupt supply chains in manufacturing sectors like the automotive industry).

The available options stretch from EEA membership on the one end to a free trade agreement on the other, with intermediate solutions like a Switzerland-type agreement or membership in the EU customs union. While they all imply a trade-off between sovereignty and economic benefits, they do so to different degrees. The rule is that higher economic benefits are associated with higher integration but can only be had with sovereignty sharing or pooling. Put differently, a UK preference for more control comes at the expense of lower economic benefits.

A full account is beyond this chapter, but suffice it here to draw attention to some features of agreements with relevance for the UK discussion:

1) The UK may apply for joining the EEA, like Norway. It gives unfettered access to the EU single market, which is inseparable from the four freedoms, that is, the free movement of goods, services, capital and persons, and implies that the UK must respect all the rules that come with membership (among which free movement of persons, EU regulation and European Court of Justice (ECJ) jurisdiction) and also contribute to the EU budget, without having the right to vote[20];
2) The UK could also try to have a lesser, Swiss-style agreement to get access to the single market (in reality a plethora of some 120 agreements that emulate EEA membership, where the violation of one single agreement triggers the termination by the EU of all the others). While it requires the free movement of labour it does not extend to financial services;
3) The UK could also aim to just be in the EU Customs Union (like Turkey). In that case there is limited market access (goods only) without customs barriers, it can control immigration but is not free to strike trade deals with third countries;

4) The UK could aim at a deeper free trade agreement, for which the Canada-EU Comprehensive Economic and Trade Agreement (CETA) has been referred as a possible blueprint (the EU regards CETA as its most advanced free trade agreement). In this case the UK would be free to control immigration and make trade deals with other countries but face limited market access (most notably, CETA does not include financial services). Any agreement would moreover be complicated in practice due to the fact that it requires the unanimous ratification by all EU member states but in addition, because of its comprehensive nature, even by some regions[21];

5) Last but not least, there is also the option to reapply to join the EU, and thereby the single market and the customs union, at some point. This option comes with the well-known sovereignty constraints. In addition, however, different entry conditions from those that the country enjoyed at the time of exit would apply. The UK would not be granted the aforementioned special conditions (among which the rebate on its budgetary contribution) and multiple opt-outs and exemptions that made its membership so problematic for the Union.

One may of course question whether the above options are realistic at all in light of the UK's preferences. Rather, the UK's options amount to the same: exiting the EU, including the single market. To start with, this is because its options are constrained by the EU interest and also by different member state interests (Wyplosz 2016).[22] In addition, because of the UK's claims for regaining full sovereignty. As Paul de Grauwe (2017) puts it, the EU should make it clear that UK demands on sovereignty make UK access to the internal market impossible, not as a choice of the EU but as the logical consequence of the UK's quest for full sovereignty. Obviously, what applies to the internal market applies also to other common goods that come with EU membership. The hard/soft Brexit distinction may not be very meaningful, but driven as it is by sovereignty concerns, it narrows down options. In the UK, both Labour and the Conservatives have been defending the need to respect the will of the people and deliver Brexit. The latter were more explicit: hard Brexit (out of the single market and the customs union, even a no-deal, cliff edge scenario); the former remained more ambiguous: no to the single market and to the customs union but tariff-free access to the EU market.

From the EU's point of view, the issue is more that a certain level of economic integration (with higher benefits) requires sovereignty sharing or pooling and also political commitment. Countries whose electorate is deeply divided on the issue of EU membership and on the objective of an ever-closer union should then not remain in the EU. In function of their different preferences it is preferable that they rather come to establish more or less deep trade agreements with the EU (like the ones of Norway, Switzerland, Turkey or Canada). In the UK, long-standing divisions have led to the country being a member of the EU without participating in two of its most important areas of integration: the euro and Schengen. The UK's participation in the European project is essentially limited to the single market but even there it dislikes being subject to EU regulation, which ensures that the market works in the first place.[23] Arguably, in such conditions there is no point to remain a member of the Union or even of the single market, neither from the UK's nor from the EU's point of view. Besides, each time there is a treaty revision in the EU the solution turns out to be suboptimal, not least because of the UK's particular red lines. The result has been insufficient integration and a popular backlash against the Union in many EU countries and also in the UK. The situation is clearly not sustainable. The EU needs to move forward with increased political integration to deal with a host of urgent transnational issues from which Brexit is little more than a distraction. The UK may want to take a distinct approach to problems and should be free to try it out.

As for the EU, it faces a credibility (and indeed sustainability) issue with regard to the exact terms that it grants the UK post Brexit: it cannot simply accept whatever member states or third countries want to do based on their national interest, at the expense of the Union and of the European project. The UK's reported wish of a "Norway-plus" agreement, which amounts to cherry-picking within the internal market, is a case in point (De Grauwe 2016).[24]

6.4.2   Why Brexit Means a Hard Brexit and Soft Brexit Amounts to an Attempt to Free Ride on EU Club Benefits

The single market is at the centre of what the EU does. British participation in the EU has also become very much limited to it. It follows that leaving the EU for the UK logically means leaving the single market. The UK government's expressed exit negotiation demands (notably regaining full control over immigration and putting an end to being subject to the jurisdiction of the European Court of Justice) mean that the country excludes itself from the single market (De Grauwe 2017), whereas through demands to be able to strike trade deals the country excludes itself from the customs union. What else could the UK want to leave, given that it already opted out or refrained from participating in other European major institutions?

Against this background, all the various positions on Brexit, including from anti-Brexit parties (Liberal Democrats, SNP and other smaller parties) and vested interests (in industry and especially in the financial sector), just amount to different negotiating strategies, which also include the government's so-called cliff edge scenario, to extract the most from the EU. Even the Lib Dems, which assume themselves as pro-Europeans, have come to defend a totally de-characterised EU much at the image of previous Eurosceptic demands that led to the infamous UK settlement in February 2016. They all amount to defending only the UK national interest by means of a post-exit bespoke deal with the EU. Such a tailor-made deal is euphemistically called soft Brexit. In practice it amounts to the UK free riding on the EU: the UK would maintain most of EU membership advantages without the obligations and commitment of a member. It seems obvious that the EU should refuse such concessions for the sake of its own survival. In fact, trying to shift from hard to soft Brexit is just a way of trying to secure the economic benefits that come with deeper integration but without the sovereignty constraints. That is obviously not on offer. To enjoy the benefits of EU integration and membership a country has to share sovereignty with its partners.

In the end, the strategy of a bespoke deal corresponds not only to a so-called soft Brexit but is the attempt to "have the cake and eat it, too". It is congruent with suggestions that any new trade deal must deliver the "exact same benefits" the UK enjoys from being inside the single market and the customs union. Obviously that cannot happen, as that would mean that the EU would let non-EU members free ride on the benefits of membership, even more so by a member state that has unilaterally decided to abandon the club. The bespoke deal strategy became clearer after the 8 June general election given the attempts of transforming a clear majority for hard Brexit (84% of the popular vote) into a soft Brexit mandate, with pressures likely to grow to the extent that the economic consequences of Brexit become felt. Claims of the superiority of a soft Brexit solution are thus purely based on the UK national interest.

For the UK, the need for a tailor-made deal arises because otherwise a "soft Brexit" (with access to the single market and membership in the EU customs union) is neither compatible with the UK's stated objective to exit the Union nor with its preference for regaining or maintaining national sovereignty in a range of policy areas. For the rest of the EU, however, it would carry a heavy burden.

For the EU such a soft bespoke Brexit is not on offer. It is not acceptable that a country that wants to leave the Union to reaffirm its sovereignty comes to cherry-pick and extract privileges for the sake of its purely national interest, which are either not available to others (be they EU or EEA members) or go against the common good. This applies to the above-referred UK demands for being exempt from European Court of Justice (ECJ) jurisdiction, limitations to the free movement of people—one of the four freedoms, and hence a non-negotiable precondition for an unfettered access of the common market—or being free to strike trade deals with third countries, incompatible with being a member of the EU customs union.[25]

6.5   A Qualitative Change in the Nature of EU Membership

The EU faces the challenge that the club has become not only much larger over the years but by many accounts also a lot more heterogeneous, so that its decision-making and problem-solving capacity is compromised if governance is inadequate and institutions cannot be made to work properly. It ultimately raises the issue of the optimum size of the EU club.[26] Fundamentally, the Union has to come to grips not only with different country preferences (although preferences on institutions can evolve) but with a situation in which successive enlargements brought countries with different views on supranational governance and European economic integration as a political project—initially confined to different clubs, EEC and EFTA and others—into the same club.[27] As explained above, the UK is a case in point.

Article 50 plus the precedent set by the UK vote for Brexit and its decision to leave the EU has made it politically easier for any member state that is not happy in the EU to leave the club. Thereby the nature of EU membership has changed: countries will now have to make a constant effort (both with respect to their electorates and to their partners in the Union) to remain members. The fact that Brexit opened the door for any discontent member state to exit the club will most likely reduce any member state's capacity to hold up decisions that are in the common interest, and should thereby facilitate decision making and problem solving.

Member states will also have to come clear in terms of narrative, stopping scapegoating the EU for domestic failures (case of the UK but not only), which has been undermining the EU (Buti and Lacoue-Labarthe 2016).

Those developments are quite positive. It is in the interest of both the EU and discontent member states that do not wish to contribute to the club's public goods (apparently also the case of some other EU members like Denmark, Hungary or Poland). It leads us back to the idea of variable geometry or various concentric circles. The fundamental lesson from Brexit is that the EU will need to focus and deliver on EU common goods in order to be sustainable. With divergent preferences across member states, that may have to happen through variable geometry. Yet, although reinforced cooperation, for which there are already many examples of sub-clubs, offers a way out of a stalemate it only does so in the short term, as it puts the cohesiveness of the EU project at risk in the longer run. For the EU to function, the Union needs a political core and a shared identity and destiny. It is the Eurozone that has established itself as the core circle of European integration.

There are limits to what differentiated integration can achieve. Having European institutions built with more flexibility that can accommodate different preferences contributes to a better functioning of the EU (Spolaore 2013). However, a loose intergovernmental arrangement to accommodate all different preferences would come at the expense of the Eurozone and in consequence it would mean the end of the European integration project as an "ever closer Union". It is not the EU that has to adapt to the very divergent preferences of given countries (some of them joined the EU upon the condition to join all of its institutions such as the euro but seem to have changed their intentions) but rather it is those countries that have to decide whether they want to stay in the Union or leave.[28] That is why it is important to have explicit provisions not only for entry but also for exiting the EU (Spolaore 2015). Binding in third countries in existing intergovernmental agreements (as suggested in Pisani-Ferry et al. 2016) also carries the risk of a backlash on EU dynamics because it then makes the evolution of governance towards the Community sphere difficult even if preferences converged among EU member states. In our view, differentiated integration is only sustainable if anchored to a solid core, which is the Eurozone.

6.6 The Need for a Strong Core as an Anchor for Differentiated Integration: The Case of the Eurozone

If there are lessons to be learned from Brexit, one is that there are limits to differentiated integration and that the EU will need to focus and deliver on the EU common goods in order to be sustainable. With divergent interests across member states, too much differentiation through opt-outs and reinforced cooperation can erode the cohesiveness of the EU project.[29] EMU—the EU's treaty-based integration objective—is a case in point.

EMU is a political project that has triggered and still requires further integration. Making monetary union work requires completing the economic union side so that it can sustain the single currency and deliver on the EU's wider objectives (Bongardt and Torres 2016a). The single market can therefore not be seen as static. It is in the legitimate interest of present and future Eurozone members—all EU members except the UK and Denmark, which have an opt-out—that it be deepened, to make it sustainable in light of the increased interdependencies between its members.

This issue is at the heart of the EU project. And to be sustainable, the EU needs to complete its Economic and Monetary Union so that it delivers economic and social results. Member states should be prepared either to contribute to those aims or to seek alternative forms of association with the EU. The EU's capacity to shape globalisation in line with citizens' concerns (not merely growth-oriented but in a more inclusive and greener manner, in line with the Lisbon and Europe 2020 strategies' objectives) will be critical for the support of the project.

The necessary convergence of preferences for a "genuine" EMU was already difficult to achieve in light of increasing EU membership and more heterogeneous member states, but progress was further complicated by the fact that membership in the Euro area sub-club—where interdependencies are larger and the completion of EMU governance is more urgent—has remained smaller than the EU club's. The announced departure of the UK from the EU leaves only one member state with an opt-out from EMU, namely Denmark, which however shadows the Eurozone. All the other (present or future) member states are to join monetary union at some point, upon fulfilling the requisites (or at least they so committed when they joined the EU).

In a EU club whose integration objectives have advanced since the Maastricht Treaty to Economic and Monetary Union (EMU), the UK has been harbouring preferences for a stand-alone (and incomplete) economic union. Once the Eurozone became established as the de facto core of European economic and political integration, those different UK preferences became untenable. During the global (economic and financial) and especially the Eurozone sovereign debt crisis, the UK's stance started to collide with the need to make the monetary union work. It became clear that further integration and institution building were needed in the economic union sphere as to impede the unravelling of monetary union, and with it of European integration achievements like the single market (as it cannot be treated as static with regard to EMU requirements, notably with regard to financial services).

It is in the legitimate interest of present and future Eurozone members that economic union be deepened with regard to Eurozone requirements to make the monetary union sustainable; doing so requires not only structural reform at the member state level but also advances on EU-level governance. However, the requirements on the EU's economic union seemed irreconcilable with some preferences expressed by the "Remain" camp in the UK, which saw the UK staying in the single market while adhering to policies of its choice. Needless to say, such a pretension is not acceptable for the other member states.

Among all EU members, the UK stands out as the least involved in the building of European economic governance. The UK's stance had not only been limited to maintaining itself at the margins of economic governance advances during the global financial and especially the sovereign debt crisis but it also actively tried to impede them, even by employing its veto. Because of the UK's veto, the Treaty on Stability, Coordination and Governance in the Economic and Monetary Union (TSCG), also known as the Fiscal Compact, could only come to life as an intergovernmental treaty outside the EU legal framework. The UK did not participate in the Euro-plus Pact and in the European Banking Union either. Moreover, the UK also did not wish to constructively assist any of the member states whose economies underwent adjustment (bailout) programmes. It did not participate in the European Financial Stability Facility (EFSF) or the European Stability Mechanism (ESM), having made an exception only for Ireland, to whom it was in the UK's national interest to provide bilateral loans in light of financial sector interdependencies (Bongardt and Torres 2017a).[30]

Still, on economic benefit terms alone (abstracting from strong preferences for sovereignty), the UK's non-cooperative stance was somewhat puzzling since the country has benefited significantly from the Eurozone, most notably because of a high proportion of euro-denominated financial activities taking place in the city of London[31] and because of privileged access of UK banks to the ECB's liquidity operations during the global financial crisis.

Had the outcome of the UK EU membership referendum been different—not "Leave" but "Remain"— the Eurozone would have risked seeing its legitimate efforts to strengthen EMU, including where necessary by deepening the single market, to be vetoed by a country with a derogation from EMU. In other words, had "Remain" won in the referendum, the prospects for completing and sustaining EMU would have worsened and dissatisfaction with the EU would have increased.

Brexit thus ought to make it easier for the Eurozone to go ahead with necessary institutional reforms to complete EMU, which happens to be a sufficiently challenging task even without the opposition from within of a large and important member state. The departure of the UK opens up the perspective to gear financial regulation in the single market better towards the Eurozone's public good of financial stability, thereby reinforcing the economic union in a crucial area for the monetary union. It could also prove easier to bring intergovernmental economic agreements into the Community framework at some stage.

6.7   Concluding Remarks

Brexit is a priority for the UK. For the EU, it is a major and costly distraction from important common challenges such as the completion of Economic and Monetary Union and the migration crisis that it needs to respond to. It is in the interest of the UK to settle its financial liabilities and leave the EU in the least acrimonious way and as fast as possible as it will come to depend on the goodwill of each one of the EU27 for any future trade deal and post-Brexit relationship.

Looking back, the UK had access to many of the EU common goods, blocked several others, benefited for many years from many exceptions, and refused to help or to play a constructive role during the sovereign debt crisis, and has unilaterally decided to abandon its partners in a difficult juncture. In fact, the EU and all of its members (including the UK) have suffered since long from the UK's growing estrangement and especially since the negotiation of the Maastricht Treaty that enshrined the Union, from the UK's systematic opposition from within. Attempts at institutional reforms to allow for deepening integration with a view to a more efficient and a more democratic EU were systematically vetoed by the UK. This has carried a very high price, which a Eurosceptic fraction in the British main parties and business sector (more keen on a US-type less regulated environment) impinged on the European integration project.

For both the EU and the UK, especially for the UK's many friends in Europe, the best that can happen in the present setting is to avoid special EU concessions to the UK to smoothen the costs of Brexit at the expense of the good functioning of the EU. The EU has to act responsibly and protect its interests, that is, the common good. The issue has nothing to do with wanting to punish the UK, which would be contrary to the EU integration spirit and also counterproductive, but is about avoiding (to continue) punishing the EU.

One cannot exclude (after all there is already a precedent in the past) that the UK will come to realise that it is not in its national interest to stay out of the club and that it will at some point decide to reapply to join the EU. Being relegated to the world of pure intergovernmental interests, the UK is likely to experience how much closer it is to the EU countries than to other hypothetical allies. However, it will only be able to re-join the EU on very different terms: with no reservations, no rebate to the Community budget and no opt-outs from the Union's core institutions (from EMU and Schengen, among others). In that scenario, the UK would come to play a much more constructive role in EU governance and in deepening European integration as it did for instance in the case of promoting the completion of the single market, whose regulatory nature it came later to dislike. True Europeanists in the UK should focus on preparing the political terrain for a whole-hearted comeback in some years and not on subverting the democratic decision taken by UK citizens. By the same token, EU leaders and institutions should focus on preserving the cohesiveness of the European integration project instead of kicking the can down the road and allow for an ever more differentiated type of integration to accommodate Poland, Sweden and others at any cost. That road will not contribute to a shared European identity and would eventually destroy the Union.

Notes

1. The decision to have an in-out referendum came in the sequence of many years of growing unease with respect to EU membership (and opposition from within the Union), in the course of which the UK became the EU's least integrated member (see König 2015, for an illustrative graphical presentation).
2. In the well-known terminology of Hirschman (1970).

3. To avoid that outcome, the UK would need to ask for a prolongation or interruption of the process, which would require the unanimous approval by the EU27 and would almost certainly come with new conditions attached. That would constitute a rather humiliating situation for the UK and would only erode its credibility and bargaining power even more.

4. It is also a logical consequence of ever more diverging UK preferences from the EU club (see Bongardt and Torres 2016b). In truth, the UK already had different preferences with regard to the sovereignty/economic benefit trade-off at the outset: It preferred an intergovernmental preferential trade organisation—it did not want to be part of the supranational European Economic Community (EEC) and founded the intergovernmental European Free Trade Association (EFTA) instead—but ended up joining the EEC because of its larger economic benefits. And indeed that membership helped it revert the British economic decline (Campos and Coricelli 2017).

5. On 29 June 2017, 49 "Labour rebels" (about a fifth of the Labour party), with the Liberal Democrats and the Scottish National Party and others, signed an amendment to the Queen's speech, which called for the government to abandon the idea that "no deal is better than a bad deal" in the Brexit talks and to negotiate for the UK to remain in the single market and the customs union. The amendment was clearly defeated as it only got 101 votes (less than one-sixth of the House of Commons). Moreover, after the vote the Labour leader, Jeremy Corbyn, asserting his authority in the party, sacked the three shadow ministers who had voted in favour of the pretension.

6. See Bongardt and Torres (2017c, d).

7. The reason is that the Leave vote was directed at the UK's EU membership status quo—which given the manifold UK opt-outs and non-participation in policy areas essentially boils down to leaving the internal market—and that EU additional concessions offered to the UK (the UK pre-referendum settlement) had not changed the outcome. Once the British people—perhaps unexpectedly for the proponents of the referendum (which was to be used as a bargaining tool in the EU)—had voted by a majority (52% to 48%) in favour of leaving the EU, those additional and far-reaching exemptions, which the government of former Conservative prime minister Cameron had demanded and obtained as a pre-condition for running a remain campaign and staying in the EU club thereafter, became invalid.

8. Jeremy Corbyn had already voted in favour of leaving the EEC in the 1975 referendum, spoke out against the Maastricht Treaty, which established the European Union, and voted against the Lisbon Treaty in 2008.

9. The former Lib Dem leader and vice prime minister from 2010 to 2015, Nick Clegg, defended (Clegg 2017) after the general election that the EU should grant the UK access in the future to the internal market and the customs union as to minimize the negative consequences from Brexit, whereby the EU should commit to a reform of the free movement of labour (including an emergency brake against especially high EU immigration). Such a position does not differ much, if at all, from the position of David Cameron's government, which led to the referendum and to Brexit, as it only takes into account the short-term interests of the UK. Obviously such a soft Brexit stance amounts to free riding on the EU and has no chance even to be considered by most of the EU27. It shows, however, that even the traditionally pro-European Lib Dems (at least before they entered into a government coalition led by the Conservatives) do not quite defend the EU and constructive UK membership but seem aligned with other Eurosceptic postures, just aiming at some cherry-picking on its institutions.

10. Sixty-four per cent of UK respondents opted for national identity only, with only 31% feeling attached to a shared—national and European—identity (Laffan 2016).

11. The idea (put forward by Timothy Garton Ash 2017) that if the priority is the economics then one must logically argue that Britain should stay in the EU is based on a false premise. As the author recognises, David Cameron had fought the referendum even exaggerating the negative economic consequences of Brexit and lost it. In fact, people voted for Brexit, opting for regaining what they see as sovereignty in spite of risking to forgo some economic benefits. As we argue below, there is a trade-off between sovereignty and economic benefits and therefore a UK preference for control spoke stronger than the loss of possible economic benefits. This is how democracy works.

12. Defenders of a reversal of the decision argue that people did not vote what type of Brexit they wanted. The argument does not make much sense, as there is only one type of Brexit: to leave the EU. It is difficult to imagine that people voted to leave the EU but that their intention was to stay in the EU's single market. Because what else could the UK want to leave, given that it is not member of EMU, Schengen, police and justice matters

(block opt-out with selected opt-ins), secured a protocol to the treaty relating to the application of the Charter of Fundamental Rights and does not participate in many other EU institutions (most notably related to the completion of economic union and the strengthening of economic governance)? Eventually people may have different preferences on what type of relation they want with the EU in the future. However, that is irrespective of the first step (Brexit) and can only be settled after the UK leaves the EU, hinging on mutual agreement with the Union (conditioned by EU common interest and the interest of the EU27).

13. The success of anti-EU populist parties in continental Europe, especially in France, is prominently rooted on the one hand in the dislike of the EU's stance attributed to UK or Anglo-Saxon deregulated economic model and, on the other hand, in what is seen as a neglect of the European model. In that respect, the UK exit will also be helpful.

14. See Closa (2016) for an interpretation of Article 50 and its use, including its potential strategic use.

15. Such an apparently open position amounts, on the one hand, to a subversion of the democratic process that led to the country's decision to exit the EU and, on the other hand, to a (not very wise, if not naïve) invitation for any EU country to try to extract short-term dividends at the expense of the common good and the sustainability of the European project.

16. Brigid Laffan (2016) calls attention to the fact that there are real dangers to the future cohesion of the Union if the UK is seen to benefit from exiting.

17. Note that even when leaving the Union it is always in the UK's long-term national interest to have a strong and stable neighbour (the EU). That implies that the EU needs to function well and deliver.

18. A transitional agreement after 30 March 2019 seems possible but conditional on a clear perspective for a future agreement and time limits (European Parliament red line).

19. The UK accounts for only 15% of the EU's GDP.

20. It is also not clear whether countries like Norway, Iceland and Liechtenstein would welcome the UK's application given its disparate size.

21. For a critical appraisal and criticism of the EU's current strategy of pursuing comprehensive bilateral trade agreements underpinned by far-reaching bilateral rules that govern the relationship, see Bongardt and Torres (2017b).

22. The country studies yield that a larger number of EU member states is likely to support a hard Brexit, few a soft Brexit and some take a more case-by-case view.

23. However, as Gros (2016) observes, "real-world examples show, no country that wants to benefit from the European Project has been able to have its cake and eat it. Open borders and economic integration require common rules".

24. The proposal for a continental partnership by Pisani-Ferry et al. (2016), considerably less deep than EU membership but rather closer than a simple free trade agreement, is incompatible with this view and, in our opinion, with EU interests. Being very flexible to accommodate UK (or other countries') interests through ever more differentiated integration it risks limiting the evolution of governance from intergovernmental to supranational when preferences converge among club members and to lose sight of creating a strong EU core. It would also mean to give in to the strategic use of Article 50 in the pursuit of national interests in detriment of the EU27 and of the European integration process.

25. Demands on the part of some in the "remain" camp for a vote in parliament on the conditions on which the UK will leave the EU (the terms of divorce or settling the financial liabilities), which were in any case rejected by parliament (and even by the House of Lords, by 274 votes to 118 votes), do also not make sense. If the other EU 27 member states do not approve those terms and/or the European Parliament does not ratify them (and without the necessary unanimity of member states to extend the negotiations), the EU treaties will automatically cease to apply to the UK at the end of the two-year period. Those are the rules of Article 50, which was nevertheless triggered by the UK government with an overwhelming support of parliament.

26. That is, whether at the margin benefits are still larger or just equal to heterogeneity costs. On the benefit side, the internal market trade benefits loom large. They are already large, and there is scope for improving the functioning and delivery of economic results of the single market (Europe 2020 strategy, digital single market, energy union), so that the benefits from EU club membership can be significantly enhanced. On the other hand, increasing heterogeneity has made itself felt in various policy areas. To the extent that it undermines trust between member states (on which, for instance, the principle of mutual recognition relies) it also makes decision making more difficult (although countries could trade off benefits across issue areas and various common goods). This is not the case for the UK, however, whose participation in the Union is essentially associated with the single market.

27. As pointed out by Alesina et al. (2017), the main impediment to further European political integration has not been heterogeneity of tastes or of cultural traits, but other cleavages like parochial national identities.

28. Soros (2017) defends a loose and flexible EU at the expense of the Eurozone as its political core and of an ever-closer Union. He goes even further in defending that the EU should grant a special treatment to the UK, in recognition of the fact that Brexit is a step towards disintegration and thus a lose-lose proposition. We argue exactly the opposite, that is, that Brexit facilitates further EU integration.

29. For a discussion of the complex state of differentiated integration in the EU see König (2015). As we argue, it makes a shared identity difficult without a core project.

30. The same did not happen in the case of Greece, where the UK even insisted on guarantees that it would be exempt from loan guarantees granted against the EU budget.

31. This is unlikely to continue after Brexit, as normally these activities should be undertaken inside the regulatory area under the control of the ECB.

References

Alesina, Alberto, Guido Tabellini, and Francesco Trebbi. 2017. *Is Europe An Optimal Political Area?* Brookings Papers on Economic Activity, Conference Draft, March.

Bongardt, Annette, and Francisco Torres. 2016a. EMU Reform and Resilience in a Re-dimensioned EU. *Journal of Economic Policy* XXXII (3, December): 575–596.

———. 2016b. The Political Economy of Brexit: Why Making It Easier to Leave the Club Can Allow for a Better Functioning EU. *Intereconomics* 51 (4, July/August): 214–219.

———. 2017a. *Brexit Can Address Eurozone Challenges.* London: The UK in a Changing Europe, April (also in *LSE Brexit blog*).

———. 2017b. Comprehensive Trade Agreements: Conditioning Globalization or Eroding the European Model? *Review of European Economic Policy* 52(3, May/June): 165–170.

———. 2017c. Nach der Wahl: Brexit und die EU. *Wirtschaftsdienst: Zeitschrift für Wirtschaftspolitik* 97(6): 378–379; Heidelberg: Springer.

———. 2017d. *Parliament Has a Strong and Clear Mandate for Brexit, Remainers and EU Politicians Shouldn't Question It*. London: The UK in a Changing Europe (also in *LSE Brexit Blog*).

Buti, Marco, and Muriel Lacoue-Labarthe. 2016. Europe's Incompatible Political Trinities. *VoxEU.org*, September 7.

Campos, N., and F. Coricelli. 2017. *EU Membership or Thatcher's Structural Reforms: What Drove the Great British Reversal?* London: Centre for Economic Policy Research, DP 11856.

Clegg, Nick 2017. Five Steps for Theresa May's Salvation. *Financial Times*, June 11.

Closa, Carlos. 2016. *Interpreting Article 50: Exit and Voice and … What about Loyalty?* EUI Working Paper RSCAS 2016/71. Florence: European University Institute, Robert Schuman Centre for Advanced Studies (RSCAS).

De Grauwe, Paul. 2016. How to Prevent Brexit from Damaging the EU. In *Brexit Beckons: Thinking Ahead by Leading Economists*, ed. R. Baldwin. A VoxEU.org eBook, London: CEPR Press, 149–152.

———. 2017. Brexit Creates Window of Opportunities for the EU. London: *Social Europe*, April 5.

Garton Ash, Timothy. 2017. A Year After Voting for Brexit, Britain Is Divided and in Uncharted Waters. *The Guardian*, June 22.

Gros, Daniel. 2016. Britain's Moment of Truth. *Project-Syndicate*, July 7.

Hirschman, Albert O. 1970. *Exit, Voice, and Loyalty: Responses to Decline in Firms, Organizations, and States*. Harvard: Harvard University Press.

König, Nicole. 2015. *A Differentiated View of Differentiated Integration*, Policy Paper 140. Berlin: Jacques Delors Institute.

Laffan, Brigid. 2016. EU Membership Must Matter. *EurActiv.com*, November 14.

Pisani-Ferry, Jean, Norbert Röttgen, André Sapir, Paul Tucker, and Guntram Wolff. 2016. Europe After Brexit: A Proposal for a Continental Partnership. *Bruegel*, August 29.

Soros, George. 2017. Standing Up for Europe. *Project Syndicate*, June 1.

Spolaore, Enrico. 2013. What Is European Integration Really About? A Political Guide for Economists. *Journal of Economic Perspectives* 27 (3): 125–144.

———. 2015. Monnet's Chain Reaction and the Future of Europe. *VoxEU.org*, July 25.

Wyplosz, Charles. 2016. Introduction. In *What to Do With the UK? EU Perspectives on Brexit*, ed. C. Wyplosz. London: VoxEU.org eBook, October.

7

Brexit and the Reform of Economic and Monetary Union

Federico Fabbrini

7.1 Summary

The reform of Europe's Economic and Monetary Union (EMU) remains on the agenda of the institutions and the member states of the European Union (EU). While several high-level institutional reports on deepening and completing EMU have been published during the last few years, in May 2017 the European Commission has delivered a reflection paper mapping the way forward towards strengthening the Eurozone economy and institutional setup.[1] This effort has acquired a new meaning following the June 2016 decision of the United Kingdom (UK) to leave the EU, and the triggering of the withdrawal negotiations in March 2017.[2] Brexit, in fact, has produced soul-searching within the EU and created the need to strategically think anew about the future of Europe. The purpose of

F. Fabbrini (✉)
School of Law and Government, Dublin City University,
Dublin, Ireland

Brexit Institute, Dublin City University,
Dublin, Ireland

© The Author(s) 2017
N. da Costa Cabral et al. (eds.), *After Brexit*,
https://doi.org/10.1007/978-3-319-66670-9_7

this chapter is to contribute to this debate, by analyzing the legal ways and means to reform EMU—on the understanding that the success of the European integration project also depends on the successful resolution of the Euro-crisis and the consolidation of EMU.

The chapter explains that there are three legal avenues to reform EMU, completing and deepening Europe's architecture of economic governance: (1) through EU legislation adopted within the framework of the current EU treaties, (2) through amendment of intergovernmental treaties concluded outside the framework of EU law and (3) through amendment of the EU treaties themselves. As the chapter claims, EU legislation suffices to introduce a number of important innovations in EMU, including the completion of Banking Union through a European common deposit guarantee scheme and the setup of a European unemployment fund—as well as the incorporation in EU law of the Fiscal Compact and the creation of an EU fiscal capacity. Amendments of intergovernmental treaties concluded outside the framework of EU law instead are necessary to upgrade the European Stability Mechanism. Amendments of the EU treaties, finally, are needed to overhaul the Eurozone institutional architecture, mutualize debts via Euro-bonds or create a debt-restructuring mechanism.

As the chapter points out, reforming EMU through legislation is easier than by amending treaties—and many EMU reforms could be already undertaken now, *à traité constant*. Nevertheless, as the chapter suggests, Brexit creates a window of opportunity to introduce revisions to the EU treaties: in fact, whether EU member states like it or not, they will be required to amend the EU treaties to adapt the EU to the reality of a Union at 27—and this should be exploited to endow the EU with a more perfect constitutional architecture. Changes to the EU treaties are needed to overhaul the EMU institutional architecture and address the deep legitimacy deficit exposed by the Euro-crisis and its aftermath.

7.2   Proposals for Reform

Growing consensus exists on the need to reform the architecture of Europe's EMU. The leaders of the EU institutions have for several years now stressed the urge of putting EMU on a more solid basis, and devised various roadmaps to this end. In December 2012, the President of the European Council, in cooperation with the Presidents of the European Commission, the Eurogroup and the European Central Bank (ECB), released a plan "Towards a Deeper EMU."[3] In July 2014, the new President of the European Commission emphasized the importance of stabilizing EMU in his programmatic speech in front of the European Parliament.[4] And in June 2015, a new report making the case for "Completing Europe's EMU" was released by the President of the European Commission, in close coordination with the Presidents of the European Council, the Eurogroup, the ECB and also the European Parliament.[5]

At the same time, national leaders have endorsed the goal of stabilizing EMU too. Despite the emergence of new crises—from Brexit to the migration crisis, and the internal and external security threats facing the EU—EMU has remained an item on the agenda of heads of state and government of the EU member states. The Bratislava Declaration of September 2016 reaffirmed the importance of economic and social development in the EU,[6] and so did the Rome Declaration of March 2017, celebrating the 60th anniversary of the Rome Treaties.[7] Moreover a number of national governments have advanced proposals to further strengthen EMU. In particular, while the then French and German Ministers of the Economy Emmanuel Macron and Sigmar Gabriel have jointly made the case in June 2015 for a reform of the Eurozone, strengthening the institutional framework and favoring public investments,[8] the Italian Minster of Finance Pier Carlo Padoan has put forward in February 2016 a comprehensive policy strategy for growth, jobs and stability in the EMU.[9] And since the election of Emmanuel Macron as French President in Spring 2017, a new élan in favor of EMU reform has taken place, with France and Germany joinly working on a proposal for completing EMU.[10]

Finally, the European Parliament has consistently backed the efforts to strengthen EMU, calling for further steps in integration.[11] And the attention for EMU reform at the institutional level mirrors that in the public and academic debate at large. Already in 2012 the Tommaso Padoa-Schioppa report of Notre Europe advanced a roadmap towards fiscal union in Europe.[12] Calls to integrate further the Eurozone have been made by groups of public intellectuals in Germany—the Glienicker Group—in October 2013[13] and in France, the Eiffel Group, in February 2014.[14] And although public concerns for the Euro-crisis seem to have declined over the last year, recent initiatives have been taken to re-launch the debate. In particular, the Bertelsmann Stiftung and the Jacques Delors Institut in Berlin and Paris identified in a recent report the remaining weaknesses of the current EMU architecture and devised a *plan de route* to repair and prepare it for the future.[15]

Most blueprints on the reform of EMU are structured in three phases, distinguishing steps to be taken in the short-, mid-, and long-term. Hence, roadmaps towards a deeper and more genuine EMU firstly identify measures that can, and should, be taken immediately—usually because they are either politically non-controversial or economically indispensable to the stabilization of the Eurozone. Secondly, they outline a subsequent set of reforms that ought to be carried out in a clearly defined time horizon, because they usually require greater political capital (coming from national elections) or more time-consuming economic adjustments. Third and lastly, all reports conclude with more ambitious proposals for comprehensive systemic and institutional reforms to be undertaken some ten years down the road with the aim to complement EMU with a real Political Union. While all reports acknowledge the difficulty of moving towards a federal-type model for EMU, they thus stress the importance of *finalité* in Europe's future.

The purpose of this chapter is to examine the reform of EMU from a legal perspective. The chapter discusses several proposals put forward in recent institutional and policy reports and evaluates the way in which such measures may be implemented in legal terms.[16] Also this chapter distinguishes between three phases of action. However, contrary to the above-mentioned reports, this chapter does not classify the measures to be adopted in the various phases based on political or economic considerations. Rather, it distinguishes between (1) measures that can be adopted within the current EU treaty framework, through legislation; (2) measures which can be adopted without changing the current EU treaties, but by amending other intergovernmental agreements outside the framework of EU law; and (3) measures which can be adopted only by amending the current EU treaties. As the chapter posits, because changing treaties is a more complex and burdensome procedure than adopting legislation within the current EU treaty framework, measures which fall in the first group can be implemented with greater speed than measures which fall in the second and third group. However, as the chapter underlines, the need to re-adapt the EU legal order to Brexit offers a window of opportunity—which should be seized to introduce also amendments to the EU treaties as far as EMU is concerned.[17]

The chapter is structured as follows. Section 7.3 discusses a plurality of measures that have been proposed in recent reports on the future of EMU and that can be implemented within the current EU treaty framework, through legislation adopted by the Council—either on its own or jointly with the European Parliament. Section 7.4 focuses instead on several reform proposals which cannot be carried out within the EU legal framework, but which do not require a change to the EU treaties either: in particular, this section examines the Treaty establishing the European Stability Mechanism (ESM)[18] and explains the ways in which this intergovernmental agreement concluded by the Eurozone member states outside the framework of EU law can be amended and upgraded. Section 7.5, finally, considers those reforms of EMU which can only be accomplished by an amendment of the EU treaties. In discussing the legal measures to be carried out in the three above-mentioned forms, the chapter does not consider the legitimacy aspects raised by each of these proposals. However, by mapping the avenues for legal and institutional reforms in the EMU and their complexity, the chapter seeks to provide a helpful compass on what is constitutionally possible in the short-, mid-, and long-term in EMU.

7.3   Reforms Through EU Legislation

Multiple legal measures to reform EMU can be adopted within the current EU treaty framework.[19] On the one hand, on the side of stability, measures can be taken to improve economic policy coordination, and to foster the process of convergence between the Eurozone member states. Legislative steps in the direction of an "Economic Union"[20] can be adopted on the basis of Articles 121 and 126 Treaty on the Functioning of the EU (TFEU), and include the creation of Competitiveness Boards[21]—designed to provide independent advice to national governments on structural reforms—and the upgrading of the European Semester, so as to increase ownership and compliance with the Country Specific Recommendations.[22] A special legal basis, Article 136 TFEU, is then available to put in place particular measures relating to the Eurozone only—for example, the introduction of a discussion of the Eurozone overall fiscal stance in the Eurogroup debates concerning the Annual Growth Survey.[23]

Moreover, while important measures have already been adopted to strengthen the rules of the Stability and Growth Pact (SGP) in the aftermath of the Euro-crisis,[24] the current EU constitutional framework would permit further steps in the direction of enhancing fiscal surveillance, for instance by incorporating within the EU legal order the key substantive provision of the Fiscal Compact.[25] As is well known, Article 3 of the Treaty on the Stability, Coordination and Governance in the EMU—which was concluded in March 2012 by 25 of the then 27 EU member states (all, except the UK and the Czech Republic)—requires contracting parties to maintain an annual structural deficit of 0.5% of GDP, and to incorporate such requirement in domestic law "through provisions of binding force and permanent character, preferably constitutional or otherwise guaranteed to be fully respected and adhered to throughout the national budgetary process." This clause of the Fiscal Compact could already today be brought back within the framework of EU law—with all the benefits in terms of administrative and judicial enforcement that would follow from it—through a regulation based on Articles 121 and 126 TFEU, combined with the use of the enhanced cooperation procedure (foreseen in Articles 326–334 TFEU) by the 25 EU member states which signed up to the TSCG.[26]

On the other hand, the current EU treaty framework also allows for further integration steps on the side of solidarity. Hence, measures to complete Banking Union with the creation of a European Deposit Insurance Scheme (EDIS) could be accomplished without any change to the treaties by resorting to Article 114 TFEU.[27] In fact, the objective of the establishment and the functioning of the internal market at the core of Article 114 TFEU would be not only the adequate legal basis to complement the Single Supervisory Mechanism[28] and the Single Resolution Mechanism[29] with a Europe-wide risk-sharing mechanism among national deposit insurance schemes—as repeatedly demanded, not least, by the ECB[30]—but also to take steps towards the creation of a Capital Markets Union, for example, with EU legislation favoring securitization.[31]

In addition, the current treaties would permit the adoption of legal measures tackling the dire problem of unemployment. While the Euro-crisis has caused a high social cost, particularly in some EU member states,[32] new, well-articulated proposals have been brought forward to endow the EU with an unemployment insurance fund, able to tackle cyclical downturns in the level of employment experienced in one of the member states as a result of asymmetric shock occurring in the EMU.[33] In particular, Article 174 and 175 TFEU, which empower the EU institutions to develop and pursue action strengthening economic, social and territorial cohesion, would appear as a suitable legal basis to pursue the creation of a European Unemployment Insurance Scheme (EUIS). If EUIS were to be restricted to Eurozone member states only, Article 136 TFEU would then have to be used in conjunction with the above-mentioned provisions to strengthen the social dimension of EMU.[34]

Yet, besides the above-mentioned risk-sharing and sovereignty-sharing measures, the current EU legal framework would allow for much additional action impacting upon EMU. First, the EU treaties grant to the EU institutions extensive power to intervene in the functioning of the internal market. In fact, the importance of the internal market competence of the EU in the field of economic policy is explicitly enshrined in Article 119 TFEU, which states that "the economic activities of the Member States and the Union shall include, as provided in the Treaties, the adoption of *an economic policy which is based* on the coordination of the Member States' economic policies, *on the internal market*, and on the definition of common objectives."[35] Under the current constitutional regime, therefore, further legislative steps to complete the internal market, for example, in the service sectors, could be pursued through the Community method by the European Parliament and the Council,[36] with potential positive spillovers on EMU.[37]

Second, no constitutional change is actually needed to promote a broader program of public investments—a development often invoked as a mid-term reform of EMU.[38] As the example of the European Fund for Strategic Investments (EFSI) enacted by a regulation of the European Parliament and the Council in June 2015 makes clear,[39] the EU already enjoys the competence—on the basis among others of Articles 172, 173, 175(5) and 182(1) TFEU (on industry, technological development and economic, social and territorial cohesion)—to start a program of public investment designed to stimulate the economy and promote growth. In fact, additional legal bases—such as Article 170 TFEU (on trans-European networks), Article 179 TFEU (on research) and Article 194 TFEU (on energy)—empower the EU institutions to launch a comprehensive public and private investment initiative, even beyond the simple plan to extend the life of the EFSI and increase its funding recently brought forward by the Commission.[40]

Last but not least, the current EU treaty framework *already* permits the adoption of an EMU reform which is regarded by all policy and institutional reports as due in the long term: the creation of a fiscal capacity for the EU (or the Eurozone), supported by European taxes.[41] In fact, Article 113 TFEU empowers the Council, acting unanimously in accordance with a special legislative procedure and after consulting the European Parliament to adopt legislation on the harmonization of taxation. At the same time, Article 311 TFEU states that "[t]he Union shall provide itself with the means necessary to attain its objectives and carry through its policies," and although this clause does not mention EU taxation explicitly, it affirms that "[w]ithout prejudice to other revenue, the budget shall be financed wholly from own resources." As I have argued elsewhere, Articles 113 and 311 TFEU can be read in conjunction as empowering the EU institutions to raise the financial resources necessary to sustain a fiscal capacity.[42] In fact, the European Commission had proposed to use Article 113 TFEU to introduce a Financial Transaction Tax (FTT)[43] or a Common Consolidated Corporate Tax Base[44]—and had indicated that the revenues derived from this tax would be assigned to the EU budget (in lieu of other member states' financial transfers).[45] Needless to say, the use of Articles 113 and 311 TFEU raises multiple complications, connected with the requirement to reach unanimity in the Council. However, this hurdle could be overcome by adopting a single harmonized EU tax through the enhanced cooperation procedure—as it has been effectively attempted with the FTT[46]—although with obvious consequential restriction on the spending side.

In conclusion, ample room exists—from a legal viewpoint—to reform EMU within the framework of the current EU legal order, if there is political willingness to do that.[47]

7.4 Reforms Through Amendments of Intergovernmental Agreements

A second set of reforms of EMU can only be accomplished by amending intergovernmental agreements concluded by groups of EU member states outside the framework of EU law. Leaving aside here the question whether the EU principle of institutional balance should constrain the use of intergovernmental agreements,[48] it is well known that in response to the Euro-crisis member states have on multiple occasions stepped outside the framework of EU law and adopted EMU-related measures through international treaties. The ESM Treaty, in particular was concluded in February 2012 by all the member states of the Eurozone to ensure the financial stability of the euro area.[49] According to Article 3 of the ESM Treaty, "the purpose of the ESM shall be to mobilise funding and provide stability support under strict conditionality […] to the benefit of ESM Members which are experiencing, or are threatened by, severe financing problems, if indispensable to safeguard the financial stability of the euro area." To this end, the ESM is endowed with an authorized capital stock of €700 billion paid by the Eurozone countries pro quota, which is handled by a Board of Governors where the Ministers of Finance of the Eurozone member states sit.[50]

Recent proposals have made the case in favor of reforming the ESM, either by bringing it back within the framework of EU law,[51] or by strengthening it externally.[52] In particular, it has been suggested that the ESM could be upgraded by creating a rapid-response facility of €200 billion for secondary market purchases on government bonds (de facto substituting the ECB Securities Market Programme[53]), and that this revamped ESM could be used also as a back-stop for the Single Resolution Fund dealing with banks' failures.[54] Moreover, to tackle the deficiencies ensuing from the ESM's intergovernmental structure, it has been suggested that the President of the Eurogroup should take on a leading role in the management of the ESM and that national parliamentarians should be involved through an inter-parliamentary conference to improve democratic oversight.

Any proposal to modify the ESM along the previous lines would require an amendment to the ESM Treaty. The ESM Treaty does not foresee special procedures for its revision. But pursuant to customary principles of international law—codified in the Vienna Convention on the Law of the Treaties—international agreements can be modified with the consent of all the contracting parties. Hence, unanimous approval of all the 19 member states which are currently contracting parties to the ESM Treaty would be necessary to amend the Treaty. In some member states, however, modifications of the ESM Treaty would be subject to ex ante judicial review as a condition for the ratification. In Germany, in particular, the Bundesverfassungsgericht (Constitutional Court) authorized the ratification of the ESM Treaty in its final judgment of March 2014 requiring that the German government takes step to ensure that its veto power be maintained in cases of future changes to the Treaty itself.[55] Possible new changes to the ESM Treaty would therefore have to pass the test of some national constitutional courts—with all the uncertainties that follow. Assuming the amendments to the ESM Treaty do not modify Article 48 of the ESM Treaty, instead, the revised treaty could enter into force when a super-majority of contracting parties deposit their instruments of ratification.

7.5   Reforms Through EU Treaty Amendments

A last set of reforms to enhance EMU can be accomplished through a revision of the EU treaties only. In particular, amendments of the EU treaties are necessary to introduce changes to the current EMU *institutional* architecture.[56] In fact, with the exception of the proposal to ensure a unified external representation of the Eurozone in international financial institutions[57]—which is specifically foreseen by Article 138 TFEU—and the proposal to appoint the Commissioner for Economic and Financial Affairs (ECFIN) also as President of the Eurogroup,[58] which is permitted by the vague language of Article 2 of Protocol No. 14 on the Eurogroup, all other options for institutional reform would require a revision of the EU treaties. This includes, among others, the proposals to appoint the ECFIN Commissioner as permanent Chair of the Economic and Financial Affairs (ECOFIN) Council[59]—which would require an amendment to Article 16(9) Treaty on EU (TEU)—or to create a Eurozone treasury,[60] which would call for a significant re-allocation of power between the ECOFIN

Council and the Commission. In fact, a treaty change would be necessary even to bring back within the framework of EU law the institutional provisions of the Fiscal Compact, and *in primis* its Article 12, which creates the Euro Summit—a forum for decision-making between the heads of state and government of the Eurozone countries—and establishes the Euro Summit President, along the model of the European Council and its President.[61]

In addition, also a number of *substantive* reforms of EMU would be permissible only through a reform of the EU treaties. Although, as mentioned above, the current treaty framework leaves ample room for legislative actions, measures such as the creation of Euro-bonds, or the setting up of a debt redemption fund,[62] could only be possible after a treaty change. While the creation of the ESM by the Eurozone countries and the establishment of the Outright Monetary Transaction program by the ECB[63] have increased risk-sharing among EU member states, Article 125 TFEU currently prohibits the mutualization of governments' debt, and the European Court of Justice has confirmed the continuing validity of this rule in its *Pringle*[64] and *Gauweiler*[65] judgments. As a result, the only kind of Euro-bond which may be permitted today is one backed exclusively by EU assets. For the same reasons, another proposal which is made often *sotto voce* in the discussions about EMU's future—that is, the creation of an orderly debt-restructuring mechanism[66]—would necessitate a specific grounding in the EU treaties.

As is well known, the procedure to amend the EU treaties is regulated in Article 48 TEU, which distinguished between an ordinary and a simplified revision procedure. Given the nature of the constitutional changes discussed above—which amount to an expansion of the EU powers, or touch upon provisions of the EU treaties outside the current Part III of the TFEU—the simplified revision procedure could not be used, and resort should be made to the ordinary revision procedure: this requires the setting up of a Convention (unless the European Parliament consents to avoid this), the approval of the amendment by the representatives of all the member states within an intergovernmental conference and the ratification of the amendments by each member state in accordance with its constitutional requirements. It goes without saying that reforming EMU via an EU treaty amendment is more burdensome than doing so via EU legislation. But it should be also considered that EU treaties have regularly been amended at frequent intervals during the last 25 years, and that Brexit creates the need for new treaty change in the EU anyway.[67]

7.6   Conclusion

The purpose of this chapter has been to analyze from a legal perspective a number of proposals for reforming the EMU. During the last months numerous reports—by the EU institutions, national governments and European think tanks—have advanced more or less articulated blueprints for deepening and completing Europe's EMU, outlining a roadmap to repair and prepare the euro after Brexit. These reports conventionally divide the measures to be taken in three phases, distinguishing steps to be taken immediately, from interventions that should be made in a medium term (when greater political capital is available)—and more systemic institutional changes which should be sought for in the longer term, as the finality of European integration. This chapter has also classified the initiatives to reform EMU in three groups. However, the classification has been based on legal criteria. Firstly, I examined the EMU reforms that can be adopted within the current EU treaty framework, through EU legislation. Secondly, I assessed those reform proposals that would require a change of intergovernmental agreements, concluded outside the EU legal order. Thirdly, I discussed those initiatives which could be implemented through a revision of the EU treaties.

As the chapter has pointed out, the current EU treaties already allow for the adoption of a wide variety of reforms in the field of EMU—both on the stability side and on the solidarity side. While further steps to enhance multilateral fiscal surveillance remain possible, the EU treaties also allow the completion of Banking Union with EDIS, the creation of a Capital Markets Union and the establishment of a EUIS, which would contribute to tackle the dramatic problem of cyclical unemployment and to enhance the social dimension of EMU. In addition, the current EU constitutional regime provides a solid basis to take initiatives to re-launching public investments, and it offers space to contribute to Europe's growth also by unleashing the potentials of the single market. Finally, the existing treaty framework would permit also steps towards an EU fiscal capacity—based on real own resources. Given the emphasis on European public goods by the High Level Group on Own Resources chaired by Mario Monti,[68] a fiscal capacity would be a valuable instrument to restore a degree of output legitimacy in the EU.

As the chapter maintained, instead, several other thought-for reforms of EMU could not be accomplished through EU legislation only. On the one hand, calls to upgrade the ESM, strengthening its financial firepower and improving its decision-making structure, could only be achieved by amending the ESM Treaty—which would require the unanimous consent of the 19 Eurozone countries, and national ratification under the oversight of domestic constitutional courts. On the other hand, initiatives to reform the EMU institutional architecture—such as the idea to create a Eurozone treasury recently re-launched by the new French President Emmanuel Macron[69]—or proposals to set up instruments of debt mutualization through Euro-bonds or the like, could only be undertaken by amending the EU treaties, on the basis of the ordinary revision procedure enshrined in Article 48 TEU. In the end, the adoption of a number of institutional reforms in the EMU architecture appears inevitable in the long run if the EU is to gain adequate input legitimacy.[70] And the scenario of a treaty change may be less unlikely than what is often claimed—due to Brexit and the need to re-adapt the EU to the reality of a Union at 27. However, reforms of the EMU through treaty amendment—just like reforms of the EMU through EU legislation—remain dependent on the willingness, foresightedness and leadership of those national and European policy-makers who care about the future of Europe more than they care about the future of their political career.

Notes

1. European Commission, Reflection paper on the Deepening of EMU, COM(2017)291, 31 May 2015.
2. See further Fabbrini (2017a).
3. See Four Presidents report "Towards a Genuine EMU," 5 December 2012.
4. See European Commission President-elect, Juncker (2014).
5. See Five Presidents report, "Completing Europe's EMU," 22 June 2015.

6. See Bratislava Declaration and Roadmap, 16 September 2016, para. IV.
7. See Rome Declaration, 25 March 2017.
8. See Macron and Gabriel (2015).
9. See Padoan (2016).
10. See Conseil des Ministres Franco-Allemand, Paris, 13 July 2017.
11. See European Parliament Resolution of 20 November 2012 Towards a Genuine EMU, P7_TA(2012)0430 and European Parliament Resolution of 24 June 2015 Review of Economic Governance Framework, P8_TA(2015)0238.
12. Enderlein (2012).
13. The Glienicker Group (2013).
14. The Eiffel Group (2014).
15. Enderlein et al. (2016).
16. See further Federico Fabbrini (2017b), on which this chapter draws.
17. See further Federico Fabbrini (2016a).
18. See Treaty Establishing the European Stability Mechanism, 25 March 2011, available at http://www.european-council.europa.eu/media/582311/05-tesm2.en12.pdf.
19. See further Federico Fabbrini (2016b, p. 529).
20. Five Presidents report, p. 6.
21. See Commission Recommendation for a Council Recommendation on the establishment of National Competitiveness Boards within the Euro Area, 21 October 2015, COM(2015)601 final.
22. Bertelsmann report, p. 21.
23. Five Presidents report, Annex 2.
24. See Regulation (EU) No. 1173/2011 of the European Parliament and of the Council of 16 November 2011 on the effective enforcement of budgetary surveillance in the euro area, OJ 2011 L 306/1; Regulation (EU) No. 1174/2011 of the European Parliament and of the Council of 16 November 2011 on enforcement measures to correct excessive macroeconomic imbalances in the euro area, OJ 2011 L 306/8; Regulation (EU) No. 1175/2011 of the European Parliament and of the Council of 16 November 2011 amending Council Regulation (EC) No. 1466/97 on the strengthening of the surveillance of budgetary positions and the surveillance and coordination of economic policies, OJ 2011 L 306/12; Regulation (EU) No. 1176/2011 of the European Parliament and of the Council of 16 November 2011 on the prevention and correction of macroeconomic imbalances, OJ 2011 L 306/25; Council Regulation No. 1177/2011 of 8 November 2011 amending Regulation (EC) No. 1467/97 on speeding up and clarifying the

implementation of the excessive deficit procedure, OJ 2011 L 306/33; Council Directive 2011/85/EU of 8 November 2011 on requirements for budgetary frameworks of the Member States, OJ 2011 L 306/41; Regulation (EU) No. 473/2013 of the European Parliament and the Council of 21 May 2013 on monitoring and assessing draft budgetary plans and ensuring the correction of excessive deficits in euro-area Member States, OJ 2013 L 140/11; Regulation (EU) No. 472/2013 of the European Parliament and the Council of 21 May 2013 on enhanced surveillance of euro-area Member States experiencing or threatened with serious difficulties with respect to their financial stability, OJ 2013 L 140/1.

25. See Treaty on Stability, Coordination and Governance in the Economic and Monetary Union, 2 March 2012, available at http://www.eurozone.europa.eu/media/304649/st00tscg26_en12.pdf

26. See further Adams et al. (2014).

27. See Commission proposal for a Regulation of the European Parliament and the Council amending Regulation (EU) No. 806/2014 in order to establish a European Deposit Insurance Scheme, 24 November 2015, COM(2015)586 final.

28. See Council Regulation (EU) No. 1024/2013 of 15 October 2013 conferring specific tasks on the European Central Bank concerning policies relating to the prudential supervision of credit institutions, OJ 2013 L 287/63.

29. See Regulation (EU) No. 806/2014 of the European Parliament and of the Council of 15 July 2014 establishing uniform rules and a uniform procedure for the resolution of credit institutions and certain investment firms in the framework of a Single Resolution Mechanism and a Single Bank Resolution Fund and amending Regulation (EU) No. 1093/2010 of the European Parliament and of the Council, OJ 2014 L 225/1.

30. See, for example, ECB President, Mario Draghi, Introductory statement in front of the European Parliament, Brussels, 15 June 2015.

31. See Commission proposal for a Regulation of the European Parliament and the Council laying down rules on securitization, 30 September 2015, COM(2015)472 final.

32. See also European Parliament resolution of 13 March 2014 on the enquiry on the role and operations of the Troika (ECB, Commission and IMF) with regard to the euro-area program countries, P7_TA(2014)0239.

33. See Ministero dell'Economia e delle Finanze, "European Unemployment Insurance Scheme," October 2015.

34. See Commission communication on strengthening the social dimension of the Economic and Monetary Union, 2 November 2013, COM(2013) 690 final.
35. Emphasis added.
36. See already Mario Monti, "A New Strategy for the Single Market at the Service of Europe's Economy and Society" – report to the President of the European Commission, 9 May 2010.
37. Bertelsmann report, p. 26.
38. See Bertelsmann report, p. 26.
39. See Regulation (EU) No. 2015/1017 of the European Parliament and the Council of 25 June 2015 on the European Fund for Strategic Investments, the European Investment Advisory Hub, and the European Investment Project Portal and amending Regulations (EU) No. 1291/2013 and (EU) No. 1316/2013, OJ 2015 L 169/1.
40. See Commission communication on strengthening European investments for jobs and growth: Towards a second phase of the European Fund for Strategic Investments and a new European External Investment Plan, 14 September 2016, COM(2016)581 final.
41. See in particular European Parliament resolution of 20 November 2012 towards a Genuine EMU, P7_TA(2012)0430.
42. See Fabbrini (2014, p. 155).
43. See Commission proposal for a Council Directive on a common system of Financial Transaction Tax, 28 November 2011, COM(2011)594 final.
44. See Commission proposal for a Council Directive on a Common Consolidated Corporate Tax Base, 16 March 2011, COM(2011)121 final and now the new Commission proposal on a Common Consolidated Corporate Tax Base, 25 October 2016, COM(2016)685 final.
45. See Commission proposal for a Council Decision on the system of Own Resources of the European Union, 29 June 2011, COM(2011)510 final.
46. See Commission proposal for a Council Directive implementing enhanced cooperation in the area of a Financial Transaction Tax, 14 February 2013, COM(2013)71 final.
47. See further Chang (2017).
48. See further Fabbrini (2016c, p. 281).
49. See European Council Decision No. 2011/199/EU of 25 March 2011, amending Article 136 TFEU with regard to a stability mechanism for Member States whose currency is the euro, OJ 2011 L 91/1.
50. See Hinarejos (2015).
51. Five Presidents report, p. 18.

52. Bertelsmann report, p. 21.
53. See Decision of the ECB of 14 May 2010 establishing a securities market program, OJ 2010 L124/8.
54. See Agreement on the transfer and mutualization of contributions to the Single Resolution Fund, 21 May 2014 available at: http://register.consilium.europa.eu/doc/srv?l=EN&f=ST%208457%202014%20INIT.
55. See BVerfG, Case No. 2 BvR 1390/12 et al., judgment (final) of 18 March 2014, para. 193.
56. See Piris (2011).
57. See Commission proposal for a Council Decision laying down measures in view of progressively establishing unified representation of the euro area in the International Monetary Fund, 21 October 2015, COM(2015)603 final.
58. Bertelsmann report, p. 25.
59. Bertelsmann report, p. 35.
60. Five Presidents report, p. 18.
61. See Fabbrini et al. (2015).
62. See Gertrude Tumpel-Gugerell, Expert Group on Debt Redemption Fund and Eurobills, final report, 31 March 2014.
63. See ECB, Press release, "Technical Features of Outright Monetary Transactions," 6 September 2012.
64. Case C-370/12 *Pringle v. Ireland*, judgment of 27 November 2012.
65. Case C-62/14 *Gauweiler*, judgment of 16 June 2015.
66. Bertelsmann report, p. 35.
67. Fabbrini, supra note 2.
68. See Mario Monti, High Level Group on Own Resources, final report and recommendations, "Future Financing of the EU," December 2016.
69. See Macron (2016, p. 236).
70. See further Fabbrini (2016d).

References

Adams, Maurice, Federico Fabbrini, et al., eds. 2014. *The Constitutionalization of European Budgetary Constraints*. Oxford: Hart Publishing.
Chang, Michele. 2017. *Brexit and EU Economic and Monetary Union,* CSF-SSSP Working Paper No. 4/2017.
Enderlein, Henrik (Coord.). 2012. *Completing the Euro: Roadmap Towards Fiscal Union in Europe*, 26 June 2012.

Enderlein, Henrik, Enrico Letta, et al. 2016. *Repair and Prepare: Growth and the Euro after Brexit*. Gütersloh/Berlin/Paris: Bertelsmann Stiftung/Jacques Delors Institut/Berlin and Jacques Delors Institute in Paris.

Fabbrini, Federico. 2014. Taxing and Spending in the Eurozone: Legal and Political Challenges Related to the Adoption of the Financial Transaction Tax. *European Law Review* 39 (2): 155–175.

———. 2016a. *How Brexit Creates a Window of Opportunity for Treaty Reform in the EU*, Bertelsmann Stiftung Paper Spotlight Europe 2016/1.

———. 2016b. Economic Policy in the EU After the Crisis: Using the Treaty to Overcome the Asymmetry of EMU, *Diritto Unione Europea*.

———. 2016c. A Principle in Need of Renewal? The Euro-Crisis and the Principle of Institutional Balance. *Cahiers de droit européen*.

———. 2016d. *Economic Governance in Europe Comparative Paradoxes and Constitutional Challenges*. Oxford: Oxford University Press.

———, ed. 2017a. *The Law & Politics of Brexit*. Oxford: Oxford University Press.

———. 2017b. *Reforming Economic & Monetary Union: Legislation and Treaty Change*, Bertelsmann Stiftung Paper Spotlight Europe 2017/1.

Fabbrini, Federico, Ernst Hirsch Ballin, et al. 2015. *What Form of Government for the European Union and the Eurozone?* Oxford: Hart Publishing.

Hinarejos, Alicia. 2015. *The Euro Area Crisis in Constitutional Perspective*. Oxford: Oxford University Press.

Juncker, Jean-Claude. 2014. *A New Start for Europe: My Agenda for Jobs, Growth and Democratic Change*, Speech at the European Parliament, Strasbourg, July 15 2014, 7.

Macron, Emmanuel. 2016. *Révolution – C'est notre combat pour la France*. XO Éditions.

Macron, Emmanuel, and Gabriel, Sigmar. 2015. Europe Cannot Wait Any Longer. *The Guardian*, Op-Ed., June 3.

Padoan, Pier Carlo. 2016. *A Shared European Strategy for Growth, Jobs and Stability*, 22 February 2016.

Piris, Jean-Claude. 2011. *The Future of Europe: Towards a Two-Speed EU?* Cambridge: Cambridge University Press.

The Eiffel Group. 2014. *For a Euro Community*, 14 February 2014. Available at: http://bruegel.org/2014/08/for-a-euro-community/

The Glienicker Group. 2013. *Towards a Euro Union*, 17 October 2013. Available at: http://bruegel.org/2014/08/towards-a-euro-union/

8

Brexit as an Exceptional Change of Circumstance?

A.B. Menezes Cordeiro

8.1 Future Scenarios: Overview

The victory for the Leave campaign in the referendum of 23 June 2016 immediately triggered significant social and political effects throughout Europe. But from a legal perspective, the real impact of Brexit remains unknown. Everything will depend on what the British authorities actually want, the interests of the major European powers and how the negotiations proceed for the United Kingdom's exit.

In mapping out the possible scenarios for Brexit, it is important to distinguish between material scenarios and formal legal scenarios.

From a material perspective, that is, leaving aside the formal solution that may be found, three main scenarios are conceivable: (i) repeal of all European law; (ii) preservation of the core of European law, with slight adaptations, depending on the sector and local requirements; or (iii) conservation of all European law already transposed into UK law.

A.B. Menezes Cordeiro (✉)
Lisbon University School of Law, Lisbon, Portugal

© The Author(s) 2017
N. da Costa Cabral et al. (eds.), *After Brexit*,
https://doi.org/10.1007/978-3-319-66670-9_8

147

From a formal perspective, three distinct scenarios are also conceivable: (i) the United Kingdom joins the European Economic Area; (ii) bilateral negotiation between the United Kingdom and the EU; or (iii) individual negotiation with each of the Member States (Lehmann and Zetzsche 2016).

Whether or not Brexit can be classed as an exceptional change of circumstances will depend on the actual solution arrived at, from both a formal and a material point of view. The mere victory of the Leave vote in the referendum of 23 June 2016 and the subsequent invocation of Article 50 of the Treaty on European Union (TUE) will not be sufficient. No court would permit a contract to be modified or even terminated, depending on the local rules applicable, without first establishing what the changes really entail.

Contrary to what might initially have been supposed, the possible shock waves from Brexit are not restricted to contracts subject to UK law. In addition to the parties being free to choose the law governing their contracts, it is perfectly conceivable, at least in a scenario of total repeal, that the impact of this decision should have a negative influence on other contracts concluded between entities not subject to UK law. In both scenarios, the legal solution will have to be found within the framework of the applicable law.

8.2   Historical Origins

The concept of change of circumstances was unknown in Roman law (Zimmermann 1996: 579).

The issue was first tackled by philosophers and rhetoricians (Cordeiro 2016: 428–429). The words of Seneca and Cicero echo down the ages: *Omnia esse debent eadem, quae fuerunt, cum promitterem, ut promittentis fidem teneas*—"If you are to hold me to the fulfilment of my promise, all the circumstances must remain the same as they were when I promised" (Seneca 1935: 278–279) and *Sic multa, quae honesta natura videntur esse, temporibus fiunt non honesta; facere promissa, stare conventis, reddere deposita commutata utilitate fiunt non honesta*—"Thus there are many things which in and of themselves seem morally right, but which under certain circumstances prove to be not morally right: to keep a promise, to abide by an agreement, to restore a trust may, with a change of expediency, cease to be morally right" (Cicero 1951: 372–373).

The philosophy of these classical authors was taken up by St. Ambrose and St. Augustine, who filled it out with a Christian ethical content that was later expanded and taken further by canonists and scholastics (Gieg 1994: 151 sqq.).

The doctrine was carried to new heights of sophistication during the *Ius Commune*, especially through the pen of Bartolus, to whom we owe the general adoption of the formulas *rebus sic stantibus* or *rebus sic habentibus* (Feenstra 1974: 83–84): *quia quando quir renunciat in aligua re omni iuris quod habet vel habere potest vel posset: oportet enim intellegi rebus sic habentibus, hoc est, ex aliquo iure quod est de prasentis re vel spe*—"were someone, on a given occasion, to waive all their rights, that they have or may have in future, then this must only be understood 'rebus sic habentibus', in other words, only the basis of the law existing at the time or which would be expected to come into being".

The contribution of Enlightenment legal scholars to perfecting the doctrine of *rebus sic stantibus* is also recognised today, in contrast to the traditional view. However, it was the school of the *usus modernus pandectarum* that afforded the doctrine the greatest visibility. It was also expressly incorporated in the *Codex Maximilianus Bavaricus Civilis*, of 1756 (Cordeiro 2016: 430–434).

8.3   Recent Developments

8.3.1   Germany

Despite the doctrine's successful incorporation in the *Codex Maximilianus Bavaricus Civilis*, the *rebus sic stantibus* clause came in for fierce criticism by German jurists in the late eighteenth and early nineteenth centuries (Cordeiro 2016: 436–437). This carried over into late pandectism: Regelsberger expresses concern at the possibility of this clause being invoked in the face of monetary variations, with damaging consequences for trading (Regelsberger 1893: 637).

The disrepute into which the *rebus sic stantibus* clause had fallen compelled scholars to explore new paths. An early and crucial contribution to this endeavour was made by Windscheid, who first set out his theory, called the doctrine of presupposition (*Voraussetzungslehre*), in an article dealing with the invalidity of transactions in the French Civil Code (Windscheid 1847: 271–279). The construction was based on the following assumption: declarations of intention are externalised in the light of a given state of affairs, and so a change in this state of affairs or the failure of such a state of affairs to come into being allows the injured party to demand the return of the goods delivered (Windscheid 1850: 1–2). Despite Windscheid's leading influence on the drafting of the BGB, the concept was kept out of the final version of the code.

The difficulties of affirmation denoted by the doctrine of presupposition failed to solve the underlying issue: how should we react to exceptional changes of circumstances? The issue arose with special acuity in the years following the First World War, due to the runaway inflation that left its mark on the German history of that period. The courts, mindful of the injustices that the situation produced, eventually adopted (to an extent) Oertmann's 1921 construction, known as the *basis of contract* (*Geschäftsgrundlage*).[1] In general terms, the basis of contract corresponds to a representation recognised by the parties to contract, any change which will require the original contract to be reviewed, for reasons of fairness.

Decades of scholarly debate and fine-tuning in the courts culminated in the doctrine being expressly incorporated in the BGB as part of the major reform of 2001/2002, in § 313[2]:

(1) If circumstances which became the basis of a contract have significantly changed since the contract was entered into and if the parties would not have entered into the contract or would have entered into it with different contents if they had foreseen this change, adaptation of the contract may be demanded to the extent that, taking account of all the circumstances of the specific case, in particular the contractual or statutory distribution of risk, one of the parties cannot reasonably be expected to uphold the contract without alteration.

(2) It is equivalent to a change of circumstances if material conceptions that have become the basis of the contract are found to be incorrect.

(3) If adaptation of the contract is not possible or one party cannot reasonably be expected to accept it, the disadvantaged party may revoke the contract. In the case of continuing obligations, the right to terminate takes the place of the right to revoke.

8.3.2 France

Although the original version of the *Code Civil* contains no rule on this matter, the issue was debated in the French courts throughout the nineteenth century, on terms similar to those discussed in other European countries.

From an early stage, the French courts were reluctant to accept the doctrine.[3] In a famous ruling of 6 March 1876—the *Canal de Craponne* case—the *Cour de Cassation*[4] declared exceptional changes of circumstance to be irrelevant, setting a precedent that held for many decades in French law. On 21 June 1567, Adam de Craponne undertook to build an irrigation channel in return for a lump sum and, thereafter, a regular fee of three *sols* each time the beneficiaries drew the water; the builder remained responsible for maintaining the channel. The amount payable for the irrigation water gradually declined in value. In the first instance, the *Court d'Appel* in Aix ruled in favour of reviewing the terms of the contract. This ruling was quashed by the *Cour de Cassation*, which invoked Article 1134 of the *Code Civil*: "Agreements legally entered into operate as law for those who engaged in them".

The theory of *imprévision*, acknowledged by the administrative courts, and the obligation to act in good faith (also established in Article 1134 of the *Code Civil*), although allowing the *Cour de Cassation* occasional leeway, kept French law apart from the other continental systems for many years (Cordeiro 2016: 467).

The reform of the *Code Civil* in 2016 made sweeping changes to several areas of French Civil Law, which included the theory of *imprévision* in Article 1195:

> If a change of circumstances, unforeseeable when the contract was entered into, renders performance excessively onerous for a party who did not agree to run this risk, such party may request the other party to renegotiate. The requesting party continues to perform his obligations during the negotiations.

If the other party refuses to negotiate or the negotiations break down, the parties may agree to terminate the contract, on the date and on the terms they may establish, or request the judge, by mutual agreement, to adapt the contract.

or else, by mutual agreement, request the judge to adapt the contract. If agreement is not reached within a reasonable period of time, the judge, on the request of one party, may amend the contract or terminate it, on the date and terms he sees fit.

8.3.3   Italy

The *Codice Civil* of 1865, influenced by the French Civil Code, made no provision for exceptional change of circumstances. However, this did not prevent a certain current of Italian doctrine, in the early twentieth century, to acknowledge the possibility of modifying contracts as a result of developments subsequent to their conclusion (Osti 1912). The First World War and its impact on the performance of contracts also compelled the courts and lawmakers to acknowledge the real importance of these changes (Modica 1915).

The legal climate prevailing at the time led the legislator to include the construction in the *Codice Civile* of 1942, in Article 1467:

In contracts with continuous or periodical execution or adjourned execution and in case that the obligation of one of the parties has become excessively onerous due to extraordinary and unpredictable events, the party who is obliged to such performance can demand the dissolution of the contract with the effects laid down in art. 1458.

The dissolution cannot be demanded if the supervening onerosity is part of the normal risk of the contract.

The party against which the dissolution is demanded can prevent this by offering to modify equitably the conditions of the contract.

8.3.4   Portugal

The Portuguese *Código Civil* of 1867, also influenced by the French Civil Code, made no express provision for modifying or terminating contracts on the grounds of developments subsequent to their conclusion (Cordeiro 2016: 511–519).

In preparing the *Código Civil* of 1966, Vaz Serra, author of the preliminary draft of the book on the law of obligations, proposed a solution along the lines defended by Oertmann (Serra 1957).

The draft first presented was subsequently adjusted and gave rise to the current Article 437.°:

> 1. If the circumstances which formed the basis for the parties' decision to contract have undergone an abnormal change, the injured party is entitled to termination of the contract, or to modification thereof on the basis of equity, if enforcement of the obligations he accepted seriously undermines the principles of good faith and is not encompassed by the risks inherent in the contract.
>
> 2. When termination is sought, the other party may contest, declaring that it accepts modification of the contract on the terms of the preceding paragraph.

8.3.5   United Kingdom

Traditionally, common law assigned no legal effect to changes subsequent to the conclusion of contracts (Chitty 2015: 1672–1673):

> [W]here the law creates a duty or charge, and the party is disabled to perform it without any default in him, and hath no remedy over, there the law will excuse him … but when the party by his own contract creates a duty or charge upon himself, he is bound to make it good, if he may, notwithstanding any accident by inevitable necessity, because he might have provided against it by his contract.[5]

In practice, subsequent changes could only be taken into account if the parties had expressly agreed to do so.

The UK law underwent a profound change with *Taylor v Caldwell*,[6] in which the Queen's Bench acknowledged the existence of an "implied condition that the parties shall be excused in case, before breach, performance becomes impossible from the perishing of the thing without default of the contractor"[7]:

The principle seems to us to be that, in contracts in which the performance depends on the continued existence of a given person or thing, a condition is implied that the impossibility of performance arising from the perishing of the person or thing shall excuse the performance… that excuse is by law implied, because from the nature of the contract it is apparent that the parties contracted on the basis of the continued existence of the particular person or chattel.[8]

In the decades that followed, the doctrine was extended to a wide variety of situations (Chitty 2015: 1682–1706): (i) *destruction of subject-matter of contract*, the typical situation that classically falls within *Taylor v Caldwell*; (ii) *non-occurrence of a particular event*, as long as that event forms the basis on which the contract has been made[9]; or (iii) *subsequent legal changes*[10] *and supervening illegality.*[11]

The implied condition test has been superseded by the test of a radical change in the obligation, applied by the House of Lords in *Davis Contractors Ltd v Fareham Urban D.C.*[12] and confirmed, by the same court, in *National Carriers Ltd v Panalpina (Northern) Ltd*[13]:

Frustration of a contract takes place when there supervenes an event (without default of either party and for which the contract makes no sufficient provision) which so significantly changes the nature (not merely the expense or onerousness) of the outstanding contractual rights and/or obligations from what the parties could reasonably have contemplated at the time of its execution that it would be unjust to hold them to the literal sense of its stipulations in the new circumstances; in such case the law declares both parties to be discharged from further performance.[14]

8.3.6   Conclusion

The doctrine of exceptional change of circumstances has had a particularly turbulent history, with false starts and setbacks. This historical instability is in contrast with the modern-day consolidation of the construction. Its express inclusion in the BGB, in 2002, and in the *Code Civil*, in 2016—the two most influential civil codes in the world—clearly illustrates the importance assigned to it today.

Finally, we have to mention its inclusion in the *Draft Common Frame of Reference*, III. – 1:110:

(1) An obligation must be performed even if performance has become more onerous, whether because the cost of performance has increased or because the value of what is to be received in return has diminished.

(2) If, however, performance of a contractual obligation or of an obligation arising from a unilateral juridical act becomes so onerous because of an exceptional change of circumstances that it would be manifestly unjust to hold the debtor to the obligation a court may:

> (a) vary the obligation in order to make it reasonable and equitable in the new circumstances; or
> (b) terminate the obligation at a date and on terms to be determined by the court.

8.4 Delimitation of the Concept

8.4.1 Mistake and Change of Circumstances

The doctrine of exceptional change of circumstances is not to be confused with mistake. In all five of the legal systems considered, mistake concerns a misrepresentation of reality at the moment of execution of the contract and not a subsequent change in the surrounding circumstances.

As a matter of principle, mistake will only be considered by the courts if it is shown that, irrespective of the situation of error, the contract would still have been entered into on the exact same terms. The provision in § 119(1) of the BGB is representative of the dominant position in civil law,[15] except as regards the respective legal consequences[16]:

> A person who, when making a declaration of intent, was mistaken about its content … may avoid the declaration if it is to be assumed that he would not have made the declaration with knowledge of the factual position and with a sensible understanding of the case.

In UK law, the legal reality is similar, although, in principle, only a mistake shared by both parties is relevant:

> Some mistake or misapprehension as to some facts … which by the common intention of the parties, whether expressed or more generally implied, constitute the underlying assumption without which the parties would not have made the contract they did." That a mistake of this nature common to both parties is, if proved, sufficient to render a contract void.[17]

8.4.2   Impossibility and Change of Circumstances

Civil law systems draw a distinction between impossibility and exceptional change of circumstances. In principle, these are distinct mechanisms, treated differently and in separate provisions. Impossibility of performance, due to factual or legal reasons, can be classed as either original or supervening.

German law contains general provisions on impossibility in § 275 I of the BGB: "A claim for performance is excluded to the extent that performance is impossible for the obligor or for any person".

In Portuguese law, in accordance with Article 790.°/1 of the *Código Civil*: "The obligation is extinguished when the performance becomes impossible for reason not attributable to the debtor". In Italy, the *Codice Civile* establishes an identical solution in Article 1256.

The French solution stands apart from the other continental legal systems. In any case, the doctrine of *force majeure* is comparable in functional terms to the doctrine of supervening impossibility. Until the great reform of 2016, the theory was founded on Articles 1147 and 1148 of the *Code Civil* (Demogue 1931: 570 sqq.). The recent changes have made it possible to clarify how it is to be applied, article 1218:

> There is force majeure in contractual matters where an event beyond the control of the debtor, which could not reasonably be foreseen on conclusion of the contract and whose effects can not be avoided by appropriate measures, prevents the debtor from performing his obligation.

In contrast, in UK law supervening impossibility, more properly called supervening illegality, is today presented as a form of *frustration* (Chitty

2015: 1685–1686): "supervening illegality is a well-recognised head of frustration in the law of contract. This doctrine applies where a statutory power in existence at the time of making the contract is subsequently exercised in such a manner that performance of the contract is rendered illegal".[18]

8.5   The Effects of Change of Circumstances

8.5.1   Germany

Under § 313 I of the BGB, when the preconditions required by law are met, the injured party may seek modification of the contract, in the light of the new factual or legal circumstances.

If modification of the contract proves impossible or particularly prejudicial to one of the parties, the disadvantaged party may revoke the contract, § 313 III.

8.5.2   France

Likewise, in French law, in the event of performance of the contract becoming excessively onerous, the injured party may seek renegotiation. While negotiations are pending, the injured party is required to continue performing the obligations accepted.

If negotiations break down, or the other party simply refuses to negotiate, the parties may, by mutual understanding, agree to terminate the contract.

In the event of the negotiations failing, both parties may also apply to the courts to have the contract modified or terminated.

8.5.3   Italy

Article 1467 of the *Codice Civile* provides a simpler and more direct solution. If one of the legal preconditions is met—the obligation of one of the parties has become excessively onerous due to extraordinary and unpredictable events—the injured party may terminate the contract.

Faced with this scenario, the other party may object, offering to modify equitably the conditions of the contract.

8.5.4   Portugal

Under Portuguese law, the injured party is entitled to seek termination of the contract or equitable modification of its terms (Article 437.°/1). If he decides to terminate the contract, the other party may object, requesting modification of the contract on equitable terms (437.°/2). Under Article 438.°, the injured party may not seek termination/modification of the contract if he is in default at the time the circumstances change.

8.5.5   United Kingdom

Under UK law, a contract which is frustrated is automatically terminated: "The legal effect of frustration is to bring a contract to an end forthwith, without more and automatically".[19] Provisions on amounts already transferred or benefits acquired are contained in the *Law Reform (Frustrated Contracts) Act 1943*.

8.5.6   Conclusions

Despite significant differences between the five legal systems examined, the solutions identified in each case can be divided into three groups: (i) if the legal preconditions are met, the contract is automatically terminated, without the parties or courts being able to stop this: the United Kingdom solution; (ii) when the requirements established in law are met, the injured party may seek the immediate termination of the contract, and the other party may object, seeking modification on equitable terms: Italian and Portuguese solution; and (iii) when the requirements established in law are met, the injured party may initiate a procedure for modification; termination may only occur if modification proves impossible or impracticable: German and French solution.

As far as the consequences are concerned, an abstract analysis suggests that the UK solution is most beneficial for the injured party, as it precludes even a modification of the contract. However, the consequences of application of the rules cannot be divorced from the actual substantive rules, that is, the definition of a change of circumstances, which in UK law involves strict and rigid requirements without parallel in the other systems.

In clear contrast to this, we have Article 1193 of the *Code Civil*. Although the French lawmakers have opened the doors to the doctrine of change of circumstances, they have recognised a solution less beneficial to the injured party, in that it requires it to continue performing its obligations while negotiations proceed on modifying the terms, and also because it limited the courts' intervention to situations where negotiations between the parties have failed.

8.6   Possible Scenarios

It is difficult today to predict how Brexit will turn out. However, following from the scenarios presented in the introduction, it is possible (from a strictly theoretical perspective) to conceive of two distinct cases where the courts might debate the application of the different doctrines examined concerning subsequent changes of circumstances and related doctrines: (i) partial or total repeal of the European legislation undermines the legality of the contracts in force or (ii) partial or total repeal of European legislation results in an increase in the costs associated with contracts in force.

8.6.1   Supervening Illegality

We have already referred to § 275 I of the BGB: "A claim for performance is excluded to the extent that performance is impossible for the obligor or for any person". The field of application of this rule encompasses supervening impossibility regarding factual or legal changes. The textbook case is that of an obligation to supply a ship that is subsequently prohibited.[20]

This solution is identical in Portuguese and Italian laws. The Portuguese courts have applied Article 790.° of the *Código Civil* to disputes where performance of obligation has become impossible due to government intervention or change of legislation,[21] just as has happened under Italian law, through application of Article 1256 of the *Codice Civile* (Smorto 2013: 692).

Although it is acknowledged that most documented rulings in these three countries relate to administrative decisions and not actually to legislative changes, supervening impossibility provisions are fully applicable in a hypothetical scenario in which the European legislation transposed to the United Kingdom is repealed.

Likewise, in French law, Article 1218 of the *Code Civil*, relating to *force majeure*, could also be applied to similar cases. Nonetheless, the requirement of unforeseeability would make it difficult, if not actually unfeasible, to apply these rules for contracts entered to after the referendum of 23 June 2016.

In contrast to the other systems analysed, under UK law a scenario of supervening illegality will be treated on the basis of frustration, with the legal effects defined above.

8.6.2   Exceptional Change of Circumstances

Application of the various regimes for exceptional change of circumstances to a hypothetical post-Brexit scenario is of course dependent on the precise facts of the case, and in particular on how it impacts on the performance of the obligations assumed by the parties and the associated costs.

A slight increase in taxes and the creation of a new charge are changes excluded from field of application of this legal construction, in all the five legal systems. The same solution would apply to an increase in operating costs. This issue was debated with particular intensity in the Portuguese courts in disputes arising from swaps contracted prior to 2008, resulting in large losses for clients at the outbreak of the global financial crisis. Although certain rulings of the Portuguese Supreme Court came out in favour of this solution, arguing, precisely, that this was an exceptional and unexpected change of circumstances, not covered by the risks inherent in the contract,[22] we have doubts as to the internal validity of this solution and, in particular, as to whether it could be applied beyond the borders of Portugal.

In the five systems analysed, application of the respective rules on exceptional changes of circumstances depends on strict legal requirements being met. The change must be abnormal, unexpected, excessively onerous, unforeseen by the parties or not covered by the risks of the contract. It is hard to imagine a scenario where the negotiations culminate in application of this concept across the entire European continent. We should recall that similar situations were experienced only during the two world wars[23] and in the aftermath of the First World War.[24]

8.7   Conclusion

The United Kingdom's departure from the European Union, if it actually happens, will have a serious social, political and legal impact across Europe. In the field of the law of obligations, Brexit could trigger a widespread contractual crisis, if interpreted as an exceptional change of circumstances.

As all five legal systems analysed—Germany, France, Italy, Portugal and the United Kingdom——recognised today legal mechanisms that allow the injured party to terminate or request the modification of contracts due to exceptional change of circumstances, Brexit can, depending on the exact facts, be interpreted as such.

Although possible in abstract terms, this scenario would presuppose a colossal failure of the exit negotiations, leading to a shutdown in trading relations and a climate of hostility unprecedented in the past 75 years.

Notes

1. The construction was applied in the famous case RG 3-feb.-1922, RGZ 103 (1922), 328–344.
2. https://www.gesetze-im-internet.de/englisch_bgb/englisch_bgb.html#p1141.
3. CassFr 9-jan.-1856, D 1856, 1, 41–42.
4. CassFr 6-mar.-1876, D 1876, 1, 193–197.
5. *Paradine v Jane* (1646) Aleyn 26–28, 27.
6. (1863) 3 B. & S. 826–840.
7. At 826.

8. At 839.
9. *Krell v Henry* [1903] 2 K.B. 740–755.
10. *Baily v De Crespigny* (1869) L.R. 4 Q.B. 180–189.
11. *Metropolitan Water Board v Dick, Kerr & Co Ltd* [1918] A.C. 119–141.
12. [1956] A.C. 696–736.
13. [1981] A.C. 675–718.
14. At 700.
15. Italy: Articles 1428, 1429 and 1431 of the *Codice Civile*; Portugal: Articles 247.° and 251.° of the *Código Civil*.
16. In French law, mistake is grounds, as a rule, for nullity of the contract, and not mere annullability: Articles 1130–1132.
17. *Bell v Lever* [1932] AC 161–237, 206.
18. *Twentieth Century Fox Film Corporation v British Telecommunications plc (No. 2)* [2011] EWHC 2714 (Ch), [47].
19. *B.P. Exploration Co (Libya) v Hunt (No. 2)* [1981] 1 WLR 232–245, 241.
20. RG 27-may-1921, RGZ 102 (1921), 203–206.
21. STJ 20-may-2015, Proc. 1869/12.
22. STJ 26-01-2016, case 876/12.9TVLSB and STJ 10-10-2013, case 1387/11.5TBBCL. Taking a different position: STJ 29-jan.-2015, case 531/11.7TVLSB.
23. The issue was also debated in France, during the Franco-Prussian War of 1870–71 (Cordeiro 2016: 473–474). United Kingdom: *Denny, Mott and Dickson Ltd v James B Fraser & Co Ltd* [1944] AC 265–285.
24. We may also recall the runaway inflation experienced by the Weimar Republic, and the application by the German courts of the doctrine of the *basis of contract (Geschäftsgrundlage)*.

References

Chitty on Contracts. 2015. I: *General Principles.* 32nd ed. London: Sweet & Maxwell.
Cicero. *De officiis.* 1951. Trans. Walter Miller. Loeb Classical Library. Cambridge, MA: Harvard University Press.
Cordeiro, António Menezes. 2016. *Tratado de Direito civil.* Vol. IX. 2nd ed. Lisbon: Almedina.
Demogue, René. 1931. *Traité des obligations en général. II: Effets des obligations.* Vol. IV. Paris: Rosseau.

Feenstra, Robert. 1974. Impossibilitas and Clausula rebus sic stantibus: Some Aspects of Frustration of Contracts. In *Continental Legal History Up to Grotius in Daube Noster: Essays in Legal History for David Daube*, ed. Alan Watson, 77–104. Edinburgh: Scottish Academic Press.

Gieg, Georg. 1994. *Clausula rebus sic stantibus und Geschäftsgrundlage: ein Beitrag zur Dogmengeschichte*. Aachen: Shaker.

Lehmann, Matthias, and Dirk A. Zetzsche. 2016. *Brexit and the Consequences for Commercial and Financial Relations Between the EU and the UK*. Available at https://papers.ssrn.com/sol3/papers.cfm?abstract_id=2841333. Accessed 29 Dec 2016.

Modica, Isidoro. 1915. L'influenza della guerra sui rapporti di diritto privato. *Il diritto comerciale*. I: 102–112.

Oertmann, Paul. 1921. *Die Geschäftsgrundlage: ein neuer Rechtsbegriff*. Leipzig: Deichert.

Osti, Giuseppe. 1912. La cosi detta clausula "rebus sic stantibus" nel suo sviluppo storico. *Rivista di diritto civile* 4: 1–58.

Regelsberger, Ferdinand. 1893. *Pandekten*. Vol. I. Leipzig: Duncker & Humblot.

Seneca. 1935. *De beneficiis*. Trans. John W. Basore. *Moral Essays*, vol. 3, Loeb Classical Library. Cambridge, MA: Harvard University Press.

Serra, Adriano Vaz. 1957. Resolução do contrato por alteração das circunstâncias. *Boletim do Ministério da Justiça* 68: 293–385.

Smorto, Guido. 2013. Dell'impossibilità sopravvenuta per causa non imputable al debitore. In *Commentario del codice civile. Delle obbligazioni. Artt*, ed. Vicenzo Cuffaro, 1218–1276. Turim: UTET.

Windscheid, Bernard. 1847. *Zur Lehre des Code Napoleon von der Ungültigkeit der Rechtsgeschäfte*. Düsseldorf: Buddeus.

———. 1850. *Die Lehre des römischen Rechts von der Voraussetzung*. Düsseldorf: Buddeus.

Zimmermann, Reinhard. 1996. *The Law of Obligations: Roman Foundations of the Civilian Tradition*. New York: OUP.

Part II

Brexit's Sectorial Effects (I): Trade and Free Movement of Goods and Citizens

9

Which Model for Brexit?

Michael Emerson

The Prime Minister, Theresa May, has said that there is no "off-the-shelf" model suitable for the UK's future relationship with the EU. This is undoubtedly true since there is no precedent for a secession agreement, and all the EU's many complex trade agreements are unique in their precise content. But the process does not start with a blank sheet of paper. There are several "models" of how the EU relates to non-member states, which may be instructive for the UK to consider, but not to copy into a formal agreement.

Several of these "models" are well known and can be summarised briefly for their relevance to the UK, namely:

- World Trade Organization (WTO)
- European Economic Area (EEA), as for Norway, inter alia
- Customs Union, as for Turkey
- Switzerland, *sui generis*
- CETA, with Canada, as a recent example of an agreement with a non-European country

M. Emerson (✉)
Centre for European Policy Studies (CEPS), Brussels, Belgium

© The Author(s) 2017
N. da Costa Cabral et al. (eds.), *After Brexit*,
https://doi.org/10.1007/978-3-319-66670-9_9

There is also a recent addition to the collection:

- the new model of Association Agreements between the EU and its close neighbours, recently negotiated with Ukraine, Georgia and Moldova and incorporating Deep and Comprehensive Free Trade Areas (DCFTAs). Although obviously not suitable for wholesale adoption, the model has several features of potential interest to the UK.

One often hears the terms "hard" versus "soft" Brexit used in the British debate. Although they have no official definitions, they seem to be understood as meaning the WTO and EEA models, respectively.

9.1   World Trade Organization (WTO)

The UK is and will remain a member of the WTO. There are two major issues to work through here, on the UK's future bound tariff schedule in the WTO, and its schedule of reservations (if any) on trade in services and establishment for individuals and companies engaged in service sectors. With its existing WTO membership renegotiated on these points, the UK will be free to negotiate its own free trade agreements with the EU and any other WTO member, as long as it quits the EU's Customs Union (see below). A first task will be to reconstitute as fast as possible the free trade content of the EU's many preferential agreements with many countries, including some advanced industrial economies, such as Korea, Singapore and Canada, as well as many developing countries. The second step would be to negotiate agreements with countries with whom the EU has no agreement so far, including major cases that are currently under negotiation (e.g. the United States, Japan and India). Advocates of Brexit have argued that the UK could negotiate such deals faster and better on its own, but Obama said that the UK will be "at the back of the queue". Trump may be willing to go faster, but that remains to be seen.

The UK's Future Tariff Schedule at the WTO   Since this will have to be agreed with all other WTO member states, the UK will have a strong interest in making this process as easy and speedy as possible. One obvious way of proceeding would be to retain the EU's MFN (most favoured nation) tariff schedule unchanged, or to do this with exceptions only for tariff lines for which it might propose more liberal rates than the EU, including possibly a more liberal tariff-quota regime for agricultural products. But the UK could not expect to persuade the rest of the world to revise its tariffs downwards in exchange. On the contrary, other WTO member states could take the occasion to demand various concessions, since the process requires that the applicant reaches bilateral agreements with each of them.

Services This will be a highly complicated affair in negotiations with both the WTO and EU. The WTO's General Agreement on Trade in Services (GATS) contains extensive lists of sub-sectors for which member states retain reservations limiting market access. The EU's service markets (internally) are partly subject to EU-level regulation and partly remain a matter of member state competences. As a result there is a double set of reservations at the WTO for the EU as such, and for each of the 28 member states individually. The UK will therefore have to decide what list of reservations it wishes to retain. The UK might choose a relatively more liberal package than the EU's existing reservations, which of course would facilitate agreement. But as in the case of the tariff schedules, this would be done unilaterally by the UK, without any real possibility to persuade the rest of the world to reciprocate.

The UK's negotiation of its services regime with the WTO will go alongside its negotiations with the EU on the same subject. The main point to keep in mind is that while the EU's services market is far from completely integrated, it is incomparably more liberalised than the WTO regime.[1]

Overall, if the UK opted to rely entirely on WTO rules for its future trading relationship with the EU, in the absence of a free trade deal, there would be a sharp deterioration of the conditions for market access for both goods and services. The EU's existing preferential trade agreements with third countries would also cease to apply to the UK, and it would take years for the UK to reconstitute them bilaterally. The potential cost of this loss, including for the UK as a location for foreign direct investment targeting the EU market, is amply discussed in the British debate.

9.2 European Economic Area, as for Norway, Iceland and Liechtenstein

This model is clearly defined: the non-member state is treated with regard to the single market exactly as if it were an EU member state. This requires that all EU single market legislation is fully implemented, including new legislation as it becomes effective, or amendments to existing legislation. But it does not entail membership of the Customs Union, thereby permitting EEA/EFTA (European Free Trade Association) states to make their own free trade agreements with third countries, which they have done in 31 cases. It also excludes EU agricultural and fisheries policies.

This model also requires respect for all four freedoms on which the EU is based, including the free movement of people.

Significant contributions are made to the EU budget by Norway (as also by Switzerland—see further below).

Enforcement is assured by specially created institutions, namely the EFTA Surveillance Authority and the EFTA Court, while this Court is subordinated to the rule that it cannot contradict the case law of the Court of Justice of the European Union.

The advantage of this model is that it exists, offers legal clarity and actually works. It is the closest among other options to sticking to the status quo in economic terms and it would avoid uncertainty and thereby minimise damage to the UK as a destination for foreign investment aimed at the EU market.

Of all the models one can entertain for the UK, it is the closest to continuing membership, that is, full inclusion in the single market, but it would not allow the country to have any say in how single market policies are determined.

A detail regarding Liechtenstein is worth noting. In its negotiations with the EU, this very small state secured the right to impose quantitative limits on immigration from the EU; but it is so small that the EU would doubtless say that it does not amount to a relevant precedent for the UK.

9.3   Switzerland

In evaluating the EU–Swiss arrangements as a possible model for the UK's future relationship with the EU, there are two aspects to keep in mind: firstly, how the existing EU–Swiss relationship developed as a set of separate agreements, following its referendum of 1992, which rejected ratification of its negotiated inclusion in the EEA, and secondly how it has handled the free movement of persons.

Swiss Model of Multiple Agreements with the EU Following its 1992 referendum that rejected accession to the EEA, Switzerland and the EU entered into a long and complex process of negotiating many sector-specific agreements, which had the effect of reconstituting much of the content of the EEA agreement. These were negotiated over many years and were grouped into successive packages. For the first and main package adopted in 1999, the EU insisted that failure to implement any single agreement would lead to automatic suspension of the other components of the package. This was intended to ensure a holistic quality to the whole relationship, since the EU is categorically averse to "cherry-picking" only those elements of the EU system that the partner state likes. This is why the EU has become highly critical of the status quo regime with Switzerland, and will surely be loath to allow the UK to negotiate something similar. The selectivity and perceived flexibility of the Swiss model are reasons why it has been advocated as a model for the UK. But the UK should have no illusions about the likelihood that the EU would find this acceptable. The EU will surely insist on a single and comprehensive agreement for its future relationship with the UK. Overall the "old" Swiss model can be excluded, while the conditions for a "new" Swiss model have been set out explicitly by the EU Council, which seem to more closely approximate the EEA model.[2]

Switzerland and the Free Movement of Persons A second and more relevant aspect of the Swiss experience concerns the free movement of people. Switzerland agreed in 1999 to the free movement of people, subject however to a "safeguard clause", which provided that: "In the event of serious economic or social difficulties, the Joint Committee shall meet, at the request of either Contracting Party, to examine appropriate measures to remedy the situation. … The scope and duration of such measures shall not exceed that which is strictly necessary to remedy the situation. Preference shall be given to measures that least disrupt the working of this Agreement". This clause has never been activated, however, and so there is no experience with how it might have been applied.

In February 2014, it was in any case overtaken politically by a referendum that was passed by a narrow majority of 50.3% "against Mass Immigration", effectively requiring the government to establish within three years a system of quantitative limits to immigration from all sources, including the EU. This was against a background of immigrants having risen to represent 23.4% of the population, with around 1.3 million from the EU (which is several times higher on a per capita basis than immigration from the EU into the UK).

Given that the Swiss government was obliged under its own law to adopt implementing legislation no later than three years after the referendum, that is, by February 2017, it proposed in March 2016 new legislation to manage immigration for the EU in the following terms: "The proposed unilateral safeguard clause provides for annual limits to be set by the Federal Council on the number of permits issued to people from EU and EFTA countries if immigration exceeds a certain threshold. When setting these limits the Federal Council will take Switzerland's general economic interests into account as stipulated in the Federal Constitution, and consider the recommendations of a newly established immigration commission".[3] Attempts to reach agreement with this proposal with the EU failed, however, and the proposed bill never passed into law.

More recently, the Swiss parliament's lower house adopted on 21 September 2016 a new law favouring the recruitment of local residents for new vacancies, including already established EU residents, in an effort to reach a compromise solution with the EU. The Swiss believe that this should be acceptable to the EU, and that the referendum of 2014 will now be overtaken by this law if passed by the upper house. European Commission President, Jean-Claude Juncker, has said that in his view the EU could be satisfied with this new law.

Finally, in a further twist to this Swiss affair, a petition is being circulated to hold a second referendum to annul the one of February 2014, and it has apparently already gained 100,000 supporters. While this number is sufficient to justify calling for a new referendum, it remains to be seen whether the petition is now dropped in view of the new law.

The new law appears to be a soft measure aimed at ending the confrontation with the EU. After a couple of years of reflection, the Swiss seem to have judged it to be in their interests to make a concession rather than let the 2014 referendum inflict major damage on their economy. This may not solve the British problem, but as a case study in Swiss management of the referendum process, it gives the UK food for thought.

9.4   Customs Union, as with Turkey

This model would mean retaining the EU's common external tariff (as bound at the WTO as its MFN tariff schedule) and also the import conditions imposed under the EU's many free trade or preferential trade agreements. The big advantage is that exports pass freely into the EU without being subject to customs controls or administratively costly "rules-of-origin" documentation.

As regards the EU's free trade or preferential agreements with the rest of the world, the UK would have to negotiate bilaterally with these countries in order to gain preferential access to their markets, but in general it would be plausible for the UK to secure the same preferential terms as the EU, although this would not be automatic. While the UK would not be free to do free trade deals with other countries ahead of entry into force of the Brexit, it is notable that the EU has ongoing negotiations with major trading nations, including the United States, Japan and India. As and when these negotiations result in new free trade agreements for the EU, the UK should in principle be able to follow through on the same terms.

Staying in the Customs Union would also have the important political advantage of avoiding renewal of custom controls at the Northern Ireland/ Ireland frontier. Abolition of those frontier controls was one of the signal achievements of the Good Friday Agreement of 1998, which ended 30 years of violent conflict. Nobody wants to destabilise that agreement.

It is fair to say that both the EU and Turkey find the Customs Union to be an uncomfortable arrangement, because of the constraints imposed on Turkey's own trade policy and resulting tensions. It is worth noting that Turkey sought but was refused participation in the EU's negotiations with the United States over the Transatlantic Trade and Investment Partnership (TTIP).

Nevertheless, the Customs Union option for the UK would have the great merit of being a much simpler route for maintaining free trade for goods than the other models described in this paper. A question would arise over associated conditions, beyond compliance with the customs code and procedures, that the EU side would require. As pointed out (in Sect. 9.6), however, it is highly likely that the UK will retain in any case conformity with European technical standards.[4]

9.5   The CETA with Canada

This Comprehensive Economic and Trade Agreement (CETA) is an advanced model of a quite deep trade agreement, except that it is very limited in the service sectors. It is comprehensive in coverage and is the most up-to-date example of a free trade agreement between advanced economies that applies comparably high regulatory standards. The EU's free trade agreement with Korea is another but somewhat older example in the same category. The relevance of this model for the UK, however, is much reduced, since it ignores the large amount of EU market law that the UK will most likely retain in order to maximise its access to the EU single market. The CETA could be a useful template to expedite future UK negotiations of its own bilateral trade agreement with Canada and other advanced economies, but not with the EU.

9.6   The New Association Agreement Model with Neighbouring Countries

The new Association Agreements that came into force in 2016 with Ukraine, Georgia and Moldova have several interesting features for the UK, which have been curiously ignored so far in London.[5] These concern their comprehensive structure and high degree of inclusion in the single market for three of the four freedoms (free movement of goods, service and capital, but not people). The reason for the exclusion of free movement of people is not explained in the Agreements, but is surely because the EU was worried about the prospect of large flows of migrants, a point that coincides with a prime UK interest for itself. This is a departure from the doctrine that all four freedoms always come together in an indivisible package, a doctrine that applies to the EU itself and the EEA, but not necessarily now between the EU and other close neighbours. Going further afield, the EU's free trade agreements with the rest of the world invariably exclude the free movement of people.

These Agreements set out in legally precise terms the entire agenda for defining the relationship with the EU, sector by sector, for almost all EU competences. This structure is more or less used in many of the EU's association or partnership agreements with third countries. If the UK chose to go for a deep and comprehensive future relationship, the EU would probably want to work along the lines of the same structure:

   I. General principles
  II. Foreign and security policy
 III. Justice, freedom and security
  IV. Trade and trade-related matters (i.e. the DCFTA)
   V. Economic and sector cooperation
  VI. Financial cooperation
 VII. Institutional provisions

An organisational advantage of this structure and its content is that it provides clear and explicit listings of all the EU directives and regulations that are considered relevant, numbering over 300 in the case of Ukraine (listed in the annexes to the agreement), with another 300 food safety regulations added subsequently.

9.7 Towards a Bespoke Association Agreement for the UK

In this section the standard structure of an advanced Association Agreement is followed, hypothetically adapted to British circumstance and interests.

General Principles This section defines common commitments to political values including democracy, human rights and the rule of law. The UK would have no problem here.

Foreign and Security Policy This chapter would be of great importance to the UK, given its substantial diplomatic, security (intelligence) and military capabilities. The UK's interests are overwhelmingly in accordance with mainstream EU interests, and the EU has often been described as a "multiplier" of British interests. However the content of this chapter would be open-ended, without fixed and pre-determined obligations. The UK would align itself with EU foreign policy positions when it wanted to do so, and could participate in military and security (European Security and Defense Policy - ESDP) missions on a case-by-case basis.

Justice, Freedom and Security (JFS) While the UK has had a general opt-out from Schengen and JFS legislation, it has also profited from a selective opt-in procedure, under which Theresa May as the then Home Office Minister negotiated inclusion in about 30 specific police and security measures. The UK government has already signalled that it would wish to continue with these provisions under Brexit, and an Association Agreement would be the place to do this.

Core Trade Policy Conditions of a DCFTA The core constituent parts of a "deep" free trade area are in institutional terms the subject matter for which the EU has exclusive competences. These make for a primary package of conditions for a free trade agreement, but there will be further conditions (under Sect. 9.7.1—see further below). Some comments are offered below on how the UK and the EU might handle the inevitable chapter headings.

First, however, is the strategic question of what the UK will want to do with the huge stock of EU market law with which it is today compliant. The Prime Minister on 2 October 2016 at the Conservative Party conference went some way towards explaining how the government intends to handle the stock of EU laws, with reference to a forthcoming "Great Repeal Bill". The Bill appears to be based on the idea that this law will, on the day following secession, retain all relevant EU legislation as sovereign UK law unchanged in the first instance.

In so doing, the distinction between the EU's *directives* and *regulations* is of major practical importance. The point here is that all directives, which are implemented by national legislation, are already, as a result, fully part of sovereign UK national jurisprudence, and thus for these nothing changes.

Regulations have the opposite logic, being directly applicable in the member states without any further supporting national legislation. Upon secession, since all EU laws will cease to apply, the substance of regulations will cease to apply unless the UK takes the step to reinstall their content in national legislation. This poses the important need to avoid an unintended legal void, which would be especially important for some sectors such as food safety. Since there are hundreds of such regulations with much technical and scientific content, the UK will have to work out how to devise some short-cut legal technique for "copying and pasting" various blocks of EU regulations into UK law, either to avoid a legal void as a temporary measure, or to assure continued market access in various sectors for the foreseeable future. The idea of the Great Repeal Bill seems precisely to avoid the legal void.

The Brexit minister, David Davies, is reported as saying that most existing market legislation will be retained. For EU laws that it proposes to keep, the UK will need to decide what to do with the continuous flow from Brussels of amendments and replacements to existing laws. Will the UK keep its stock of EU laws up-to-date? If not, there will be a break in legal homogeneity, with the risk of reduced market access.

The main chapters of a plausible Association Agreement are now discussed briefly, item by item.

Access to the EU Market for Goods (Elimination of Almost All Tariffs) The UK wants this as a priority, and the EU has an interest here too, but the question will be on what conditions, which involves many of the following headings.

Ability to Make Own Free Trade Deals with the Rest of the World The UK wants this also as a high priority, and it would be able to do this in all circumstances bar joining the Customs Union.

Trade Remedies (e.g. Anti-dumping Duties) The EU generally relies on basic WTO rules here, which the UK would automatically comply with by virtue of its WTO membership.

Customs Procedures (Including Rules of Origin) The UK would want to remain compliant with the EU's basic customs codes, but will inevitably have to introduce customs clearance procedures and "rules of origin" paperwork if it leaves the Customs Union.

Technical Standards for Industrial Goods The UK will surely wish to remain a full member of the European standards organisations, which are pan-European rather than EU institutions. These bodies define technical standards for industrial products, which amount to around 5000 in number, in many cases at the request of the European Commission.[6] As one British minister supporting Brexit (C. Grayling) has said, "There is no point in defining new British standards for the safety of lawnmowers" – an argument that is valid 5000 times over.

There is provision in the DCFTAs for making Agreements on Conformity Assessment and Acceptance of Industrial Products (ACAA), as long as EU technical standards are respected, upon which "[t]he ACAA will provide that trade between the Parties in goods in the sectors that it covers shall take place under the same conditions as those applying to trade between the Member States of the European Union" (Article 57.2 of the Ukraine DCFTA). This is a matter of major economic significance.

In addition, European technical standards are mostly "voluntary" in the sense that manufacturers remain free to produce according to other standards for supplying foreign markets, and also for the domestic market as long as they meet the "essential requirements" of the EU's framework directives. This means that the EU regime is in practice more flexible than some observers suggest.

Food Safety Regulations The same broad arguments apply here as for the technical standards above. The UK will want to avoid non-tariff barriers for agri-food products, and so will see the value of retaining EU product regulations here too. The UK might want to deviate from EU regulations in exceptional cases.

Services This is a fiendishly complex field in which there remain considerable restrictions on cross-border services provision within the EU itself, but these are much less onerous than all other models (WTO, Canada) except for the EEA.[7] The UK would presumably want to remain compliant with the 2006 Services Directive in order to get the best possible market access.

For the important *financial, transport and electronic communications services*, however, the DCFTA has special provisions for "internal market treatment" on the condition that relevant EU legislation is fully implemented,[8] which, under these conditions, more closely resembles the EEA model.

This means that for city interests in *financial markets* in particular, the DCFTA model suggests in principle a possible route to retain access to the EU's financial market, if the UK remains fully compliant with EU legislation in this area. This compliance, however, has to be "dynamic" in the sense of updating for amended or new EU legislation in the field, as illustrated by the decision on 30 September 2016 for the EEA states such as Norway to adopt a large package of 31 new EU laws in the financial market domain in order to continue to ensure legal homogeneity with the EU. The main features of this extremely complex field, including "passporting" provisions, are explained in another CEPS publication.[9] In the Bank of England's document defining passporting, the key language is identical to that found in the DCFTA.[10] This suggests that the DCFTA offers in principle the possibility of passporting, but of course there has been be no testing of these provisions yet so far, and there may be further secondary legal complications for this to be done in practice.

Civil Aviation The UK would be interested in negotiating a Common Aviation Area (CAA) Agreement to retain access to the single European sky, for which the UK is wholly qualified in terms of regulatory standards.

Public Procurement The DCFTA relies largely on WTO provisions in this area, but it goes further towards full market access as long as EU legislation is fully implemented. Presumably the UK would be interested in this.

Intellectual Property Rights (IPRs) Again there are basic WTO provisions in this area, but EU law goes deeper in various ways that the UK has been keen to advance, and presumably would want to retain.

Competition Policy The UK has been a major driving force for sustaining a rigorous EU competition policy for both anti-trust and subsidies. The British government's general ideology seems unchanged here, and in any case the EU would require continued consistency with this block of policy as one of the sure conditions for tariff-free trade.

Trade-Related Energy EU law excludes subsidised or dual pricing for energy inputs into industry, and the UK would have no problem in remaining consistent with these rules.

Overall on Core DCFTA Chapters The important conclusion from this summary review of core trade policies is that the UK could not only easily remain consistent with these prerequisites for free trade with the EU, but it would in all likelihood want to do so as a matter of policy choice.

9.7.1   Economic and Sectoral Cooperation Chapters

Of these chapters of EU policies some are also hard-core elements of the EU market regulatory policies, such as for the energy, environment and climate domains. But for other areas that are less directly, or not at all trade-related, there might be agreement over a selective approach to continued commitment to EU law.

Energy Cooperation The UK took a leading role in framing EU policies in this area, including the 3rd Energy Directive, which requires the de-monopolising or "unbundling" of energy supply networks. It is plausible that the UK would wish to remain at least broadly in line with these EU policies, although there may be questions over forthcoming EU energy legislation under the label "Energy Union".

Environment Here there is much extremely important trade-related regulation (e.g. emissions standards for industrial enterprises), alongside other elements that are not at all trade-related or without cross-border spillover impacts (e.g. the quality of bathing water or nature reserves). Here, as under other chapters, as and when the UK seeks to lighten the extent of EU regulations, the key criterion must be to separate those that do, or do not, have trade-related and cross-border spillovers.

Climate The EU's Emission Trading System (ETS) lies at the heart of EU climate policy, and the UK took a leading role in getting it established. The UK is now of course party to the Paris Agreement of December 2015, at which the EU took commitments that were only incompletely disaggregated by individual member states. The UK will surely wish to remain faithful to the Paris Agreement, but in principle it could do so by retaining its own ETS alongside that of the EU, or remaining fully integrated with the EU system with the aid of a new Protocol.[11]

Agriculture The UK would not be under pressure from the EU to continue to apply various instruments of EU farm policy.

Fisheries There will necessarily be a need to negotiate afresh over access to territorial waters both with the EU as well as with Iceland and Norway.

Labour Market and Social Policies The Brexit minister, David Davies, is reported to have observed (quite correctly) that EU law in this area, although controversial in the UK, has not prevented the UK from having one of the most flexible labour markets in Europe, and therefore these directives could be retained. If this were the government's choice, it would be an important argument for heading off objections in the EU to free trade with the UK on grounds of "social dumping".

Movement of Persons To regain control over immigration from the EU has been the single-most powerful driving force for secession. It is not yet known, however, how the UK will define its policy in this area, and the government says it is looking at various options, including work permits. While the political imperative to act here is evident, it is equally clear that many sectors of the British economy are crucially dependent on migrants from the EU (financial services, health services, higher education, construction, farm workers, etc.). The search is therefore on for the least-damaging means of achieving the objective of lower immigration numbers. The Swiss experience here is worth noting, both for the 1999 safeguard clause, which was accepted by the EU but never activated, and for how its 2014 referendum led after more than two years to a different solution that was finally acceptable to the EU (see above on Switzerland). It is possible that there may soon be a spontaneous reduction of immigration numbers into the UK from the EU, due to the uncertainty factor now created, as well as the unfortunate spread of xenophobic attitudes and behaviour that emerged with the referendum campaign, for which there is anecdotal evidence.

For the future UK–EU relationship, some "grandfathering" of the acquired rights of EU citizens resident in the UK, and vice versa, may be expected. However, there seems to be no hard legal basis or obvious precedent for this.

Other Areas, Including Company Law, Consumer Protection, Public Health Some parts of these chapters are strongly related to market access, such as for labelling of consumer products and for public health (e.g. technical regulations for pharmaceuticals and medical equipment). For this category, continued compliance by the UK would be plausible. But there are other elements of these chapters that are not so closely market-related, and where the EU would not pose conditions.

Macroeconomic Cooperation Macroeconomic cooperation would be established via soft "dialogue", without binding obligations towards the quantitative norms of the Stability Pact. On *taxation,* however, continued use by the UK of the value-added tax would be a prerequisite for free trade.

Agencies and Programmes There are explicit provisions for the participation by the non-member state in many of the sector-specific agencies and operational programmes of the EU, including some of great importance for the UK, such as Horizon 2020 for scientific research, the Erasmus programme for higher educational exchanges and the European Defence Agency, to name just three. There is a standard formula for pro-rata GDP financial contributions. Participation in these agencies and programmes has to be governed by specific agreements.

For some of the programmes, notably in the fields of scientific research and higher education (Horizon 2020 and Erasmus), it is already apparent that key UK interests are being damaged by the Brexit uncertainty factor, with the undermining of existing research and university networks. It is therefore a matter of urgency for the UK that agreements are reached permitting full participation in these cases.

Financial Cooperation No doubt the question of financial contributions from the UK to the EU budget will arise in the course of negotiations, with the precedents of Norway and Switzerland surely to be cited by the EU. The outcome of such negotiations cannot be anticipated, but it will undoubtedly relate to the degree of access to the single market that would be negotiated. It is already clear that the EU will not want the overall package to appear to be so favourable to the UK that it might be interpreted in other member states as an attractive secession model.

Institutional Provisions There are standard models in the EU's external agreements. It may be anticipated that a ministerial-level Cooperation Council would be created for the UK, supported by an array of sector-specific committees and sub-committees of officials. As in the case of the EU's "strategic partnerships", there would be provision for the whole process to be guided by summit-level meetings between the British Prime Minister and the Presidents of the Commission and European Council.

The powers of the Association Council will need to be carefully defined. In the case of the new Association Agreements, the Association Council has some limited powers to amend the Agreement, not the main text, but the annexes, which define much of the detail of the legal obligations. This links to the issue of updating of the future UK–EU agreement for new legislation by the EU. Such updating is automatically required for the EEA and is enforced directly by the "EFTA Court" if necessary. For the Association Agreements there is a provision for updating, but this has to be decided jointly by the Association Council, which on political grounds would presumably be viewed more favourably by the UK.

Dispute Settlement The Association Agreements have two regimes. The first mechanism of general application relies on the Association Council to settle disputes by agreement. For the DCFTA part of the Agreement, however, there is a system of binding arbitration that draws largely on the WTO model of dispute settlement, consisting of three arbitrators, one each from the two parties, and a third from another country as chairperson. There is also a role here for the Court of Justice of the European Union (CJEU), where issues of interpretation of EU laws are at stake – a highly sensitive issue for both sides. The Great Repeal Bill would put all EU laws under strictly British jurisdiction and the Prime Minister has stressed the political objective to escape the authority of the CJEU. In any comprehensive agreement between the UK and the EU, however, there would have to be a strong dispute settlement system, and the EU side will want to retain a role for the CJEU to assure legal coherence with EU jurisprudence. The EEA, for example, has a special "EFTA Court", which is obliged not to deviate from case decisions of the CJEU.

Negotiation Process Under Article 50   Given that the Article 50 procedure was triggered into action at the end of March 2017, the clock has started ticking for the negotiations to reach an agreement within two years by end-March 2019. Complex trade and cooperation agreements typically take several years to complete, normally longer than two years (even assuming that the UK–EU negotiations for their future trade regime can proceed in parallel with the separate withdrawal agreement, but this is still unclear as of now).

Two years later, if there is no agreement defining future UK–EU relations, the guillotine falls, meaning that the UK will be "out", all EU laws will cease to apply to the UK and its relations with the EU will for trade purposes be governed essentially by the terms of WTO membership. In the absence of an agreement, this means introducing tariffs at the level of their WTO MFN levels.

The two-year period can be extended if there is unanimous agreement by all member states to do so, but this might well be difficult to achieve if the failure to reach an agreement on time reflected a period of harsh negotiations. The Great Repeal Bill, entering into force on the day of withdrawal, only covers against the risk of legal void within the UK.

While there is little publicly known, even at the time of writing (July 2017) after the Article 50 Declaration in March, there is much speculation in the media that the government may be willing to go for a "hard Brexit". This has immediately played into political statements suggesting a "hard" response from the EU, notably from the President of France.[12] The negotiators have to think through what their respective bargaining positions would be if there were still an impasse as the two-year period approached its end. There is a paramount need for correct evaluations of each other's likely bottom-line positions. Here there seems to be some risk of miscalculation on the British side, to judge by various "hard Brexit" statements. In particular, there is the frequently heard argument that because the EU has a trade surplus with the UK, it will have a compelling interest in making a tariff-free trade deal. This argument is an incomplete assessment, for two reasons. First the prospect of UK withdrawal has ignited serious interest in the rest of the EU in gaining market share from the UK for both foreign direct investment in manufactured goods aiming at the EU market (e.g. Japanese car producers), and, of course, for financial markets, with the "red carpet" already being rolled out in other EU financial centres. Secondly, as the French President already said explicitly, the remaining EU will have a strong and indeed existential interest in preventing "disintegration contagion", meaning that the terms of UK withdrawal should not appear potentially attractive to others. Moreover it is already clear that financial markets are highly sensitive to the perceived risks of a "hard Brexit", and these sensitivities are bound as the Article 50 clock ticks on.

At the technical level, it may be noted that the Association Agreement model has two potentially useful features. First, much of the technical legal drafting could be carried over if a similar structure were adopted, thus shortening the time needed to assure the technical adequacy of the legal drafting. Second, the Association Agreements provide for a very large degree of "provisional application" (indeed for all the DCFTA provisions) from the moment of signature, without waiting for the necessary ratification of the full treaty text by all EU member states and the European Parliament.

9.8   Conclusion

All five of the familiar models have their qualities, but each suffers from one defect or another for the UK, which validates the "no off-the-shelf model" remark of the Prime Minister. Simple WTO membership would mean serious damage to access to the EU market for both goods and services; the EEA regime is incompatible with the wish to control immigration; staying in the Customs Union would limit the possibilities to conduct free trade with the rest of the world; the Swiss model would not be acceptable for the EU and the Canadian model is not really relevant for a future UK–EU trade deal, but more for third-country cases. There is a new sixth model for the Association Agreement with neighbouring countries, including the DCFTA formula for trade. This model is also not suitable for wholesale copying, but it offers some features of potential interest to the UK: a structure to frame the forthcoming UK–EU negotiations, a high degree of single-market inclusion for three of the four freedoms (goods, services, capital, but not labour) and other legal and institutional features that the UK would find not inappropriate.

Whether the EU would be willing to engage in something like this is not known. Several EU leaders, however, have already staked out political markers. The two main points being made concern the indivisibility of the four freedoms and the need to avoid a British solution that would risk encouragement by contagion for other member states to escalate disintegration, which, as mentioned earlier, is a concern of existential proportions for the EU as a whole.

For the time being, however, the general view on the continent seems to be, as at the battle of Fontenoy in 1745, that it is for *Messieurs les anglais de tirer les premiers.*

Notes

1. Federica Mustilli and Jacques Pelkmans, "Access Barriers to Service Markets – Mapping, tracing, understanding and measuring", CEPS Special Report No. 77, CEPS, Brussels, June 2013.
2. Council of the EU, Council Conclusions on a Homogenous Single Market and EU Relations with Non-EU Western European Countries,

16 December 2014. Extract, para. 44: "A precondition for further developing a bilateral approach remains the establishment of a common institutional framework for existing and future agreements through which Switzerland participates in the EU's internal market, in order to ensure homogeneity and legal certainty in the internal market. The Council welcomes the opening of negotiations on such a framework in May 2014, expects further efforts in order to progress with these negotiations and reiterates that without such a framework no further agreements on Swiss participation in the internal market will be concluded."

3. See www.sem.admin.ch/sem/en/home/aktuell/news/2016/ref_2016-03-04.html.

4. The EU also shares its Customs Union with some European micro-states such as Andorra, and currently the EU seeks to bring these states into much more extensive alignment on EU law, as explained in Council of the EU, op. cit.

5. The AA-DCFTA text for Ukraine in the *Official Journal of the EU* runs to 2000 pages of legal and technical matters, which is the main reason why its essence is not easily understood. With the aim of making these complex texts more accessible, CEPS decided to write shorter explanatory books, which have recently been published. See Michael Emerson and Veronika Movchan, *Deepening EU-Ukraine Relations – What, Why and How?*, CEPS and Rowman and Littlefield International, 2016. This text is freely downloadable at:

    www.ceps.eu/publications/deepening-eu-ukrainian-relations-what-why-and-how, with a short guide available at: www.ceps.eu/publications/ukraine-and-europe-%E2%80%93-short-guide.

    Comparable books are published on the EU's similar agreements with Georgia and Moldova, accessible at www.ceps.eu.

6. CEN (European Committee for Standardisation), CENELEC (European Committee for Electrotechnical Standardisation), and ETSI (European Telecommunications Standards Institute).

7. See Mustilli and Pelkmans, op. cit.

8. See the AA-DCFTA with Ukraine at Article 124 on p. 61, and Annex XVII, Article 4, on "Regulatory Approximation", pp. 1725–1729 of the *Official Journal of the EU*, L161, Vol. 57, 29 May 2014. Internal market treatment is defined as: "No restrictions on the freedom of establishment of juridical persons of the EU or Ukraine in the territory of either of them and that juridical persons formed in accordance with the law of an EU Member State or Ukraine and having their registered office, central administration or principal place of business within the territory of the

Parties shall, for the purposes of this Agreement, be treated in the same way as juridical persons of EU Member States or Ukraine. This shall also apply to the setting up of agencies, branches or subsidiaries by juridical persons of the EU or Ukraine established in the territory of the other Party; and – no restrictions on freedom to provide services by a juridical person within the territory of the other Party in respect of persons of EU Member States and Ukraine who are established in the EU or Ukraine".

9. Karel Lannoo, "EU Financial Markets after Brexit", *CEPS Policy Brief*, September 2016.

10. This is the same wording as that reproduced in footnote 9. The Bank of England source can be found at:

     www.bankofengland.co.uk/pra/Pages/authorisations/passporting/default.aspx.

11. For further details on this complicated question see Milan Elkerbout, "Brexit and climate policy: Political choices will determine the future of EU-UK cooperation", CEPS Commentary, CEPS, Brussels, 15 July 2016.

12. See *Financial Times*, "Hollande demands tough Brexit negotiations" and "French president seeks to avoid contagion and protect principles of single market", 7 October 2016.

10

Economic Implications of Alternative Trade Relationships: Post-Brexit Options for the UK

Mark Baimbridge and Philip B. Whyman

10.1 Introduction

The project of European integration has been viewed by many as a continuing process of tightening the economic relationships between member states, based upon a common set of institutions and restrictions placed upon national economic autonomy ultimately intended to forge a single European economy. Whenever there is a problem that may impact upon this project, the tendency is to ask how the deepening of economic integration can provide a solution. However, not all European citizens accept this basic premise. Many consider the imposition of constraints upon national governments and parliaments to be illegitimate, whilst that the one-size-fits-all model of European integration, and especially the model surrounding the single

M. Baimbridge (✉)
School of Management, Faculty Management and Law, University of Bradford, Bradford, UK

P.B. Whyman
Lancashire Institute for Economic and Business Research (LIEBR), Lancashire Business School, University of Central Lancashire, Lancashire, UK

© The Author(s) 2017
N. da Costa Cabral et al. (eds.), *After Brexit*,
https://doi.org/10.1007/978-3-319-66670-9_10

European currency, impinges upon the ability of national governments to manage their economies in their own interests. When offered the option of either reaffirming the UK's continued progress towards ever-deeper political and economic integration, or to reassert national self-determination over many areas affecting their lives, UK citizens voted to withdraw from the European Union (EU).

Brexit, therefore, provides the means of escaping constraints imposed by the EU upon the UK's economic development. It allows UK policy makers to design their own regulations for the 94% of UK firms who do not trade with the EU. Further, it releases a significant sum of money that the UK annually transfers to the EU budget that could be used to fund infrastructure aimed at boosting the UK's future growth potential and/or promote reindustrialisation by nurturing strategic industries through the early and unknowable stages of their development until they achieve their own international competitive advantage (Baimbridge 2016). Additionally, an independent UK has the option of rejecting austerity and stimulating growth rates through a variant of national Keynesianism, by making use of fiscal, monetary and exchange rate policy instruments to prioritise economic growth, low unemployment and low inflation (Baimbridge et al. 2012). Thus, Brexit provides the freedom to develop alternative economic policies that are distinctly different from those pursued across the EU.

One key area where the UK has been consistent in its desire for a closer economic relationship with other EU member states has been in the area of free trade, and this will be a feature of the forthcoming exit negotiations as (hopefully) both sides seek to forge a sustainable future trade relationship that benefits all concerned. Certainly, the UK's trade relationship with the EU will remain important in the short- to medium-term, both for the UK, which currently exports around 40% of its goods and services to the continent, and also for those EU member states who have a substantial trade surplus with the UK. Indeed, as illustrated in Table 10.1, the UK's very large trade deficit with the EU implies that the UK has been living beyond its means and, since this deficit has continued to rise, it would seem that membership of the EU Single Market may have exacerbated this structural problem. Brexit offers a potential solution in that the UK would have more flexibility to rebuild its industrial base

Table 10.1 UK current account balance (2014) with selected trade blocs

Regional trade bloc	Current account (£m)
European Union (EU)	−89,468
European Economic Area (EEA)	−92,261
European Free Trade Association (EFTA)	−1,220
North American Free Trade Agreement (NAFTA)	28,664
Mercosur	1,976
ASEAN Free Trade Area (AFTA)	3,255
Commonwealth (India, Canada, South Africa, Australia)	−2,707

Source: ONS (2015)

and seek future trade agreements with the rest of the world, where incidentally, the UK enjoyed a trade surplus of £24 billion in 2014.

This chapter, therefore, seeks to discuss how Brexit may provide a means of escaping constraints imposed by the EU upon the UK's economic development, before outlining a few of the alternative economic relationships that could be forged between the UK and the EU. These could, for example, include:

(i) The 'Norway model', involving participation in the European Economic Area (EEA) to preserve full access to the single internal market (SIM), but at the cost of accepting free movement of capital and labour, the retention of most EU-determined regulation and the UK having to pay EU budgetary contributions;

(ii) The 'Swiss model', involving bilateral trade deals, negotiated piecemeal with the EU to gain free trade in goods but not most services that would still involve accepting free movement of capital and labour, together with (smaller) budgetary contributions;

(iii) The 'Canadian model', based upon the negotiation of a free trade agreement with the EU covering goods and some services but without having to accept free movement or budgetary contributions; or

(iv) The 'World Trade Organization (WTO) model', where if a preferential trade agreement cannot be reached with the EU, then trade would automatically revert back to trade based upon WTO 'most favoured nation' (MFN) rules that would involve trade subject to tariffs.

10.2   The Myth of Globalisation and Economic Interdependence

One of the most influential arguments in favour of continued European integration relates to the assertion that an increased internationalisation, or globalisation, of the world economy has created a new environment which has eroded the efficiency of traditional policy instruments and with it the relevance of individual nation states. This partially derives from conceptions of a 'borderless world' (Ohmae 1990), within which 'the stateless corporation' operates, relocating the location of production facilities with relative ease on the basis of calculations that optimise profits and productivity (Holstein 1990; Reich 1992). Simultaneously, technological advances have produced cost reductions in transport and communications and facilitated the development of a light, information-knowledge-based, service-centred economy (Katz 1988; Carnoy et al. 1993; Castells 1996).

This hyper-globalisation thesis suggests that the integration of financial markets, the free movement of capital, the rising importance of transnational corporations (TNCs) in global manufacturing production and their use of foreign direct investment (FDI) to expand their control into an increasing number of national markets have undermined the abilities of nation states to successfully manage their own affairs (Ohmae 1990, 1993, 1995; Reich 1992; Hay 1999). Hence, the authority of national governments has 'leaked away, upwards, sideways, and downwards', with states being 'hollowed out' by a combination of ease of evasion of regulation and dramatic increases in capital mobility (Cerny 1990; Strange 2000). As a result, advocates for European integration suggest that it can provide a bulwark against the worst effects produced by these global forces (McGrew and Lewis 1992).

The problem with this thesis is that globalisation is quite possibly 'the most contested concept in contemporary social science' (Grant 2002:41), being 'invariably over-used and under-specified' (Higgott and Payne 2000:ix). Indeed, Wiseman (1998:1) has been prompted to identify it as 'the most slippery, dangerous and important buzzword' of modern economic discourse. Certainly, the cost of communications and transportation of goods has declined substantially over the past half a century

(Rustin 2001:18), facilitating pan-national supply chains and an expansion of international trade exceeding global growth rates (OECD 1986:9), whilst FDI has enabled TNCs to gain dominance in many global markets (Ruigrok and Van Tulder 1995). Yet, the clearest evidence of globalisation does not derive from trade but rather the spectacular increase in short-term financial capital flows and speculation. Whereas in 1971, 90% of all financial transactions were made to facilitate international trade and long-term productive investment (Eatwell 1995; Watson 2002), trading on the major foreign exchange markets today is around 100 times greater than the equivalent value of international trade and dwarfing the total world expenditure on crude oil (Eatwell 2000; Helleiner 2000). Indeed, one estimate suggests that derivatives trading alone accounts for more than twelve times global GDP (Castells 2000).

Yet despite these dramatic changes, there is little convincing evidence to indicate that globalisation has undermined the efficiency of institutional frameworks within which economic policy operates (Garrett 1995; Scholte 2000; Whyman 2007). Careful examination of the data leads a number of theorists to conclude that contemporary phenomenon relates more closely to internationalisation than globalisation (Hirst and Thompson 1996; Wade 1996). Indeed, it is perhaps worth noting that claims of 'the end of the nation state' have coincided with more nation states existing than during any previous historical period of world history. National macroeconomics remains a viable alternative for any nation to pursue (Baker et al. 2002). Nation states remain essentially sovereign, influenced by the international economy, certainly, and with their freedom of movement constrained by the consequences of specific actions, naturally, yet remaining sufficiently autonomous to devise and implement a distinctive, self-determined economic strategy tailored to the needs of its economy and preferences of its electorate.

Given the continued viability of national economic self-determinism, the question turns to the selection of the type of economic strategy that best meets the objectives of the individual nation. This could, for example, draw inspiration from the low-tax, deregulated, neo-liberal market-orientated economics, as hinted at in UK Prime Minister May's recent speech on her perceived options for Brexit,[1] or alternatively it could embody a more interventionist, active macroeconomic policy evolving from Keynesian principles. Whatever option is selected, this will be based upon the democratic will of the UK citizenry, expressed through its election of representatives to the House of Commons and thereby the formation of the national government, rather than being stymied by the over-exaggerated claims of the hyper-globalists that would dismiss the relevance of any such discourse. It is this that motivated the expression of electoral will that resulted in Brexit and it is to consideration of alternative aspects of national economic policy in relation to new trade relationships open to the UK post-Brexit that we now turn.

10.3   Alternative Trade Relationships: Within the European Sphere

There are various options that the UK could choose, including:

10.3.1   Norway Model

This strategy would involve the UK formally withdrawing from the EU and re-joining the European Free Trade Association (EFTA) that it helped found four decades ago. In the process, the UK would be eligible for membership of the European Economic Area (EEA). Article 41 of the convention establishing EFTA states that any state may accede provided it receives the approval of the EFTA Council, or alternatively the Council may negotiate bilateral agreements with individual states subject to its unanimous approval by all member states. Article 42 establishes the right to withdraw from the convention after 12 months advance notice. Similarly, Article 128 of the EEA Agreement states that any European state becoming a member of EFTA can apply to the EEA Council to be party to the agreement, with the terms and conditions subject to negotiation. All future EU members are required to apply to become party to the agreement.

The EEA is an agreement made between EFTA (less Switzerland) to extend the internal market of the EU and that of the EFTA participants to create a trading area of 28 countries and some 462 million people. This is the world's largest and most comprehensive multinational trading area that came into force on 1 January 1994. Under the agreement, there is free movement of goods, services and capital across the entire area, whilst Article 28 provides for the free movement of persons and a single labour market across all member countries. Participants are encouraged to co-operate in the fields of environmental protection, social policy, education and research and development programmes. Exceptions to coverage include agriculture and fisheries, whilst the EEA has no common external tariff and therefore requires the identification of country of origin for all goods and services.

As a member of the EEA, the UK would possess full access to the SIM and retain some influence over the rules that affect trade with EU nations. The EEA ensures free trade without the discrimination against external nations created by a customs union. The terms of the EEA stipulate that the UK business sector would operate under the same general conditions as its EU competitors whilst ensuring that EEA member states develop relevant legislation jointly without the EU imposing standards arbitrarily. The EEA provides member states with the right to oppose and veto EU law if they feel that it operates against their national interest. It also offers the possibility to participate in EU research projects and co-operation on the environment and the social dimension of EU legislation should any EEA participants find these beneficial.

A net transfer of income to the EU budget is part of the requirement for EEA membership, but it would be significantly lower than the high budgetary burden imposed by full EU membership upon UK taxpayers. Taking into account differences in per capita GDP compared to Norway, the UK's fiscal contribution might be anticipated to be around 0.2% of UK GDP, which is around 40% of the UK's current net contributions to the EU budget. Membership of the EEA also releases the UK from pressure to participate in the Exchange Rate Mechanism (ERM), stipulated by the Treaty on European Union (TEU). Given the UK's previous unfortunate experience of ERM membership, and the still larger disadvantages it would suffer through participation in Economic and Monetary Union (EMU), this constitutes a significant advantage. Thus, the EEA provides many of the advantages of EU membership without some of the costs.

Norway can also be used as a political precedent since their electorate rejected EU membership in a national referendum and yet was able to participate in the EU Single Market by means of the EEA. The EU have not sought to 'punish' Norway for failing to persuade its people to become full members and on the contrary appear eager to take advantage of their addition to the Single Market to export goods and services, whilst having Norway pay a contribution towards the EU bureaucracy that manages the market.

An advantage is that EFTA is a similar type of trade agreement to NAFTA in that it does not impose undue costs and restrictions upon member governments, barring those minimum rules necessary to maintain the effectiveness of the free trade area. The only significant differences are that the EEA is not as explicit on the issues of intellectual property and foreign investment, whilst it progressively adopts updated rules on trade harmonisation once these are agreed between the EU and EFTA members. Thus, UK membership of the EEA and NAFTA could establish closer co-operation between the two trade blocks around two very similar free trade agreements.

The main disadvantage of the EEA involves participants having to accept EU-determined rules and regulations relating to SIM trade with little effective input. In effect, EEA members become 'rule takers' rather than, as full EU members, they are 'rule makers'. This difference can be over-emphasised, of course, since the UK is currently one of 28 member states and therefore can only influence the drafting of new rules and regulations through argument and/or building effective majority alliances with other members. Nevertheless, as an EEA member, the UK would have less ability to shape the trade rules within which it would have to operate. It is possible that, with the UK joining the existing EEA members, this might reduce the power imbalance with the EU somewhat and facilitate greater partnership rather than subservience between EFTA and the EU; however, there have been no such proposals made in this direction to date.

Partly as a result of the lack of influence over rules governing its own industries and trade, the Norwegian government has expressed a degree of dissatisfaction with aspects of the operation of the EEA. It has, furthermore, welcomed the free movement of labour as a means of resolving what had become persistent skill shortages within its economy, and yet the Norwegian government had registered its concern that free movement simultaneously undermines high quality working conditions and can lead to social dumping (NOU 2012). In addition, SIM rules would stifle independent policymaking (Baimbridge et al. 2010; Swidlicki et al. 2016).

10.3.2   Swiss Model

One further option that the British government could consider relates to formal withdrawal from full EU membership and its replacement with a bilateral trade agreement between the EU and UK. It is sometimes referred to as the 'Swiss position' as, following rejection of EU membership by a majority of its citizens and cantons voted against EEA membership in December 1992, Switzerland negotiated a series of over 100 bilateral treaties with the EU, including a 1972 free trade agreement, which covers industrial goods (Church 1993).

Since the UK is ill served by participating in the Common Agricultural Policy (CAP) and the Common Fisheries Policy (CFP), a restriction of free trade with EU nations to industrial and financial goods and services would prove more beneficial than the present status quo. The remaining EFTA countries negotiated such a free trade agreement with the EU in 1972, after the UK, Denmark and Ireland had joined the EU, thus escaping from the financial burdens and policy constraints imposed by EU membership. As with membership of the EEA, this approach would allow the UK to re-orientate its economic policy to serve its own perceived national interest rather than those of competitor EU countries. The money saved by non-contribution to the EU budget could be used to increase incentives for productive investment within the UK and for state expenditure on infrastructural and research-based projects that increase long-term competitiveness. This option provides greater freedom than EEA membership.

These decisions did not haemorrhage economic vitality; instead they strengthened the Swiss economy. Amongst OECD countries, agriculture apart, there is no economy more open to the outside world than Switzerland. Exposure to such competitive pressures encouraged the development of some of the world's most international-orientated companies. Switzerland is the 14th trading nation in the world and the 2nd trade partner with the EU (after the USA) and the 3rd supplier after the USA and Japan. Switzerland has managed to maintain relatively low levels of inflation, interest rates and unemployment, together with a significant balance of payments surplus, particularly when compared to the larger continental EU member states. Thus, Switzerland is benefiting from its arm's-length relations, despite a continued eagerness amongst its political elite for future

EU membership. Consequently non-membership of the EU has failed to hamper its economic development or its trading potential.

Despite economic success outside the EU, the Swiss authorities express two fears, which are familiar to UK citizens when confronted with the possibility of a change in relations with the EU. First, since the majority of trade is done with EU nations, membership may prove essential to protect it. Second, absence from the EEA may result in EU discrimination against Swiss-made goods through technical barriers. These concerns may be over-exaggerated. For example, in the Swiss case only 58% of exports and 71.5% of imports relate to the EU, so that its economy is less orientated towards the EU than most commentators claim. Additionally, like the UK, an increasing proportion of its international trade is being conducted with the fast growth areas in Asia and the USA rather than with the slow-growing EU. Thus, Switzerland's dependence upon the EU market is likely to diminish in the future. The trend would be accelerated if the UK, Switzerland's fifth most important trading partner, left the EU.

In answer to the second point, the EU nations benefit far more than Switzerland from their trade so that they are unlikely to engage in discriminatory practices that could endanger their own more sizeable exports. Moreover, the Uruguay GATT (latterly WTO) agreement prevents arbitrary treatment of a nation's exports in any market, thus preventing active discrimination against Swiss, or any other countries', exports by the EU. Of course unofficial barriers to trade do exist, but EU membership is no guarantee that these will be dismantled.

The Swiss option does involve acceptance of the free movement of capital and labour, and the latter has created difficulties for this relationship with the EU. For example, a 2014 referendum decision instructed the Swiss government to introduce immigration quotas, which would have terminated the bilateral relationship with the EU had the Swiss government not decided to effectively sideline the referendum result in favour of less drastic policies intended to curb the impact of migration rather than placing restrictions upon the inward flow. This experience raises difficult questions for the UK, should the government seek to pursue the 'Swiss option', since regaining some measure of control over immigration was a key issue in the UK European referendum (Booth et al. 2015).

The 'Swiss option', therefore, provides a more flexibly means of securing a close relationship between the EU and the UK, but the insistence upon acceptance of the free movement of capital and labour is likely to prove to be difficult, if not impossible, for the UK to accept, as it goes against the expressed democratic will of its people.

10.4   Alternative Trade Relationships: A Global Vision

Successive British governments have sought to place the UK at 'the heart of Europe' and in the process have accepted the idea of the inevitability of a drift towards broader and deeper economic and political integration across a large swathe of the European continent. This is not to say that leading British political figures have not made personal stances against this process, together with a larger number who have argued for a loosening of the constraints imposed upon nation states by the integration process (Abbott 2000; Redwood 2000; Benn 2006; Gould 2006; Mitchell 2006; Owen 2006; Shore 2006). Moreover, both Conservative and Labour governments have drawn their 'red lines' or vetoed specific new initiatives usually seeking to limit national self-determination. However, notwithstanding these efforts, the process of ever-closer unification has progressed from the trade-related common market, through the creation of a SIM, to the establishment of EMU.

Withdrawal from the EU provides one means of escaping these increasing constraints imposed by the EU upon the UK's economic behaviour, and which are not fully eliminated by those options involving retained EU membership. Renegotiation could reduce many of these direct costs, but would be exceptionally difficult because a gain for the UK would involve a net cost for other member states. The Swiss option is the most palatable, but if this is achieved with the UK remaining bound by the Treaty of Rome, then economic policy remains fundamentally constrained and speculators could therefore 'punish' sterling for non-compliance with EMU rules. Therefore, in view of the varying but substantial costs implied by any form of EU membership, a further option for the UK is complete withdrawal, so that it can repatriate the ability to employ those policy tools it sees fit to better manage the country in its natural interests.

Once attained, the UK is free to operate any economic policy it wishes. It could take the form of a determined effort to rebuild large sections of the UK's industrial base, decimated by EU, and accelerated by ERM, membership. Burkitt et al. (1997) outlined the essential elements of one such strategy. It could pursue a low-tax, market-orientated strategy, or else seek to stimulate growth rates through a combination of national Keynesianism, an active labour market and industrial policy. However, the crucial point is that UK citizens would possess the power to decide how they are governed and how the economy is run, rather than exercising merely a token vote at election time because important decisions concerning fiscal, monetary, exchange rate and trade policy are taken in Brussels. The economy would be free to react to external shocks in a way that suited its particular circumstances, not what suited Germany as the strongest EU state, or the 'average' member state, whether or not such a creation of statistical indexes actually exists! Indeed, as the German and Japanese economic 'miracles' were partially based upon a competitive currency and long-term low-interest rates for industrial finance, the UK could adopt a similar approach to compete more successfully with EU members rather than be restricted by EU economic policies that are not in its interest.

The argument that the UK can only exercise any influence on world events within the EU is perverse, appearing to be simultaneously defeatist yet hankering for a world leadership role. The UK lost its former dominant world position because of economic problems. Decades of slow economic growth reduced the UK from being the leading world economy before the turn of the century to a medium-sized economy in the 1990s, with political power declining accordingly. Japan and Germany obtained increased international influence not because of foreign policy or military might, but because their economic strength compels attention. If the UK is to regain influence, it must be based upon economic success, which is less likely to be secured within the monetarist-inspired EU-EMU policy straitjacket. Furthermore, the UK could secure international influence far in excess of its size through less conventional means. The Scandinavian countries, for example, achieved significant prestige for their environmental and human rights campaigns. The UK, when it established the National Health Service, was likewise a model that countless other countries used when constructing their own welfare systems. Likewise, the British democratic system is still admired by many sections of the globe as the 'mother of parliaments'. International influence does not, therefore, have to be of the traditional type. Even the latter can be more effectively attained through UK participation in the G7 summits than by being one voice amongst 28 (or more) within the EU.

The belief that withdrawal would reduce the flow of foreign investment into the UK is widely held, but a UK economy growing faster outside the EU with a permanently competitive exchange rate may prove to be equally attractive to foreign investors. Foreign-based companies locate productive facilities in the UK to enhance their profits through producing output it can sell in the British and European markets, utilising the skills and abilities of a well-educated and flexible labour force. If firms remain profitable irrespective of British membership of the EU, they will continue to invest in the British economy in large numbers, as they currently do with few indications that the UK will participate in the most visible extension of European economic integration, namely the single currency.

Nor is the idea that withdrawal from the EU would provoke retaliation from current EU 'partners' any more probable. It is likely that EU negotiators will impart political pressure upon the UK, either to seek to persuade the UK to reverse its decision to withdraw or else to persuade those amongst the citizenry in other EU member states that withdrawal is not an attractive proposition. Nevertheless, this rhetoric will be tempered by the fact that the erection of any significant trade barriers between the EU and the UK will harm EU member states, given their large trade surplus with the UK and their reliance upon continued access to inexpensive capital through the City of London. It may also prove counter-productive in the medium term because any such restrictions placed upon trade with the EU would encourage the UK to complete a more rapid and substantial reorientation of its trade towards global markets, sourcing goods and services from outside of Europe and accelerating its programmes to rebuild UK industrial capacity and to ensure the continued international competitiveness of its produce. Were this successful, it would create the very example of a successful Brexit that might prove attractive to those EU citizens who find the current model of European integration unappealing. The EU negotiators, in pursuing a hard line in their negotiations, would in effect have scored an own goal.

10.4.1   Canadian Model

Withdrawal from the EU is only a first, necessary step. Once achieved, the UK can develop whatever trading relations with other nations. It may, for example, seek to negotiate a free trade agreement (FTA) with various Commonwealth nations. Indeed, the Prime Ministers of Australia and New Zealand have already expressed their interest in pursuing such an agreement. In addition, the new US administration has stated its interest in negotiating a FTA with the UK. Given this likely modus operandi for the UK to pursue free trade with multiple partners, the negotiation of a FTA with the EU would, therefore, seem to be an obvious choice for a future trade relationship between the two parties. Depending upon the scope of the agreement, it would extend free trade between the UK and the EU to goods and some services, but excluding agricultural products. It would secure continued free trade between the UK and EU member states without the necessity of insisting upon continued budgetary contributions, the harmonisation of regulations, the acceptance of free movement of capital and people, and the unwelcome (to the British people) pretensions of economic and political union.

One possible starting point for negotiations could be the FTA recently completed between Canada and the EU, although it is likely that the UK would seek to add financial services to the existing Canadian agreement. This might not prove to be an insurmountable obstacle, given EU industry's reliance upon the continued access to inexpensive capital through Europe's premier financial centre, based in London, and the likely financial instability that may be caused if this link were to be broken.

A FTA would require 'rule of origin' regulations, which is where a UK company exporting into the EU Single Market would have to state the proportion of the value of the good or service which originated in the UK. The reason is to prevent UK companies acting as re-importers of finished goods from elsewhere into the Single Market, and thereby evading the Common EU tariff. This does add a minor cost to UK exporters, estimated at between 2% and 7% of the value of the goods traded (Cadot et al. 2006), yet it would enable the UK to achieve free trade in goods, and possibly some services, without having to accept additional elements of political and social integration (Milne 2004).

10.4.2   World Trade Organization (WTO) Model

Should it prove impossible to negotiate a FTA, or other form of preferential trade agreement, then trade would revert to reliance upon WTO 'most favoured nation' (MFN) rules. Trade between the UK and EU would no longer be free from restriction, but rather be based upon tariffs no higher than those offered by the EU to other nations. Calculated on a trade-weighted basis, the EU's average tariff is only around 2.3% for non-agricultural goods,[2] which is a relatively modest level and should prove to have only minimal cost implications for UK exporters. This average figure, however, obscures the fact that, for certain sectors, the tariff rates are significantly higher. Vehicle production, for example, may face tariffs of around 8.5%, whilst plastics are likely to face a tariff of 5.9% and beverages 8.5% (Business for Britain 2015:777–8). It should be noted that since the value of sterling has depreciated by more than 12% since the European referendum result, none of these increases in tariff costs would offset the boost to international competitiveness resulting from this shift in the exchange rate. Moreover, independence from EU rules would enable the UK government to offset any negative impact, through a range of other measures taken to enhance the competitiveness and productive potential of the UK industrial base. These could include additional tax credits to stimulate R&D, or measures to enhance technical skills formation.

The WTO model provides the UK with the greatest policy flexibility but greater restrictions placed upon continued access to EU markets. Nevertheless, given the relatively modest level of average MFN trade-weighted tariffs that would be levied, the price for gaining this additional degree of policy autonomy might be considered to be worthwhile by UK policy makers. Indeed, this is probably the meaning of UK Prime Minister's comment that 'no deal for Britain is better than a bad deal for Britain'.[3]

10.4.3   Membership of NAFTA

There are compelling reasons why both the USA and the UK should actively promote closer cooperation; potentially even culminating in the UK joining the North American Free Trade Agreement (NAFTA) comprising the USA, Canada and Mexico (United States International Trade Commission (2000); Baimbridge et al. 2004; Philippidis 2004). NAFTA countries have already expressed interest in establishing closer trading relations with EFTA and Chile. If Britain participated in such a grouping, a revamped NAFTA could ultimately be transformed into a global free trade association, which could potentially incorporate such countries as Australia, New Zealand, South Africa, Denmark, Sweden, Norway, Ireland and Switzerland, together with the Caribbean. It would be a grouping, based solely upon a commitment to free trade between them. It would seek no control of member states' trade relation with non-members nor would it possess the motivation to pursue 'ever closer union' that renders the EU unpalatable to many people within the UK. By contrast, NAFTA would prove more consistent with the democratically accountable sovereignty of each individual participating nation state.

The UK and the US economies are closely intertwined through trade, investment and the business cycle; so that further trade liberalisation would result in immediate benefits, in terms of trade creation, for both. From the past, the USA and UK share a common culture and language, which make a contemporary trade relationship between them more likely to prove successful. A free trade area centred on an Anglo-American nexus is a more efficient fit than any conceivable alternative economic arrangement.

One important factor for potential partners in a free trade area to consider relates to the degree of comparability of the economies in question—in particular, what possibilities for economies of scale exist for firms taking advantage of the larger free trade area and whether trade creation will exceed trade diversion resulting from the creation of the larger trade bloc. The former benefit will result from companies currently stymied from expanding to their optimum size due to the limited size of the domestic market and therefore are unable to offer consumers products as cheaply as would be the case in a larger market. This potential for lower prices will also be more likely to be realised in a larger market, where competition will prevent former national monopolies or oligopolies from exploiting their market power and maintaining high prices.

A second type of potential benefit accruing from the enlargement of NAFTA would refer to the degree of trade creation less diversion. This relates to the fact that in a global market characterised by free trade, the most efficient producer(s) in a given commodity should specialise in its production, thereby optimising consumer benefits from low prices and efficient production. However, the existence of trade restrictions (i.e., tariffs) means that less efficient internal producers might be able to produce goods and services more cheaply, thereby transferring production from more to less efficient companies and consequently wasting precious resources through this unwarranted diversion of trade. The benefit of a free trade area is where former tariffs levied on foreign firms now inside the tariff barriers might result in more efficient producers taking market share from less efficient domestic firms, thereby consuming less scarce resources and thus potentially increasing world production.

Since its withdrawal from the ERM, the British economy has been convergent, both structurally and cyclically, with North America. Consequently, sterling tracks the US dollar, not the euro, whilst its divergence from continental euro has widened. Thus, sterling has fluctuated in a range of 13% against the dollar since September 1992 but over a range of 37% against the (former) deutschemark. Such oscillations determine the efficiency of interest rate harmonisation, leading to the conclusion that the American and British economies are more convergent with each other than either is with the euro zone. Such a conclusion is supported by analysis of the growth rates of the UK, the USA, France and Germany.

In terms of business cycle, the UK has traditionally had a closer statistical relationship with USA than with Germany and other leading EU member states (Bayoumi and Eichengreen 1993). Indeed, whilst the USA and UK economies have enjoyed years of relatively rapid economic expansion, many continental EU economies have been trapped in conditions of slow economic growth and high unemployment. In the decade prior to the Global Financial Crisis/Great Depression, the USA created 22 million new jobs, whilst UK unemployment stood at a 20-year low. Comparable unemployment figures for leading EU member states were

9.1% in Germany, 11.7% in France and 12% in Italy whilst standing at approximately 5% for the UK and USA.

Additionally, a noticeable change in both US and UK economies has been the transition in their respective labour markets. The shift towards non-standard contracts, whether part-time, temporary or fixed-term working, together with the deregulation of the labour market, has increased the flexible adaptation of both economies to deal more effectively with industrial restructuring. One notable feature of this change is a decline in the non-accelerating inflation rate of unemployment (NAIRU) that denotes that level of unemployment associated with a stable rate of inflation. Consequently, both economies have little tendency towards inflationary wage pressure despite low unemployment levels. Moreover, productivity has been rising quickly in both nations, with US productivity growth outstripping average wage growth. This, together with the high value of both currencies, has dampened remaining inflation pressure from increasing oil prices and property market booms.

One factor stimulating productivity increases, running at double the average of the previous 25 years in USA, is due to the impact of information technology. One estimate calculates that computers account for about a quarter of the overall increase in productivity, with increases in the use of information technology accounting for approximately half of this rise. The UK accounted for 44% of all EU venture investment in high technology, with Germany a poor second with 17% of the investment total. The diffusion of information technology and especially the internet throughout the economy is incomplete, thereby allowing for continued high rates of future economic expansion. Stock market asset expansion has further stimulated consumer expenditure, with high technology shares securing the greatest value accumulation, before more recent market adjustment.

Macroeconomic strategy is similar for the UK and USA, with restrained fiscal policy enabling a greater role for monetary policy loosening to facilitate economic growth and increased levels of investment though lower real interest rates. Supply-side policy seeks to reduce taxation to encourage entrepreneurship, together with stimulation of investment in human capital. Consequently, both nations are ranked in the top ten most competitive nations in the world; the USA maintaining its premier position. Moreover, of the most competitive EU nations, it is the smaller Scandinavian economies that tend to score well in the World Economic Forum international competitiveness index, with the larger continental EU member states such as France, Germany and Italy receiving significantly poorer rankings.

Furthermore, if Britain joins NAFTA, the larger group will help to protect both the USA and the UK from whatever outcome emerges from the EU experiment in supranationalism where a more broadly based NAFTA can counter the impact of either an imploding or a successfully integrating but by necessity largely inward-looking EU. Third, the telecommunications revolution has led to the 'death of distance'; sharing borders no longer necessarily translates into increased trade and financial transactions, compared to a geographically distant country, as it has tended to do throughout history. A US-UK focal trading relationship would not work well in the era of the sailing ship or even when the Treaty of Rome was signed in 1957. Today information technology makes it eminently practical.

It is, moreover, possible that a revamped NAFTA could ultimately be transformed into a global free trade association. It would seek no control of member states' trade relations with non-members nor would it possess the motivation to pursue 'ever closer union' but respect each member's democratically accountable sovereignty. The last point is important because the now stalled Trans-Atlantic Trade and Investment Partnership (TTIP) contains clauses that are problematic for the ability for future democratically elected governments to protect the integrity of the NHS, public services and indeed any publically owned industries, from penetration by large US transnational corporations[4].

10.4.4 Commonwealth FTA

The greatest visible sign of economic weakness is the persistence of mass unemployment within EU nations, which is not matched by the North American, Asian 'Tiger' and Latin American areas. Indeed, it is interesting to note that many Commonwealth countries offer potentially faster growing markets than do other EU member states and hence the development of a Commonwealth free trade area. Indeed, Commonwealth nations include a number of the fastest growing markets in the world, particularly in South and East Asia (World Bank 1993) where historic links may give the UK a potential advantage in re-establishing trade links with these dynamic economies (Burkitt and Baimbridge 1990; West 1995). Again the potential exists to develop the Commonwealth into a FTA, since for too long the UK has been distracted from taking advantage of such export opportunities by the emphasis focused upon trading with European neighbours and by the EU's common external tariff, which encourages other nations to place tariffs upon EU exports, thereby putting UK companies at a competitive disadvantage with the rest of the world.

Historic links with Commonwealth nations could give the UK a potential advantage in establishing trading links with these dynamic economies. These include Singapore, India, Pakistan, Malaysia, New Zealand, Australia, Canada and the 'new' South Africa. This trade potential is likely to have become even more favourable as those regions with close Commonwealth connections outperform the IMF's estimated world growth rate of 3.7%, whilst the USA, Eastern Europe and non-EU industrial countries were all anticipated to grow faster than the EU. Indeed, the World Bank (1993) estimated that the areas of the world which grew most during the past two decades, namely South and East Asia, will continue to expand more rapidly. Additionally, growth potential is expected to result in significantly higher rates amongst most developing, than amongst the developed, economies. Latin America, Africa and the Middle East join Asia in offering UK companies superior potential for increased export sales than does the EU Single Market. Brexit highlights these developments in the world economy and reduces the danger of the Single Market distracting UK firms from pursuing their widest options for sales and discourage a parochial European mentality at a time when a more international focus is indicated, for both short- and long-term trade prospects.

Naturally enough, predictions relating to future market shares must always be taken with more than a degree of scepticism due to the tendency to fail to predict external, or even internal shocks, which may alter national growth and competitiveness figures substantially. Suitable examples concern currency and financial crises involving EU member states in 1992, Asian economies in 1997 and Russia in 1998. Nevertheless, even including these effects, East Asia appears likely to expand more rapidly than continental EU economies over the next few years, and therefore trade relations are more likely to grow in importance over this medium-term time period.

10.5   Conclusion

Even in light of the 2017 General Election outcome where the incumbent Conservative Party failed to receive the mandate regarding Brexit that it was seeking in terms of a larger parliamentary majority, the arguments contained in this chapter remain valid concerning the potential alternative trade relationships that Britain could pursue, where each possesses advantages and disadvantages. Hence, the choices made by policy makers needs to be mindful of this potential trade-off between policy autonomy and trade access, and a final selection should rest at least partly on the basis of a cost-benefit analysis following an informed public debate.

Whichever option is selected, the crucial common factor is that it permits the UK sufficient freedom to craft an independent economic policy based upon national priorities and interests, thereby enabling the formation of new trade relationships that better represent the dynamic elements of the world economy.

Rather than being tied into regional economic integration, where distinctive areas of British competitive advantage are sacrificed in pursuit of harmonisation across the European continent, British workers and companies could benefit from a change in focus, from a narrow vision of the future, to a global, more enriching alternative.

Notes

1. https://www.gov.uk/government/speeches/the-governments-negotiating-objectives-for-exiting-the-eu-pm-speech.
2. http://stat.wto.org/TariffProfile/WSDBTariffPFView.aspx?Language=E&Country=E28.
3. https://www.gov.uk/government/speeches/the-governments-negotiating-objectives-for-exiting-the-eu-pm-speech.
4. http://labourlist.org/2016/06/corbyn-a-labour-government-will-block-ttip/; https://www.theguardian.com/business/2015/aug/03/ttip-what-why-angry-transatlantic-trade-investment-partnership-guide.

References

Abbott, D. 2000. The Case Against the Maastricht Model of Central Bank Independence. In *The Impact of the Euro: Debating Britain's Future*, ed. M. Baimbridge, B. Burkitt, and P. Whyman. London: Macmillan.

Baimbridge, M. 2016. The Economic Costs of Membership. In *The Labour Case for Brexit*, ed. K. Hickson and J. Miles, 17–21. London: Labour Leave.

Baimbridge, M., J. Harrop, and G. Philippidis. 2004. *Current Economic Issues in EU Integration*. London: Palgrave Macmillan.

Baimbridge, M., P.B. Whyman, and B. Burkitt. 2010. Britain Beyond the EU. In *Britain in a Global World: Options for a New Beginning*, ed. M. Baimbridge, P. Whyman, and B. Burkitt, 19–26. Exete/Charlottesville: Imprint Academic.

———. 2012. New International Political and Economic Relationships. In *Building an Economy for the People: An Alternative Economic and Political Strategy for 21st Century Britain*, ed. J. White, 37–45. London: Manifesto Press.

Baker, D., A. Gamble, and D. Seawright. 2002. Sovereign Nations and Global Markets: Modern British Conservatism and Hyperglobalism. *British Journal of Politics and International Relations* 4 (3): 399–428.

Bayoumi, T., and B. Eichengreen. 1993. Shocking Aspects of European Monetary Integration. In *Adjustment and growth in the European Monetary Union*, ed. F. Torres and F. Giavazzi. Cambridge: Cambridge University Press.

Benn, T. 2006. The Establishment of a Commonwealth of Europe. In *Implications of the Euro: A Critical Perspective from the Left*, ed. P. Whyman, M. Baimbridge, and B. Burkitt. London: Routledge.

Booth, S., C. Howarth, M. Persson, R. Ruparel, and P. Swidlicki. 2015. *What If…?: The Consequences, Challenges and Opportunities Facing Britain Outside EU, Open Europe Report 03/2015*. London. Available at: http://openeurope.org.uk/intelligence/britain-and-the-eu/what-if-there-were-a-brexit/.

Burkitt, B., and M. Baimbridge. 1990. The Performance of British Agriculture and the Impact of the Common Agricultural Policy: A Historical Review. *Rural History* 1 (2): 265–280.

Burkitt, B., M. Baimbridge, and P.B. Whyman. 1997. *A Price Not Worth Paying: The Economic Cost of EMU*. Oxford: Nelson & Pollard.

Business for Britain. 2015. *Change or Go: How Britain Would Gain Influence and Prosper Outside an Unreformed EU*. London: Business for Britain. Available at: https://forbritain.org/cogwholebook.pdf.

Cadot, O., C. Carrère, J. de Melo, and B. Tumurchudur. 2006. Product-Specific Rules of Origin in EU and US Preferential Trading Arrangements: An Assessment. *World Trade Review* 5 (2): 199–224.

Carnoy, M., et al. 1993. *The New Global Economy in the Information Age*. University Park: Pennsylvania State University Press.

Castells, M. 1996. *The Information Age: Economy*. Blackwell/Oxford: Society and Culture.

———. 2000. Information Technology and Global Capitalism. In *On the Edge: Living with Global Capitalism*, ed. W. Hutton and A. Giddens, 52–75. London: Jonathan Cape.

Cerny, P.G. 1990. *The Changing Architecture of Politics: Structure, Agency and the Future of the State*. London: Sage.

Church, C. 1993. *Switzerland and Europe: Problem or Pattern?* London: European Policy Forum.

Eatwell, J. 1995. The International Origins of Unemployment. In *Managing the Global Economy*, ed. J. Michie and J. Grieve Smith. Oxford: Oxford University Press.

———. 2000. Unemployment: National Policies in a Global Economy. *International Journal of Manpower* 21 (5): 343–373.

Garrett, G. 1995. Capital Mobility, Trade and the Domestic Politics of Economic Policy. *International Organisation* 49: 657–587.

Gould, B. 2006. Preface. In *Implications of the Euro: A Critical Perspective from the Left*, ed. P. Whyman, M. Baimbridge, and B. Burkitt. London: Routledge.

Grant, W. 2002. *Economic Policy in Britain*. London: Palgrave.

Hay, C. 1999. *The Political Economy of New Labour: Labouring Under False Pretences?* Manchester: Manchester University Press.

Helleiner, E. 2000. Explaining the Globalization of Financial Markets: Bringing States Back In. In *The New Political Economy of Globalisation*, ed. R. Higgott and A. Payne, vol. 1. Cheltenham: Edward Elgar.

Higgott, R., and A. Payne. 2000. Introduction: Towards a New Political Economy of Globalisation. In *The New Political Economy of Globalisation*, ed. R. Higgott and A. Payne, vol. 1. Cheltenham: Edward Elgar.

Hirst, P., and G. Thompson. 1996. *Globalisation in Question: The International Economy and the Possibilities of Governance*. Cambridge: Polity.

Holstein, W.J. 1990. The Stateless Corporation. *Business Week*, 52–59, May 14.

Katz, P.L. 1988. *The Information Society: An International Perspective*. New York: Praeger.

McGrew, A., and P. Lewis. 1992. *Globalisation and the Nation States*. Cambridge: Polity Press.

Milne, I. 2004. *A Cost Too Far? An Analysis of the Net Economic Costs and Benefits for the UK of EU Membership*. London: Civitas. Available at: http://www.civitas.org.uk/pdf/cs37.pdf.

Mitchell, A. 2006. Euro Versus the People. In *Implications of the Euro: A Critical Perspective from the Left*, ed. P. Whyman, M. Baimbridge, and B. Burkitt. London: Routledge.

NOU [Official Norwegian Report]. 2012. *Utenfor og Innenfor: Norges avtaler med EU* [Outside and Inside: Norway's Agreement's with the EU], NOU 2012:2. Oslo: Norwegian Ministry of Foreign Affairs. Available at: https://www.regjeringen.no/contentassets/5d3982d042a2472eb1b20639cd8b2341/no/pdfs/nou201220120002000dddpdfs.pdf.

OECD. 1986. *Flexibility in the Labour Market*. Paris: OECD.

Office for National Statistics (ONS). 2015. *United Kingdom Balance of Payments – The Pink Book: 2015*. London: Office for National Statistics.

Ohmae, K. 1990. *The Borderless World: Power and Strategy in the Interlinked Economy*. London: Collins.

———. 1993. The Rise of the Region State. *Foreign Affairs* 71 (2): 78–87.

———. 1995. *The End of the Nation-State: The Rise of Regional Economies*. London: Harper Collins.

Owen, D. 2006. Foreword. In *Implications of the Euro: A Critical Perspective from the Left*, ed. P. Whyman, M. Baimbridge, and B. Burkitt. London: Routledge.

Philippidis, G. 2004. Membership of NAFTA: A Viable Alternative for UK Agro-Food Producers? *Economic Issues* 9 (2): 21–42.

Redwood, J. 2000. Sterling Democracy or European Bureaucracy? In *The Impact of the Euro: Debating Britain's Future*, ed. M. Baimbridge, B. Burkitt, and P. Whyman. London: Macmillan.

Reich, R. 1992. *The Work of Nations*. New York: Vintage.

Ruigrok, W., and R. van Tulder. 1995. *The Logic of International Restructuring*. London: Routledge.

Rustin, M. 2001. The Third Sociological Way. In *The Economics of the Third Way: Experiences from Around the World*, ed. P. Arestis and M. Sawyer, 11–25. Cheltenham: Edward Elgar.

Scholte, J.A. 2000. *Globalisation: A Critical Introduction*. Basingstoke: Macmillan.

Shore, P. 2006. Fighting Against Federalism. In *Implications of the Euro: A Critical Perspective from the Left*, ed. P. Whyman, M. Baimbridge, and B. Burkitt. London: Routledge.

Strange, S. 2000. The Defective State. In *The New Political Economy of Globalisation*, ed. R. Higgott and A. Payne, vol. 1. Cheltenham: Edward Elgar.

Swidlicki, P., R. Ruparel, and S. Booth. 2016. *As the UK Searches for a POST-BREXIT PLAN, Is the EEA a Viable Option?* London: Open Europe.

United States International Trade Commission. 2000. *The Impact on the US Economy of Including the United Kingdom in a Free Trade Arrangement with the United States, Canada and Mexico.* Investigation No. 332–409, Publication 3339, August.

Wade, R. 1996. Globalization and Its Limits: Reports of the Death of the National Economy Are Greatly Exaggerated. In *National Diversity and Global Capitalism*, ed. S. in Berger and R. Dore, 60–88. Ithaca: Cornell University Press.

Watson, M. 2002. Sand in the Wheels, or Oiling the Wheels of International Finance? New Labour's Appeal to a 'New Bretton Woods'. *British Journal of Politics and International Relations* 4 (2): 193–221.

West, K. 1995. *Economic Opportunities for Britain and the Commonwealth.* London: Royal Institute for International Affairs.

Whyman, P.B. 2007. The Nature of Globalisation and Its Impact on the UK Economy. In *House of Commons Treasury Select Committee, Globalisation: Prospects and Policy Responses*, No. 137, 165–172. London: The Stationary Office Ltd.

Wiseman, J. 1998. *Global Nation: Australia and the Politics of Globalisation.* Cambridge: Cambridge University Press.

World Bank. 1993. *The East Asian Miracle: Economic Growth and Public Policy.* Oxford: Oxford University Press.

11

The Position of EU Citizens in the UK and of the UK Citizens in the EU27 Post-Brexit: Between Law and Political Constitutionalism

Samo Bardutzky

11.1 Introduction

This chapter addresses the issue of the position of the EU citizens in the UK and of the UK citizens in the remaining Member States of the EU after the exit of the UK from the EU (throughout the chapter, they will generally be referred to as "citizens affected by Brexit" to avoid the long descriptive label). The chapter is written on the basis of the persuasion of the present author that the prevailing view of this issue, which frames it as a political issue and a matter for negotiations, is wrong. The chapter thus presents the argument that there is a strong legal dimension of this issue, based predominantly on the European Convention of Human Rights (ECHR) and the case law of the European Court of Human Rights (ECtHR). Combined, these two groups of persons are very likely more than 5 million (Mantouvalou 2016). This means, on the one hand, that the legal question of their continuous right to reside and enjoy the access to health, education and so on

S. Bardutzky (✉)
Faculty of Law, University of Ljubljana, Ljubljana, Slovenia

© The Author(s) 2017
N. da Costa Cabral et al. (eds.), *After Brexit*,
https://doi.org/10.1007/978-3-319-66670-9_11

affects a large number of persons, comparable with one of the smaller Member States of the EU.

First, the chapter remarks on the context in which the question, discussed in the chapter, has arisen. An analysis of the majority of issues, related to the future post-Brexit, has to take into consideration that the exit of the UK from the EU will take place as a result of exercise of direct democracy. Next, the chapter recounts the political discussion on the position of the citizens affected by Brexit and discusses the approach to using these citizens as a "chip" in the negotiations between the UK and the remaining 27 EU Member States (EU27[1]). It then presents the case for understanding the position of the affected citizens as a matter of law, recounting the contributions made by other authors and drawing attention to case law that had previously not been quoted in this context. The final part of the chapter recognizes that the premise that (especially) the UK will continue to be a Party to the ECHR is dubious. It links the aversion to the bounds of international human rights to the idea of political constitutionalism and presents a critique of a political constitutionalist argument for withdrawal from the ECHR.

11.2   The Context: A Few Thoughts on Decision Making in Direct Democracy

Decision making in direct democracy is, in the majority of cases, dangerously binary. The voters choose one of the—regularly two—options on the ballot sheet. The alternative, namely, that the ballot sheet would include more than one option, or alternative options, is rarely desirable as it may make the interpretation of referendum results ambiguous, reducing or obliterating the arguably massive potential for democratic legitimation offered by direct ballot.[2] Consequently, the expressive power of the referendum decision is limited in that it does not articulate the will of the electorate on a number of questions inseparably linked to the question on the ballot sheet. Of course, this partly depends also on a number of modalities of the referendum. Where the referendum functions as a popular veto, deciding the fate of an already adopted legislative reform, the reductionist effect of a binary decision is smaller. A positive vote will bring into force the new law with all its details. A negative vote will keep status quo. When the question is more prospective, as was the case with the Brexit referendum, direct democracy will render nothing more than a very general decision, with myriad details to be decided afterwards.

The Brexit referendum probably stands out and might as well make constitutional history as one where the binary, all-or-nothing logic of direct democracy contributed to a record volume of uncertainties. This problem was graphically described by Neil Walker (2016a), positing that "[h]aving donned the referendum straitjacket", even the pre-referendum debate in the UK was framed "mutually reinforcing all-or-nothing terms". The referendum question on 23 June 2016, that is, "Should the United Kingdom remain a member of the European Union or leave the European Union?",[3] thus did not per se answer a number of other, perhaps almost equally important questions which surfaced after it was clear that the British electorate had voted to leave. The question whether the UK should—in the case of choosing to leave—nevertheless purport to remain a part of the single market is perhaps the most pertinent one.

The question that concerns us in this chapter, that is, what will be the (legal) position of citizens, affected by Brexit, of course, also remained unanswered on 23 June 2016 when the referendum ballots returned. What is worth noting, however, is that both official campaigns that supported the vote to leave seemed to have assumed that a decision to leave would not mean a change in the legal status of the affected EU and UK citizens, although their documents phrased this assumption quite inexpertly. "Vote Leave", the "cross-party" organization that attracted to its ranks a high number of ministers from David Cameron's cabinet, stated on its website that "EU law forbids the collective expulsion of British citizens living in the EU after we Vote Leave. Even the former legal adviser to EU's Council of Ministers has said that 'those with permanent residency in EU states could stay'" (Briefing: The EU immigration system is immoral and unfair 2016). "Leave.EU" was similarly confident of the rights of UK citizens in EU27 but at least also mentioned the EU citizens in the UK in the "Frequently Asked Questions" section of its website (FAQs 2016).[4]

However, the Brexit case will most likely serve as a potent illustration of a stark contrast between, on the one hand, direct democracy and on the other hand, representative democracy. The different "pledges" and "statements" made by campaign spearheads in the run up to a referendum become irrelevant once the decision of the people is left to be implemented by the government or parliament.[5] In comparison to the manifestos of the political parties competing for a mandate to lead the nation, their weight is infinitesimal. This is particularly so in the UK system, where the party manifesto has been accorded constitutional value through the Salisbury doctrine (MacLean 2011). In the tale of the Brexit, the vote for Leave swept the existing, pro-Remain cabinet away; the successor Prime Minister was chosen in an internal party election. Immediately after the referendum, it seemed that a general election had the potential to partly remedy the problem described. The expectation was that the political parties would lay down their "Brexit plans" in their manifestos, giving the electorate a further choice to decide on the details of the planned exit from the EU. A general election, however, only took place almost a year later—shortly before completing this manuscript. Notably, a number of parties included in their manifestos that the rights of citizens, affected by Brexit, should be guaranteed. But most interestingly, on the one hand no such guarantee was provided by the winning Conservative Party, whereas on the other hand, this was one of the guarantees of the manifesto of the Democratic Unionist Party (DUP) (Democratic Unionist Party 2017, 19). Of course, it is the DUP with which the Conservatives were planning, at the time this manuscript was completed, to govern jointly (Oppenheim 2017).

So, while in the months after the referendum, it seemed that the Conservative Party with its comfortable majority in the House of Commons would be more or less free to start tailoring a Brexit according to its political vision, the situation is at the moment significantly less predictable. This, we may note, is however entirely due to the unexpected outcome of the 2017 general election, and not, as many expected, due to the control over the Parliament over the Article 50 TEU notification process. The latter was won in the court battle that came to be known as the *Miller* case.[6] But it became clear that the Parliament will do little more but rubberstamp the decision of the Government to formally start the two-year negotiating period envisaged in Article 50 TFEU.[7]

11.3   The Prevalently Political Discussion on the Post-Brexit Position

It is a slight understatement that the political leaders in the UK were unprepared for the outcome of the referendum. In fact, the Remain-supporting Cameron government had chosen not to prepare contingency plans for Brexit before the referendum.[8] We may speculate that the key people in the Conservative Party, amidst the post-referendum hangover, realized that the exit-bound UK had found itself in an undesirable situation and with a tough negotiating partner on the other side of the table. On the day after the referendum, the presidents of all the main EU institutions had called on the UK to "leave as soon as possible" (Rankin et al. 2016). After the resignation of David Cameron, the new leader of the Conservative Party became former Home Secretary Theresa May, the only party leadership candidate who supported the Remain vote during the referendum campaign, but also the only candidate who refused to promise any unilateral guarantees to EU citizens resident in the UK during the party leadership contest (Peter Walker 2016b). She was nevertheless not alone in the assessment that the weak negotiating position of the UK should be improved by counting on the EU27 citizens resident in the UK. The head of the permanent representation of the UK to the EU, Sir Ivan Rogers, is said to have advised May that "the rights of EU citizens living in Britain [were] one of the 'few cards' she ha[d] to play in the Brexit negotiations". Accordingly, it would be unwise to give any guarantees a priori (Wright 2016).

This put the position of the affected citizens on the negotiating table, making them, as was then often mentioned, a "bargaining chip". To the present author it seems that it significantly framed the discussion on this issue from which legal arguments, such as the one made here, were by and large absent (with the notable exception of the ones recounted below). We should be cautious, however. It cannot be said that the UK Government has made it its official position that it will not give any a priori guarantees on the right to remain of the EU citizens. What can be said is that the Government has not given or promised any a priori guarantees to this day.[9]

In addition to that, the ministers of the government have, on occasions, sent signals that the position of the affected individuals will indeed be subject to negotiations between the UK and EU27. Perhaps most noticed was the statement made by Liam Fox, a Leave supporter who in the May cabinet was given one of the three key roles connected to the exiting process, that of the Secretary of International Trade.[10] Speaking at a fringe event of a Conservative Party conference, Fox said that the government would "like to be able to give a reassurance to EU nationals in the UK, but that depends on reciprocation by other countries". Acting differently than that "would be to hand over one of our main cards in the negotiations and doesn't necessarily make sense at this point" (Elgot 2016).

11.4   A "Bargaining Chip"

The present chapter does not wish to argue that the issue of the affected citizens would not—in the harsh reality of the complex EU27–UK relations post-referendum—represent a strong, to refer once again to the odious term, "bargaining chip". The instincts of Sir Ivan Rogers were probably right. The negotiating position of the UK probably is, or at least in June 2016 appeared weaker compared to the EU27. In a hypothetical situation where everything or almost everything is on the table in the Brexit negotiations (we will later show why this is not the case), the position of the affected citizens can indeed serve as a powerful element of the negotiating process.

It may, in principle, be used to the advantage of either the UK or the EU27; however it would—beyond the remarks made by the permanent representative—indeed seem that the UK Government understands it as primarily benefitting the UK in the negotiating process. And it may be right: the most obvious argument would be that there are significantly more EU citizens in the UK than there are UK citizens in EU27. However, in my view, this is additionally so as for the different members of EU27, the stakes are incredibly differently high when it comes to the question whether Brexit means that their citizens will lose the right to remain in the UK.

The stakes are differently high, to begin with, as there are very different numbers of citizens of the different Member States that are resident in the

UK. Of the five countries where most usual residents of the UK who do not hold UK nationality come from, in 2015, four were EU States: Poland (916,000 residents), Republic of Ireland (332,000), Romania (233,000) and Portugal (219,000) (Office of National Statistics 2016). Leaving aside Ireland, which we will not discuss as there is a particular historical and geographical context to its case, we can establish that the three largest countries of origin are all countries of the European Union's periphery (Kukovec 2015, 2017). Accordingly, an important part in the economic relationship between the UK and the top countries is also played by the remittances sent by EU27 citizens resident in the UK to their home countries. Poland, for example, exports US$13 billion to the UK and is estimated to receive more than US$1 billion yearly in remittances from the UK. In contrast, the three EU States among the top import origins of the UK are Germany, the Netherlands and France: countries at the very core of the economic and political centre of the EU (Observatory of Economic Complexity 2016). I am not trying to posit here that the richer, more economically powerful countries of the centre of the EU would not fight for the rights of their citizens in post-Brexit UK. However, what can be speculated is that the periphery countries with large numbers of citizens settled in the UK might be particularly interested in the status of their citizens and may prioritize their status over issues that might be more pertinent to the countries of the centre of the EU—the "passporting rights" for the financial institutions can serve as an example (Martin 2016).

While it was initially the UK Government that had managed to frame the issue of the position of the citizens as a matter for negotiations, this framing was accepted on the other side of the Channel as well. It has to be noted that May's post-referendum UK Government was prepared to exclude the issue of the guarantees for the affected citizens from the wider negotiations. Perhaps under the pressure of some of the domestic media and politicians, May offered to exclude the issue of the position of the affected citizens from the bulk of the Brexit negotiations and conclude an "early deal" with EU27 on this separate issue (Khan 2016). However, that offer was squarely rejected by the political leaders on the other side (Cowburn 2016). The stated reason for the rejection was the categorical refusal of the EU leaders to negotiate any of the Brexit issues before the formal beginning of the process of exiting the European Union (Penny 2016).

The negotiations between the UK and the EU27 started on the 19 June 2017 (Bendix 2017). In the run up to this date, neither of the sides has expressed the conviction that the position of the affected citizens is by and large a matter of law and of the human rights of the individual citizens and as such will not be negotiated with. As a result of the positions of both of the sides described in the preceding paragraph, the issue of the position of the affected citizens is thus currently negotiated together with the bulk of other Brexit issues (access to the single market, contributions to the EU budget, jurisdiction of the European Court of Justice—to name the most pertinent ones).

The initial reports on the negotiations of the status of the citizens, affected by Brexit, have expressed disappointment with the level of protection offered (O'Carroll 2017; Merrick 2017). The paper, published by the UK Government a week after the beginning of the negotiations, promised "settled status" to the EU27 citizens resident in the UK for five years and temporary status to the ones with a shorter residence history (HM Government 2017).

Thus, the initial phases of the negotiations show that in the neglect of international human rights obligations, the rights of the citizens affected by Brexit can slump to significantly lower levels than those guaranteed by Article 8 ECHR. While the level of rights protection may still improve in the course of negotiations, it has—generally speaking—not been recognized that the right of the citizens, affected by Brexit, to remain is to a large part determined by human rights law. In the continuation, some of the arguments along this line that had already been made will be recounted and an additional argument will be made supporting the claim for a legal, rights-based view of the position of the affected citizens.

11.5   Position of the Affected Citizens as a Matter of Law

Purporting to demonstrate how the position of the affected citizens is a legal question, it is logical to turn for arguments to the law of the European Convention on Human Rights. It is widely regarded as the most advanced regional system of human rights protection in the world on account of individual access to the European Court of Human Rights and wide acceptance of its judgments by the governments of the States Signatories, partly due to the power of the ECtHR to order the government to pay "just satisfaction" to the successful applicant (Art. 41 ECHR). Indeed, the first negative reactions to the mentioning of EU citizens in the UK as "bargaining chips" sought support in the case law of the ECtHR, pointing primarily to the Article 8 ECHR right to private and family life. Virginia Mantouvalou pointed out to the fact that specifically the right to private life is not limited to activities in one's own home, rather it has to be seen to an extent as extending to the "right to establish and develop relationships with other human beings" (Mantouvalou 2016).

In his analysis, Matthew White listed several ECtHR cases essentially stemming from applications of migrants from third countries, that is, individuals that were not able to rely on EU freedom of movement but rather were subject to "ordinary" immigration law when entering or settling down in the different European countries: *Gul v Switzerland* (23218/94), *Moustaquim v Belgium* (12313/86), *Berrehab v the Netherlands* (10730/84) (White 2016). And of course, there are principles established in this case law that do pose limits onto the States Parties of the ECHR's right to decide whether an alien can reside on its territory or not. We can, however, also see that the utility of the Article 8 rights for the migrants residing in a foreign country can be limited. *Gul* is perhaps the best example. The Court finds that a Turkish asylum seeker in Switzerland cannot demand family life with his Turkey-based family in Switzerland if they can have it in Turkey.

The setting of these cases is—in my view—much too binary. The contrast between Inside (i.e. the territory of the respondent state) and Outside (i.e. the country that the applicant is to be returned to) is too stark. The migrant applicant is too clearly recognizable as "the Other" even if this is not directly articulated in the Court's reasoning. Against the background of this stark contrast, the Court can effortlessly frame the legal issue before it as a conflict between—on the one hand—the right of a sovereign state to decide who can reside on its territory and, on the other hand, the limitations on this sovereign right imposed by international law (*Gul v Switzerland*, para. 38, *Berrehab v the Netherlands*, para. 28).

It seems to me that it makes a notable difference whether the interference with Article 8 rights is causally linked to, on the one hand, a subject of law crossing boundaries of territorial jurisdiction, or on the other hand, it is what Kostakopoulou and Tataryn (2017) called a "conditioning event" which—practically completely detached from the subject's action—transforms the subject into an object of events and developments. I am of the opinion that we should seek case law analogical to the potential future analysis of Article 8 rights of citizens affected by Brexit among the cases where it was a "conditioning event" that lied at the base of an interference with Article 8. Cases, where subjects—exaggerating only slightly—go to bed at night in one country and wake up the next morning in another one. These are not cases of migrants but of persons who did not have to travel a single mile to find themselves subjected, overnight, to a new legal system, a new political reality, a new territoriality.[11] Such cases—in the jurisprudence of the ECtHR—stem from the geopolitical transformations at the beginning of the last decade of the previous century: the disintegration of federal (or quasi-federal) systems of the Soviet Union and Yugoslavia.

11.6   The Usefulness of Case Studies from Disintegrated Federal Systems

Matthew White, in his analysis, for example, points to the case of *Slivenko v Latvia*, which definitely merits our attention. After the conditioning event, that is, the restoration of the independence of Latvia, there was a special regime for "ex-USSR citizens", which provided a legal status for mostly ethnic Russians that had settled in Latvia during the existence of the Union of Soviet Socialist Republics (USSR). However, the applicants were still ordered to leave the territory of Latvia as Latvia and Russia had concluded a treaty, according to which Russian military personnel that had also come to Latvian territory during the existence of the USSR, and their families, were to return to Russia. It had been submitted to the Court that even if the obligation for them to leave Latvia was an interference with their right to private life, this was justifiable invoking Latvia's legitimate concern for national security posed by the presence of foreign military personnel on its territory.

The importance of this case for our discussion lies in the fact that the Court recognized the importance of the "network of personal, social and economic relations that make up the private life of every human being" of a person who is in a foreign country and his human rights as protected by the ECHR. This led the Court to the conclusion that the interference with the Article 8 was not one "necessary in a democratic society" due to the fact that the applicants had developed "personal, social and economic ties" in Latvia (Para. 124).

Thanks to the submission by the Latvian government that the applicants were not proficient in the Latvian language, we also have a useful Court's position on the influence of language proficiency on the migrant's right to private life: "As regards the respondent Government's argument about the level of the applicants' proficiency in Latvian, the Court observes that, in so far as this is a relevant consideration, it has not been shown that the degree of the applicants' fluency in the language – although the precise level is in dispute – was insufficient for them to lead a normal everyday life in Latvia" (Para. 125).

For the first time, the Court recognized the "wider social relations that constitute the foreigners' private life" and consequently accorded "autonomous human rights protection" to long-term residents in a foreign country (Thym 2014, 115). Obviously, this already represents a strong legal argument for the protection of citizens affected by Brexit. UK citizens in the EU27 or EU27 citizens in the UK with jobs, networks of friends and acquaintances, social activities and so on in the country of their residence can rightly see *Slivenko* as a beacon of legal hope when refusing to be treated as bargaining chips.

There are, however, a couple of issues with the utility of *Slivenko* in showing exactly how strong the legal dimension of the issue of citizens affected by Brexit really is. Firstly, the fact that the applicants belonged to the military personnel of a foreign country means puts the judgment in *Slivenko* in a particular context that ought not to be neglected. This context led the Court to frame the discussion on the necessity of the interference with Article 8 right as a conflict between the interests of the individual and the interests of the community.

Second, since *Slivenko*, human rights protection for long-term residents has evolved into an important legal safeguard that was further developed through ECtHR case law but also led, for example, to the adoption of a special EU directive. However, as this safeguard now offers important and tangible protection to migrants in the States Parties to the ECHR, the Court has also limited its applicability. As was noticed by Daniel Thym (2014, 119), for example, when it comes to the line of cases that involve "illegal" migrants and their right to private life, even though a generous reading of private life that accommodated for shorter periods of residence would have been possible, the Court insists that the applicants relying on their right to private life have spent extensive periods of time in the relevant country. Again, with full awareness that this is a position taken in cases regarding people who did not comply with immigration law and so on, I find it a tangible risk that in a potential Brexit Art. 8 case, the quantitative criterion of the length of stay would come to play a central role.

For these reasons, I submit here that the human rights oriented argumentation on the position of the citizens affected by Brexit should inform itself by the outcome of another case, which shares with *Slivenko* an important fact: that it is casually linked to a "conditioning event"—a geopolitical transformation within a federal system.

11.7   The Case of the Erased: *Kurić and Others v Slovenia*

Similar to the USSR, the Socialist Federal Republic of Yugoslavia (SFRY) also began to disintegrate in the beginning of the 1990s. The six former constituent republics of SFRY are now all independent states.[12] In SFRY, the citizenship of the federation coexisted with the citizenship of the constituent republic. At least as defined by law, every Yugoslav citizen had a federal citizenship as well as a citizenship of his republic.[13] The latter was most commonly assigned following the principle of jus sanguinis and did not change when a citizen moved from one constituent republic from the other (*Kurić*, Judgment of third section, para. 23). This bears resemblance to the coexistence of the European Union citizenship and the Member State citizenship, especially as after a certain point in time, the citizenship acquisition and registries were in the hands of the constituent republics (Štiks 2010, 8). The difference, nevertheless, is that it was the federal citizenship that carried practical importance and many people were not aware that they also held the citizenship of the republic. However, citizens of SFRY were also registered as permanent residents in the constituent republic where they lived. Unlike the obscure legal status of the citizenship of the republic, permanent residence gave access to a number of public services: health, education and so on.

Slovenia was the first former constituent republic to declare independence in 1991. The newly created state needed to define its corpus of citizens and the decision was made that all citizens of the former constituent republic would automatically become citizens of the new Republic of Slovenia. All citizens of other constituent republics (i.e. simultaneously also citizens of the SFRY) who were permanent residents of Slovenia had an opportunity to apply for the citizenship of the new state and a vast number of this group of persons also acquired the new Slovenian citizenship (*Kurić*, Judgment of third section, paras. 33–37). The problem is that the persons who either did not apply, could not apply or whose applications were rejected not only failed to become citizens of the new state. On 26 February 1992, approximately 26,000 people in this position were also removed—or rather "erased"—from the registry of permanent residents (*Kurić*, Judgment of third section, paras. 38–45) This had devastating consequences as they many were forcibly removed from the country even though they had lived in Slovenia their whole life. Access to health care, housing, education, employment, social assistance and so on was denied to thousands. The erased residents reported visiting the authorities to try to sort out their status only to have their personal identity documents confiscated and destroyed before their eyes (*Kurić*, judgment of the Grand Chamber, para. 356. Zorn 2003, 104).

Six years later, in 1998, the Slovenian Constitutional Court declared that the erasure was contrary to the Constitution of the Republic of Slovenia. It violated the principle of the state governed by law (*pravna država*, Art. 2), to be precise, its subprinciple of the protection of trust in the law.[14] The Court ordered the legislature to repair the inconsistency of the legislation with the Constitution. This was the beginning of a long and arduous process in the course of which several attempts at remedying the situation were found inadequate by the Constitutional Court, and the rights of the erased residents became a bitter and conflicting political issue.[15] An application to the ECtHR was made in 2006, and on 26 June 2012, the Grand Chamber issued a judgment confirming that there was a violation of Article 8 and finding that Slovenia had not yet resolved the issue despite several legislative endeavours.

Already the judgment of the third section (para. 359) acknowledges, referring to *Slivenko*, that the erased residents, applicants in the case, had in Slovenia a "network of personal, social, cultural, linguistic and economic relations that make up the private life of every human being". Particularly relevant for our discussion, however, is the following passage from the judgment of the third section (para. 357, emphases added by SB):

> It is important to note that prior to 1991 the applicants **did not enter Slovenia as aliens but settled there as SFRY citizens** and registered their permanent residence in the same way as citizens of the then Socialist Republic of Slovenia […]. At the moment of the "erasure" on 26 February 1992, the applicants therefore had a **stronger residence status than long-term migrants**, whose status is protected in a number of Contracting States, and in comparison with aliens seeking to enter or remain in a state after only a short period of time.

The analogies have been underlined. European Union citizenship, as was remarked before, is not the same as SFRY citizenship once was: but these two statuses and their relevance in the life of an individual are definitely comparable. This, I believe, confirms the thesis set out above: as far as the right to private life under Art. 8 ECHR is concerned, there is an important difference between subjects who cross borders and settle in a country other than their own, on the one hand, and the "homo objectus" (Kostakopoulou and Tataryn 2017) who is redefined and reconstituted by the changing law in his or her status as a citizen, resident and human being with a private life, on the other hand.[16]

What is the origin of this difference? From a human point of view, there is little difference between an individual that enters a foreign country and within the next two decades or so creates a family, buys a home, develops a career and becomes an active member of his local community, on the one hand, and the individual who moves from one part of his country to another, creates the same network of social, personal and economic ties and then one day finds herself in a completely new situation due to, for example, disintegration of a federal system. The aggrieved individuals that we are comparing face practically the same difficulties: they may lose their job, friends and home (to say the least). It would seem to me that what strengthens the residence status and human rights position of the latter individual is linked precisely to the constitutional principle that was invoked in the above cited judgment on the erased residents' case by the Slovenian Constitutional Court: the principle of confidence/trust in law.

The principle of confidence in law as a subprinciple of a "state governed by law" is far from an exotic feature of the Slovenian constitution. Rather, it is a serious candidate for a place among the principles and values of common European constitutional heritage. In several systems, a similar idea will be considered an element of the protection of rule of law (or analogous concept such as *Rechtsstaat*).[17] In that sense, the choice of the words of the justices of the Estonian Supreme Court that prohibit the lawmaker from changing law in a way that is "perfidious towards the subjects of the law"[18] is particularly apposite as it resonates with the previously mentioned connection between the subjects of law and conditioning events: it is constitutional protection of trust in law that will prevent conditioning events from stripping subjectivity of the subjects of law. Not only that: the phrase seems to be particularly felicitous at a moment when perfidiousness towards the Brexit-affected subjects of law abounds among the politicians not only in Albion (Schmidt 1953), but in continental Europe as well.

11.8 Continued Relevance of the ECHR as a Precarious Premise

A reader that has been following the developments directly prior to and after the referendum might present the following objection to the premise of the discussion in the preceding paragraph. The premise is that both the UK as well as the EU27 States[19] will continue to be bound by the ECHR. The premise is not a dubious one as far as the EU27 States are concerned. I cannot recall any calls for withdrawal from the ECHR, and I believe it safe to say that on the Continent, such proposals, if there are any, are located on the deep political fringe. The UK is another story altogether. As Mantouvalou (2016) succinctly phrased it, "Theresa May is no friend to the ECHR". Three months before the Brexit referendum, the then Home Secretary May stated that the UK should withdraw from the ECHR regardless of the decision on EU Membership: "The ECHR can bind the hands of parliament, adds nothing to our prosperity, makes us less secure by preventing the deportation of dangerous foreign nationals – and does nothing to change the attitudes of governments like Russia's when it comes to human rights" (Asthana and Mason 2016). May scrapped this claim as part of her bid for the leadership of the Conservative Party, stating as reason that there was no majority in the House of Commons to support the withdrawal (Elgot and Mason 2016). Given that the reason is not May's change of heart, but rather lack of political backing for such a move, it should come as no surprise that at the time of drafts this text, in the last days of 2016, it was reported that May planned to campaign to withdraw from the ECHR in 2020 UK general election (Wagner 2016). In the manifesto released before the 2017 early election, however, the Conservatives promised that the UK would remain signatory to the ECHR (Conservative Party 2017, 37).

The relationship of the Tory Party with the ECHR has been an uncomfortable one more generally.[20] A 2014 document produced by the Party, *Protecting Human Rights in the UK*, promised that the Human Rights Act, that had been adopted by the Labour government in 1998, will be replaced by a "new British Bill of Rights and Responsibilities" (p. 5; see also Dimelow and Young 2015). The objective that this approach wanted to achieve, inter alia, was to prevent that the ECtHR would be "binding over the UK Supreme Court", that it would be able to "order a change in UK law", effectively rendering the Court "an advisory body only" (p. 5).

A Twitter comment by Human Rights Law Professor Fiona de Londras (2016) provided for a succinct explanation of Theresa May's once again intention to take the UK out of the European human rights protection system.[21] According to her, what is perceived as the fundamental problem with the ECHR by the proponents of the withdrawal is not the rights per se but rather judicial supervision by the ECtHR and the accountability to this Court for the adherence to the ECHR rights.

While at the time of finishing the manuscript, the withdrawal from the ECHR seems to be off the table for the moment, the fact that in the past two years, important political figures have seriously discussed withdrawal from the UK should suffice for us to recognize how precarious it might become in a crucial moment to rely on the ECHR as a source of legal guarantees. But in the continuation, we turn to the next challenge: how are we to understand the aversion of a sizeable part of the UK politics (as well as the current leader of the country) to international human rights documents with independent, supranational mechanisms of review and enforcement? The present chapter looks at this problem through the prism of political constitutionalism and presents a critique.

11.9   Citizens Affected by Brexit and Political Constitutionalism

Drawing a line in the sand between substantive (fundamental) rights on the one hand and the mechanism for their implementation, elaboration and enforcement on the other is an established theme—especially in British scholarship—of the dispute between legal and political constitutionalism. In Richard Bellamy's account (2011, p. 90), political constitutionalists will maintain that while people do have rights, there are also reasonable disagreements on the origin, substance, scope and so on of rights. Furthermore, rights cannot take an elevated position of "higher law" which would hierarchically outrank the outcomes of political decisions. Reasonable disagreements will be best solved by political, democratic decision making processes in the legislature. Courts are suboptimal fora for answering these questions. This is particularly so as judicial procedures are in no way capable of treating all members of the society equally: the plaintiff or claimant (e.g. in a procedure for review of legislation before the constitutional court) will be in a privileged position as far as submitting arguments and defending their own interests are concerned (Bellamy 2007, 12, 2011, 91–92).

It seems that the opposition to the ECHR among the British politicians, especially as it was captured in de Londras' comment in the previous section, would indeed fall within a broader rubric of political constitutionalism

(Elliot 2012). Especially if we take into consideration the plans for a new "British Bill of Rights" (and Responsibilities!). The idea behind the plans seems to be nothing against rights, but one needs to allow for a redefinition of their scope. Most important, however, is that a principal agreement on the necessity of recognizing, upholding and indeed codifying rights is severable from odious (i.e. for the proponents of these changes) ideas of "judicial supremacy".

While politicians-political constitutionalists and scholars-political constitutionalists may agree that parliament is the more adequate venue for the resolution of rights-based disputes, I believe that there is an important difference between them. The difference is in the reason why they find parliament to be more adequate. In Bellamy's account, the reason for opposition to judicial review is the arbitrariness of the judicial decision making stemming from the fact that members of the community are no longer equal. The judges possess no superior trait that would legitimize their imposition of their view (Bellamy 2007, 14):

> A key advantage of a democratic vote lies in its overcoming this arbitrary arrangement. Under majority rule each person counts for one and none for more than one. All citizens are treated equally in this respect – including judges and members of the currently incumbent government. The reason that the legislature favours certain peoples' views more than others is because more people have voted for a given party's representatives than for those of other parties. […] But whatever the supposed failings of democratic decision-making, this very mechanical aspect of democracy has a decided advantage in the context of disagreement. It allows those on the losing side to hold on to their integrity. They can feel their views have been treated with as much respect as those on the winning side, counting equally with theirs in the vote, and that the winners are not thereby 'right', so that they are 'wrong', but merely the current majority.

The reason why politicians advocate a political species of constitutionalism is, in my view, somewhat different. They try to prevent being bound by commitments. Instead, they prefer to have the broadest possible freedom to shape policies, uninhibited by legal bounds created at a previous point in time.[22] The idea is to be constantly prepared to check whether there is still consent among the members of the society for a certain policy. As soon as consent is absent, the policy can (and ought to) be scrapped.[23] Nations more inclined towards legal constitutionalism[24] have long made commitments and imposed bounds upon themselves by adopting a written constitution and judicial review of legislation. In those communities, the idea of making commitments can resolve the democratic dilemma of judicial review through an idea such as "commitmentarian freedom" (Rubenfeld 2001, 97). In my view, the tension between political constitutionalism and the idea of committing oneself only came to light in the UK with the supranational integration—the European Union and the Council of Europe.[25]

What I wish to posit here is that commitments, made not only by a nation to itself (e.g. enacting a written constitution), but rather commitments made between a group of sovereign nations, will often require some kind of a precommitment device which will ensure that all the parties keep faithful to the commitments made to each other (Elster 2000, 34; Peters 2008, 244; Ratner 2004, 81) To be more precise: treaties in international law can be and are concluded without designating an agent who will enforce them, with the states left with nothing to rely upon but classical methods of enforcement (reprisal, threat to the partner's reputation, etc.). However, treaties where States agree to relinquish large portions of their sovereign powers in order to develop high standards and efficient protection of human rights of the individuals in their territories have commonly also included mechanisms or bodies independent from the States. This was to assure the parties that when a decision on whether a State violated human rights or not was taken, this decision was not simply a subjective result of political alliances, animosities or amities between the States. An argument based in political constitutionalism, which in the name of superiority of the legislature over the courts to define the scope and nature of rights serves to reject, domestically, judicial review of conformity of legislation with the constitution, therefore loses much of its power when deployed against enforcement of human rights treaties in a supranational context.

This is particularly pertinent for the discussion in the present chapter given that the issues here are the rights of foreign citizens. It is not only the multilateral context that will increase the need for an independent agent in control of the commitment that the States had made to each other.

The reason is also the exceptional inadequacy of parliament to represent the citizens affected. In Bellamy's account of political accountability, "necessity for legal constitutional protection might appear undeniable" in the case of certain groups which in US constitutional doctrine might be referred to as "discrete, insular minorities" (his example are Roma and asylum seekers) with "little or no ability to engage in politics" (Bellamy 2007, 21–22). Bellamy adds another condition: legal constitutional protection will only be needed "if it is assumed that such minorities are at risk from widespread prejudice from a majority of the population and their elected representatives, and the judiciary are free from such prejudices".

It should firstly be pointed out to the fact that the franchise for the Brexit referendum, which followed the rules for the electoral franchise in UK general elections, completely excluded both UK citizens residing in EU27 as well as citizens of the majority of the EU27 residing in the UK (citizens of Malta, Cyprus and Ireland (residents in the UK) have the right to vote in the UK general election). Both exclusions have been characterized as anomalies as the people most likely to be affected by the result of the referendum were denied a vote (Ziegler 2015). While, of course, neither UK citizens in EU27 nor EU23 citizens in the UK are what might be described as an insular/discrete minority—on the contrary, these are highly diverse groups—we should nevertheless seriously consider the possibility that there is a strong necessity for legal constitutional protection of their position and rights. They may not be a target of widespread prejudice as Roma and asylum seekers frequently are (although see Dearden 2016). It is nevertheless reasonable to expect that after a historic popular vote that set the country on a diametrically opposite strategic course, with a myriad of details of a 40 years of long relationship in need of redefinition and renegotiation, the well-being of the disenfranchised non-voters whose interests are directly contrary to the direction the country is taking will be almost entirely disregarded. A persuasive case for legal constitutional protection, for honouring the commitments to fundamental rights and dignity of the individual, and for continuous respect for ECHR and ECtHR case law, can undoubtedly be made.

11.10   Conclusion

More often than not, the democratic message from the electorate, received by way of referendum, is an impoverished one. It may provide an answer to a general question and leave a host of questions, connected to the subject matter of the referendum, unanswered. It does not come as a surprise that the politicians in charge of "implementing" the referendum decision may feel strongly legitimized by the referendum, including as far as answering the other, connected questions is concerned. In the case of the Brexit referendum, this led to the question on the position of the citizens affected by Brexit being framed by and large as a matter for negotiations and a decision to be made by the politicians. The citizens affected by Brexit found themselves in the detestable position of "bargaining chips". Arguments were presented in this chapter why this framing is wrong and there is a strong legal dimension to the issue that should not be neglected.

Attempts to justify the withdrawal of the UK (or any other State, for that matter) with the doctrine of political constitutionalism should be squarely rejected. The present author is certain that if such endeavours will be undertaken, an extensive debate will soon ensue. Embarking on a detailed discussion of the issue at this point would lie beyond the scope of the present chapter. But the arguments have been sketched. And in an era, where searching for different species of loud rhetoric with arguable potential to help renounce international obligations seems to be very much in fashion, they might just come in handy.

Notes

1. Refers both to the 27 Member States of the European Union (all but the UK) but it on occasions overlaps with the institutions of the European Union.
2. See the controversial decision of the Slovenian Constitutional Court Case No. U-I-12/97 of 8 October 1998 (Official Gazette no. 82/98) that established which of the three concurrent proposals for an electoral reform won the national referendum (English translation is available at http://odlocitve.us-rs.si/documents/aa/0c/u-i-12-97-english2.pdf).

3. The possible responses were "Remain a member of the European Union" and "Leave the European Union".
4. The text on the website reads: "13. What will happen to British citizens working in the EU, and EU citizens working in the UK? The EU would be obliged to grant permanent settlement rights to Britons living in Ireland and mainland Europe, and the UK would do the same".
5. The pledges may just as well be disowned by the campaigners themselves. Perhaps the most notorious of such "quickly forgotten" promises made by the Leave campaigners was printed on the side of a red campaign bus and read: "We send the EU 350 million a week – let's fund our NHS instead" (Bulman 2016).
6. *R (Miller) v Secretary of State* for Exiting the European Union [2016] EWHC 2768.
7. European Union (Notification of Withdrawal) Act 2017, Ch. 9. Amendments to the Act were proposed introducing guarantees for citizens affected by Brexit, but all were rejected by the Commons majority. The veto of the House of Lords came with a signal that the Commons should include the guarantees in the Act—but to no avail (Asthana in O'Caroll 2017).
8. A fact considered "regrettable" by the Foreign Affairs Committee of the House of Commons (2016). According to media reports mid-November 2016, based on a leaked memo, the Government had at that point still not had any defined plans on how to implement the exit from the UK (Singh 2016).
9. In contrast, the Scottish government that does not possess the powers to guarantee the rights to EU citizens in Scotland nevertheless made clear its intentions in a letter sent to all EU citizens resident in Scotland that stated: "The immediate status of EU nationals living in Scotland has not changed and you retain all the same rights to live and to work here. I believe those rights for the longer term should be guaranteed immediately and have written to the Prime Minister and all of the candidates to succeed him, calling for all EU citizens living here to be given an assurance that their residency will be unaffected" (First Minister of Scotland 2016).
10. The other two key positions, the Foreign Secretary and the newly created post of Secretary of State for Exiting the European Union, were given to two important Remain campaigners: Boris Johnson and David Davis (respectively) (Hefer 2016).
11. "Territoriality" in the sense understood by Preuss (2010).

12. Kosovo also declared independence and is effectively the seventh state to appear on the territory of former SFRY, however, has only been partly recognized.
13. I write "at least by law" as there are also cases where apparently, maladministration had caused certain individuals with federal citizenship of the SFRY to be without the citizenship of any of the republics. See the facts pertaining to Mr Velimir Dabetić (*Kurić*, Judgment of third section, paras. 119 ff).
14. The Constitutional Court (Judgment in case U-I-284/94) found that "[t]he principle of protection of confidence in the law guarantees an individual, that the state shall not impair his/her legal status without a justified reason. The citizens of other countries, who had not decided to apply for Slovene citizenship, where quite justified not to expect to have the same status as foreigners, who had just arrived to the Republic of Slovenia and they had no reason to expect to lose their permanent residence without due notice". Unofficial English translation which is cited here is available from http://www.refworld.org/docid/3ae6b74a10.html [accessed 16 January 2017].
15. Recounted in *Kurić*, Judgment of third section, paras. 50–69.
16. For a discussion of legal subjects as constituted and defined by law in the context of European Union Law, see Bardutzky and Fahey (2017).
17. For a discussion on the German concept of *Vertrauensschutz*, see Grimm et al. (2017), Section 2.1.3.
18. The Constitutional Review Chamber of the Supreme Court of Estonia held that the rule of law and the principle of protection of legitimate expectations also meant that "[e]veryone has a right to conduct his or her activities in the reasonable expectation that applicable Acts will remain in force. Everyone must be able to enjoy the rights and freedoms granted to him or her by law at least within the period established by the law. Modifications to the law must not be perfidious towards the subjects of the law". Judgment 16 December 2013, 3-4-1-27-13, para. 61., cited in Ernits et al. (2017), Section 2.1.3.
19. All Member States of the EU are Parties to the ECHR. The EU is not itself a party to the ECHR (see Opinion 2/13 of the Court (Full Court) of 18 December 2014, ECLI:EU:C:2014:2454). At the same time, according to the TEU, "fundamental rights, as guaranteed by the European Convention for the Protection of Human Rights and Fundamental Freedoms and as they result from the constitutional traditions common to the Member States, shall constitute general principles of the Union's law" (Art. 6/III).

20. At the time when this manuscript was completed, the Conservatives had just recently lost the majority in the Commons and were negotiating support for their government with the Democratic Unionist Party (from Northern Ireland). It is unclear whether the agreement between the parties will affect the UK's relationship with the ECHR.

21. I have not found any indication as to whether the Tories' plans (or wishes) also included withdrawal from the 1949 Treaty of London that established the Council of Europe. Considering Theresa May's quote, the answer probably depends on whether the Council of Europe will be deemed to contribute to UK's prosperity and whether it does enough to change the attitude of the Russian government towards human rights.

22. Indeed, it is considered an element of the doctrine of parliamentary sovereignty that no parliament can bind its successors.

23. In my observation, this way of thinking is relatively widespread in the British society, beyond the political circles or the ranks of the Conservative opponents to the European Union and the ECHR. Anecdotally, compare the recently articulated opinion of "radical social democrat" and journalist Paul Mason (2017) that Brexit could still be prevented provided there is a little tweak to freedom of movement. The UK should join the European Economic Area (EEA) and rely on the flexibility provided by Art. 112 of the EEA Treaty which "allows us to suspend freedom of movement, for an unspecified period and unilaterally, due to serious economic, societal or environmental difficulties. Well, we have a serious societal difficulty: we have lost consent for high inward migration, and we need to regain it". Imagine any bilateral contract—an apartment lease, if you will—where the parties agree to include a similar safeguard measure that will essentially allow either party to get out the contract if they come to face serious difficulties. What a waste of ink and paper is it even to draft such a contract if the parties know that they will be able to invoke the safeguard measure by saying: "There's simply no consent between my spouse and me anymore on letting you stay in our property".

24. Best examples are the nations of Central, Eastern and Southern Europe, especially those with painful experiences of totalitarian regimes in the twentieth century (Albi 2017).

25. Compare *Thoburn v Sunderland City Council*, [2002] EWHC 195. A concept of "constitutional statutes" which cannot be repealed implicitly, was introduced to draw a symbolic line between the decisions that the Parliament can change at any moment and those where it honours prior

commitments. It is fair to note that when listing examples of constitutional statutes, Laws LJ included other pieces of legislation that were not connected to the UK's participation in supranational integration (such as the 1707 Act of Union).

List of References

Albi, A. 2017. Comparative Report. In *National Constitutions in European and Global Governance*, ed. A. Albi and S. Bardutzky. The Hague: TCM Asser Press (forthcoming).

Asthana, A., and R. Mason. 2016. UK Must Leave European Convention on Human Rights, Says Theresa May. *Guardian*, April 25. Available at: https://www.theguardian.com/politics/2016/apr/25/uk-must-leave-european-convention-on-human-rights-theresa-may-eu-referendum.

Asthana, A. in L.O'Carroll. 2017. Lords Urge Tories to Back Brexit Bill Amendment on EU Citizens. *Guardian*, May 2. Available at: https://www.theguardian.com/politics/2017/mar/01/lords-defeat-government-over-rights-of-eu-citizens-in-uk-brexit-bill.

Bardutzky, S., and E. Fahey. 2017. Subjects and Objects of EU Law: Exploring a Research Platform. In *Framing the Subjects and Objects of Contemporary EU Law*, ed. S. Bardutzky and E. Fahey. Cheltenham: Edward Elgar.

Bellamy, R. 2007. *Political Constitutionalism*, School of Public Policy Working Paper Series 26.

———. 2011. Political Constitutionalism and the Human Rights Act. *International Journal of Constitutional Law* 9 (1): 86–111.

Bendix, A. 2017. Brexit Negotiations Begin. *The Atlantic*, June 19. Available at: https://www.theatlantic.com/news/archive/2017/06/brexit-negotiations-begin/530901/.

Briefing: The EU Immigration System Is Immoral and Unfair. 2016. Available at: http://www.voteleavetakecontrol.org/briefing_immigration.html.

Bulman, M. 2016. Brexit: 'Vote Leave Camp Abandon £350m-a-Week NHS Vow in Change Britain Plans'. *Independent*, September 11. Available at: http://www.independent.co.uk/news/uk/home-news/brexit-nhs-350m-a-week-eu-change-britain-gisela-stuart-referendum-bus-a7236706.html.

Conservative Party. 2017. *Forward, Together: Our Plan for a Stronger Britain and a Prosperous Future: The Conservative and Unionist Party Manifesto 2017*. Available at: https://www.conservatives.com/manifesto.

Cowburn, A. 2016. Brexit: Theresa May's Call for Deal on EU Migrant Rights 'Blocked by Angela Merkel'. *Independent*, November 29. Available at: http://www.independent.co.uk/news/uk/politics/brexit-theresa-may-angela-merkel-eu-migrants-deal-a7445261.html.

de Londras, F. 2016. *May's Fundamental Prob w the ECHR Is Not the Rights Per se But Judicial Supervision in Strasbourg. It Is Accountability that Troubles Her* [Twitter], December 29. Available from: https://twitter.com/fdelond/.

Dearden, L. 2016. Damning Report Condemns Rising 'Racist Violence and Hate Speech' by Politicians and Press in post-Brexit UK. *Independent*, October 4. Available at: http://www.independent.co.uk/news/uk/home-news/brexit-david-cameron-nigel-farage-council-of-europe-report-racist-violence-intolerance-hate-speech-a7345166.html.

Democratic Unionist Party. 2017. *Standing Strong for Northern Ireland: The DUP Manifesto for the 2017 Westminster Election*. Available at: http://dev.mydup.com/images/uploads/publications/DUP_Wminster_Manifesto_2017_v5.pdf.

Dimelow, S., and A.L. Young. 2015. *'Common Sense' or Confusion? The Human Rights Act and the Conservative Party*. London: Constitution Society.

Elgot, J. 2016. Liam Fox: EU Nationals in UK One of 'Main Cards' in Brexit Negotiations. *Guardian*, October 4. Available at: https://www.theguardian.com/politics/2016/oct/04/liam-fox-refuses-to-guarantee-right-of-eu-citizens-to-remain-in-uk.

Elgot, J., and R. Mason. 2016. Theresa May Launches Tory Leadership Bid with Pledge to Unite Country. *Guardian*, June 30. Available at: https://www.theguardian.com/politics/2016/jun/30/theresa-may-launches-tory-leadership-bid-with-pledge-to-unite-country.

Elliot, M. 2012. Legal Constitutionalism, Political Constitutionalism and Prisoners' Right to Vote. *Public Law for Everyone*, December 5. Available at: https://publiclawforeveryone.com/2012/12/05/legal-constitutionalism-political-constitutionalism-and-prisoners-right-to-vote/.

Elster, J. 2000. *Ulysses Unbound: Studies in Rationality, Precommitment, and Constraints*. Cambridge: Cambridge University Press.

Ernits, M., C. Carri Ginter, S. Laos, M. Allikmets, P.K. Tupay, R. Värk, and A. Laurand. 2017. The Constitution of Estonia: The Unexpected Challenges of Unlimited Primacy of EU Law. In *National Constitutions in European and Global Governance*, ed. A. Albi and S. Bardutzky. The Hague: TCM Asser Press (forthcoming).

First Minister of Scotland. 2016. *Letter to European Union Citizens Living in Scotland of 5th July 2016*. Available at: http://www.gov.scot/Resource/0050/00502733.pdf.

Grimm, D., T. Reinbacher, and M. Wendel. 2017. European Constitutionalism and the German Basic Law. In *National Constitutions in European and Global Governance*, ed. A. Albi and S. Bardutzky. The Hague: TCM Asser Press (forthcoming).

Hefer, S. 2016. Meet the Three Brexiteers: The Men Who Could Change How We Exit the EU. *The New Statesman*, September 13. Available at: http://www.newstatesman.com/politics/uk/2016/09/meet-three-brexiteers-men-who-could-change-how-we-exit-eu.

Hillion, C. 2016. Leaving the European Union, the Union Way: A Legal Analysis of Article 50 TEU. *European Policy Analysis* 2016:8epa. Available at: http://www.sieps.se/sites/default/files/Leaving%20the%20European%20Union,%20the%20Union%20way%20(2016-8epa).pdf.

HM Government. 2017. *The United Kingdom's Exit from the European Union: Safeguarding the Position of EU Citizens Living in the UK and UK Nationals Living in the EU: Policy Paper*. Available at: https://www.gov.uk/government/publications/safeguarding-the-position-of-eu-citizens-in-the-uk-and-uk-nationals-in-the-eu/the-united-kingdoms-exit-from-the-european-union-safeguarding-the-position-of-eu-citizens-living-in-the-uk-and-uk-nationals-living-in-the-eu.

House of Commons, Foreign Affairs Committee. 2016. *Equipping the Government for Brexit, Second Report of Session 2016–17*. Available at: http://www.publications.parliament.uk/pa/cm201617/cmselect/cmfaff/431/431.pdf.

Ian MacLean, I. 2011. The Salisbury Convention that Avoided Complete Lords Reforms for the Last Century Is Dead, but Achieving Any Mandate for Change that Peers Must Accept Remains Very Difficult. *LSE Politics and Policy*, July 4. Available at: http://blogs.lse.ac.uk/politicsandpolicy/salisbury-lords-reform-history/.

Khan, M. 2016. Theresa May Pushes for Citizenship Guarantees in Early Brexit Talks. *Financial Times*, November 30. Available at: https://www.ft.com/content/afee21fb-4365-338c-a56b-8e4a44c4a56d.

Kis, J. 2009. Constitutional Precommitment Revisited. *Journal of Social Philosophy* 40 (4): 570–594.

Kostakopoulou, D., and A. Tataryn. 2017. Homo Objectus, Homo Subjectus and Brexit. In *Framing the Subjects and Objects of Contemporary EU Law*, ed. S. Bardutzky and E. Fahey. Cheltenham: Edward Elgar.

Kukovec, D. 2015. Law and the Periphery. *European Law Review* 21 (3): 406–428.

———. 2017. Subject-Object Dialectics and Social Change. In *Framing the Subjects and Objects of Contemporary EU Law*, ed. S. Bardutzky and E. Fahey. Cheltenham: Edward Elgar.

Leave.EU. 2016. *Faqs*. Available at: http://leave.eu/en/faqs.

Mantouvalou, V. 2016. EU Citizens as Bargaining Chips. *UK Constitutional Law Blog*, July 14. Available at: https://ukconstitutionallaw.org/2016/07/14/virginia-mantouvalou-eu-citizens-as-bargaining-chips/.

Martin, W. 2016. 'Never Waste a Good Crisis'—Paris and Frankfurt Are Fighting to Steal London's Banking Crown Post-Brexit. *UK Business Insider*, October 19. Available at: http://uk.businessinsider.com/brexit-london-financial-passporting-euro-clearing-banking-frankfurt-paris-2016-10.

Mason, P. 2017. We Can Escape Brexit Doom with One Small Tweak to Free Movement. *Guardian*, January 16. Available at: https://www.theguardian.com/commentisfree/2017/jan/16/we-can-escape-brexit-doom-with-one-small-tweak-to-free-movement.

Merrick, R. 2017. Brexit: Donald Tusk Says Theresa May's Offer to EU Citizens Will Make Their Situation 'Worse'. *Independent*, June 23. Available at: http://www.independent.co.uk/news/uk/politics/brexit-latest-donald-tusk-theresa-may-citizens-offer-below-expectations-eu-european-council-brussels-a7804751.html.

O'Carroll, L. 2017. EU Citizens 'Bitterly Disappointed' with post-Brexit Rights Offer. *Guardian*, June 26. Available at: https://www.theguardian.com/politics/2017/jun/26/eu-citizens-bitterly-disappointed-with-post-brexit-rights-offer.

Observatory of Economic Complexity. 2016. *United Kingdom*. Available at: http://atlas.media.mit.edu/en/profile/country/gbr/.

Office of National Statistics. 2016. *Statistical Bulletin: Population of the UK by Country of Birth and Nationality: 2015*. Available at: https://www.ons.gov.uk/peoplepopulationandcommunity/populationandmigration/internationalmigration/bulletins/ukpopulationbycountryofbirthandnationality/august2016#poland-is-the-most-common-non-uk-country-of-birth-and-polish-is-the-most-common-non-british-nationality.

Oppenheim, M. 2017. Election Results: DUP Says It Will Form Government with Theresa May with No Need for Formal Coalition. *Independent*, July 9. Available at: http://www.independent.co.uk/news/uk/politics/dup-conservatives-election-results-hung-parliament-theresa-may-coalition-deal-a7781281.html.

Penny, T. 2016. U.K. Lawmakers Demand pre-Brexit Deal on EU Resident Rights. *Bloomberg*, November 27. Available at: https://www.bloomberg.com/news/articles/2016-11-27/u-k-lawmakers-demand-pre-brexit-deal-with-eu-on-resident-rights/.

Peters, A. 2008. Precommitment Theory Applied to International Law: Between Sovereignty and Triviality. *University of Illinois Law Review* 1: 239.

Preuss, U.K. 2010. Disconnecting Constitutions from Statehood: Is Global Constitutionalism a Viable Concept? In *Twilight of Constitutionalism*, ed. P. Dobner and M. Loughlin. Oxford: Oxford University Press.

Rankin, J., J. Henley, P. Oltermann, and H. Smith. 2016. EU Leaders Call for UK to Leave as Soon as Possible. *Guardian*, June 24. Available at: https://www.theguardian.com/politics/2016/jun/24/europe-plunged-crisis-britain-votes-leave-eu-european-union.

Ratner, S.R. 2004. Overcoming Temptations to Violate Human Dignity in Times of Crisis. *Theoretical Inquiries in Law* 5 (1): 81–110.

Rubenfeld, J. 2001. *Time and Government: A Theory of Constitutional Self-Government*. New Haven: Yale University Press.

Schmidt, H.D. 1953. The Idea and Slogan of "Perfidious Albion". *Journal of the History of Ideas* 14 (4): 604–616.

Singh, A.R.J. 2016. Theresa May Still Has No Plan for Brexit, Leaked Document Reveals. *Independent*, November 15. Available at: http://www.independent.co.uk/news/uk/politics/brexit-theresa-may-leaked-document-reveals-still-no-plan-article-50-a7417931.html.

Štiks, I. 2010. *A Laboratory of Citizenship: Shifting Conceptions of Citizenship in Yugoslavia and Its Successor States*, CITSEE Working Paper Series 2010/02. Available at: http://www.citsee.ed.ac.uk/__data/assets/pdf_file/0009/108828/179_alaboratoryofcitizenshipshiftingconceptionsofcitizenshipinyugoslaviaanditssucces.pdf.

Thym, D. 2014. Residence as De Facto Citizenship? Protection of Long-Term Residence Under Article 8 ECHR. In *Human Rights and Immigration*, ed. Ruth Rubio-Marin. Oxford: Oxford University Press.

Wagner, A. 2016. Theresa May Plans UK Withdrawal from European Convention on Human Rights—Report. *Human Rights Views, News and Info*, December 28. Available at: http://rightsinfo.org/theresa-may-plans-uk-withdrawal-human-rights-convention-reports/.

Walker, N. 2016a. The Brexit Vote: The Wrong Question for Britain and Europe. *Verfassungs Blog*, June 16. Available at: http://verfassungsblog.de/walker-brexit-referendum/.

Walker, P. 2016b. Government Refuses to Guarantee EU Citizens Living in UK Can Stay. *Guardian*, July 4. Available at: https://www.theguardian.com/politics/2016/jul/04/government-refuses-guarantee-eu-citizens-living-in-uk-can-stay.

White, M. 2016. Bargaining Chips No More: The Status of EU and UK Citizens After Brexit. *EU Law Analysis*, December 11. Available at: http://eulawanalysis. blogspot.co.uk/2016/12/bargaining-chips-no-more-status-of-eu.html.

Wright, O. 2016. May Was Warned Against Migrant Guarantees. *The Times*, August 20. Available at: http://www.thetimes.co.uk/article/may-was-warned-against-migrant-guarantees-kskf7p67w.

Ziegler, R. 2015. The 'Brexit' Referendum: We Need to Talk About the (General Election) Franchise. *UK Constitutional Law Blog*, October 7. Available at: https://ukconstitutionallaw.org/2015/10/07/ruvi-ziegler-the-brexit-referendum-we-need-to-talk-about-the-general-election-franchise/.

Zorn, J. 2003. The Politics of Exclusion During the Formation of the Slovenian State. In *Erased: Organized Innocence and the Politics of Exclusion*, ed. J. Dedić, V. Jalušič, and J. Zorn, 93–151. Ljubljana: Mirovni inštitut.

12

Post-Brexit Models and Migration Policies: Possible Citizenship and Welfare Implications for EU Nationals in the UK

Ioanna Ntampoudi

12.1 Introduction

Britain's historical relationship with Europe has not always been easy, while the country has been described as a traditionally Eurosceptic nation on more than one occasions (Ash 2001; George 2000; Gifford 2014). After two unsuccessful British applications to join the then called European Economic Community (EEC) in 1961 and 1967, Britain was finally admitted in 1973 under the rule of the Conservative PM Edward Heath (Gifford 2014). Soon after, the first British referendum on EEC membership was held on 5 June 1975, and the British people voted to stay in by 67–33% (Gifford 2014). Forty-one years later, the decision to remain in the now called European Union (EU) is reversed with a second membership referendum on 23 June 2016, whereby a small majority of 51.9% of British voters chose to depart from the union (Menon and Fowler 2016). This time around, the initiative of Conservative PM David Cameron found Europe in some of its most troubling times with the Greek and Euro economic crisis still raging on after several years, a refugee

I. Ntampoudi (✉)
Aston University, Birmingham, UK

© The Author(s) 2017
N. da Costa Cabral et al. (eds.), *After Brexit*,
https://doi.org/10.1007/978-3-319-66670-9_12

245

crisis coming in forcefully from the Middle East, and terrorist attacks in European cities crippling the public sense of security (Laffan 2016).

The main motivations behind the Leave vote were concerns about national and popular sovereignty, the state of the economy, and immigration (Hobolt 2016; Menon and Fowler 2016). Immigration, especially EU immigration, was a key factor in the referendum politics, with Leave supporters asking for the significant reduction of the numbers of EU migrants coming into the UK (Goodwin 2016a; Portes 2016b). Political rhetoric and public perceptions focused on negative representations of not only excessive quantities of immigrants but also scarcity of 'jobs for the British' and lowering of salaries due to over-employment of foreigners, the vexing issue of 'benefit tourism', and a national economy in a 'state of emergency' (Moagar-Poladian et al. 2015; Roos 2016).

Regardless of statistical evidence suggesting that immigration does not actually hurt the British economy, immigrants are more economically active and receive fewer social benefits than British citizens, therefore make greater contributions to public funds rather than subtractions (Roos 2016; Thielemann and Schade 2016), the Leave campaign was successful in capitalising on preoccupations over immigration and turning them into an important political asset towards achieving an electoral victory (Menon and Fowler 2016). Since nothing ever occurs in a vacuum, all these dynamics necessarily took place in the wider context of increasing populism, nationalism, xenophobia, and Euroscepticism around Europe (Hobolt 2016).

There are numerous consequences for multiple political actors that are intimately related to Brexit, such as governments, institutions, parties, politicians, and citizens. The British government, for instance, needs to artfully navigate the politics of delivering a satisfying and fair Brexit outcome (Doherty 2016; Thielemann and Schade 2016). On the one hand, significant changes to the British immigration system will need to be implemented if the demands of Leave supporters are to be satisfied. This can only mean that one of the fundamental principles and practices of the EU, namely that of free movement of persons, will need to be partially or even fully abandoned. On the other side, the aspirations of Remain supporters, British citizens living in the EU, and EU citizens living in the UK will also need to be taken seriously into account and fairly addressed (Portes 2016a). The EU, on its side, will have to coordinate collective decisions about Brexit between its 27 member-states and its various institutions, while trying to avoid the risk of new referenda on EU membership and other countries following the example of Britain.

Although, as exemplified above, multiple actors will be affected by Brexit, the present chapter shall focus on the ways EU nationals living, or wishing to live, in the UK may be affected in the future by the forthcoming changes in British immigration policies. As will become apparent during the discussion, the category 'EU nationals in (post-)Brexit Britain' does not comprise a homogenous mass of individuals, but instead presents us with variable socioeconomic subcategories. As such, attempts will be made to refer to different kinds of EU migrants in the UK. There will be references to the possibly changing circumstances of British nationals living in the EU, because their political predicament is as important as that of the EU nationals in Britain and changes to these two groups will depend on reciprocal agreements between Britain and the EU. However, for the purposes of this chapter, the focus will remain on EU migrants in Britain to address recent changes that are peculiar to the British immigration system. In the event of a clean-cut full Brexit, resulting in EU and British citizens on either side becoming third country nationals, peculiarities would need to be addressed in 27 EU member-states, which is not within the scope of this chapter.

The first part of this chapter concentrates on three important notes: (a) uncertainty as a distinct consequence in itself, (b) the EU principle and practice of free movement, and (c) residence rights and permanent residence applications. The first note argues that although several commentators refer to the uncertainty that Brexit breeds, we need to look at uncertainty as a distinct consequence in itself with multiple implications for individuals. The second note provides a reflective commentary on the EU principle of free movement and its political desirability, as well as the ways it historically helped to empirically substantiate the vague concept of European citizenship. The third note analyses pre-existing or recent immigration policy, specifically pertaining to procedures and requirements for permanent residence applications.

In the second part, this chapter focuses on the EU's external relations with non-EU countries and various existing models of economic and political engagement. These relations are assessed with reference to their implications for a number of intertwined issues, such as trade and access to the Single Market or the Customs Union, EU budget contributions, EU law, and, most importantly for this chapter's purposes, free movement of persons. The models are allocated within two possible scenarios of Britain's negotiation with the EU, namely those of a 'soft' or a 'hard' Brexit. Within a soft Brexit possibility, the models of Norway, Iceland, and Lichtenstein, as well as Switzerland, are discussed. In the category of hard Brexit, the cases of Ukraine, Georgia, and Moldova are discussed, along with Turkey, Canada, and the World Trade Association options. The models are also critically analysed with reference to their plausibility, based on the ways they accommodate the interests and objectives of the two negotiating parties.

12.2   Uncertainty Is the Only Certainty

Many commentators mention that Brexit brings with it great uncertainty for the future of immigration policy and EU citizens in the UK (Doherty 2016; Vargas-Silva 2016). In this respect, multiple questions arise regarding the nature of change: what kind of new policies will be decided? How much will they affect immigrants? Will different immigrants be affected equally or variably? Which groups will be affected the most? Although there can be vast speculations on these questions, they remain to be decidedly defined by the outcome of the negotiations. Furthermore, there is an important temporal dimension to Brexit's uncertainty: When will changes to immigration policy be implemented? Will they be enforced immediately or will there be transitional arrangements for gradual change? Will the immigration issue be settled early in the negotiations or later on? At the moment, EU law prescribes that a country wishing to withdraw from the EU needs to formally inform of its intentions by triggering Article 50, after which two years are provided for the completion of the withdrawal arrangements. Will two years offer adequate time for such purposes or will negotiations take longer, if EU member-states agree to do so? Finally, there is always the possibility of intervening factors with unforeseen and unpredictable consequences.

Another area of ambiguity resides with legal voids and legal uncertainty under British, EU and international law, while the lack of historical precedent of a country withdrawing from the EU does not offer any guarantees (Emerson 2016; Hobolt 2016). At the absence of these, all appears to rely on the political will of the negotiators (Doherty 2016). However, even in this respect, declarations by both British and EU officials remain vague, since no negotiating party would desire to outline all its intentionalities before or too early in the formal negotiations. At the moment of writing this chapter, the closest we have come to clarifying Brexit has been the recent PM May's speech on 17 January 2017, whereby she outlined several of Britain's priorities (GOV.UK 2017a). Regarding safeguarding the rights of both EU and British nationals living on either side of the English Channel and North Sea, PM May stated that the objective was to 'control immigration', clarifying that it is impossible to do so 'when there is free movement to Britain from Europe' (GOV.UK 2017a). Furthermore, the PM stated that the rights of both EU and British expats could be 'guarantee[d]… as early as we can…' so that people are given 'the certainty they want straight away', because 'this is the right and fair thing to do' (GOV.UK 2017a). Although the British PM's words exhibit good will and cooperative spirit, as most experienced negotiators would assert, it is the process and outcome of a challenging negotiation that ultimately matter, not early announcements.

As such, a large space for uncertainty still remains. However, with the Brexit negotiations initiated at the end of March 2017 to be processed and concluded by 2019 and delayed or obstructed by various national elections, including the British ones in June 2017, we need to understand uncertainty as a consequence in itself with multiple unpleasant implications for people. In the interim, immigrants on both sides will face various economic, political, legal, social, and psychological challenges (Portes 2016b). At the economic register, EU nationals may find it more difficult to be recruited by some British employers, since they might not be able to reassure them of their right to work in Britain in the near future. Simultaneously, some suggest that anecdotal evidence indicates that British businesses and institutions find it more difficult to recruit and keep skilled EU workers (Portes 2016a). This can be attributed to the difficulty faced by EU nationals in Britain to make long-term life plans in face of Brexit

(Portes 2016b). Many are pessimistic about the possibility that the life that they had planned before the referendum will still be realistic in the new socio-legal context. Consequently, the factor of uncertainty could cause reduction in the numbers of EU migrants (Emerson 2016).

Additionally, some mention that there is anecdotal evidence that the insecurity sensed by the increase of racist and xenophobic sentiments in British society may drive some EU nationals away from the UK (Emerson 2016; Portes 2016b). Moreover, the rights and status of EU citizens in the UK will depend on how the rights of British citizens living in the EU are negotiated with the EU partners (Portes 2016b; Vargas-Silva 2016). This political dynamic could be said to indicate possibilities for acrimonious and mutually punishing debates between Britain and the EU. Correspondingly, many commentators and politicians have contested the condition of ordinary EU and UK citizens being treated as 'bargaining chips' in the negotiation process (Islam 2016; Simons 2016). Alternatively, a political settlement might easily be reached on the question of expats, since neither side would wish to appear insensitive by allowing words like 'deportation' to enter the public debate (Portes 2016b). Nevertheless, until this is concluded, many migrants may feel as if they are standing still in a previously unexplored 'limbo land' of precarious rights and waning citizenship.

12.3   Free Movement, EU Citizenship, and Acquired Rights

Since the 1950s, as European integration progressed, the rights of EU citizens have been continuously expanding (Roos 2016). As shall be demonstrated below, the language of EU law outlining the rights of individuals has been changing from the mere economic register to a more political one. The motivation behind this development was the belief that there were both utilitarian and normative benefits for an EU that wanted to secure the success of the Single Market and later on, the monetary union, and simultaneously politically involve citizens in order to overcome the ever-present 'democratic deficit' (Warleigh 2001: 22). The expansion of citizens' rights occurred gradually over time through the advancement of EU law and the updating of EU treaties.

The EU's principle of free movement comprises four indivisible freedoms across borders: capital, goods, services, and labour (Doherty 2016). It was originally introduced in the Treaty of Rome (Treaty of the European Economic Community, TEEC, 1957), whereby obstacles to workers' movement across member-states were removed to allow for labour mobility (Portes 2016a). At the time, the focus was on 'workers' rather than 'citizens' and persons were primarily defined as economic, rather than political units. As specified by the treaty, people could move freely for the purpose of employment or self-employment (Article 48, 52: 21–22), not mere residency. The treaty further explains that measures should be adopted in the field of social security, such as unemployment benefits and vocational training, funded by a European Social Fund and the member-states (Article 51, 125: 22, 43–44). Welfare rights were subject to restrictions and previously employed persons were more facilitated, compared to economically inactive ones, although there was mention of encouraging young workers (Article 50: 22).

With the progression from the EEC to the EU, the Maastricht Treaty (Treaty on European Union, TEU, 1992) introduced the concept of EU citizenship. According to the TEU, every national of an EU member-state was automatically a citizen of the EU (Article 9: 20). EU citizenship was meant to function as an additional layer to national citizenship, not a replacement. In line with this new specification, EU citizens could now reside freely anywhere in the EU, irrespective of their economic status (Doherty 2016; Roos 2016), being legitimate citizens. As prescribed in TEU, the EU was meant to provide its citizens 'an area of freedom… without internal frontiers in which the free movement of persons is ensured…' (Article, 3: 17). As seen, the new language speaks of 'persons' and 'citizens' not only 'workers'. In time, the TEEC was revised into the Treaty on the Functioning of the European Union (TFEU 2009) to reinforce the rights of both persons and workers to reside freely, albeit subject to conditions.

As the Citizens Directive (2004) specifies, economically inactive citizens could reside in an EU country other than their own as long as they (a) had sufficient resources for themselves and their families so as not to become a burden on the social system of the host country and (b) were covered by a 'comprehensive sickness insurance'. If EU nationals fulfilled these conditions, also known as 'exercising treaty rights', for a continuous period longer than five years, they and their non-EU family members could acquire the right of permanent residence in the host country. According to the directive and the principle of non-discrimination, EU nationals could now have the right to equal treatment to that of nationals of the host state, which in effect provided access to social benefits (Portes 2016a), after three months of residence.

Within the discussion of EU citizenship and post-Brexit Britain, the legal concept of 'acquired rights' has gained a considerable momentum (HL/EUC 2016). Acquired rights are defined as rights that once they have been granted and vested legally, should not be altered or reduced by a subsequent legislation. According to this legal doctrine, it would follow that the rights of EU citizens living in the UK and British citizens living in the EU should not be reversed and downgraded, because they were previously granted by the legal frameworks of EU citizenship. Unfortunately, neither EU, nor international law can safeguard these rights after Brexit. International law is narrow in scope and enforceability, thus cannot protect against the loss of such rights. However, as will be demonstrated next, voids in prior practices may cause many EU nationals in Britain to lose their residence rights, ironically even under pre-existing EU law.

12.4   Residence Rights and Permanent Residence Applications

Brexit has indicated that the residence rights of EU nationals in Britain are not automatically granted after the country's withdrawal; hence their status can only be clarified in the withdrawal agreement between Britain and the EU (Vargas-Silva 2016). Amid looming uncertainty, it is anticipated that growing numbers of EU nationals will seek ways to secure future residence in the UK by applying either for permanent residence or British citizenship (Migration Observatory 2016). However, given that the first has recently become a prerequisite for the latter, the current policy for acquiring permanent residence in the UK is a relevant and good starting of the discussion regarding EU nationals' future status in post-Brexit Britain (Vargas-Silva 2016).

One of the first problems for EU nationals wishing to apply for permanent residence that is currently reported is the fact that several socioeconomic categories of EU citizens living in the UK are not qualified to apply. As it currently stands under EU law, based on the Citizens Directive and adopted by Britain in February 2017, the application process is straightforward only for those EU nationals who have been employed in the UK for the last five years without any interruptions (Migration Observatory 2016). Social groups that have resided in the UK for years, but have been irregularly employed or economically inactive, such as students, homemakers, stay-at-home parents and carers, the self-funded, the retired, casual workers, and the disabled, may be particularly adversely affected.

The clause for 'comprehensive sickness insurance', either by medical insurance in EU citizens' own country or private medical insurance in the UK, is reported as an important obstacle for EU nationals wishing to apply for permanent residence. One reason is that many EU nationals in the economically inactive categories, that is, students, never opted for health insurance since access to the NHS was open in the UK. Another misgiving is that several EU citizens were previously unaware of such a requirement (Vargas-Silva 2016). This becomes particularly acute, since as specified in the Citizens Directive the host member-state is not required to seek evidence that EU nationals residing in its territory fulfil the conditions of sufficient funds and comprehensive sickness insurance. As a result, many citizens were not informed upon arrival and remained unaware of these requirements throughout their residence, especially since according to prior EU law after five years of residence citizens were directly assumed as permanent residents. As a result of such exclusions of people who have lived in the UK for several years, some British politicians, such as MP Sarah Wollaston, have asked for this regulation to be removed (O'Carroll 2016a).

Given that the question of who can qualify for permanent residence becomes controversial within a Brexit context, changes might be made. For instance, there may be room for future migration policy to grant EU citizens indefinite residence rights through a more flexible and simplified procedure, such as by providing proof of physical presence in the country before a specified cut-off date (Migration Observatory 2016; Vargas-Silva 2016). This date could be determined as the date of the referendum, the date the UK triggered Article 50, or the date of its official departure from the EU (Vargas-Silva 2016). However, applying for permanent residence through such a migrant-friendly system may still be intractable for people who lack the evidence. For instance, older documents that can testify to individuals' residential address, such as gas, electricity, and council tax bills (GOV.UK 2016c), may be impossible to retrieve, especially since EU nationals never had to gather such paperwork before (Vargas-Silva 2016).

The Citizens Directive (2004) suggests, but does not demand, that a host member-state could ask EU citizens to register at the appropriate authorities and acquire a 'registration certificate'. Although some EU member-states have been following this practice in the past, Britain has not. As such, an important tool in efforts to prove past residence status is unavailable. Permanent residence applications were not previously needed for EU citizens and were predominantly directed towards non-EU family members of EU nationals, rather than EU citizens themselves, as shown in both the EU's Citizens Directive (2004: 36) and its regulation adopted by the British government (GOV.UK 2016c). Consequently, most EU nationals residing in the UK never before had solid reasons for applying for permanent residence. Ultimately, between a Union that does not ensure its member-states implement its laws properly, a member-state that does not, because it does not have to, combined with the lack of sufficient communication of legal requirements to the public by both Union and member-state, topped by several citizens not being aware of their rights and duties, one can sadly conclude that the state of the Union verges on the embarrassing.

Additional embarrassment is presently caused by numerous stories of EU nationals in the British press that face bureaucratic obstacles in their applications for permanent residence and have been sent rejection letters by the Home Office asking them to make preparations to leave the country (i.e., O'Carroll 2016a, b). The public emergence of these occurrences has led MEP Sophie in't Veld to call for an investigation of the British government as regards to cases where EU citizens have felt harassed and unfairly treated by the state or British employers after the referendum (Boffey and O'Carroll 2017). Simultaneously, various activist groups have sprung up demanding that the rights of EU nationals living in Britain are addressed (O'Carroll 2016d). Although such disturbances to established EU nationals' lives can be attributed to a possibly over-whelmed bureaucracy and an absence of responsive policy or governmental direction regarding the treatment EU nationals during Brexit, they could also be interpreted as glimpses of what the future holds for many EU nationals living in a UK that may be becoming less and less cosmo-politan. The next section will assess different post-Brexit models based on pre-existing relations between the EU and non-EU countries in order to infer the possible implications for EU migrants in post-Brexit Britain.

12.5 Post-Brexit Models and EU External Relations

Although PM May announced that Britain will not be choosing an 'off-the-shelf' available model for its future relationship with the EU (McTague 2016), there are various existing such models that can assist us in inferring future Britain-EU relations and their implications for EU citizens in the UK (Emerson 2016). As aptly put, the whole process does not start with a 'blank sheet of paper' (Emerson 2016: 1). These models include examples of several countries' relations with the EU, and although it is most likely that none of these models shall be implemented as is, features of them shall be present in the final negotiation product.

In public language, many terms were coined to describe possible Brexits, such as 'clean', 'dirty', 'black', 'white', and 'grey' (BBC News 2017). Nevertheless, its possible character has mostly been defined by the terms 'soft' and 'hard' (Menon and Fowler 2016). The softness, or hard-ness thereof, of Brexit is defined by the degree of access to, or acceptance of, a number of interrelated issues, which are (a) the Single Market, (b) the Customs Union, (c) financial contributions to the EU budget, (d) endorsement of EU laws, and (e) free movement of people. A hard Brexit entails Britain leaving the Single Market and the Customs Union, ceasing making EU budget contributions or being subject to EU law, and finally disconnecting itself from the four freedoms, including free movement of people. In contrast, a soft Brexit would presuppose some form of partial membership or substantial access to the Single Market or the Customs Union, and a certain degree of acceptance of EU law, financial contributions, and free movement of individuals. While these two options can be understood as two schematic extremes, it is likely that the result of the negotiations may resemble a combination of features falling between these two poles.

As it currently stands, the key themes of the successful Leave campaign over sovereignty and immigration make it difficult to imagine the likelihood of a soft Brexit since media and political actors appear keen on holding the British leadership accountable for its ability to deliver the mandate of the referendum (Menon and Fowler 2016). Most importantly, the recent speech by PM May where she provided clarifications about British goals and intentions (GOV.UK 2017a) indicated the determination of Britain to lead a harder, rather than a softer, version of Brexit. Some have even speculated that a Brexit could be reversed and Britain could still remain an EU member if its relationship was devised in such a way as to accommodate the concerns of Brexiters regarding immigration (McDougall 2016). However, the repeated messages coming from both sides with PM May declaring that 'Brexit means Brexit' and EU officials warning that Britain cannot 'cherry-pick' from the EU (BBC News 2016; Mardell 2016) illustrate the implausibility of avoiding Brexit and its challenging negotiations.

Still, as determined as these messages may be, they still leave us with a significant space for speculation (Mardell 2016; McDougall 2016). As there is major uncertainty over future UK migration policy, Brexit implies a spectrum of immigration regimes, ranging from EU nationals' residency rights remaining largely unaffected or minimally affected to EU nationals being situated somewhere between their previous status and that of non-EU nationals through a semi-preferential system, or the two types of immigrants being equated, which would result in EU nationals facing the same expansive restrictions as non-EU nationals (Portes 2016b; Vargas-Silva 2016). The following case studies situate these possibilities.

12.5.1 Soft Brexit Options and Possible Implications for Free Movement

Two pre-existing models of relating to the EU present possibilities for a soft Brexit for EU migrants, since they retain forms of membership and association to the EU and its economic institutions, hence allow for greater degrees of free movement. However, as shall be illustrated, their plausibility may not be as great.

EEA: Norway, Iceland, and Lichtenstein

Within the spectrum of soft Brexit, Britain has the option to safeguard access to the Single Market through membership of the European Economic Area (EEA) that contains EU member-states and non-EU members of the European Free Trade Association (EFTA), such as Norway, Iceland, and Lichtenstein (Menon and Fowler 2016; Portes 2016a). Non-EU EEA members make financial contributions and are impacted by EU law due to regulations upheld by the EFTA Court which cannot contradict decisions of the European Court of Justice, and as such, are subordinated to the latter (Emerson 2016; Menon and Fowler 2016). EEA countries are not members of the Customs Union and therefore are not bound by common external tariffs and can negotiate their own trade deal with third countries (Goodwin 2016b).

Most importantly, with reference to immigration, non-EU EEA members are required to accept the four principles of free movement, including that of people (Menon and Fowler 2016). This would allow greater EU residency rights to EU nationals who could continue living, studying, and working in the UK, but would not satisfy Leave voters because of the narrow changes as regards to regaining control over immigration (Doherty 2016; Goodwin 2016a). Moreover, this model would leave Britain unable to influence future reforms, despite being subject to them, which contradicts the sovereignty principle proclaimed by Leavers (Goodwin 2016b; Thielemann and Schade 2016).

Regarding limiting immigration, Liechtenstein managed in prior negotiations with the EU to be granted the right to impose quantitative limits on EU migrants (Emerson 2016). However, taking into consideration that Liechtenstein is much smaller than the UK and receives much fewer numbers of EU migrants, it appears unlikely that the EU would grant Britain the same right. The EEA option would be the most optimistic and gratifying one for EU nationals living in the UK, as their EU citizenship rights would not be adversely affected. However, the possibility currently seems bleak, since latest developments indicate that Britain will not be seeking access to the Single Market, as stated by PM May in her Brexit speech (GOV.UK 2017a).

EFTA: Switzerland

In 1992, a Swiss referendum rejected accession to the EEA and since then Switzerland has been trading with the EU through a series of numerous sector-specific bilateral agreements (Doherty 2016; Emerson 2016). Although Switzerland is not an EEA member, it is an EFTA member (Moagar-Poladian et al. 2015) and has a separate agreement with the EU on free movement of people (Roos 2016). As an EFTA member, Switzerland makes some financial contributions to the EU, which are proportional to a member's GDP, and smaller than those of EEA members, while it has to partially follow some EU regulations for trade purposes (Moagar-Poladian et al. 2015).

In terms of EU immigration, in 1999 Switzerland accepted the free movement of persons on the condition that in the event of serious economic and social difficulties, the country could take measures to regulate the inflow of migrants (Emerson 2016). This echoes the similar clause in Cameron's negotiations with the EU before the British referendum, which were criticised as ineffective in satisfying public demands regarding the reduction of immigration, therefore an agreement like that would probably not be relevant in the negotiations after the referendum.

Recent developments in Switzerland indicate that some concessions could be made by Britain in the future. In 2014, a Swiss referendum resulted in rejecting mass immigration from inside and outside the EU, but negotiations with the EU about imposing quantitative limits on migration through a safeguard clause came to a stall and the policies were never implemented (Emerson 2016; Portes 2016a). At a later stage, the Swiss government passed a law that favoured recruitment of local residents for new job openings and was extended to include established EU residents (Emerson 2016). While this law was intended to reach a compromise with the EU and to resolve tensions in Swiss-EU relations (Emerson 2016), it further indicates that Britain could opt for favourably accommodating established EU residents by facilitating their stay and employment in the UK. However, this would necessarily disadvantage EU immigrants that arrived later in the UK. As such, the Swiss example could only be a soft Brexit for some EU migrants in the UK, but not all. Ultimately, however, it appears questionable how acceptable this model would be for Leave voters, a doubt which reduces the plausibility of this option.

12.5.2   Hard Brexit Options and Possible Implications for Free Movement

Once we move away from any form of membership, EEA or EFTA, Britain is in an empowered position to redefine its immigration policy and have greater control of migrants from the EU (Peers 2016; Thielemann and Schade 2016). Leaving the EU and abandoning its principle of free movement will inevitably lead to significant changes in the British immigration system (Katwala et al. 2016) and as a consequence to the lives of EU nationals in Britain.

Customs Union: Turkey, Andorra, and San Marino

The negotiations could conclude with an agreement on Customs Union membership, following the example of Turkey, Andorra, and San Marino (Moagar-Poladian et al. 2015). However, in this case, Britain would not be able to negotiate its own free trade agreements with other countries ahead of the EU, while the latter holds ongoing negotiations with significant trading partners, such as the USA, Japan, and India (Emerson 2016; Goodwin 2016b). These issues render this option much less desirable for Britain, especially since one of the priorities of the British government is to secure free trade agreements with third countries, such as the USA and Canada (Goodwin 2016b). Nevertheless, in the event that such an option was followed, no EU budget contributions would be necessitated and tariff-free trade with the EU could continue (Goodwin 2016b; Moagar-Poladian et al. 2015). Most importantly, Britain would not need to accept immigration generated from EU member-states (Moagar-Poladian et al. 2015).

PM May's declaratory speech clarified her position on the Customs Union, saying that 'full Customs Union membership prevents us from negotiating our own comprehensive trade deals… I want Britain to be able to negotiate its own trade agreements. But I also want tariff-free trade with Europe and cross-border trade… Common Commercial Policy [and] Common External Tariff… prevent us from striking our own comprehensive trade agreements with other countries. But I do want us to have a customs agreement with the EU' (GOV.UK 2017a). As is illustrated, some elements of the Customs Union are desirable for the British side. Since such matters remain to be negotiated and accounted for by the EU, it is possible that some permissive policies are asked of Britain on the immigration issue in return for favourable tariff mechanisms. In the event that negotiations granted such concessions, EU nationals in the UK could probably benefit from them to some degrees.

DCFTA: Ukraine, Georgia, and Moldova

A model that has often been overlooked in the literature is the Deep and Comprehensive Free Trade Areas (DCFTAs) based on the Association Agreements between the EU and neighbouring countries, such as Ukraine, Georgia, and Moldova (Emerson 2016). These agreements include a high degree of Single Market access for all movement freedoms, except that of people (Emerson 2016). To the degree that Britain simultaneously valued Single Market access and reduction of immigration above all other considerations, this model would be highly satisfying for the British side. However, the abandonment of the principle of free movement of persons would be undesirable for the EU and detrimental for EU nationals in Britain. Given that PM May stated that Britain's objective is to achieve 'a new, comprehensive, bold and ambitious Free

Trade Agreement' with the EU, it is most possible that a model like this could be pursued by Britain. In this occasion, EU nationals could be disadvantaged severely by such an agreement.

This case study presents us with some peculiar dynamics. Although many EU officials and commentators emphasise the indivisibility of the four freedoms (Roos 2016), these association agreements clearly undermine these claims. One could perhaps question the EU's selectivity here, pointing out the unwillingness to receive supposedly large flows of immigrants from these Eastern European countries (Emerson 2016). More widely, the limited mention of this model as a possible choice for Britain appears unusual in light of its seeming advantages for British objectives. One could hypothesise that this omission may be due to the unwillingness of Britain to be symbolically associated with models that were designed for countries that are stereotypically seen as underdeveloped and war-torn, or simply the fact that these agreements are quite new and untested yet, having only been signed in 2016. Nonetheless, the DCFTAs could be one of Britain's negotiating cards for pressurising the EU to confer comprehensive trade benefits, without having an uncompromised moral ground to claim free movement of persons. As stated by policy researcher Andrew Duff, for the EU27 'the Ukrainian deal provides a precedent which it would be difficult to deny its former Member State' (Parliament.UK 2016).

CETA: Canada

The EU free trade agreement with Canada is another model that appears highly desirable for British interests (Singapore's agreement is another example). Canada and the EU negotiated the Comprehensive Economic and Trade Agreement (CETA) for the last seven years, although this has not yet been fully ratified, or implemented (Goodwin 2016b). If the UK followed this example, there would be access to the Single Market in those sectors that would be covered by the agreement, which would create the incentive to secure as many sectors as possible (Goodwin 2016b). However, this could mean that Britain would have to follow a large amount of EU market law in order to maximise its access to the EU

Single Market, which reduces the desirability of this model (Emerson 2016). In any case, free movement of people would not be guaranteed under this arrangement and EU nationals could face difficulties remaining in the country.

WTO: 'Global Britain'

At the far extreme of Brexit options, which could be the result of no deal being agreed during the negotiations, Britain could rely solely on its existing membership of the World Trade Organization (WTO) (Emerson 2016; Goodwin 2016b). This option would leave it without Single Market access and with imposition of tariffs on goods traded with the EU (Menon and Fowler 2016). Although Britain would not need to follow EU law, its traded products with the EU would still need to meet EU standards, while UK businesses would need to trade with the same non-tariff barriers with which all third countries with no preferential agreement with the EU trade (Goodwin 2016b). Within this regime, Britain would not be obligated to comply with free movement of people and could proceed to imposing barriers on EU migration (Goodwin 2016b). Although it seems questionable that Brexit negotiations could result in no agreement, PM May (GOV.UK 2017a) declared that 'no deal for Britain is better than a bad deal for Britain'. However, no clear agreements on the fundamental issues of the negotiation could mean a 'bad deal' for EU nationals in the UK. As 'Global Britain' appears to be becoming the new national mantra for Britain's future international identity, unsuccessful negotiations could result in Britain abandoning the EU for the world.

12.5.3   Visas for Europeans?

In these hard Brexit cases where no free movement is maintained, a system of work permits and visas could begin to apply to EU citizens wishing to be in the UK (Doherty 2016), which renders current British visa policies towards non-EU/non-EEA nationals a relevant area to explore (Vargas-Silva 2016). Such a policy would enable the UK to direct immigration to those sectors of the economy that the domestic labour market cannot cover due to skills shortage (Goodwin 2016a), while simultaneously achieving the government's goal to continue to attract 'the best and the brightest' of the world, as declared by PM May (GOV.UK 2017a). However, there are speculations over how satisfactory such a selective system can be for the UK, given that 'no system can select perfectly or even close to it' (Portes 2016a: 17). Simultaneously, it is questionable how well such a system could work for the 'brightest' since in these times of precarious employment, many bright, qualified people are forced to work for lesser contracts and salaries than their skills would suggest.

The main visa scheme for non-EU nationals in the UK is the Tier 2 visa, which presupposes a £25,000 'appropriate' salary and £945 in savings (GOV.UK 2017b). This salary threshold used to be £20,800, but was revised in November 2016. Moreover, the government has announced that this threshold will be increased to £30,000 in April 2017 (GOV.UK 2016a), a policy that indicates the government's intention to limit immigration. If this policy was applied to EU nationals, it would make it even more challenging for them to work and live in the UK. Vargas-Silva (2016), based on the 2015 UK Labour Force Survey, reports that only 14% of EU nationals working in the UK as employees, not self-employed, meet this requirement. At the same time, British employers will be burdened with additional fees and procedural tasks for the purposes of employing EU citizens (Portes 2016a; Vargas-Silva 2016). Given increasing complications, there is concern that illegal employment could increase (Portes 2016a), which can only be damaging to workers' labour rights.

Nevertheless, there may be a possibility for EU nationals to be treated differently from non-EU ones (Vargas-Silva 2016), through a preferential EU migration system regardless of the controversial character of such policy that discriminates between Europeans and non-Europeans. Nevertheless, this policy could better safeguard some of the rights that many EU nationals lived with for years in the UK, which would partly address the issue of acquired rights. In this case, less restrictive criteria could be applied to EU nationals for the purposes of skilled work visas (Portes 2016a; Vargas-Silva 2016). For example, in terms of skilled labour, there could be lower qualification thresholds, wider spectrum of occupations, higher quota for Tier 2 visas, fewer or no boundaries on intra-company transfers, and other provisions (Portes 2016a). Furthermore, low-skilled worker immigration programmes could be created anew to accommodate British needs for this type of labour, since they currently do not exist (Vargas-Silva 2016). Such needs could be directed through the British established scheme of Temporary Tier 5 visas that last from six months to two years (GOV.UK 2016b). This arrangement would allow EU nationals to work in the UK, but only for a strictly defined period, hence permanent residence could not apply. A similar example is that of sector-specific migration schemes, like the Seasonal Agricultural Workers Scheme (Portes 2016a).

In terms of other immigration routes, family unification could become more difficult than it currently is for EU nationals who wish to bring spouses and children with them when they settle in the UK, since salary thresholds and charges per child may apply (Vargas-Silva 2016). Immigration of students may be affected if EU nationals have to pay more tuition fees in the future and can no longer access benefits such as the student loan for undergraduate studies. In terms of travelling visas, it is possible that a pre-entry registration scheme might be introduced, similar to Electronic System for Travel Authorisation (ESTA) in the USA, for movements of people to and from the EU (Portes 2016a). Such an initiative would impose changes to travelling habits of both British and European citizens who will need to plan differently and pay an individual fee per traveller. Although there might be an all-embracing policy on immigration, there may also be bilateral arrangements between countries (Vargas-Silva 2016), which would facilitate only those nationals whose countries sign such agreements.

Ultimately, the letting go of the EU's free movement and the equation of EU migrants with non-EU migrants would alter the lives of EU nationals living in the UK substantially. Although nobody can tell at this point what criteria may be established, suffice to say that salary and skills set will be defining features in the selection process (Vargas-Silva 2016), which would create inequalities among EU migrants. Furthermore, those EU nationals who would not be able to fulfil these criteria would need to leave the country to return to their homelands or seek employment in other EU countries. The introduction of such admission requirements would have a great impact on EU communities in the UK, since most EU nationals come to the UK with the intention to work (Vargas-Silva

2016). Alternatively, those EU nationals who are skilled enough to have wider spectrums of options may find other migratory destinations more desirable than the British one.

12.6   Conclusions: A Global, but Not Cosmopolitan, Britain?

Britain's relationship with the EU has never been easy, but as Brexit would suggest, this relationship is bound to become even more uneasy. During the last few years, Europe has been going through some of its most challenging times and Brexit can be understood as a symptom of these times. While national sovereignty claims, Euroscepticism and anti-immigration voices were raised across Europe as a response to economic and security crises, it was the British referendum that spoke the loudest. EU immigration was one of the major issues in this political debate and based on the results of the referendum the British government is accountable to deliver a substantial reduction of the numbers of EU migrants coming into the UK. This in effect has created an enormous uncertainty and speculation over the future of British immigration policy and the fate of EU nationals in the UK.

This chapter argued that although uncertainty is often mentioned with regard to the Brexit aftermath, we should understand uncertainty as a particular consequence in itself, since this is the defining condition of many EU migrants in the UK at the moment. Furthermore, given the unprecedented character of the Brexit negotiations, this moment may be suspended in time to last for several years, which breeds various problems to professionals and families who need to plan their lives and feel confident about the society they live in. As Brexit has brought to the fore several ambiguities that remain to be negotiated, the only certainty is uncertainty, and all appears to depend on the political will of both British and EU negotiators.

If anything, Brexit presents a blow to some of the EU's political foundations, such as those of free movement and EU citizenship. Although the rights of EU citizens have been expanding over the years, Brexit has put these rights into question for millions of EU nationals living in the

UK. While the legal concept of 'acquired rights' has gained significant momentum in the Brexit debate, implying that previously granted rights cannot be taken away, both EU and international law provide limited protection. Within the context of threatened residence rights, the only formal route for securing the right to reside in the UK available to EU nationals is the application for permanent residence and the number of applications has increased since the referendum. However, given several ambiguities in EU law regarding the enforcement of registering EU nationals and the previously obscure issue of 'comprehensive sickness insurance', several socioeconomic groups within the wider category of EU nationals are not eligible to apply. If permanent residence applications are the future of immigration policy for EU nationals in the UK, many of them will be excluded and inequality will be created between the economically active who can easily acquire a permanent residence card and the economically inactive who cannot qualify for one.

As the future of EU nationals depends on the outcome of the Brexit negotiations, several models of non-EU countries' engagement with the EU can help us understand post-Brexit models and their implications for free movement. These models can be categorised in line with the distinction between soft and hard Brexit. Within the soft Brexit category, the case studies of EEA or EFTA memberships are examined, and it is concluded that these options offer great scope for the maintenance of free movement; therefore they would secure the rights of EU nationals to continue residing in Britain. However, as illustrated, emerging statements by PM May point to the possibility of a harder Brexit. Hard Brexit options are similarly examined, looking at Customs Union and WTO scenarios, as well as the free trade agreements of the EU with Canada or the Eastern neighbourhood countries. It is concluded that the last two possibly constitute the most appealing models for Britain in its attempts to build a new international identity for itself as a 'Global Britain' that trades with the world. However, as these options do not allow much scope for free movement, it is expected that they would severely reduce the capacity of EU nationals to stay in the UK. This could lead to EU immigrants being equated to non-EU immigrants, which in effect would subject the first to the same increasingly restrictive immigration policies that apply to the latter. In this sense, within this context of reduction of both EU and non-EU migration, Britain could build an economically global identity over time, but it would lose the inclusivity and egalitarianism that a politically cosmopolitan identity stands for.

Bibliography

Ash, Timothy Garton. 2001. Is Britain European? *International Affairs* 77 (1): 1–13.

BBC News. 2016. Brexit: UK Cannot Cherry Pick, EU Negotiator Says. Available at http://www.bbc.co.uk/news/world-europe-38224834. Last accessed 24 Jan 2017.

———. 2017. Brexit Options: Hard, Soft, Grey and Clean Versions, January 13. Available at http://www.bbc.co.uk/news/uk-politics-38611676. Last accessed 22 Jan 2017.

Boffey, Daniel, and Lida O'Carroll. 2017. Plight of EU Nationals Seeking UK Residency to Be Investigated. *The Guardian*, January 25. Available at https://www.theguardian.com/politics/2017/jan/25/plight-of-eu-nationals-seeking-uk-residency-to-be-investigated-brexit-vote. Last accessed 3 Feb 2017.

Citizens Directive. 2004. Directive 2004/58/EC of the European Parliament and of the Council. *Official Journal of the European Union*, April 29. Available at http://eur-lex.europa.eu/LexUriServ/LexUriServ.do?uri=OJ:L:2004:229:0035:0048:en:PDF. Last accessed 2 Feb 2017.

Cohen, Russell, and Elena Hinchin. 2016. Brexit: Impact on EU Nationals and Non-Europeans. *Trusts & Estates* 155 (11): 62–68.

Doherty, Michael. 2016. Through the Looking Glass: Brexit, Free Movement and the Future. *King's Law Journal* 27 (3): 375–386.

Emerson, Michael. 2016. *Which Model for Brexit?* CEPS Special Report, No. 147, October. Centre for European Policy Studies. www.ceps.eu.

George, Stephen. 2000. Britain: Anatomy of a Eurosceptic State. *Journal of European Integration* 22 (1): 15–33.

Gifford, Chris. 2014. *The Making of Eurosceptic Britain*. Farnham: Ashgate.

Goodwin, Andrew. 2016a. Brexit and Immigration. *Oxford Economics* 40(April): 20–25.

———. 2016b. Brexit – Velvet Divorce or Messy Breakup? *Oxford Economics* 40(October): 5–12.

GOV.UK. 2016a. *Migration Advisory Committee Reviews of Tier 2*, first published on 24 March 2016. Available at https://www.gov.uk/government/news/migration-advisory-committee-reviews-of-tier-2. Last accessed 24 Jan 2017.

———. 2016b. *Tier 5 (Temporary Worker – International Agreement) Visa.* Available at https://www.gov.uk/tier-5-international-agreement. Last accessed 26 Jan 2017.

———. 2016c. *Prove Your Right to Live in the UK as an EU Citizen.* Available at https://www.gov.uk/eea-registration-certificate/permanent-residence.   Last accessed 2 Feb 2017.

———. 2017a. *The Government's Negotiating Objectives for Exiting the EU: PM Speech*, January 17. London: Lancaster House, Full Transcript. Available at https://www.gov.uk/government/speeches/the-governments-negotiating-objectives-for-exiting-the-eu-pm-speech. Last accessed 1 Feb 2017.

———. 2017b. *Tier 2 (General) Visa*, last updated on 6 January 2017. Available at https://www.gov.uk/tier-2-general/eligibility. Last accessed 24 Jan 2017.

Hobolt, Sara B. 2016. The Brexit Vote: A Divided Nation, a Divided Continent. *Journal of European Public Policy* 23 (9): 1259–1277.

House of Lords / European Union Committee (HL/EUC). 2016. *Brexit: Acquired Rights*, 10th Report of Session 2016–17, published on 14 December 2016 by the Authority of the House of Lords, 1–54. https://www.publications.parliament.uk/pa/ld201617/ldselect/ldeucom/82/82.pdf.

Islam, Faisal. 2016. Don't Use Expats as Brexit 'Bargaining Chips', Says EU Chief Donald Tusk. *SKY News*, November 29. Available at http://news.sky.com/story/angela-merkel-rejects-theresa-mays-advances-on-eu-citizen-hostages-10676859. Last accessed 26 Jan 2017.

Katwala, Sunder, Jill Rutter, and Steve Ballinger. 2016. *Britain's Immigration Offer to Europe: How Could a New Preferential System Work?* 1–24. British Future, October. www.britishfuture.org.

Laffan, Brigid. 2016. Europe's Union in Crisis: Tested and Contested. *West European Politics* 39 (5): 915–932.

Mardell, Mark. 2016. *What Does 'Brexit Means Brexit' Mean?* Available at http://www.bbc.co.uk/news/uk-politics-36782922. Last accessed 24 Jan 2017.

McDougall, Derek. 2016. Australia and Brexit: Déjà Vu All Over Again? *The Round Table* 105 (5): 557–572.

McTague, Tom. 2016. *Theresa May Calls for 'Unique' Brexit Deal.* Politico, published on 31 August 2016. Available online at http://www.politico.eu/article/theresa-may-calls-for-unique-brexit-deal-outside-european-union-cabinet/. Last accessed 22 Jan 2017.

Menon, Anand, and Brigid Fowler. 2016. Hard or Soft? The Politics of Brexit. *National Institute Economics Review* 238(November): 4–12.

Migration Observatory. 2016. *Here Today, Gone Tomorrow? The Status of EU Citizens Already Living in the UK*, 1–9. Centre on Migration, Policy and Society, University of Oxford. www.compas.ox.ac.uk.

Moagar-Poladian, Simona, George-Cornel Dumitrescu, Ionela Baltatescu, Emilia-Mary Balan, Mariana-Camelia Taranu, Alexandra Rusu, and Cristinel Claudiu Cocosatu. 2015. *Brexit: The Economic and Political Impact of a Possible Withdrawal of Great Britain from the European Union,* 36–51. Bucharest: Institute for World Economy, Romanian Academy.

O'Carroll, Lisa. 2016a. Scrap Insurance Rule for Stay-at-Home Parents from EU, Says Tory MP. *The Guardian*, December 30. Available at https://www.theguardian.com/uk-news/2016/dec/30/scrap-insurance-rule-stay-at-home-parents-eu-tory-mp-sarah-wollaston. Last accessed 26 Jan 2017.

———. 2016b. Dutch Woman with Two British Children Told to Leave UK After 24 Years. *The Guardian*, December 28. Available at https://www.the-guardian.com/politics/2016/dec/28/dutch-woman-with-two-british-children-told-to-leave-uk-after-24-years. Last accessed 3 Feb 2017.

———. 2016c. German Neuroscientist Also Told to Leave UK After Residency Rejection. *The Guardian*, December 29. Available at https://www.theguard-ian.com/uk-news/2016/dec/29/german-neuroscientist-told-to-leave-uk-resi-dency-application-rejected-monique-hawkins. Last accessed 3 Feb 2017.

———. 2016d. Campaigners Urge PM to Give EU Nationals in UK Permanent Right to Stay. *The Guardian*, December 12. Available at https://www.the-guardian.com/politics/2016/dec/12/the3million-campaign-group-letter-the-resa-may-eu-citizens-in-uk-right-to-remain. Last accessed 3 Feb 2017.

Parliament.UK. 2016. Chapter 5: A UK-EU Free Trade Agreement. *Brexit: The Options for Trade.* Available at https://www.publications.parliament.uk/pa/ld201617/ldselect/ldeucom/72/7208.htm. Last accessed 3 Feb 2017.

Peers, Steve. 2016. Migration, Internal Security and the UK's EU Membership. *The Political Quarterly* 87 (2): 247–253.

Portes, Jonathan. 2016a. Immigration, Free Movement and the EU Referendum. *National Institute Economic Review* 236 (May): 14–12.

———. 2016b. Immigration After Brexit. *National Institute Economic Review* 238 (November): 13–21.

Roos, Christof. 2016. *The Brexit and EU Freedom of Movement: Legal Uncertainty on Both Sides of the 'Border'*, Policy Brief, Issue 2016/17. Institute for European Studies, Vrije Universiteit Brussel, April. www.ies.be.

Simons, Ned. 2016. MPs to Debate Theresa May's 'Disgraceful' Use of EU Nationals as Brexit 'Bargaining Chips', *Huffpost Politics United Kingdom*,

October 19. Available at http://www.huffingtonpost.co.uk/entry/mps-to-debate-theresa-mays-disgraceful-use-of-eu-nationals-as-brexit-bargaining-chips_uk_580634cae4b0dcd0298fe88d. Last accessed 26 Jan 2017.

Thielemann, Eiko, and Daniel Schade. 2016. Buying into Myths: Free Movement of People and Immigration. *The Political Quarterly* 87 (2): 139–147.

Treaty of Rome. 1957. *Treaty of the European Economic Community (TEEC)*. Available at http://ec.europa.eu/archives/emu_history/documents/treaties/rometreaty2.pdf. Last accessed 2 Feb 2017.

Treaty on European Union. 1992. Consolidated Version of the Treaty on European Union. *Official Journal of the European Union*, 26.10.2012, C 326/13-45. Available at http://eur-lex.europa.eu/resource.html?uri=cellar:2bf140bf-a3f8-4ab2-b506-fd71826e6da6.0023.02/DOC_1&format=PDF. Last accessed 2 Feb 2017.

Treaty on the Functioning of the European Union. 2009. Consolidated Version of the Treaty on the Functioning of the European Union. *Official Journal of the European Union*, 26.10.2012, C 326/47-390. Available at http://eur-lex.europa.eu/legal-content/EN/TXT/PDF/?uri=CELEX:12012E/TXT&from=EN. Last accessed 2 Feb 2017.

Vargas-Silva, Carlos. 2016. EU Migration to and from the UK After Brexit. *Intereconomics* 5: 251–255.

Warleigh, Alex. 2001. Purposeful Opportunists? EU Institutions and the Struggle Over European Citizenship. In *Citizenship and Governance in the European Union*, ed. Richard Bellamy and Alex Warleigh, 19–40. London: Continuum.

13

New Forms of Social Security for Persons Moving Between the EU and the UK?

Yves Jorens and Grega Strban

13.1 Introductory Remarks

Since the title of the present book is "After Brexit: Consequences for the European Union", the question might be whether the UK has ever been fully integrated in the EU. Or have special arrangements between the UK and the EU shaped a special relationship between them, especially in the field of social policy and social security? The history of the UK in the EU could shed a light on the UK's recent decision to leave the EU and possible paths of regulating the EU and UK's future relationship.

Free movement of workers and the coordination of social security systems have always played a prominent role in the EU-UK relationship. One of the reasons might be a strong border culture resulting from the UK's position as an island state with land borders only to Ireland, which led to a specific understanding of free movement.[1] Due to various reasons,

Y. Jorens (✉)
Faculty of Law, Ghent University, Ghent, Belgium

G. Strban
Faculty of Law, University of Ljubljana, Ljubljana, Slovenia

© The Author(s) 2017
N. da Costa Cabral et al. (eds.), *After Brexit*,
https://doi.org/10.1007/978-3-319-66670-9_13

also internal political reasons, fear of immigration, especially coupled with the refugee crisis in 2015 and 2016, various measures have been taken in the UK to restrict access to social security benefits.

This paper presents a brief history of the UK in the EU, followed by an analysis of the so-called Brexit agreement, especially in relation to family benefits. Before concluding, the possibly ways of shaping the future EU-UK relationship are tested.

13.2 The UK and the European Union

The UK only joined the European Economic Community (EEC at that time; today the European Union, hereafter "EU") on the 1st of January 1973, together with Denmark and Ireland, after applying to join the EEC in 1961. The UK failed to join the Community for more than ten years, since its membership was vetoed by Charles de Gaulle in 1963. It was argued that Denmark and Ireland were so economically linked to the UK, that they considered it necessary to join the EEC if the UK did. The UK was thereby not an initial signatory to the Treaty of Rome, which established the EEC in 1957 and also included a special chapter on social policy (Articles 117–128 of the EEC Treaty).

Interestingly enough, in 1982, after gaining more independence from Denmark, Greenland voted to leave the EEC, which actually materialised in 1985. This led to the so-called Greenland Treaty[2] and a comprehensive partnership between Greenland and the EU. Social security issues are regulated in Council Regulation (EEC) No 1661/85 of 13 June 1985 laying down the technical adaptations to the Community rules on social security for migrant workers with regard to Greenland.[3] Greenland's particular position is emphasised by the EU nationality of Greenlandic nationals (by having the Danish citizenship).

Nevertheless, the UK was a signatory to the Single European Act of 1986, a document that also contributed to the Community's competence to adopt legislation in the field of social policy. By then, health and safety at work and the furthering of good living and working conditions of workers in the Community had become a relevant issue that in 1989 led to the adoption of the Community Charter of the Fundamental Social

Rights of Workers (the so-called Community Social Charter). However, the UK was the only Member State not to adopt the Charter.[4]

In 1992 the Treaty on European Union (the so-called Maastricht Treaty) further developed the (now) European Union's activities and policies in the social sphere, also creating a European Social Fund. Nevertheless, the most important novelty of the Treaty was the Social Policy Agreement and the Social Policy Protocol, together forming the so-called Social Chapter annexed to the Maastricht Treaty in the form of a Protocol.

However, the UK opted out of this Chapter. The UK chose not to participate in the Social Chapter initially and so was not originally bound by it. As a result, the Chapter applied to all Member States except the UK. The Social Chapter provided the EU with greater legislative competences and enhanced the role of the social partners and collective agreements at EU level. In 1997 the Amsterdam Treaty introduced a new title on Social Policy that included the existing Treaty Articles and the Social Chapter. The Protocol was deleted and the Agreement on Social Policy was incorporated into the revised Social Chapter after the newly elected UK labour government of Tony Blair decided not to opt out any longer. As a result, these provisions now apply to all Member States, and the two-tier system of employment, industrial relations, and social policy that was present in the EU between 1992 and 1997 came to an end.

The other important consequence of the Social Chapter's incorporation into the EC Treaty was that all legislation adopted during the period of the UK's opt-out and based on Articles in the Social Protocol were extended to the UK without an opportunity for the UK to negotiate changes to make the legislation fit with UK employment practices.[5]

As a result of the newly inserted Article 63 into the Treaty of Amsterdam (now Articles 78–80 of the Treaty on the Functioning of the EU, hereafter "TFEU"), the Community gained the competence to legislate on measures of immigration policy and rights of third-country nationals residing in one Member State while being legal residents of another Member State.

Since only workers who were nationals of a Member State enjoyed freedom of movement,[6] also the protection offered by the social security coordination regulations in order to enable such free movement was provided to nationals of a Member State. This was the case with the initial Regulation (EEC) 3/58 and the subsequent Regulation (EEC) 1408/71.[7]

However, it was quite early that the extension of the Regulations to third-country nationals was raised. The Luxembourg delegation was of the opinion that the Regulations should be extended to third-country nationals already in 1959.[8] Only after many years Member States could agree to extend the scope of Regulation 1408/71 to third-country nationals moving within the EU, but not on the basis of Article 51 (and then 235)[9] of the EC Treaty, but on the grounds of Article 63 of the EC Treaty (on immigration).

Hence, Regulation (EC) 859/2003 was adopted. It extended the scope of Regulation 1408/71 to third-country nationals, who are legally residing in the EU and moving between two or more of its Member States. The Treaty of Amsterdam contained two protocols that enabled the UK and Ireland to opt in or opt out of the legislation based on Title IV EC Treaty (on immigration).[10] In May 2002, both the UK and Ireland announced that they had decided to participate in the discussion of the Commission's proposal and that the legislation would apply to them, without requesting exemptions or special provisions.[11] Both the UK and Ireland opted in, whereas Denmark opted out.

After Regulation (EEC) 1408/71 was repealed and Regulation (EC) 883/2004 came into force in 2010, it again did not include third-country nationals[12] in its material scope. Therefore, again a so-called bridging regulation, that is, a regulation extending the personal scope of the basic Regulation (EC) 883/2004, had to be adopted, and again based on the immigration chapter of the Treaty.[13] This was achieved by Regulation (EU) 1231/2010.[14] Denmark and Ireland straightaway decided to go for the same legal regime as before, that is, Denmark opted out and Ireland opted in.

However, this time the UK changed its mind and did not opt in. Therefore, the Regulation 883/2004 does not apply to third-country nationals moving between a Member State and the UK. The question is whether or not third-country nationals are covered in the UK. It could be argued that Regulation (EC) 1408/71 and its implementing Regulation (EC) 573/72 remain applicable to third-country nationals moving between the UK and another Member State (apart from Denmark) on the basis of Regulation (EC) 859/2003 and Article 90(1)(a) of Regulation (EC) 883/2004. This is one clear example of the UK's changing social policy towards migration.

13.3 Family Benefits for Persons Moving Between the EU and the UK

Two of the most prominent topics regarding the EU-UK relationship are family benefits and benefits of or related to social assistance, especially when provided to persons moving to the UK from other Member States. Therefore, it is hardly surprising that special provisions on the coordination of family benefits can be found also in the Conclusions of the European Council meeting of 18 and 19 February 2016,[15] the so-called (anti-)Brexit agreement or the New Settlement.[16]

13.3.1 New Settlement for the UK

One of the main concerns of the New Settlement was the so-called export of family benefits. However, it should be noted that the notion of the "export" of family benefits might be misleading from a legal point of view. The social security coordination regulation, that is, Regulation (EC) 883/2004, obliges Member States to pay family benefits, for example, to workers whose children reside in another Member State. In this case, there is no actual payment (export) to another country. However, benefits might be provided to a person actually caring for a child[17] (living together with the entitled person or being divorced)[18] and exported to another country. Nevertheless, the export of family benefits is usually understood in a broader way, that is, when family benefits have to be paid for children residing in another country.

Such exporting is contested by some Member States, arguing that paying for children in another country might not follow the policy aims behind these benefits. These concerns found their way into the New Settlement with the UK. An appropriate response to the concerns of the UK should also be found in the "Declaration of the European Commission on the indexation of child benefits exported to a Member State other than that where the worker resides".[19]

This Declaration can actually be found in Annex V to the Council Conclusions. The European Commission commits itself to making a proposal for amending Regulation (EC) 883/2004. It would *"give the*

Member States, with regard to the exportation of child benefits to a Member State other than that where the worker resides, an option to index such benefits under the conditions of the Member State where the child resides" (emphases added). *The Commission considered that these conditions included "the standard of living and the level of child benefits applicable in that Member State."*

13.3.2   Limitation to "Child Benefit(s)"?

There are certain problems related to the Declaration mentioned above. It is not exactly clear which benefits are meant by the notion of "child benefits". The notions used in Regulation (EC) 883/2004 are "family benefits" and "family allowances".[20]

The notion of "family benefits" encompasses all benefits in kind and in cash intended to meet family expenses, excluding advances of maintenance payments[21] and special childbirth and adoption allowances (mentioned in Annex I to Regulation (EC) 883/2004).[22]

This new definition, compared to the previous distinction in the former Regulation (EEC) 1408/71, demonstrates the comprehensive approach to family benefits. According to the goal of simplification, the distinction between family benefits and family allowances was as a rule abolished. The subject of social security coordination is not only child benefits, but also child-raising benefits (which may in some Member States be linked to maternity) and child-care benefits.[23] Not only cash benefits but also benefits in kind are covered.[24]

Moreover, tax benefits for dependent children may fall under the coordination rules,[25] although at the same time they could be subject to double taxation avoidance treaties.[26] This leads us to another hot topic in the EU, that is, the distinctive coordination of social security and tax systems, which might lead to unwanted legal consequences.[27]

Therefore, would it be possible that the New Settlement with the UK covers only "classic child benefits", or even only the most common child benefit in each Member State, despite the use of the plural form, that is, "child benefits"?

13.3.3   Only for Workers Residing in the UK?

Moreover, it seems that a "worker's residence" may be decisive. This might exclude frontier and seasonal workers, not establishing (habitual) residence in the UK, despite the UK being the Member State of work and the main rule for applicable legislation would have to be used, that is, the *lex loci laboris*.

The Court of Justice of the European Union (hereafter "CJEU") already argued that seasonal workers have to be entitled to family benefits in the Member State of their work. In the *Hudziński and Wawrzyniak* cases, there was an entitlement to family benefits in Poland. Polish seasonal and posted workers were not disadvantaged by exercising the right to free movement and working in Germany. They neither lost nor suffered any reduction of family benefits.

The CJEU argued that it would be against Regulation (EC) 883/2004 and Article 48 TFEU to rule that the non-competent Member State is prohibited from granting workers and members of their family broader social protection than those granted under the Regulation. The Regulation cannot be applied in such a way as to deprive a migrant worker of benefits granted solely by virtue of the legislation of a single Member State. In this case, the entitlement to child benefits also existed for any person who did not reside in Germany (also the children were not residing there) and was subject to unlimited income tax liability (from which the child benefits are financed).

The argument that a non-competent Member State is not deprived or is allowed to pay family benefits might be misleading. Family benefits were indeed refused. Otherwise, there would be no case before the CJEU. The exclusion from family benefit provisions is actually prohibited, since it could constitute a disadvantage for migrant workers, regardless of their residence.[28]

However, the CJEU argued that in order to prevent overlapping of benefits, the German court was allowed to deduct the Polish family benefit from the German one and pay only the difference. This rule of deducting the amount of family benefits from another Member State applies (and there is no discretion), even if the entitlement to family benefits exists but family benefits would actually not be claimed in that Member State.[29]

The question in relation to the UK was what the legal nature of the New Settlement was. Could it overrule the CJEU judgments? It was not planned that all Member States would ratify the New Settlement in order to give it a power of primary law. Or was it even hoped that the CJEU would overrule the New Settlement? Moreover, such limitation to residence in the UK might also place pressure on family reunification, since family members would have an incentive to reside with the worker. In this case not less, but more persons might have moved to the UK.

13.3.4 What Kind of Indexation of Family Benefits?

The New Settlement also opens the question which rules should be applied for indexation, what data should be used to determine the standard of living and the level of benefits, and will the national legislation have to foresee such option for indexation?[30]

Some argue that wages and some social benefits are also adjusted for EU civil servants residing outside of Belgium and Luxembourg under the EU Staff Regulations.[31] Another solution to reduce family benefits would be to reverse the priority rules and make the Member State of residence (solely) competent for all family benefits (which might prove to be impossible for contribution-based schemes) or to classify some family allowances as special non-contributory cash benefits (which are not exported).

However, there are other problems with adjusting family benefits which are of a more general nature. The CJEU already argued that the old rule under which France could restrict the export of family benefits to the national level in the Member State of the children's residence is contrary to the provisions of the TFEU.[32] The heads of state have now decided in the New Settlement that the arrangements for the UK (including the indexation of child benefits), if it decided to remain in the EU, are "fully compatible with the Treaties".[33] The final decision on such compatibility would probably have to be taken by the CJEU and not the heads of states in the European Council.

There is also a question whether the possibility of indexation not only by one, but by all Member States would really lead to more equality? Probably not, especially if the indexation could go both ways. The indexation could be not only downward, that is, when providing higher "child benefits", the UK could pay less for workers whose children are residing in another (lower income) country, but also upwards. In the latter case, Member States with lower "child benefits" could be obliged to pay higher family benefits for children residing in the UK, if this provided higher "child benefits".[34]

If such indexation were only optional,[35] the lower income Member States might not foresee such upward adjustment in their legislation. Hence, it would remain a measure to reduce "child benefits" by the UK as one of the Member States which has been profiting most from the EU.[36]

The export of family benefits is established, in the first place, to enable economic mobility within the EU. Usually, contributions and taxes are paid in the Member State of work and family benefits are mainly financed by these contributions and taxes. Additionally, living costs may also be distinct within a single Member State, and this might have no influence on family benefits' levels. The same rule currently applies among the Member States.

13.3.5   New Settlement for the UK: Role Model for Other Member States?

The New Settlement with the UK should have become effective on the date the UK government informed the Secretary-General of the European Council that the UK has decided to remain a member of the EU. However, this did not materialise, since at the referendum held in the UK on the 23rd of June, the majority voted to leave the EU. Therefore, the set of arrangements of the New Settlement for the UK ceased to exist.[37]

Nevertheless, "concerns" expressed by the UK and "responded to" by the European Council continue to live a life of their own. Some Member States argue that if such a settlement could be agreed for the UK, it should also be possible for some other (high income) Member States.

The European Commission responded mid-December 2016 by presenting a revision of the EU legislation on social security coordination.[38] It appears that the Commission has (at least for now) refused the arguments on indexation of family benefits within the EU. It is emphasised that the proposal of the Commission does not modify the existing rules on the export of child benefits. No indexation of child benefits is planned: the country of work of the parent(s) remains responsible for paying the child allowances, and that amount cannot be adjusted if the child resides elsewhere. The position is supported by the fact that less than 1% of child benefits in the EU are exported from one Member State to another.

13.3.6 Family Benefits: Role Model for Coordinating Social Assistance?

The coordination of family benefits might be a model for coordinating social assistance, which is currently outside of the material scope of Regulation (EC) 883/2004.[39] It could be argued that the relation between social security and social assistance (as understood in international law)[40] used to be clear. Social security regulations applied to social security and the regulations concerning free movement of workers[41] included also social assistance.

Later on, the Free Movement Directive (sometimes also referred to as the Citizenship Directive or Residence Directive)[42] was adopted and construed by the CJEU. It seems that for categorical social assistance, that is, assistance linked to one of the traditional social risks, such as old age, invalidity, or unemployment, the rules of the Directive prevail over the rules of the Regulation. The former excludes equal treatment of Union nationals in an initial period of residence in a host Member State,[43] whereas the latter contains no transitional period for so-called special non-contributory cash benefits (SNCB).[44]

Not to dwell on the case law of the CJEU, especially cases like *Brey*,[45] *Dano*,[46] *Alimanovic*,[47] or *Garcia Nieto*,[48] since these have already been analysed in detail,[49] it should be mentioned that the CJEU seems to be giving the Member States more space for decisions on social assistance. Nevertheless, the need to coordinate social assistance was already expressed.[50] Developments in Member States show that many of them have also linked the entitlement to benefits which under the national system are perceived as social assistance to legal entitlements (at least Member States have opted for solutions which give the persons concerned a legally described situation which could also be invoked before national courts). Thus, one element of a social assistance benefit[51] (discretionary nature of social assistance) no longer exists. If the benefit is clearly dedicated to a specific group (e.g. unemployed or old-aged persons or persons in need of care), also the second element of social assistance (no link to one of the risks enumerated in the material scope of Regulation (EC) 883/2004) no longer applies. Also benefits in kind do not exclude the application of the Regulations. To avoid distinctive rules for similar benefits under various legal instruments, social assistance could be subject to social security coordination.[52]

There are at least two questions related to this. The first one is whether family benefits could be a role model for coordinating social assistance. For instance, social assistance could be provided at the level of the new Member State, but the former Member State should reimburse a certain amount, similarly as it currently is with family benefits.[53] For social assistance it might be envisaged that the reimbursement of the former Member State is progressively reduced as the link with the host Member State gets stronger.[54]

The second question is whether only the UK should "make a success of the Brexit" or should also the EU make a success of it? It could be in the sense of closely linking the Union citizens, also by linking social assistance schemes, drawing not only from the examples of the European Convention on Social and Medical Assistance, but also the Nordic Convention on Social Assistance and Social Services,[55] which exists next to the Nordic Convention on Social Security.[56]

Moreover, it seems that the CJEU itself could not stay entirely unaffected by the changing relations towards the UK. It modified the conditions for access to social (assistance) benefits for economically inactive persons in a judgment involving the UK, passed just several days before the Brexit referendum.[57] It no longer concerned the right to reside test only for social assistance benefits as in previous case law, but also for "classic" social security benefits under Regulation (EC) 883/2004 (in this case family benefits).

The right to reside test is being considered as part of substantive national law, not affected by conflicting norms of Regulation (EC) 883/2004, and not subject to the proportionality test. This judgment must be considered in the political context in which economically inactive EU citizens claiming benefits in a host Member State are often regarded as "benefit tourists" who should not have access to social benefits (and the solidarity circle) of the host Member State. Nevertheless, this judgment concerns family benefits, which might be very diverse and may show similarities to social assistance (be linked to a certain threshold and provided to a family). Hence, the consequences of this judgment should not be applicable to all "classic" social security benefits.

13.4   The Future UK-EU Relationship: Some Options for a Potential Relationship Between the EU and the UK

Now that the UK has decided to leave the EU, we would like to ask the question what the options are to regulate the potential relationship between the EU and the UK. We would like to address this question by comparing a number of topical examples of relationships between certain third countries and the EU. These current examples show that the relationship with the EU can be either strong or less strong depending on the situation. Exactly because the free movement of persons was one of the key aspects in the voting behaviour, it is important to examine to what extent free movement is still covered by these relationships; in other words, the hard Brexit or the soft Brexit.

13.4.1   The Norwegian Option

By far the least drastic option is the option after the example of Norway. The UK could decide to become an EFTA member and that way join the EEA.[58] This entails that the UK would keep its access to the internal market and that the four economic freedoms, and in particular also the free movement of workers, would remain applicable (goods, persons, services and capital). However, the following fall outside the scope of application of the EEA agreement[59]:

- – Treaties and agreements with third countries with regard to foreign trade;
- – EU citizenship;
- – EU policy on direct and indirect taxes and the monetary policy;

- there is no joint regional relief programme;
- the policy on the monetary union, the customs union, justice, and home affairs;
- there is no joint agricultural policy, nor is there a joint fisheries policy.[60]

When concluding its own trade agreements, the UK would be able to better guarantee that these agreements are adjusted to British companies' needs, and it does not so much need to reckon with EU Member States.[61] For example, it may be pointed out that the trade agreements which EFTA has already concluded with third states[62] do not mention anything about the free movement of workers, contrary to, for example, the free trade agreements which the EU has concluded with certain third states.[63] The latter is rather significant, as the free movement of workers is manifestly present in the Brexit debate.

However, this autonomy is also relative, as a horizontal policy remains to exist to protect and strengthen the internal market, such as social policy (occupational health and safety, labour law, equal treatment), consumer protection policy, environmental and company law. [64]

In the EEA agreement, a separate decision-making procedure has been elaborated. According to this procedure, the EEA/EFTA Member States have to implement EU legislation that concerns EEA domains. However, in addition Norway sometimes also collaborates with the EU in fields that are not related to the EEA. For example, Norway is a member of the Schengen area. The EEA/EFTA States have not transferred any legislative competences to the EEA institutions and they are unable, constitutionally, to accept direct decisions by the Commission or the CJEU. To cater for this situation the administration of the EEA agreement is done by the EFTA Surveillance Authority and the European Commission. Both authorities thereby have to safeguard a uniform application of the EEA rules. For the interpretation of the rules, an EFTA court was established, and the case law by the CJEU dating before the EEA agreement is binding for the EFTA Member States.[65] With regard to legal questions dating after the agreement, the EFTA court is competent. Still, this court generally applies the reasoning by the CJEU.[66]

Although Norway thus has no direct influence on the decision-making process in the EU, to a certain extent, it does indirectly. For example, Norway is a member of certain "expert groups" (e.g. the Administrative Commission on social security for migrant workers) and also participates in the preparatory works of the European Commission. Norway can forward its comments to Parliament and the Council by means of a green paper. Furthermore, EFTA and EU representatives meet in the EEA Council, where they exercise political supervision, and joint interests are discussed in the EEA Joint Parliamentary Committee. Finally, Norway is also involved in the budget of different EU programmes such as Erasmus+, Galileo, Copernicus, and Horizon 2020.

The other way around, the EU also has no direct influence on Norway. EEA-relevant legislation has to be incorporated in the EEA agreement, through the EEA Joint Committee. Once a Regulation has been incorporated, with the consent of both parties, it can affect Norway. Furthermore, the national parliaments of the EFTA have a right of reservation. Only once did Norway try to make a reservation, namely with regard to the third Directive on postal services. This led to the EU threatening to exclude Norway from certain parts of the internal market, which resulted in the Directive being incorporated after all.[67]

In other words, the Norwegian option implies more of a soft Brexit, as the UK would be to a great extent bound by the rules of free movement. In that respect, not much would change, and when in future the EU were to adopt new legislation concerning workers' rights, the UK would most likely have to apply this legislation as well.

The fact that Norway is bound by EU policy and EU law to such a fairly large extent originates from the fact that Norway cannot survive without the highly skilled workers coming from the EU. The internal market is thus essential for the Norwegian economy.[68] Whether the same line of reasoning would be followed in the UK is, however, far less clear.

The Norwegian model does have a number of pros and cons. For instance, some authors point to the fact that this model could maintain the unity of Great Britain. It could indeed be a good compromise for Scotland and Ireland, as they would still enjoy free movement. This could be an argument for Scotland to refrain from holding a new referendum on the Scottish independence. On the other hand, this option would also meet a number of concerns of the Leave camp. The UK would, for example, have a bigger say in tax policy, it would be free from the Brussels bureaucracy, and it would have a bigger say in fisheries and agricultural policy. Moreover, trade would become more flexible and the UK would be able to conclude its own trade agreements. Membership of the single market would safeguard London as a centre for trade and finances, which would in turn result in the protection of jobs.[69] Because, if Great Britain can no longer enjoy the internal market, financial institutions may as a result no longer automatically provide their services in the EU. This model would keep companies from being forced to move to another EU Member State to be able to trade from London with companies in the EU. [70] Besides, Boris Johnson claimed that, even in the event of a Brexit, the UK would still have access to the internal market.[71]

As stated above, next to advantages, this option also has disadvantages. A first issue has to do with sovereignty. The UK would lose influence in the EU, while still having to adhere to a large part of EU legislation.[72] After all, one consequence of the EEA agreement is that EU legislation generally has to be accepted without really having a vote in it. Moreover, the UK would still have to pay for the EEA.[73] On top of this, however, the domain of free movement also gives rise to quite a number of issues. For instance, EU migrants would still be able to live and work in the UK, while this was actually a very important element in the British people's decision to leave the EU. Research has already shown that these concerns are mainly felt by persons with a low income, low-skilled persons, persons with an older age profile, and persons who perform low-skilled work and that it is these people who voted Leave.[74] Another study has shown that a high number of persons who voted Leave are actually far less confronted with immigration in their region. It is in fact so that areas where clearly most people voted Leave are areas with the least number of non-British immigrants. Conversely, areas in which more Remain votes were counted are areas with more non-British immigrants.[75] The British government was fast to make clear that it's the concerns of this working class which they intend to take into account.[76]

The question rises whether the free movement of persons should be considered as an all-encompassing "take it or leave it" package? All the more so since the fear of the negative consequences of an unrestrained free movement of persons has become a problem which various Member States are confronted with. For example, some argue in favour of negotiations about the restriction of rights that were conferred on EU citizens by the CJEU, derived from Directives. The access to social benefits and public services and the rights of non-working family members could, for instance, be limited.[77] Although this is as such possible, this should rather be evaluated negatively. The former President of the European Parliament Martin Schulz, for example, claimed that the UK will not be able to get a deal that is more advantageous than EU membership. There is, nevertheless, room for negotiation with the UK, but this entails taking into account the Member States' interests. If the UK wants access to the internal market, this comes with all four freedoms, and not three or three and a half.[78] In the recent past, the European Commission has indeed reacted negatively to Switzerland's wish to introduce quota as a type of "safeguard clause" to limit free movement of persons.[79] This does not mean, however, that this moment cannot be used to evaluate the entire process of the internal market. Martin Schulz pointed out that many British people voted for a Brexit because they felt marginalised in the EU. Schulz does recognise that this deserves attention, but he also emphasises that this cannot be done without the support of all Member States. Schulz thus suggests a "reset": a fresh start for the EU to safeguard prosperity, social justice, and our values within a globalised world.[80]

13.4.2   The Swiss Option

A second option to consider is the EU's special relationship with Switzerland. After World War II, Switzerland did not fully participate in the European integration because of its image of neutrality. In addition, Switzerland was sceptical about the European project and preferred to safeguard its independent image. On the other hand, Switzerland did want to participate in the free trade area in the EU.[81] For that reason, numerous bilateral agreements concerning trade were concluded and Switzerland thus became a significant trade partner for the EU. It was initially also intended that Switzerland would become a member of the EEA, to create an internal market between the EU and the EFTA Member States, but due to a negative referendum it never came to that.[82]

Contrary to Norway, Switzerland has no full access to the internal market. Switzerland does apply the principle of free movement of persons, however. The Swiss option is characterised by a sectorial approach, which entails that there is collaboration with the EU within certain domains—including the free movement of persons.[83] By contrast, the EEA—and thus Norway—is characterised by a more integrated approach, entailing that legislation and policy that relate to the four freedoms still have to be incorporated.[84] However, the bilateral agreements are static in nature, contrary to EEA membership, which means that there are no mechanisms to adapt the agreements to new tendencies and evolutions. Contrary to the EEA agreement, there is no dispute settlement or supervisory body.[85]

Nevertheless, the Swiss model is important because also in Switzerland concerns have been expressed about issues related to the free movement of persons.

Free Movement of Persons in Switzerland

The free movement of persons was legally enshrined in the first bilateral agreement.[86] The first bilateral agreement regulates in particular three topics: the free movement of workers, the mutual recognition of diplomas, and the coordination of social security.[87] The agreement on the free movement of persons does not, however, comprise the rights of EU citizens. That is why important CJEU cases on EU citizenship (case law regarding Article 18 *iuncto* Article 20 TFEU[88]) are not applicable in Switzerland.[89]

The agreement did provide for a number of transitional measures.[90] After two years, Swiss citizens received an unconditional right to free movement within the EU, together with all other rights related to this right. The transitional measures agreed on for EU citizens were more extensive. The free movement for EU citizens in Switzerland becomes unconditional after twelve years. In the first five years, EU citizens were allowed to access Switzerland within the limits of a *quotum* that gradually decreased.[91] Within the first two years, the Swiss authorities could also give priority to national workers in the access to certain employment. The principle of non-discrimination was thus not applicable during the first two years of the agreement. As from the sixth year from the entry into force of the agreement, Switzerland had to apply an unconditional right for EU citizens who wished to reside in Switzerland. Since that date Switzerland nevertheless also has the right to again implement quota in the event that there is a substantial increase in immigration.[92] After twelve years Switzerland had to unconditionally respect the principle of freedom of establishment of EU citizens. A "safeguard clause" could be invoked if there is mutual consent by the parties.[93] From 1 June 2016, the same conditions apply to all citizens of Member States of the EU-27/EFTA. Only for Croatia there are still some transitional provisions.

However, further measures to fight social dumping could still be implemented at national level, and in particular to protect both the Swiss working population and foreign employees sent to Switzerland from efforts to undercut salaries and the working conditions that apply in Switzerland. This entailed that cantons were able to introduce rules on minimum wages in certain sectors. Furthermore, as conditions were relaxed, it became possible to extend collective contracts with regard to terms of employment.[94] With respect to the free movement of persons, the bilateral agreement had to be amended when new Member States entered the EU. Switzerland was thereby allowed to set restrictions for the new Member States, in the event that their entry caused mass immigration by the new EU citizens. Also concerning cross-border service provision Switzerland was allowed to impose restrictions. It may do so in the construction sector, the industrial cleaning sector, the horticultural sector, and the security sector.[95]

The existence of a certain "guillotine clause" is thereby important. The first bilateral agreement contains seven agreements that are linked to each other. When one of these agreements is not renewed or is terminated, the other agreements also expire.[96] Therefore, if Switzerland were to opt to end the free movement of persons, this would also mean the termination of the agreements on research, technical barriers to trade, civil aviation, overland transport, agriculture, and public procurement.[97]

The contracting parties thereby have to interpret the sectorial agreements themselves. Contrary to the EEA agreement no joint judiciary body was established for this purpose.[98] The agreement states that Switzerland has to take into account the relevant case law of the CJEU dating before the date of the agreement. The agreement does not, however, throw much light on how to deal with CJEU case law dating after the date of the agreement.[99] The Swiss Federal Supreme Court is in this respect not bound by the case law of the CJEU on the free movement of persons dating from after the date of the agreement, although they can draw inspiration from the CJEU. In the event that the UK were to follow this model, this might imply that they would be bound by all CJEU case law dating before the date on which the agreement was concluded. Nevertheless, the UK would in future have more autonomy.

The Swiss Referendum Against Mass Immigration

The EU was, however, recently confronted with a special issue concerning migration. The referendum and a right of initiative are enshrined in the Swiss constitution. A referendum is held when 50,000 signatures are collected from Swiss voters. The referendum gives people the right to vote on parliamentary decisions.[100] In the event of an initiative, supported by 100 0000 signatures, it is possible to request that the federal constitution is amended or partly revised. An amendment to the constitution requires a majority of votes and of the number of cantons.[101]

On 9 February 2014, Switzerland voted in favour of the initiative "Against mass immigration" with 50.3% votes in favour and a majority in 14.5 of the 23 cantons. This resulted in a new article being inserted in the constitution, entailing that the stay of migrants in Switzerland had to be limited by means of quota and maximum numbers.[102] The treaties that are not in line with this article have to be renegotiated within three years.

As a consequence, according to Swiss law the bilateral agreement between the EU and Switzerland on the free movement of persons had to be renegotiated. Furthermore, Switzerland also refused to sign a protocol that would expand the scope of application of the free movement of persons to Croatia. For the EU, however, this is non-negotiable. The EU has indeed more than once emphasised that the free movement of persons cannot be considered separately from the other three freedoms and therefore constitutes an inseparable part of the internal market.[103]

In this respect, the European Commission adopted the following declaration:

Declaration of the European Commission following the popular vote in Switzerland on the 'mass immigration' initiative

The European Commission regrets that an initiative for the introduction of quantitative limits to immigration has been passed by this vote. This goes against the principle of free movement of persons between the EU and Switzerland. The EU will examine the implications of this initiative on EU-Swiss relations as a whole. In this context, the Federal Council's position on the result will also be taken into account.[104]

On top of this, the European Commission also sanctioned Switzerland by suspending Switzerland's participation in Horizon 2020 and Erasmus+.[105] Furthermore, because of the guillotine clause the other agreements risk to expire should the new constitutional provision be implemented. Because the EU refuses to renegotiate the agreement on the free movement of persons, the Swiss government is caught between its constitutional obligations on the one hand and its European obligations on the other.

The amended Swiss constitution not only causes problems in the EU; it also gives rise to problems in other areas of international law. For example, Switzerland has concluded numerous international treaties with international organisations that are based in Switzerland, most of which state: "*All measures [...] aimed at restricting the entry into Switzerland of foreigners, or of controlling the conditions of their stay, will not be applicable*". Thus, the question is whether Switzerland will have to renegotiate each of these treaties.[106] Chances are that this could undermine Switzerland's strong position as host country for international organisations. To solve this problem, Switzerland could exclude migrants employed by order of international organisations from the quota. The clause in Article 121a of the Swiss Constitution furthermore also causes problems with regard to the Geneva Convention. If Switzerland were to apply quota to political refugees, this would be contrary to the UN Convention against Torture and the Geneva Convention with regard to the status of refugees. Quota may thus not be applied to persons who risk prosecution, torture, or inhumane treatment in their own country.[107]

The Swiss federal council therefore sought to find a solution and declared that it was endeavouring to agree on a solution with the EU so as not to endanger the bilateral agreements. Should that ultimately prove impossible, the Federal Council proposed introducing a unilateral safeguard clause as a means of controlling the immigration of persons covered by the bilateral agreement with the EU. Simultaneously there were intensive consultations with EU representatives, which continued through to the summer of 2016. However, following the UK's vote to leave the European Union, it became clear that an agreement with the EU would not be possible. On 21 September 2016, the national Council adopted a "light" version of the proposal to assure preferential treatment of Swiss nationals on the labour market. An agreement was reached on a new law which is believed to be compatible with the existing rules on the free movement of persons so as not to jeopardise Switzerland's bilateral agreements with the EU. New rules on unemployment were agreed which should limit the impact of foreign workers on the domestic job market. Employers will be obliged to advertise vacant positions to job centres and invite selected Swiss jobseekers for an interview. The Federal Council instructed the discussion of some variants. The first variant includes a provision that would require any measures for controlling immigration to take account of international conventions that have far-reaching consequences for Switzerland's status in Europe. In addition, it calls for the repeal of the transitional provision under which international conventions that are inconsistent with the new immigration amendment would have to be renegotiated and amended within a three-year time limit. The second variant calls only for the repeal of the transitional provision.

The Swiss Model in the UK?

The Swiss model seems attractive for the UK because of the à la carte concept and the sectorial approach. For example, the UK could choose to only conclude a tailor-made bilateral agreement on the free movement of services and goods, and not on the free movement of persons.[108] Or, it might conclude a bilateral agreement on the free movement of persons, however, thereby negotiating certain exceptions to be included for the UK.

It is highly debatable whether the EU would be willing to accept such an à la carte scenario. It is very time-consuming and laborious, and it is furthermore doubtful whether the EU would allow the UK a cherry-picking mechanism. Still, the UK will have to contribute to the budget, although this contribution would be lower in comparison to the scenario where the UK remained a member of the EEA.[109]

13.4.3   Greenland Copycat?

It should not be forgotten that the UK is not the first country to leave the European Union. Greenland left the then European Community without really breaking away from Denmark. It is a distinct community of Denmark.[110] Greenland's situation was special. It is a small area (55,847[111] inhabitants), fishery being its main economic activity. Moreover, as a result of the Home Rule Act, the competences regarding finances, the executive power, and local legislation in various domains (including social welfare and the labour market) were transferred from Denmark to Greenland.[112] Greenland's integration was rather difficult, as it wanted full control of its fishery and did not want to be dependent on fishing quota. As there was fishing only in the territory of Greenland, there was no interest in fishing in foreign waters. There are, however, some similarities with the current Brexit. The fear of a domino effect, like at the time that Greenland left the EU, is also present today. However, this fear was dismissed by the fact that it concerned an overseas, non-European territory, and developing area. Greenland could, nevertheless, set a precedent for territories in the same position, such as the French overseas territories. It was important for both the EU and Greenland to maintain a good relationship and carry on trade. These interests were to be safeguarded, which was for the most part solved by making Greenland one of the EU's Overseas Countries and Territories (OCT). The OCT Association provides in particular for the development of these territories.[113]

Exactly because Greenland was allowed to join the OCTs and no special arrangement was made, this probably also prevented other Member States to see Greenland as an example.[114]

Then again, there also are a number of considerable differences with the Brexit. For Greenland the main issue was the fishing industry. Practically no changes had to be made to the treaties and the relationship between Greenland and the EU was kept since Greenland's interests are represented by Denmark.[115] Certainly the free movement of workers was not really an issue. Furthermore, representation in the EU institutions—Parliament or European Council—posed no problems. If the EU had prevented Greenland from leaving the EU or had "punished" Greenland, this would have damaged the EU's reputation because of its history with European colonialism.[116]

In this respect, the Greenland scenario does not really appear to be an option for the UK.

"Greenland in Reverse"?

Some people advocate using Greenland as a precedent "in reverse" for Scotland, Northern Ireland, and Gibraltar,[117] as the Danish precedent has shown that one sovereign Member State within the EU can allow certain of its territories not to be a member of the EU. As Greenland and the Faroe Islands are not part of the EU, whereas they are part of the Kingdom of Denmark, in the reverse sense, certain regions within the UK are provided with opportunities.[118]

However, this would give rise to problems with regard to border checks, the representation in EU bodies, and the (im)possibilities for the Schengen membership. Furthermore, the Spanish prime minister—keeping Catalonia in the back of his mind—has already stated that in the event of a Brexit, Scotland has to leave as well. Put forward as an advantage of this option is that British companies would be able to resettle within the UK and still enjoy the benefits which the EU entails. It would also mean more freedom for England and Wales to experiment with relationships between the EU and the UK and to, for example, not remain a member of the EEA. On the other hand, this scenario would be more easily executable if England and Wales remained a member of the internal market. The more free trade there is with the UK, the easier it would also be for Scotland to stay in the EU.[119] Also, Gibraltar staying within the EU would prevent Spain from exerting more pressure to transfer the sovereignty over Gibraltar to Spain.[120] It is feared that Spain would again close its borders, which also happened between 1969 and 1985. Furthermore, Gibraltar's economy depends on Spanish frontier workers.[121] In order to retain this, the UK could use the precedent of Greenland, or it could remain a member of the EEA.

13.4.4   Turkey: A Customs Union

At a certain point, the EU also established a special relationship with Turkey by concluding an association agreement with this country. As a result, there has been a customs union since 1 January 1996.[122] It is, however, rather unlikely that this could serve as an example for the UK. After all, the objective of these agreements was that they would serve as preparations for a future membership, whereas the UK wants to leave the EU. This would be putting the cart before the horse.

Besides, it should be noted that this agreement offers only a limited number of advantages.[123] It would therefore be more of a step backwards for the UK and thus be considered far from attractive.

13.4.5   'Go It Alone': The WTO Model

Another option is probably the most drastic. It entails that the UK fully retreats from the EU. The UK would in that case get full sovereignty to conclude trade agreements. It should of course be noted, though, that the UK would have to negotiate separately and that it would thus have a less strong negotiating position than the EU. Also, negotiations would take a lot of time. The UK would not be obliged to incorporate rules on the internal market and to follow the EU's economic policy. Moreover, there would neither be a common agricultural policy, nor a common fishery policy. On the other hand, British service providers would have less access to the EU markets.

The biggest advantage would perhaps be that the UK would have more control over immigration, as it would no longer have to comply with the free movement of persons. As a result, the UK would regain control over migration into the UK. Nevertheless, some have already warned that a full exit from the free movement of persons will not automatically result in a decrease in migration into the UK. In addition, problems with immigration in the UK might increase. As the situation will remain the same for two years, first this could in the short term lead to an increase in immigration in the UK.[124]

Second, family reunification could cause a rise in migration into the UK. To this end, economic migrants, refugees, and students could invoke Article 8 of the European Convention on Human Rights (ECHR).[125]

Third, irregular (illegal) migration could increase. The British economy depends on cheap labour, and thus an exit from the internal market does not necessarily mean the end of cheap labour in the UK; the chance that this will happen under the radar even more will only increase.[126]

Fourth, EU citizens might try to reach the UK via Ireland. This is politically very sensitive, as it was decided not to have border checks between Ireland and the UK exactly because this border is too extensive and too porous.[127]

Fifth, the UK might introduce an Australian inspired points-based system. This entails that migrants are allowed access to the British labour market based on certain qualities, and not so much based on the fact that an employer has selected them to fill a vacancy.[128] In countries such as Australia and New Zealand, this resulted in an increase in migration, as the emphasis of this system is on the selection of migrants and not so much on limiting migration.[129] Nevertheless, this would not necessarily have the same consequence in the UK. After all, this type of system has a more limiting effect for EU citizens than the current system. This system thus entails increased central planning by the government, which immediately attracts the criticism that it is not adjusted to the needs of employers, whereas it is to the government's perception. It allows people to be given access who are then not able to find employment. Or the other way around: people are refused access who would be able to find employment.[130]

Finally, an exit from the EU increases pressure on the British border control services. It is not certain whether they will better succeed in preventing irregular migration. The past few years, the British government has been making personnel cuts in the British border control. The yearly budget will have to be increased considerably in order to control the Irish border, but also to meet the British people's expectations.[131]

Acquired Rights?

Another problem which could arise is that British citizens who currently enjoy free movement of persons in the EU will in future no longer be able to do so, and vice versa for EU citizens within the EU. Will these persons lose all their "acquired" rights?

To determine acquired rights on the basis of a treaty that is terminated, Article 70 of the Vienna Convention on the Law of Treaties can be referred to. Article 70 of the Vienna Convention states:

"*Consequences of the termination of a treaty*

1. *Unless the treaty otherwise provides or the parties otherwise agree, the termination of a treaty under its provisions or in accordance with the present Convention:*

    (a) *releases the parties from any obligation further to perform the treaty;*
    (b) *does not affect any right, obligation or legal situation of the parties created through the execution of the treaty prior to its termination.*

2. *If a State denounces or withdraws from a multilateral treaty, paragraph 1 applies in the relations between that State and each of the other parties to the treaty from the date when such denunciation or withdrawal takes effect.*"

The key question here is whether the withdrawal agreement as provided for by Article 50 of the Treaty of the European Union[132] can be considered as the exception to Article 70 (1) (b) of the Vienna Convention, in the sentence "unless the treaty otherwise provides or the parties otherwise agree". If nothing is agreed in the withdrawal agreement, Article 50 TEU may be considered as the exception to this provision, as a result of which all rights and obligations would be cancelled after two years.[133] That is why chances are real that the withdrawal agreement will regulate the rights of EU citizens in the UK and of British citizens in other Member States. For this reason, it has already been proposed to provide for a settlement for this, in particular to include such a clause in the agreement, for example:

1. *Any citizens of the UK residing in the EU as of [Brexit Day], and any EU citizens residing in the UK as of that date, shall retain any rights which they acquired pursuant to EU free movement law before that date. They shall also continue to acquire rights which were in the process of acquisition as of that date.*
2. *The parties shall give full effect to this principle in EU or national law, as the case may be.*
3. *The EU/UK Joint Committee may adopt further measures to implement this rule.*[134]

EU citizens based in the UK could also invoke the ECHR for the protection of their rights. They could invoke Article 8 ECHR to protect their property. On the other hand, Article 14 of the ECHR could make sure that it is no longer justifiable that a certain category of third-country nationals are treated differently from all other third-country nationals.[135]

Looking at the past, the UK could withdraw the European Communities Act 1972, as a result of which Regulations implemented in British law no longer have effect in the UK.[136] It is rather unlikely that the UK would take such a drastic step. Besides, it may be expected that certainly in the beginning courts will still follow the case law of the CJEU.

13.4.6   The Canadian Model

The UK could also adopt the Canadian model. Canada has a free trade agreement with Mexico and the USA (NAFTA), and an agreement was negotiated with the EU that gives limited access to the internal market (CETA[137]). This agreement has not yet entered into force, however.[138] The free trade agreement among other things entails that the parties to the agreement still have separate, external tariffs, but that internally almost all tariffs have been abolished for goods and services, which entails an almost free movement of goods and services. Nevertheless, there is no free movement of persons and capital.[139]

This model seems suitable for the UK, as it would gain control over its borders and as it would no longer be bound by the free movement of persons. The UK would also have to contribute less to the EU budget.[140] However, it could be expected that concluding such an agreement would take a very long time.[141] Also, it is not certain that the EU would want to offer such an agreement to the UK. As repeatedly emphasised above, the four freedoms are an inseparable part, and a too advantageous deal is dangerous as it could cause a domino effect in other Member States.[142]

13.5   Concluding Thoughts

It could be argued that UK-EU relations have always been specific and not easy-going. It started with the delay in acceding to the EU and it continued with reservations to the Community Social Charter, the Social Policy Agreement, and a changing legal regime for third-country nationals moving within the EU, leading to the New Settlement and the Leave vote by the UK.

Although the New Settlement, which was concluded before the so-called Brexit vote, never became applicable, it may have consequences for the future shaping of EU social policy and social security coordination, especially in the field of family benefits and social assistance. It is argued that the UK vote to leave the EU might not only present a success for the UK, but also a success for the EU. The European Commission already announced that there will be no indexation of family benefits in the (near) future, despite distinctive aspirations of certain Member States. However, pressure from some Member States and certain CJEU judgments may still be a matter of concern for the EU.

Nevertheless, the UK leaving the EU will have a certain impact, and it might be a good time to reconsider certain established rules and practices in order to prepare the EU and its citizens for turbulent times still to come. For the UK, it remains an issue to what extent it will still be a "united" country as Brexit has relaunched the move to Scottish independence and may possibly lead to an Irish unification.

For the UK, but also for EU citizens, it will be important to find out as quickly as possible what the situation will be. Currently, however, it is far from clear. On 1 March 2017, the House of Lords, by 358 votes to 256, a majority of 102, voted in favour of amending the European Union (Notification of Withdrawal) Bill to guarantee the rights of EU nationals living in the UK after Brexit. The amendment states that:

> Within three months of exercising the power under section 1(1), Ministers of the Crown must bring forward proposals to ensure that citizens of another European Union or European Economic Area country and their family members, who are legally resident in the United Kingdom on the day on which this Act is passed, continue to be treated in the same way with regards to their EU derived-rights and, in the case of residency, their potential to acquire such rights in the future.[143]

On 13 March 2017, the UK Government overturned the House of Lords' amendment in the House of Commons, leaving EU citizens in the UK with a continuing uncertainty.[144] For new people entering the EU, this would imply that they will have to rely on UK migration law (as modified under the influence of EU law until the moment of leaving the EU?). That would enable the UK to discriminate directly and indirectly against EU nationals through a mix of immigration laws and entitlement conditions such as residence, presence, and so on.[145] Similarly, UK nationals who work or live in the EU might lose the general application of fundamental principles under the EU Coordination Regulations such as equal treatment, export of benefits, and aggregation of periods.

Concerning the option for a new relation between the EU and the UK, Prime Minister Theresa May has recently declared that she is opting for a hard Brexit, leaving the single market. The UK cannot accept the four freedoms regarding goods, capital, services, and people attached to the single market. "Being out of the EU but a member of the single market would mean complying with the EU's rules and regulations that implement those freedoms, without having a vote on what those rules and regulations are", she pointed out. She insisted that the message from British voters was clear: "Brexit must mean control of the number of people who come to Britain from Europe. And that is what we will deliver". May added that a post-Brexit UK could not accept the case law of the CJEU. "We will not have truly left the European Union if we are not in control of our own laws", she said, adding that "leaving the European Union will mean that our laws will be made in Westminster, Edinburgh, Cardiff and Belfast".[146]

On March 29, May triggered Article 50, notifying the European Council that the UK withdraws from the European Union. In this letter she indicates, as a second principle for discussion, "We should always put our citizens first". "There is obvious complexity in the discussions we are about to undertake, but we should remember that at the heart of our talks are the interests of all our citizens. There are, for example, many citizens of the remaining member states living in the UK, and UK citizens living elsewhere in the European Union, and we should aim to strike an early agreement about their rights".[147]

These declarations clearly show several possible future judicial challenges concerning free movement between the EU and the UK, and it raises the question about the new "unique" model arrangement to be concluded between the UK and the EU.

Notes

1. Shaw, J. "Where does the UK belong?", in Verschueren, H. (ed.), *Residence, employment and social rights of mobile persons. On how EU law defines where they belong*, Antwerpen, Intersentia, 2016, p. 12.
2. Treaty amending, with regard to Greenland, the Treaties establishing the European Communities, OJ L 29, 1.2.1985, pp. 1–7.
3. OJ L 160, 20.6.1985, pp. 7–8. See also Article 90 of Regulation (EC) 883/2004.
4. The UK subsequently adopted the Charter in 1998. For more on the Community Social Charter, see Bercusson, B. "The European

Community's Charter of Fundamental Social Rights of Workers", *Modern Law Review*, Vol. 53 (1990), No. 5, New Perspectives on European Law, p. 624.

5. This included Directive 94/95 on European Works Council, Directive 97/80 on burden of proof, Directive 96/34/EC on parental leave and Directive 97/81/EC on part-time workers. HM Government, Review of the Balance of Competences between the United Kingdom and the European Union: Social and Employment Policy (Summer 2014), p. 18.

6. Article 48 EEC Treaty. Social security coordination was based on Article 51 EEC Treaty.

7. The social security regulations are accompanied by implementing regulations, that is, Regulation (EEC) 4/58 and Regulation (EEC) 574/72, respectively.

8. R. Cornelissen, ("50 Years of European Social Security Coordination", European Journal of Social Security (EJSS), Vol. 11 (2009), No. 1–2), p. 25 cites the document CASSTM/59/6 of the Administrative Commission on social security for migrant workers.

9. Today Articles 48 and 352 TFEU.

10. Cornelissen, R., "50 Years of European Social Security Coordination", *European Journal of Social Security (EJSS)*, Vol. 11 (2009), No. 1–2, p. 26.

11. *Ibid.*, p. 28.

12. Apart from refugees and stateless persons, who were covered also by Regulations (EEC) 3/58 and 1408/71.

13. Articles 78 and following TFEU.

14. Regulation (EU) No 1231/2010 of the European Parliament and of the Council of 24 November 2010 extending Regulation (EC) No 883/2004 and Regulation (EC) No 987/2009 to nationals of third countries who are not already covered by these Regulations solely on the ground of their nationality OJ L 344, 29.12.2010, p. 1.

15. Brussels, 19 February 2016, EUCO 1/16. The UK referendum was held on 23 June 2016.

16. Or the New Settlement Decision. Barnard, C.: "Could free movement of persons be confined to free movement of workers in any Brexit deal?", http://www.cels.law.cam.ac.uk/brexitfree-movement-persons-and-new-legal-order/catherine-barnard-could-free-movement-persons-be (December 2016), p. 3.

17. Article 68a of Regulation (EC) 883/2004. It is interesting to observe that for family benefits, a distinction can be made between the entitling

person (a child), the entitled person (one of the parents) and the receiving person (another parent or other person caring for a child). STRBAN, G. "Family benefits in the EU - is it still possible to coordinate them?", *Maastricht Journal of European and Comparative Law*, Vol. 23 (2016), No. 5, p. 783.

18. See Case C-363/08 *Slanina*, EU:C:2009:732 or Case C-378/14 *Trapkowski*, EU:C:2015:720.
19. Point 2(e) of Chap. I. The United Kingdom and the European Union.
20. Family allowances are still mentioned in Article 15 of Regulation (EC) 883/2004.
21. "Advances of maintenance allowances" are recoverable advances intended to compensate for a parent's failure to fulfil his/her legal obligation of maintenance to his/her own child, which is an obligation under family law. These advances should not be considered as a direct benefit from collective support in favour of families and the coordination rules should not apply to them anymore. Recital 36 of the Preamble to Regulation (EC) 883/2004.
22. Article 1(z) of Regulation (EC) 883/2004. An insertion in the annex is a constitutive element and in the case that childbirth allowances are not mentioned in this annex, they would be fully subject to the coordination rules (and thus exportable to other Member States).
23. In Case C-333/00, *Maaheimo*, EU:C:2002:641, the CJEU argued that home child-care allowance, provided by the Finish local community, is intended to meet family expenses and has to be considered as a family benefit.
24. Case C-75/11, *Commission v Austria*, EU:C:2012:605. Here, the granting of reduced fares on public transport only to students whose parents are in receipt of Austrian family allowances was contrary to EU law.
25. In Case C-177/12, *Lachheb*, EU:C:2013:689, the CJEU established that the fact that a benefit is governed by national tax law is not conclusive for the purpose of evaluating its constituent elements, which determine whether a benefit is subject to coordination or not. Hence, tax reduction (child bonus in Luxembourg) is a family benefit in social security coordination law.
26. Case C-303/12, *Imfeld and Garcet*, EU:C:2013:822 (on tax exemption for dependent children under the German tax law and the supplementary tax-free income allowance for dependent children under the Belgian tax law).

27. Spiegel, B. (ed), Daxkobler, K., Strban, G., Van Der Mei, A P., "Analytical report 2014: The relationship between social security coordination and taxation law", FreSsco, European Commission, April 2015

28. National courts followed the arguments of the CJEU in the mentioned cases and granted the family benefit. The German Federal Central Tax Office even issued special guidelines for family benefits, that is, Bundeszentralamt für Steuern: Dienstanweisung zur Durchführung des Familienleistungsausgleichs nach dem X. Abschnitt des Einkommensteuergesetzes (DA-FamEStG) Stand 2011.

29. Case C-4/13, *Fassbender-Firman*, EU:C:2014:2344. More on anti-overlapping rule after the judgment in Case C-347/12, *Wiering*, EU:C:2014:300, Strban, G. "Family benefits in the EU - is it still possible to coordinate them?", *Maastricht Journal of European and Comparative Law*, Vol. 23 (2016), No. 5, p. 791.

30. Probably yes (*Fassbender-Firman* EU:C:2014:2344). See Spiegel, B. (ed.), Carrascosa Bermejo, D., Henberg, A., Strban, G., "Assessment of the impact of amendments to the EU social security coordination rules on export of family benefits", Analytical Report 2015, FreSsco, European Commission, June 2015.

31. Regulation (EEC) 31, and (EAEC) 11, laying down the Staff Regulations of Officials and the Conditions of Employment of Other Servants of the European Economic Community and the European Atomic Energy Community, [1962] OJ P 45/1385, as amended. However, under Article 67(4) of Regulation (EEC) 31, and (EAEC) 11, adjustment only applies if family allowance is directly paid to a person other than the official to whom the custody of the child is entrusted.

32. Case C-41/84, *Pinna,* EU:C:1986:1.

33. Point I. (2) of the European Council Conclusions (18 and 19 February 2016).

34. On indexation, with practical examples, see also Spiegel, B. (ed.), Carrascosa Bermejo, D., Henberg, A., Strban, G., "Assessment of the impact of amendments to the EU social security coordination rules on export of family benefits", Analytical Report 2015, FreSsco, European Commission, June 2015.

35. In Annex V to the Council Conclusions Member States should have "an option to index" such benefits to the conditions of the Member State where the child resides.

36. Reference could be made also to cross-border healthcare, where many go for treatment to high income Member States, including the UK, and the reason why lower income Member States cannot provide (high quality, equally accessible and sustainable) healthcare seems irrelevant (e.g. Case C-268/13, *Petru*, EU:C:2014:2271).
37. Article 4 of Chap. I of the Council Conclusions from February 2016.
38. European Commission, Fairness at the heart of Commission's proposal to update EU rules on social security coordination, Brussels, 13 December 2016.
39. Article 3(5)(a) Regulation (EC) 883/2004.
40. C.f. ILO Convention 102 concerning minimum standards of social security or Council of Europe Convention on social and medical assistance.
41. Currently Regulation (EU) 429/2011 on freedom of movement for workers within the Union, OJ L 141, 27.5.2011, pp. 1–12.
42. Directive 2004/38/EC, OJ 158, 30.4.2004, pp. 77–123.
43. Article 24 Directive 2004/38/EC.
44. Articles 4 and 70 Regulation (EC) 883/204. For more on SNCBs see VERSCHUEREN, H., "Special non-contributory benefits in Regulation 1408/71, Regulation 883/2004 and the case law of the ECJ", *European Journal of Social Security (EJSS)*, Vol. 11 (2009), No. 1–2, p. 217; Lhernould, J-P. (ed.), Eichenhofer, E., Rennuy, N., Van Overmeiren, F., Wollenschläger, F., "Assessment of the impact of amendments to the EU social security coordination rules to clarify its relationship with Directive 2004/38/EC as regards economically inactive persons", Analytical Report 2015, FreSsco, European Commission, June 2015, 71 p.
45. Case C-140/12, *Brey*, EU:C:2013:565.
46. Case C-333/13, *Dano*, EU:C:2014:2358. The British Daily Mail actually tracked down Ms Dano ('The Roma gipsy who sparked a crackdown on benefit tourism: Elisabeta Dano, 25, tracked down to German city after finding herself at centre of landmark welfare case') and published her picture, at www.dailymail.co.uk/news/article-2835442/The-Roma-gipsy-sparked-crackdown-benefit-tourism-Elisabeta-Dano-25-tracked-German-city-finding-centre-landmark-welfare-case.html#ixzz4Vr1FbLSK
47. Case C-67/14, *Alimanovic*, EU:C:2015:597.
48. Case C-299/14 *García-Nieto and Others*, EU:C:2016:114. See also the CJEU's decision in case C-308/14, *Commission v United Kingdom*, EU:C:2016:436.

49. Verschueren, H., "Free Movement or Benefit Tourism: The Unreasonable Burden of Brey", *European Journal of Migration and Law*, Vol. 16 (2014), Issue 2, pp. 147–179; Minderhoud, P., "Sufficient Resources and Residence Rights under Directive 2004/38", in Verschueren, H. (ed.), *Residence, employment and social rights of mobile persons. On how EU law defines where they belong*, Antwerpen, Intersentia, 2016, pp. 47–74; Pfeil, W. J., "Social benefits for migrating unemployed persons", *Rivista del Diritto della Sicurezza Sociale* (RDSS), 2016, No. 2, pp. 271–288.
50. Jorens, Y. (ed.), Spiegel, B. (ed.), Fillon, J-C., Strban, G., "Key challenges for the social security coordination Regulations in the perspective of 2020", trESS Think Tank report 2013, European Commission, 2013, p. 18.
51. See, for example, CJEU decision in Case C-249/83, *Hoeckx*, EU:C:1985:139.
52. For more on this, see, for example, Jorens, Y. (ed.), Spiegel, B. (ed.), Fillon, J-C., Strban, G., "Key challenges for the social security coordination Regulations in the perspective of 2020", trESS Think Tank report 2013, European Commission, 2013, p. 46.
53. STRBAN, G. "Family benefits in the EU – Is it still possible to coordinate them?", *Maastricht Journal of European and Comparative Law*, Vol. 23 (2016), No. 5, p. 789.
54. Compare with the idea of N. Rennuy of gradual transition where the level of social assistance should also be adjusted in time. However, it might be required that minimum subsistence in the host Member State is provided from the day of arrival and not only gradually. On ideas of delayed transition and a pro-rata *temporis* solution, see N. Rennuy, "The Role of the EU Legislature, presentation at the FreSsco seminar on 'Social Tourism' within the EU: Legal and Practical Reflections on a Political Debate", Leiden, 28 October 2016.
55. http://www.norden.org/en/om-samarbejdet-1/nordic-agreements/trea-ties-and-agreements/social-and-health-care/nordic-convention-on-social-assistance-and-social-services (January 2017).
56. http://www.norden.org/en/om-samarbejdet-1/nordic-agreements/trea-ties-and-agreements/social-and-health-care/nordisk-konvention-om-social-trygghet-1 (January 2017).
57. Case C-308/14, *European Commission v UK*, EU:C:2016:436 (14 June 2016).

58. See Agreement on European Economic Area: (OJ No L 1, 3.1.1994, p. 3) for text, see http://www.efta.int/media/documents/legal-texts/eea/the-eea-agreement/Main%20Text%20of%20the%20Agreement/EEAagreement.pdf; see also Burke, C., Isberg Hannesson, O., Bangsund, K., "Life on the Edge: EFTA and the EEA as a Future for the UK and Europe", *EPLJ*, 2016, 77.

59. See http://www.efta.int/eea/eea-agreement/eea-basic-features#5 and NORDLING, H., "The EEA Agreement and the 'Norway option': integration without co-determination", Eutopia Law 2016, https://eutopialaw.com/2016/07/05/the-eea-agreement-and-the-norway-option-integration-without-co-determination/

60. This does in no way imply that these domains completely fall outside the influence of EU law and policy. For example, EFTA Member States get free access to the European market for unprocessed fish products, but for processed fish products, higher tariffs apply. With regard to agricultural policy, there are rules and standards for additives.

61. Dhingra, S. and Sampson, T., "Life after Brexit: what are the UK's options outside the European Union?", Centre for Economic Performance, London School of Economics, 10. http://eprints.lse.ac.uk/66143/

62. See, for example, the EFTA agreement with Canada, which entered into force in July 2009, contrary to the agreement between the EU and Canada, which has not entered into force yet. For the text of this agreement, see http://www.international.gc.ca/trade-agreements-accords-commerciaux/agr-acc/eu-ue/efta.aspx?lang=eng

63. See, for example, Stabilisation and Association Agreement between the European Communities and their Member States, of the one part, and the Republic of Albania, of the other part (L107, 28/04/2009), p. 166, which states:

Article 46

  1. *Subject to the conditions and modalities applicable in each Member State:*

     – *treatment accorded to workers who are Albanian nationals and who are legally employed in the territory of a Member State shall be free of any discrimination based on nationality, as regards working conditions, remuneration or dismissal, compared to its own nationals;*

> — *the legally resident spouse and children of a worker legally employed in the territory of a Member State, with the exception of seasonal workers and of workers coming under bilateral Agreements within the meaning of Article 47, unless otherwise provided by such Agreements, shall have access to the labour market of that Member State, during the period of that worker's authorised stay of employment.*

The Euro-Mediterranean Agreement establishing an association between the European Communities and their Member States, of the one part, and the Republic of Tunisia, of the other part (*OJ L 278, 21.10.2005, p. 9–169*), for example, states:

Article 64

> 1. *The treatment accorded by each Member State to workers of Tunisian nationality employed in its territory shall be free from any discrimination based on nationality, as regards working conditions, remuneration and dismissal, relative to its own nationals.*
> 2. *All Tunisian workers allowed to undertake paid employment in the territory of a Member State on a temporary basis shall be covered by the provisions of paragraph 1 with regard to working conditions and remuneration.*
> 3. *Tunisia shall accord the same treatment to workers who are nationals of a Member State and employed in its territory.*

64. Article 66-76 EEA Agreement.
65. See article 6 EEA Agreement: "*Without prejudice to future developments of case law, the provisions of this Agreement, in so far as they are identical in substance to corresponding rules of the Treaty establishing the European Economic Community and the Treaty establishing the European Coal and Steel Community and to acts adopted in application of these two Treaties, shall, in their implementation and application, be interpreted in conformity with the relevant rulings of the Court of Justice of the European Communities given prior to the date of signature of this Agreement.*"
66. See, for example, Case E-3/04, *Athanasios* on the E101 form (now A1 posting form): "*It follows from the principle of sincere cooperation and the aims of the choice of law rules contained in Title II of Regulation 1408/71, that once form E 101 has been issued, it is binding on other Contracting Parties in so far as it establishes a presumption that the individual in ques-*

tion falls under the social security legislation of the issuing State (see Case C-202/97 Fitzwilliams, at paragraphs 52 to 53; and Case C-178/97 Barry Banks, at paragraphs 39 to 40). The same applies with respect to equivalent official statements. If the competent institution of the flag State doubts the correctness of the issued form, the competent institution of the State of residence is obliged to reconsider whether the form was properly issued and, if appropriate withdraw it (see Fitzwilliam, at paragraph 56; and Barry Banks, at paragraph 43). 32 In a situation, such as the one at hand, where no form E 101 has been issued, the States concerned are similarly under an obligation to ensure the correct application of the choice of law rules contained in Title II of Regulation 1408/71. That follows from the principle of sincere cooperation which is laid down in Article 3 EEA. The flag State must assess whether the conditions of Article 14b(4) of Regulation 1408/71 are fulfilled, and for that purpose evaluate other evidence presented to it, including unofficial evidence. Any other solution would impair legal certainty and thereby undermine the aims of the choice of law rules in Regulation 1408/71 and restrain the free movement of workers." (paragraph 31–32), see http://www.eftacourt.int/cases/detail/?tx_nvcases_pi1%5Bcase_id%5D=69&cHash=57c1d80b929ecf591de1fa9537a5576e

67. Nordling, H., "The EEA Agreement and the 'Norway option': integration without co-determination", Eutopia Law 2016, https://eutopialaw.com/2016/07/05/the-eea-agreement-and-the-norway-option-integration-without-co-determination/

68. Helgesen, V., "Brexit, a Norwegian View", https://www.regjeringen.no/no/aktuelt/brexit_norway/id2402031/

69. Mark Stanford, King's College http://www.telegraph.co.uk/news/2016/06/27/after-brexit-only-one-thing-can-keep-britain-together-the-norway/. See also PEERS, S., "What next after the UK vote to leave the EU?", http://eulawanalysis.blogspot.be/

70. Munchau, W., "Brexit: The Norway option is the best available for the UK", http://www.ft.com/cms/s/0/eb8dbe8c-3d0c-11e6-9f2c-36b487ebd80a.html#axzz4EOM3bgmo

71. "What is the single market? How is it different from the EEA? Can the UK stay in after Brexit?" http://www.independent.co.uk/news/business/news/single-market-what-is-it-brexit-eu-referendum-eea-boris-johnson-economy-effects-a7106066.html

72. "BREXIT, Employment law consequences of Brexit", Addleshaw Goddard, http://www.lexology.com/library/detail.aspx?g=1a6e17d9-abc5-4269-9ad2-ae3e086e4d52

73. http://eeagrants.org/Who-we-are/Norway-GrantsFor example, indirectly Norway helps to pay, through "EEA Grants", to tackle inequalities between the different EEA Member States. In 2009–2014, the EFTA Member States reserved €993 million to even out these inequalities. 95.8% was contributed by Norway.

74. "How Britain voted", https://yougov.co.uk/news/2016/06/27/how-britain-voted/

75. "Hard Evidence: how areas with low immigration voted mainly for Brexit",https://theconversation.com/hard-evidence-how-areas-with-low-immigration-voted-mainly-for-brexit-62138

76. Theresa May stated: "*When we take the big calls, we'll think not of the powerful, but you. When we pass new laws we'll listen not to the mighty, but to you. When it comes to taxes we'll prioritise not the wealthy but you*", see "Theresa May appeals to centre ground but cabinet tilts to the right", http://www.theguardian.com/politics/2016/jul/13/theresa-may-becomes-britains-prime-minister

77. Portes, J., "The 'EEA minus' option: amending not ending free movement",http://ukandeu.ac.uk/the-eea-minus-option-amending-not-ending-free-movement/

78. Schulz, M., "The EU must not treat the UK as a deserter – we can negotiate without rancour", https://www.theguardian.com/comment-isfree/2016/jul/12/brexit-eu-uk-negotiate-without-rancour

79. Peers, S., "What next after the UK vote to leave the EU? http://eulawanalysis.blogspot.be/

80. Schulz, M., "The EU must not treat the UK as a deserter – we can negotiate without rancour", https://www.theguardian.com/comment-isfree/2016/jul/12/brexit-eu-uk-negotiate-without-rancour

81. Vahl, M., and Grolimund, N., *Integration without membership: Switzerland's Bilateral Agreements with the European Union*, Brussels, Centre for European Policy Studies, 2006, 9.

82. Marescau, M., *Bilateral Agreements concluded by the European Community*, Leiden, Martinus Nijhoff Publishers, 2006, 413.

83. See (2002) OJ L114; other policy areas of common interest are research, public procurement, reciprocal recognition of conformity assessments, access to the market in agricultural products, and transport.

84. Vahl, M., and Grolimund, N., *Integration without membership: Switzerland's Bilateral Agreements with the European Union*, Brussels, Centre for European Policy Studies, 2006, 78.

85. The European Economic Area (EEA), Switzerland, and the North, http://www.europarl.europa.eu/atyourservice/en/displayFtu.html?ftuId=FTU_6.5.3.html

86. Agreement between the European Community and its Member States, of the one part, and the Swiss Confederation, of the other, on the free movement of persons—Final Act—Joint Declarations—Information relating to the entry into force of the seven Agreements with the Swiss Confederation in the sectors free movement of persons, air and land transport, public procurement, scientific and technological cooperation, mutual recognition in relation to conformity assessment, and trade in agricultural products *Official Journal L 114, 30/04/2002 P. 0006 – 0072*.

87. Felder, D., and Kaddous, C., "Accords bilatéraux Suisse – UE (Commentaires")", Basel, Helbing & Lichtenhahn, 2001, 260.

88. Which took a start with the case *Martinez Sala* (see Case 85/96, *Martinez Sala*, ECLI:EU:C:1998:217.

89. Breitenmoser, S., "Sectoral Agreement between the EC and Switzerland: contents and context", *Common Market Law Review* 2003, 1162.

90. Article 10 of the Agreement between the EU and Switzerland on free movement of persons.

91. Article 10 of the Agreement: this in respect of access to an economic activity for the following two categories of residence: residence for a period of more than four months and less than one year and residence for a period equal to, or exceeding, one year.

92. Article 10, §4 of the Agreement between the EU and Switzerland on free movement of persons; see also Schwok, R., and Levrat, N., "Switzerland's Relations with the EU after the Adoption of the Seven Bilateral Agreements", *European Foreign Affairs Review* 2001, 338. https://www.kluwerlawonline.com/abstract.php?area=Journals&id=383251

93. *Ibid.*

94. *Ibid.*

95. Marescau, M., "Bilateral Agreements concluded by the European Community", Leiden, Martinus Nijhoff Publishers, 2006, 420.

96. Breitenmoser, S., "Sectoral Agreement between the EC and Switzerland: contents and context", *Common Market Law Review* 2003, 1160. See, for example, Article 25 of the Agreement on free movement of persons: "*The seven Agreements referred to in paragraph 1 shall cease to apply six months after receipt of notification of non-renewal referred to in paragraph 2 or termination referred to in paragraph 3*".

97. Vahl, M., and Grolimund, N., "Integration without membership: Switzerland's Bilateral Agreements with the European Union", Brussels, Centre for European Policy Studies, 2006, 24.

98. Breitenmoser, S., "Sectoral Agreement between the EC and Switzerland: contents and context", *Common Market Law Review* 2003, 1155.

99. Article 16, §2 Bilateral Agreement between EU and Switzerland on free movement of persons: "Insofar as the application of this Agreement involves concepts of Community law, account shall be taken of the relevant case-law of the Court of Justice of the European Communities prior to the date of its signature. Case-law after that date shall be brought to Switzerland's attention. To ensure that the Agreement works properly, the Joint Committee shall, at the request of either Contracting Party, determine the implications of such case-law."

100. Vahl, M., and Grolimund, N., "Integration without membership: Switzerland's Bilateral Agreements with the European Union", Brussels, Centre for European Policy Studies, 2006, 15.

101. Pedersen, T., "European Union and the EFTA Countries", London, Pinter Publishers, 1994, 121.

102. Article 121a van de Zwitserse Grondwet.

103. Ambuhl, M., and Zurcher, S., "Immigration and Swiss-EU Free Movement of Persons: questions of a Safeguard Clause", *SPSR* 2015, 77. See further, for example, "*For us, EU-Swiss relations come as a package*", said Hannes Swoboda, a member of the European Parliament. "*If Switzerland suspends immigration from the EU, it will not be able to count on all the economic and trade benefits it is currently enjoying. We will not allow […] cherry-picking*". "EU-Swiss relations in turmoil after immigration vote", http://www.euractiv.com/section/justice-home-affairs/news/eu-swiss-relations-in-turmoil-after-immigration-vote/; https://www.theguardian.com/world/2014/feb/10/switzerland-talks-eu-immigration-referendum

104. http://europa.eu/rapid/press-release_MEMO-14-96_fr.htm

105. Carrera, S., Guild, E., and Eisele, K., "No Move without Free Movement: the EU-Swiss Controversy over quotas for free movement of persons", CEPS Policy Brief 2015.

106. Chetail, V., "The Swiss vote against mass immigration and international law: A preliminary assessment", Migration Policy Practice 2014, 13. http://papers.ssrn.com/sol3/papers.cfm?abstract_id=2426824

107. Chetail, V., "The Swiss vote against mass immigration and international law: A preliminary assessment", Migration Policy Practice 2014, 14. http://papers.ssrn.com/sol3/papers.cfm?abstract_id=2426824

108. Dhingra, S., and Sampson, T., "Life after Brexit: what are the UK's options outside the European Union?", Centre for Economic Performance, London School of Economics, 6. http://eprints.lse.ac.uk/66143/

109. Dhingra, S., and Sampson, T., "Life after Brexit: what are the UK's options outside the European Union?", Centre for Economic Performance, London School of Economics, 9. http://eprints.lse.ac.uk/66143/

110. In a referendum in 1982, the people of Greenland expressed the desire to leave the European Community. By means of an amendment to the European Treaties, they do not apply to Greenland as from 1 February 1985 (see Treaty of 13 March 1984 amending, with regard to Greenland, the Treaties establishing the European Communities, (1985), OJ L 29/1). But Greenland remains part of Denmark and therefore falls under the association arrangements of the EC Treaty.

111. http://www.stat.gl/default.asp?lang=en

112. For the text, see http://www.stm.dk/_p_12712.html

113. Association of the overseas countries and territories: Article 198-204 TFEU

Article 198 […] *The purpose of association shall be to promote the economic and social development of the countries and territories and to establish close economic relations between them and the Union as a whole.* […]

  Article 199 […] *Association shall have the following objectives:*

1. *Member States shall apply to their trade with the countries and territories the same treatment as they accord each other pursuant to the Treaties.*

2. *Each country or territory shall apply to its trade with Member States and with the other countries and territories the same treatment as that which it applies to the European State with which is has special relations.*

3. *The Member States shall contribute to the investments required for the progressive development of these countries and territories.*

4. *For investments financed by the Union, **participation in tenders** and supplies shall be open on equal terms to all natural and legal persons who are nationals of a Member State or of one of the countries and territories.*

5. *In relations between Member States and the countries and territories the right of establishment of nationals and companies or firms shall be regulated in accordance with the provisions and procedures laid down in the Chapter relating to the right of establishment and on a non-discriminatory basis, subject to any special provisions laid down pursuant to Article 203.*

114. Harhoff, F., "Greenland's withdrawal from the European communities", *CML Rev.* 1983, 13–33, https://www.kluwerlawonline.com/abstract.php?area=Journals&id=COLA1983002

115. Nicolaides, P., "Is Withdrawal from the European Union a Manageable Option? A Review of Economic and Legal Complexities." http://aei.pitt.edu/58466/

116. Friel, R.J., "Providing a constitutional framework for withdrawal from the EU: article 59 of the draft European Constitution." *ICLQ* 2004, 411.

117. Sarmiento, D., "Brexit or the art of 'doing a Greenland'", https://despiteourdifferencesblog.wordpress.com/

118. Pram Gad, U., "Could a 'reverse Greenland' arrangement keep Scotland and Northern Ireland in the EU?", http://blogs.lse.ac.uk/europpblog/2016/07/07/reverse-greenland-arrangement/#Author

119. Keating, M., "How could Scotland remain in the EU?", http://ukandeu.ac.uk/how-could-scotland-remain-in-the-eu/

120. O'leary, B., "Detoxifying the UK's exit from the EU: a multi-national compromise is possible", http://blogs.lse.ac.uk/brexitvote/2016/06/27/de-toxifying-the-uks-eu-exit-process-a-multi-national-compromise-is-possible/

121. "Gibraltar is dragged from Europe against its will", http://www.economist.com/news/europe/21702147-peninsula-now-faces-uncertain-future-outside-eu-gibraltar-dragged-europe

122. See Agreement of September 12, 1963 establishing an Association between the EEC and Turkey ((1973) OJ C C113/1) with an additional protocol of November 23, 1970 (OJ L 293/73). Decision No 1/95 of

the EC-Turkey Association Council of December 22, 1995 on implementing the final phase of the Customs Union ((1996) OJ L 35/1).

123. For instance, the free movement of workers is very limited. The right of Turkish nationals to move to an EU country to work depends entirely on the laws of that country. There is also no free movement of Turkish workers between EU countries. There are only some rights granted to Turkish workers who are legally employed in an EU country and who are duly registered as belonging to the labour force. (see also Additional Protocol to the Association Agreement of 23 November 1970 (OJ EC No C 113/17, 24.12.1973) and Decision 1/80 of the Association Council).

124. MCGOVERN, P., "Five Problems with UK immigration control post-Brexit", http://blogs.lse.ac.uk/brexitvote/2016/07/11/five-problems-with-uk-immigration-control-post-brexit/

125. *Ibid.*

126. *Ibid.*

127. *Ibid.*

128. Commentary: "What would UK immigration policy look like after Brexit?", The migration observatory at the University of Oxford, http://migrationobservatory.ox.ac.uk/commentary/what-would-uk-immigration-policy-look-after-brexit

129. Mcgovern, P., "Five Problems with UK immigration control post-Brexit", http://blogs.lse.ac.uk/brexitvote/2016/07/11/five-problems-with-uk-immigration-control-post-brexit/

130. Commentary: "What would UK immigration policy look like after Brexit?", The migration observatory at the University of Oxford, http://migrationobservatory.ox.ac.uk/commentary/what-would-uk-immigration-policy-look-after-brexit

131. Mcgovern, P., "Five Problems with UK immigration control post-Brexit", http://blogs.lse.ac.uk/brexitvote/2016/07/11/five-problems-with-uk-immigration-control-post-brexit/

132. "1. *Any Member State may decide to withdraw from the Union in accordance with its own constitutional requirements.*

   2. *A Member State which decides to withdraw shall notify the European Council of its intention. In the light of the guidelines provided by the European Council, the Union shall negotiate and conclude an agreement with that State, setting out the arrangements for its withdrawal, taking account of the framework for its future relationship with the Union. That agreement shall be negotiated in accordance with Article 218(3) of the Treaty on the Functioning of the European Union. It shall*

be concluded on behalf of the Union by the Council, acting by a quali-fied majority, after obtaining the consent of the European Parliament.

3. *The Treaties shall cease to apply to the State in question from the date of entry into force of the withdrawal agreement or, failing that, two years after the notification referred to in paragraph 2, unless the European Council, in agreement with the Member State concerned, unanimously decides to extend this period.*

4. *For the purposes of paragraphs 2 and 3, the member of the European Council or of the Council representing the withdrawing Member State shall not participate in the discussions of the European Council or Council or in decisions concerning it.*

   A qualified majority shall be defined in accordance with Article 238(3)(b) of the Treaty on the Functioning of the European Union.

5. *If a State which has withdrawn from the Union asks to rejoin, its request shall be subject to the procedure referred to in Article 49."*

133. "Could EU citizens living in the UK claim 'acquired rights' if there is a full Brexit?", Interview with Tim Eicke, *Lexis PSL* 2016, http://www.lexisnexis.com/uk/lexispsl/immigration/document/412012/5K4J-X7D1-DYW7-W4M6-00000-00/What-should-EEA-citizens-living-in-the-UK-do-next

134. Peers, S., "What next after the UK vote to leave the EU?", http://eulawanalysis.blogspot.be/.

135. *Ibid.*

136. Lang, E., Hunter, I., Froud, J., Walsh, P., and Goldsworthy, J., "Brexit: Employment and Immigration Law implications", http://www.twobirds.com/en/news/articles/2016/uk/brexit-employment-and-immigration-law-implications

137. Comprehensive Economic and Trade Agreement (CETA) between Canada and the European Union and its Member States signed on 30 October 2016.

138. The EU and Canada approved and signed CETA on 30 October 2016. In February 2017 the European Parliament approved this text. In September 2017 CETA entered into force provisionally. As such most of the agreement now applies. National parliaments have to approve CETA before it can take full effect.

139. "The Canadian model for trade deals", http://www.economist.com/blogs/economist-explains/2016/06/economist-explains-26

140. *Ibid.*

141. The negotiations with Canada started in 2007.

142. See, for example, the statement by Marianne Thyssen: "vier vrijheden vormen samen de Europese interne markt" [*The four freedoms together form the European internal market*], http://deredactie.be/cm/vrtnieuws/videozone/programmas/terzake/2.45486?video=1.2713130

143. House of Lords Hansard European Union (Notification of Withdrawal) Bill, 01 March 2017, Volume 779, European Union (Notification of Withdrawal) Bill.

144. Independent, 14 March 2017, "EU nationals express 'utter desperation' following MPs rejection of Lords amendment", author May Bulman: http://www.independent.co.uk/news/uk/home-news/brexit-eu-nationals-mps-lords-amendment-article-50-utter-desperation-commons-a7628291.html.

145. Guild, E. (2016) "Brexit and Social Security in the EU", *CEPS Commentary: Thinking ahead for Europe*, 17 November 2016 https://www.ceps.eu/publications/brexit-and-social-security-eu.

146. See https://euobserver.com/uk-referendum/136569.

147. https://www.gov.uk/government/publications/prime-ministers-letter-to-donald-tusk-triggering-article-50/prime-ministers-letter-to-donald-tusk-triggering-article-50

Literature

Ambuhl, M., and S. Zurcher. 2015. Immigration and Swiss-EU Free Movement of Persons: Questions of a Safeguard Clause. *Swiss Political Science Review* 21 (1): 76–98.

Barnard, C. 2016. *Could Free Movement of Persons be Confined to Free Movement of Workers in Any Brexit Deal?* http://www.cels.law.cam.ac.uk/brexitfree-movement-persons-and-new-legal-order/catherine-barnard-could-free-movement-persons-be. December 2016.

Bercusson, B. 1990. The European Community's Charter of Fundamental Social Rights of Workers. *Modern Law Review* 53 (5): 624–642. New Perspectives on European Law.

Breitenmoser, S. 2003. Sectoral Agreement Between the EC and Switzerland: Contents and Context. *Common Market Law Review* 40 (5): 1137–1186.

Brexit, Employment law consequences of Brexit. Addleshaw Goddard. 2016. *BREXIT—Employment Law Consequences of Brexit.* http://www.lexology.com/library/detail.aspx?g=1a6e17d9-abc5-4269-9ad2-ae3e086e4d52

Bundeszentralamt für Steuern: Dienstanweisung zur Durchführung des Familienleistungsausgleichs nach dem X. Abschnitt des Einkommensteuergesetzes (DA-FamEStG) Stand 2011. http://www.bzst.de/DE/Steuern_National/Kindergeld_Fachaufsicht/Familienkassen/Dienstanweisung/DA_FamEStG_2011.html

Burke, C., O. Isberg Hannesson, and K. Bangsund. 2016. Life on the Edge: EFTA and the EEA as a Future for the UK and Europe. *European Public Law* 22 (1): 69–96.

Carrera, S., E. Guild, and K. Eisele. 2015. *No Move Without Free Movement: The EU-Swiss Controversy Over Quotas for Free Movement of Persons*, CEPS Policy Brief No. 331. April 2015.

Chetail, V. 2014. The Swiss Vote Against Mass Immigration and International Law: A Preliminary Assessment. *Migration Policy Practice* 4: 12–16. http://papers.ssrn.com/sol3/papers.cfm?abstract_id=2426824

Church, C. 2007. *Switzerland and the European Union*, 263 p. London: Routledge.

Cornelissen, R. 2009. 50 Years of European Social Security Coordination. *European Journal of Social Security (EJSS)* 11 (1–2): 9–45.

Denton, R.L. 2016. *UK to Start Preliminary Trade Talks with India*. http://brexit.bakermckenzie.com/2016/07/12/uk-to-start-preliminary-trade-talks-with-india/

Dhingra, S., and T. Sampson. 2016. *Life After Brexit: What Are the UK's Options Outside the European Union?* Centre for Economic Performance, London School of Economics, 10. http://eprints.lse.ac.uk/66143/

European Commission. 2017. *Fairness at the Heart of Commission's Proposal to Update EU Rules on Social Security Coordination, Brussels*, 13 December 2016. http://europa.eu/rapid/press-release_IP-16-4301_en.htm. Last accessed January 2017.

Felder, D., and C. Kaddous. 2001. *Accords bilatéraux Suisse – UE (Commentaires)*, 260. Basel: Helbing & Lichtenhahn.

Friel, R.J. 2004. Providing a Constitutional Framework for Withdrawal from the EU: Article 59 of the Draft European Constitution. International and Comparative Law Quarterly, 53411.

Gad, U. P. 2016. *Could a 'Reverse Greenland' Arrangement Keep Scotland and Northern Ireland in the EU?* http://blogs.lse.ac.uk/europpblog/2016/07/07/reverse-greenland-arrangement/#AuthorPortes

Gstohl, S. 1996. *Switzerland, Norway and the EU: The Odd Ones Out?* Genève, l'institut européen de l'Université de Genève, 27 p.

Guild, E. 2016. *Brexit and Social Security in the EU, CEPS Commentary: Thinking Ahead for Europe*, 17 Nov. 2016. https://www.ceps.eu/publications/brexit-and-social-security-eu

Harhoff, F. 1983. Greenland's Withdrawal from the European Communities. *Common Market Law Review* 20: 13–33. https://www.kluwerlawonline.com/abstract.php?area=Journals&id=COLA1983002

Helgesen, V. 2015. *Brexit, a Norwegian View*. https://www.regjeringen.no/no/aktuelt/brexit_norway/id2402031/

HM Government. 2014. *Review of the Balance of Competences Between the United Kingdom and the European Union: Social and Employment Policy* (Summer 2014), 78 p. Available at: https://www.gov.uk/government/uploads/system/uploads/attachment_data/file/332524/review-of-the-balance-of-competences-between-the-united-kingdom-and-the-european-union-social-and-employment-policy.pdf. Last accessed January 2017.

Jenni, S. 2016. *Is the Swiss Model a Brexit Solution?* http://ukandeu.ac.uk/is-the-swiss-model-a-brexit-solution/

Jorens, Y., Spiegel, B (ed.)., Fillon, J-C., Strban, G. *Key challenges for the social security coordination Regulations in the perspective of 2020*, trESS Think Tank report 2013, European Commission, 2013, 64 p.

Keating, M. 2016. *How Could Scotland Remain in the EU?* http://ukandeu.ac.uk/how-could-scotland-remain-in-the-eu/

Lang, E., I. Hunter, J. Froud, P. Walsh, and J. Goldsworthy. 2017. *Brexit: Employment and Immigration Law Implications*. http://www.twobirds.com/en/news/articles/2016/uk/brexit-employment-and-immigration-law-implications

Lhernould, J-P. (ed.), E. Eichenhofer, N. Rennuy, F. Van Overmeiren, and F. Wollenschläger. *Assessment of the Impact of Amendments to the EU Social Security Coordination Rules to Clarify Its Relationship With Directive 2004/38/EC as Regards Economically Inactive Persons*, Analytical Report 2015, FreSsco, European Commission, June 2015, 71 p.

Marescau, M. 2006. *Bilateral Agreements Concluded by the European Community*, 413. Leiden: Martinus Nijhoff Publishers.

Mcgovern, P. 2016. *Five Problems with UK Immigration Control Post-Brexit*. http://blogs.lse.ac.uk/brexitvote/2016/07/11/five-problems-with-uk-immigration-control-post-brexit/

Minderhoud, P. 2016. Sufficient Resources and Residence Rights Under Directive 2004/38. In *Residence, Employment and Social Rights of Mobile Persons. On How EU Law Defines Where They Belong*, ed. H. Verschueren, 47–74. Antwerpen: Intersentia.

Mullock, J. 2016. Brexit—A Data Protection Perspective. *Privacy & Data Protection* 16 (6): 14–17.

Munchau, W. 2016. *Brexit: The Norway Option Is the Best Available for the UK.* http://www.ft.com/cms/s/0/eb8dbe8c-3d0c-11e6-9f2c-36b487ebd80a. html#axzz4EOM3bgmo

Nicolaides, P. 2014. *Is Withdrawal From the European Union a Manageable Option? A Review of Economic and Legal Complexities.* Bruges: College of Europe. http://aei.pitt.edu/58466/

Nordling, H. 2016. *The EEA Agreement and the 'Norway Option': Integration Without Co-Determination*, Eutopia Law. https://eutopialaw.com/2016/07/05/ the-eea-agreement-and-the-norway-option-integration-without-co-determination/

O'brien, C. 2017a. *Brexit, Free Movement and Welfare: We Must Bring Evidence Back Into Fashion.* http://www.cels.law.cam.ac.uk/brexitfree-movement-persons-and-new-legal-order/charlotte-obrien-brexit-free-movement-and-welfare-we. Last accessed January 2017.

———. 2017b. The ECJ Sacrifices EU Citizenship in Vain: Commission v. United Kingdom. *Common Market Law Review* 54 (1): 209–244.

O'leary, B. 2016. *Detoxifying the UK's Exit From the EU: A Multi-National Compromise Is Possible.* http://blogs.lse.ac.uk/brexitvote/2016/06/27/ de-toxifying-the-uks-eu-exit-process-a-multi-national-compromise-is-possible/

Pedersen, T. 1994. *European Union and the EFTA Countries*, 121. London: Pinter Publishers.

Peers, S. 2017. *What Next After the UK Vote to Leave the EU?* http://eulawanalysis.blogspot.be/

Pfeil, W.J. 2016. Social Benefits for Migrating Unemployed Persons. *Rivista del Diritto della Sicurezza Sociale (RDSS)* 2: 271–288.

Portes, J. *The "EEA Minus" Option: Amending Not Ending Free Movement.* http:// ukandeu.ac.uk/the-eea-minus-option-amending-not-ending-free-movement/

Sarmiento, D. 2017. *Brexit or the Art of 'Doing a Greenland'.* https://despiteour-differencesblog.wordpress.com/

Schmidt, V. 2016. *Brexit and the EU: A New Deal for the EU or No Deal at All?* https://www.socialeurope.eu/2016/07/brexit-eu-new-deal-eu-no-deal/

Schulz, M. 2016. *The EU Must Not Treat the UK as a Deserter – We Can Negotiate Without Rancour.* https://www.theguardian.com/commentisfree/2016/ jul/12/brexit-eu-uk-negotiate-without-rancour

Schwok, R., and N. Levrat. 2001. Switzerland's Relations with the EU After the Adoption of the Seven Bilateral Agreements. *European Foreign Affairs Review* 6 (3): 335–354.

Shaw, J. 2016. Where Does the UK belong? In *Residence, Employment and Social Rights of Mobile Persons. On How EU Law Defines Where They Belong*, ed. H. Verschueren, 301–322. Antwerpen: Intersentia.

Spiegel, B. (ed.), K. Daxkobler, G. Strban, A P. VAN DER MEI. *Analytical Report 2014: The Relationship Between Social Security Coordination and Taxation Law*, FreSsco, European Commission, April 2015, 61 p.

Spiegel, B. (ed.), D. Carrascosa Bermejo, A. Henberg, and G. Strban. 2015. *Assessment of the Impact of Amendments to the EU Social Security Coordination Rules on Export of Family Benefits*, Analytical Report, FreSsco, European Commission, June 2015, 81 p.

Strban, G. 2016. Family Benefits in the EU – Is It Still Possible to Coordinate Them? *Maastricht Journal of European and Comparative Law* 23 (5): 775–795.

———. 2017. Brexit and Social Security of Mobile Persons. *ERA Forum 2/2017*, 18 (2): 165–185.

Vahl, M., and N. Grolimund. 2006. *Integration Without Membership: Switzerland's Bilateral Agreements with the European Union*, 79. Brussel: Centre for European Policy Studies.

Verschueren, H. 2009. Special Non-Contributory Benefits in Regulation 1408/71, Regulation 883/2004 and the Case Law of the ECJ. *European Journal of Social Security (EJSS)* 11 (1–2): 217–234.

———. 2014. Free Movement or Benefit Tourism: The Unreasonable Burden of Brey. *European Journal of Migration and Law* 16 (2): 147–179.

Zahn, R. 2016. *After the Referendum and Before Brexit… Where Now for Workers' Rights in the EU?* http://europeanlawblog.eu/?p=3248

Links

http://eeagrants.org/Who-we-are/EEA-Grants

http://www.europarl.europa.eu/atyourservice/en/displayFtu.html?ftuId=FTU_6.5.3.html

http://europeanlawblog.eu/?p=3248

http://www.telegraph.co.uk/news/2016/06/27/after-brexit-only-one-thing-can-keep-britain-together-the-norway/

http://www.independent.co.uk/news/business/news/single-market-what-is-it-brexit-eu-referendum-eea-boris-johnson-economy-effects-a7106066.html

How Britain voted, https://yougov.co.uk/news/2016/06/27/how-britain-voted/

Hard Evidence: How areas with low immigration voted mainly for Brexit, https://theconversation.com/hard-evidence-how-areas-with-low-immigration-voted-mainly-for-brexit-62138

Theresa May appeals to centre ground but cabinet tilts to the right, http://www.theguardian.com/politics/2016/jul/13/theresa-may-becomes-britains-prime-minister

The European Economic Area (EEA), Switzerland and the North, http://www.europarl.europa.eu/atyourservice/en/displayFtu.html?ftuId=FTU_6.5.3.html

EU-Swiss relations in turmoil after immigration vote, http://www.euractiv.com/section/justice-home-affairs/news/eu-swiss-relations-in-turmoil-after-immigration-vote/

http://www.stat.gl/default.asp?lang=en

Gibraltar is dragged from Europe against its will, http://www.economist.com/news/europe/21702147-peninsula-now-faces-uncertain-future-outside-eu-gibraltar-dragged-europe

Commentary: What would UK immigration policy look like after Brexit? (The migration observatory at the university of Oxford), http://migrationobservatory.ox.ac.uk/commentary/what-would-uk-immigration-policy-look-after-brexit

Could EU citizens living in the UK claim 'acquired rights' if there is a full Brexit?, Interview met Tim Eicke, *Lexis PSL* 2016, http://www.lexisnexis.com/uk/lexispsl/immigration/document/412012/5K4J-X7D1-DYW7-W4M6-00000-00/What-should-EEA-citizens-living-in-the-UK-do-next

The Canadian model for trade deals, http://www.economist.com/blogs/economist-explains/2016/06/economist-explains-26

http://www.bakermckenzie.com/en/insight/publications/2016/06/brexit-what-it-means-for-your-business

http://players.brightcove.net/3653334463001/default_default/index.html?videoId=5016529117001

https://euobserver.com/uk-referendum/136569

Independent, 14 March 2017, "EU nationals express 'utter desperation' following MPs rejection of Lords amendment", author May Bulman: http://www.independent.co.uk/news/uk/home-news/brexit-eu-nationals-mps-lords-amendment-article-50-utter-desperation-commons-a7628291.html

https://www.gov.uk/government/publications/prime-ministers-letter-to-donald-tusk-triggering-article-50/prime-ministers-letter-to-donald-tusk-triggering-article-50

Part III

Brexit's Sectorial Effects (II): Free Movement of Capital and the Financial Markets

14

Free Movement of Capital and Brexit

Ana Paula Dourado

14.1 Introduction[1]

The exit of the United Kingdom from the European Union—known as Brexit—has been activated by Article 50 of the Treaty on the European Union, according to which:

1. Any Member State may decide to withdraw from the Union in accordance with its own constitutional requirements.
2. A Member State which decides to withdraw shall notify the European Council of its intention. In the light of the guidelines provided by the European Council, the Union shall negotiate and conclude an agreement with that State, setting out the arrangements for its withdrawal, taking account of the framework for its future relationship with the Union. That agreement shall be negotiated in accordance with Article 218(3) of the Treaty on the Functioning of the European Union. It shall be concluded by the Council, acting by a qualified majority, after obtaining the consent of the European Parliament.

A.P. Dourado (✉)
Lisbon University School of Law, Lisbon, Portugal

© The Author(s) 2017
N. da Costa Cabral et al. (eds.), *After Brexit*,
https://doi.org/10.1007/978-3-319-66670-9_14

3. The Treaties shall cease to apply to the State in question from the date of entry into force of the withdrawal agreement or, failing that, two years after the notification referred to in paragraph 2, unless the European Council, in agreement with the Member State concerned, unanimously decides to extend this period.

On the basis of Article 50(2), different agreements can be concluded. The United Kingdom can exit the EU and neither become a Member of the European Economic Area (EEA) nor conclude any special bilateral agreements with the EU providing for some benefits similar to those in the Treaty on the Functioning of the European Union (TFEU) and benefits similar to those resulting from EU secondary law.

Differently from that scenario, the United Kingdom can conclude an association agreement with the EU, with non-discrimination clauses, the range of which can vary from free movement of goods to free movement of persons. That would be the case if the United Kingdom were to conclude an association agreement with the EU, similar to others, such as those concluded with Russia, Tunisia and Lebanon (see the *Secil* case).[2]

The United Kingdom can also become a third state with no special agreement with the EU. It will then benefit only from the free movement of capital and will likely have no legal obligations towards the EU.

The United Kingdom could also become a member of the EEA or obtain special treatment from the EU, for strategic reasons, as has happened between the EU and Switzerland (e.g. the agreement on the free movement of persons, between the EU and Switzerland, of 21 June 1999).

14.2 Brexit, EU Free Movement of Capital and Third Countries

In the scenario assumed in this chapter, the United Kingdom is regarded as a third country, in the same category with the United States and Brazil, for example. In the bilateral relationship between the United Kingdom and the EU Member States, there will be no legal obligations for the United Kingdom deriving from either primary or secondary EU law. However, due to Article 63 of the TFEU, the EU Member States will still be forbidden to restrict capital movements from and to the United Kingdom.

The meaning and scope of free movement of capital is considered here, taking Brexit as an example.

The movement of capital was harmonized by Directive 88/361/EEC, which defined capital and provided for free movement of capital.[3] However, the scope of the Directive was limited to Member States of the then European Economic Community and their nationals. Article 56 of the EC Treaty (current Article 63 of the TFEU) extended the scope of the free movement of capital to third countries.

Thus, since 1 January 1994, the date of entry into force of the EC Treaty, any restriction on the movement of capital between Member States, as well as between Member States and third countries, is prohibited. The beneficiaries of this prohibition are EU nationals and third-country nationals, individuals and corporations.

This prohibition is a unilateral obligation assumed by EC/EU Member States towards third states in the Maastricht Treaty (ex-Article 56), the origin of which can be justified by the introduction of the European and Monetary Union, strong promotion of the euro as an international currency and in the context of the worldwide globalization movement.[4] The Treaty does not define capital, and even though the 88/361/EEC Directive has been obsolete since 1 January 1994, it is settled case law that the meaning of capital is to be found in the Directive, more specifically in its Annex I.[5]

Directive 88/361/EEC does not contain a condensed definition of capital, but rather enumerates and defines it. The movement of capital is defined in a very broad sense. Capital covers any right concerning assets, such as portfolio investment across States; different types of direct investment and establishment, including transfers related to insurance contracts and the establishment of branches and subsidiaries; and inheritance. In general terms, any right concerning assets is capital for purposes of the TFEU, and the movement of capital is the transfer of any rights concerning assets.[6] This broad concept of capital and the movement of capital means that, in most cases, it will overlap with other fundamental freedoms in the Treaty, namely, freedoms related to establishment, services, and workers.

Apparently, the consequences deriving from Article 63 of the TFEU for direct taxes were not taken into consideration when the EC Treaty was approved: in direct tax cases, the ECJ grants a scope to the free movement of capital that is inversely proportional to the importance ("the size") of the investment.[7]

It is *acte clair* that Article 63 of the TFEU has the same object and scope independently of only Member States or a Member State and a third country being involved (*Sanz de Lera*, para. 24 et seq.; 41, 47; *Bordessa*, para. 24; *A.*, para. 21, *Orange, Commission v. Netherlands*). Article 63 therefore implies that corporate income taxes and income taxes on individuals, property taxes, and any other direct taxes in the Member States cannot be discriminatory towards the movement of capital.

Since 2006 (the *Van Hilten*[8] case), there have been many ECJ/CJEU direct tax cases concerning the meaning and scope of the free movement of capital, although—in respect of some topics—it is difficult to conclude that there is settled case law.[9]

For the purposes of assessing the consequences for direct taxes in the Brexit extreme scenario, the discussion below reviews the problem of the overlap between the free movement of capital and the free movement of workers, freedom of establishment and the free movement of services.

14.3   Overlap Between Free Movement of Capital and Other Fundamental Freedoms

Although protection of the free movement of capital covers any legal transaction that is necessary to attain the transfer of those assets, and although the TFEU does not contain a hierarchy among the freedoms, the overlapping of the free movement of capital with the aforementioned fundamental freedoms in the Treaty has created problems of interpretation.[10]

In fact, the free movement of workers, the freedom of establishment and the freedom to provide services benefit only nationals of a Member State. If the free movement of capital overlaps with the free movement of workers (e.g. in the case of inheritance and inheritance taxes),[11] establishment (in the case of setting up a company, subsidiary or permanent establishment in a Member State)[12] and services (in the case of financial services or insurance contracts),[13] and if all of them apply simultaneously, nationals of third states would ultimately be protected under all fundamental freedoms at stake.

The overlapping among freedoms and the fact that—except for movement of capital—all other freedoms benefit only nationals of EU Member States has been an argument for the ECJ/CJEU to limit the scope of the free movement of capital in direct tax cases. In most cases involving an overlap, the Court gives precedence to the freedom other than the free movement of capital. According to the Court, the free movement of capital is "an indirect consequence of" the freedom to provide services. The facts show a "predominant consideration" of establishment/services: "The rules in dispute impede access to the [...] market for companies established in non-member countries; they affect primarily the freedom to provide services" (*Bachmann*,[14] *Fidium Finanz*,[15] *Van Hilten*,[16] *Burda*[17]). The holding in the capital of a company established in another Member State "which gives him definite influence over the company's decisions and allows him to determine its activities is exercising his right of establishment" (*Baars*).[18] The purpose of the legislation at issue (*FII*,[19] *Holboeck*[20]) and the analysis of the factual situation (*Burda*, *KBC*),[21] as well as abuse of a freedom, has been subsequently developed as complementary, more refined arguments to resolve issue of overlap.

Curiously, this hierarchy has also been asserted by the Court in respect of (some) cases involving only Member States (e.g. *Bachmann*, *Baars*, and *Burda*), but not all of them (e.g. *Bouanich*). But when the Court uses a tie-breaker criterion in an EU case, it has no consequences, as the scope of the fundamental freedoms is identical.

More recently, in direct tax cases involving investment and non-distribution of dividends, freedom of establishment has been related to the exercise of an activity in a Member State, whereas the free movement of capital does not require that activity (*Olsen* and *Commission v. UK*).[22]

Although the case law on the topic is erratic and unclear, there is a *de minimis* protection that the Court has never denied to movement of capital (it is *acte clair*). This protection relates to portfolio investments, as they do not fall under any other freedom.

From the internal market and European Monetary Union perspective, however, the purpose of extending the free movement of capital to third countries and nationals goes far beyond the protection of portfolio investments. Expanding EU multinationals worldwide and promoting the euro both required a broad concept of capital, including direct investments, with "definite influence" and services provided from EU companies to third countries.

The fact that Article 63 of the TFEU does not restrict protection to outbound movements (from a Member State to a third state), but covers inbound movements (from a third state to a Member State), at least as it has been always interpreted by the Court, reveals a strong belief in free movement at the worldwide level.

Finally, the grandfather clause in Article 64 of the TFEU demonstrates that the scope of Article 63 goes beyond portfolio investments. In fact, Article 64 introduces an exception to Article 63 of the TFEU, by excluding from its regime those restrictions which existed on 31 December 1993 under national or Union law, adopted in respect of the movement of capital to or from third countries involving direct investment—including in real estate—establishment, the provision of financial services and the admission of securities to capital markets. Article 64 is necessary only if Article 63 covers direct investment, establishment and services.

CJEU case law that uses the overlapping of freedoms to restrict the scope of capital movement is hardly compatible with Article 64. However, this issue was never directly addressed by the Court.

Taking the above discussion on the overlap between capital movements and other fundamental freedoms, in the Brexit extreme scenario, it remains to be seen how much investment from the United Kingdom in an EU Member State (and vice versa) can benefit from Article 63.

14.4   Investment, Establishment, Capital and Brexit

One significant example, in the consideration here of the consequences of Brexit for the overlap between freedoms of establishment and capital, concerns inbound and outbound dividends resulting from "definite influence" situations and direct investments ("involving long and lasting links"). The issue concerns whether participations with "definite influence" from a national of an EU Member State in a company in the United

Kingdom and vice versa, in a Brexit extreme scenario, is protected by the free movement of capital, or excluded because it falls exclusively under the freedom of establishment.

14.5 Portfolio Investments

From an EU perspective, the free movement of capital will cover any portfolio investments in the United Kingdom and inbound dividends, as well as any UK portfolio investments in an EU Member State. This means that inbound dividends from the United Kingdom to an EU Member State, resulting from a portfolio investment, cannot be subject to a less favourable tax treatment than domestic dividends (vertical comparison). However, they can be subject to less favourable tax treatment than that granted by a Member State to another Member State or an EEA State, because so far, the Court has not accepted the so-called horizontal comparison and horizontal discrimination (see *D*.[23] and *ACT GLO*[24]).

Taking into account *Holboeck*,[25] *FII GLO 1*[26] and *FII GLO 2*,[27] inbound dividends from direct investment are also protected if the purpose of the Member State tax legislation is to cover both types of income. For example if domestic dividends are granted an exemption independently of the amount of participation, the exemption is to be extended to dividends coming from the United Kingdom, no matter what the amount of participation is. If the exemption is granted domestically (and in this way, economic double taxation eliminated), applying the credit method to dividends from the United Kingdom may be discriminatory unless a switch-over clause were to be applicable (see *Haribo and Salinen*).

In the *FII GLO 2* case—by coincidence, a UK case—decided prior to the Brexit referendum, the Court departed from the purpose of the UK legislation. National legislation applied not only to dividends received by a resident company on the basis of shareholding that conferred definite influence over the decisions of the company paying the dividends, but also to dividends on the basis of a shareholding not conferring that influence (para. 91). The Court furthermore considered that (inbound) dividends were not an issue concerning market access, and therefore even investments with definite influence were protected by the free movement of capital:

Since the Treaty does not extend freedom of establishment to third countries, it is important to ensure that the interpretation of article 63(1) of the TFEU as regards relations with third countries does not enable economic operators who do not fall within the limits of the territorial scope of freedom of establishment to profit from that freedom. Such a risk does not exist in a situation such as that at issue in the main proceedings. The legislation of the Member State in question does not does not relate to the conditions for access of a company from that Member State to the market in a third country or of a company in a third country to the market in that Member State. It concerns only the tax treatment of dividends which derive from investments which their recipient has made in a company established in a third country.[28]

Thus, under the aforementioned circumstances, both inbound and outbound dividends are covered by Article 63(1) of the TFEU.

Assume that in EU Member States, no withholding is applicable to domestic dividends, in respect of participations, independently of the holding amount. In such case, a Member State may not withhold taxes on dividends being paid to a UK holder, even if the latter has a 100% participation, following *Holboeck, FII GLO 1* and *FII GLO 2*. Thus, as long as a UK company is set up in an EU Member State, and national legislation applies to both portfolio and definite influence situations, the taxation of dividends will be protected by the free movement of capital.

However, it is still difficult to say that this jurisprudence is *acte clair*, taking into account cases such as *Burda* and *KBC* where, besides the purpose test, the factual situation was taken into account. If there was definite influence in the concrete situation, freedom of establishment prevailed and free movement of capital did not apply. Even in the absence of a "precedent rule" with *stare decisis* in EU law, the fact that *FII GLO 2* was decided after *Burda* and *KBC* and by the Grand Chamber is not irrelevant, and these are sound arguments for the *FII GLO 2* decision to prevail over *Burda* and *KBC*.

Unfortunately, when a case on the scope of the free movement of capital seems to settle the case law, a new decision follows that relies on different arguments and ultimately brings back uncertainty.

14.6   Pursuit of an Economic Activity and Financial Investments

In the *Olse*n case (an EFTA Court case)[29] and in the *Commission v. UK case* (CJEU case),[30] the EFTA court and the CJEU, respectively, considered that financial investments, such as the setting up of a trust, or holding of more than 10% of shares in a foreign company, respectively, fell under the free movement of capital. It was not an issue covered by the freedom of establishment, because there was no "participation in the economic life of the country effectively";[31] it was an issue of attracting capital. Thus, in both *Olsen* and *Commission v. UK*, the free movement of capital was extended to the detriment of the freedom of establishment and is applicable independently of (i) the purpose of the legislation and (ii) there being a portfolio shareholding or a definite influence situation.

If financial investments are covered by the free movement of capital, independently of the level of participation, inbound and outbound investments from the United Kingdom into an EU Member State, and from an EU Member State in the United Kingdom, cannot be subject to discriminatory tax treatment.

14.7   Anti-abuse Provisions and Brexit

Fundamental freedoms, including the free movement of capital, can be circumvented. In *Glaxo*,[32] the Court considered that it was an issue concerning the free movement of capital and not the freedom of establishment, as there was no real activity exercised by the company set up in the United Kingdom by a German parent company.

Abuse of a freedom can therefore imply reclassification. If the exercise of a fundamental freedom is considered to be capital, third states will benefit from it, that is, from the prohibition of restrictions. The artificial exercise of a fundamental freedom has led to the application of national anti-abuse provisions. If they are national anti-abuse provisions, they cannot be discriminatory (or restrictive).

However, discriminatory or restrictive anti-abuse provisions can be justified, as long as they are not disproportionate. Thus, for example, CFC rules and thin capitalization rules have been held to be discriminatory by the CJEU and the EFTA Court. Discrimination can be justified if proportionate. And this proportionality requires that the presumption of abuse be rebuttable. However, national anti-abuse rules targeted at cross-border situations were traditionally aimed at aggressive tax planning by multinationals—and therefore with the freedom of establishment (their purpose was to address abuse in definite influence situations). The Court decided so in *Cadbury Schweppes*[33] and *Thin Cap GLO*.[34]

Thus, on the basis of the above-mentioned case law, a Member State may apply CFC and thin capitalization rules to a third country, including the United Kingdom in a Brexit extreme scenario, as the United Kingdom will no longer be protected by the freedom of establishment.

Contrary to the *Cadbury Schweppes* case, in the *Olsen* and *Commission v. UK* case, CFC rules applied to financial investments were considered incompatible with the free movement of capital. These cases were decided after the BEPS (base erosion and profit shifting) project was initiated and after the Action Plan and EC Recommendations against aggressive tax planning were issued. Therefore, the G20/OECD/EU fight against aggressive tax planning and avoidance influenced neither the EFTA court nor the CJEU.

If *Olsen* and *Commission v. UK* are confirmed by the CJEU, an EU Member State may not apply CFC rules or any other anti-abuse rules to a third country, including the United Kingdom, with irrebuttable presumptions.

14.8   The Anti-Tax Avoidance Directive and Brexit

However, the new Anti-Tax Avoidance Directive (ATAD) allows irrebuttable presumptions in respect of CFC rules towards third country situations (excluding EEA States). According to Article 7(2) of the Directive:

> Where an entity or permanent establishment is treated as a controlled foreign company under paragraph 1, the Member State of the taxpayer shall include in the tax base:

(a) the non-distributed income of the entity or the income of the permanent establishment which is derived from the following categories:

(i)   interest or any other income generated by financial assets;
(ii) royalties or any other income generated from intellectual property;
(iii) dividends and income from the disposal of shares;
(iv) income from financial leasing;
(v)   income from insurance, banking and other financial activities;
(vi) income from invoicing companies that earn sales and services
      income from goods and services purchased from and sold to associ-
      ated enterprises, and add no or little economic value;

Point (a) shall not apply where the controlled foreign company carries
on a substantive economic activity supported by staff, equipment, assets
and premises, as evidenced by relevant facts and circumstances.

Where the controlled foreign company is resident or situated in a third
country that is not party to the EEA Agreement, Member States may
decide to refrain from applying the second subparagraph of point (a).

The enumerated categories of income correspond to passive income,
with no economic activity, and therefore no "establishment", as described
in the *Olsen* case.

In contrast, by granting the possibility to the Member States of eliminating the test on the "substantive economic activity" when third countries
come into play, the ATAD relies on the *Cadbury-Schweppes* jurisprudence,
according to which CFC rules fall under the freedom of establishment.

It remains to be seen how the CJEU will assess national CFC rules,
transposing Article 7 of the ATAD and applying to third countries on the
basis of irrebuttable presumptions. It also remains to be seen whether it
will confirm the *Cadbury-Schweppes* or *Olsen* doctrines. If it confirms the
former doctrine, Member States may apply CFC rules with an irrebuttable presumption of abuse to the United Kingdom, in the Brexit extreme
scenario. If it confirms the *Olsen* doctrine, Member States will have to
allow evidence that a substantive economic activity exists, and cannot
treat the United Kingdom, in the Brexit extreme scenario, differently
from other Member States.

It also remains to be seen whether this is an issue regarding the compatibility of the Directive with the Treaty, or an issue of the compatibility of Member State legislation in transposing the Directive with the TFEU.

Taking into account that the Anti-Tax Avoidance Directive has de minimis rules, and that the CFC rules in the Directive distinguish between EU Member States and third countries, the transposition of those rules is the transposition of the Directive. However, there is an option (b) granted to Member States, using the *Cadbury-Schweppes* language, and this option does not distinguish between CFC rules applied to Member States and CFC rules applied to third countries other than EEA States:

(b) the non-distributed income of the entity or permanent establishment arising from non-genuine arrangements which have been put in place for the essential purpose of obtaining a tax advantage.

For the purposes of point (b), an arrangement or a series thereof shall be regarded as non- genuine to the extent that the entity or permanent establishment would not own the assets or would not have undertaken the risks which generate all, or part of, its income if it were not controlled by a company where the significant people functions, which are relevant to those assets and risks, are carried out and are instrumental in generating the controlled company's income.

It would be problematic to conclude that national legislation transposing option (a) is incompatible with the free movement of capital. It is more likely that the Directive itself will be considered incompatible with the Treaty.

14.9   Exchange of Information

Considering that an EU Member State restriction to a UK inbound or outbound situation falls under the free movement of capital, it can still be justified if the United Kingdom, as a third country, were not to comply with the exchange of information standard, that is, if the exchange of information between the EU Member State and the United Kingdom were not to occur in equivalent terms to that under the Mutual Assistance Directive.

In respect of exchange of information upon request, the United Kingdom complies with the international standard in the OECD Model Convention, and the Directive follows that standard. However, the new global standard as enacted by the OECD relates to automatic exchange of information on financial accounts. Automatic exchange of information in the EU Mutual Assistance Directive goes beyond automatic exchange of information on financial accounts and covers every type of income from 2017 onwards.

So far, the comparison carried out by the CJEU between exchange of information from a third country to an EU Member State and exchange of information under the Mutual Assistance Directive refers to the exchange of information upon request. It is not certain whether the CJEU will refer to the new global standard in order to assess whether a restriction on free movement of capital is justified, and whether it will go beyond the aforementioned automatic exchange of information on financial accounts.

14.10   Good Governance Clauses

Presumably, one of the big advantages of Brexit to the United Kingdom is to escape state aid rules (Article 107 of the TFEU) and, in this manner, introduce targeted (i.e. selective) tax benefits in order to attract strategic investment. However, the EU External Strategy for Effective Taxation may influence the relationship with the United Kingdom in a Brexit extreme scenario.

In 2012, the Commission issued a Recommendation to the Parliament and Council regarding measures intended to encourage third countries to apply minimum standards of good governance in tax matters 8C(2012) 8805, 6 December 2012). The Recommendation encouraged Member States to use transparency, information exchange and fair tax competition as the three criteria for assessing the tax regimes of third countries and, where necessary, to apply common counter-measures.[35]

On 28 January 2016, a Commission document on the external strategy was approved. This document defines fair tax competition as follows:

> means that a third country should not operate harmful tax measures in the area of business taxation. Tax measures which provide for a significantly lower effective level of taxation, including zero taxation, than those levels

which generally apply in the third country in question are to be regarded as potentially harmful. Such a significantly lower level of taxation may operate by virtue of the nominal tax rate, the tax base or any other relevant factor.[36]

The Commission recommends as good governance clauses that State aid provisions be included in bilateral agreements. In this manner, transparency on subsidies can be increased, the most harmful types of subsidies prohibited and consultations on harmful subsidies can be provided. This methodology would create more fair competition between Member States and third countries in the area of business taxation.[37]

If fair tax competition and good governance clauses are not respected by third countries, common counter-measures are suggested, such as the aforementioned anti-avoidance and anti-aggressive tax planning rules in the ATAD, domestic anti-avoidance rules, withholding taxes, and non-deductibility of costs for transactions in listed jurisdictions.

Although these tax good governance clauses are controversial and protectionist, if adopted, they would also apply to the United Kingdom in a Brexit extreme scenario.

14.11 BEPS and the United Kingdom: Concluding Remarks

Although the United Kingdom, in the Brexit extreme scenario, will not have any obligations resulting from EU law, it can be more or less cooperative in respect of the BEPS project.

It may also interpret the OECD recommendations in a manner that does not lead to worldwide coordination, but can instead have a regional, that is, a commonwealth, impact (see the example of the diverted profits tax, adopted by the United Kingdom and to be adopted by Australia).[38]

If transposition of the BEPS actions by the United Kingdom and the commonwealth is more attractive to multinationals than transposition of the BEPS Actions in the EU, tax competition between regional blocs could occur.

However, the fact that the United Kingdom, in a Brexit extreme scenario, would not benefit from the freedom of establishment can be a significant disadvantage, as the United Kingdom would lose "access to the EU market". The aforementioned conclusions on non-discrimination of inbound and outbound dividends presuppose that EU and UK companies have access to each other's markets.

Notes

1. This chapter has been first published at *Intertax* ("Free Movement of Capital, the European Union Anti-Tax Avoidance Package and Brexit", Intertax, 44, n°12, 2016, pp. 870–877), and is now republished, submitted to small changes.
2. C-464/14, *Secil Companhia Geral de Cimento S.A. v. Fazenda Pública.*
3. Before that, *Luisi and Carbone* defined capital as "financial operations essentially concerned with the investment of the funds rather than remuneration for a service": ECJ 31 January 1984, Joined Cases 286/82 and 26/83 (*Luisi and Carbone*), ECR 1984 p. 00377, para. 21.
4. Ana Paula Dourado, National Report Portugal, *The EU and Third Countries: Direct Taxation* (Lang et Pistone eds.), Linde Verlag, Wien, 2007, pp. 511–513.
5. See Daniel S. Smit, "The Relationship between the Free Movement of Capital and the other EC Treaty Freedoms in Third Country Relationships in the Fields of Direct Taxation: a Question of Exclusivity, Parallelism or Causality?", *EC Tax Review,* 2007, n. 2, p. 253; ECJ 19 March 1999, case C-222/97, *Trummer and Mayer,* para. 21, 1999 I -01661; ECJ 23 February 2006, C-513/03, *Van Hilten* para. 39, 2006 I- 01957.
6. Joined cases C-358/93 and C-416/93 *Bordessa* case 1995 I-361; Ana Paula Dourado, "Free movement of capital and capital income taxation within the EU; *EC Tax Review* 1994, p. 179; Wolfgang Schoen, "Europaische Kapitalverkehrsfreiheit und nationale Steuerrecht", in Schoen (ed.), *Gedaechtnisschrift fuer Brigitte Knobbe-Keuk,* 1997, p. 747.
7. A. Cordewener, G. W. Kofler, C.P. Schindler, "Free movement of capital and third countries: exploring the boundaries with Lasertec, A and B and Holboeck, *European Taxation*, August/September 2007.
8. ECJ 23 February 2006, C-513/03, cit.
9. See, for example, S. Hemels et al., "Freedom of establishment or free movement of capital: is there an order of priority? Conflicting visions of national courts and the ECJ", *EC Tax Review,* 2010, 1, pp. 19–27; and recent developments specifically on CFC rules, in A.P. Dourado, "The Role of CFC rules in the BEPS Project and in EU Law", *BTR*, 2015, n. 3.

10. A. Cordewener, G. W. Kofler, C.P. Schindler, "Free movement of capital and third countries...", cit. pp. 371–374. A. Dourado, "National Report", cit., pp. 508–514; S. Hemels et al., "Freedom of establishment or free movement of capital: is there an order of priority? Conflicting visions of national courts and the ECJ", *EC Tax Review*, 2010, 1, pp. 19–27; D. Smit, cit., pp. 254–262.
11. ECJ: 23 Feb. 2006, Case C-513/03, *Heirs of M.E.A. van Hilten-van der Heijden v. Inspecteur van de Belastingdienst/Particulieren/Ondernemingen buitenland te Heerlen,* para. 35.
12. ECJ: 13 Mar. 2007, Case C-524/04, *Test Claimants in the Thin Cap Group Litigation v. Commissioners of Inland Revenue,* para. 34.
13. ECJ: 3 Oct. 2006, Case C-452/04, *Fidium Finanz AG v. Bundesanstalt für Finanzdienstleistungsaufsicht,* para. 49.
14. ECJ: 28 January 1992, C-204/90 (Bachmann v Belgian state).
15. ECJ, C-452/04, *Fidium Finanz ...,* cit. para. 49.
16. ECJ: Case C-513/03, *Heirs of M.E.A. van Hilten...,* cit.
17. ECJ: 26 June 2008, C-284/06 (Finanzamt Hamburg-Am Tierpark v Burda GmbH).
18. Case C-251/98 *Baars* [2000] ECR I-2787, paragraphs 21 and 22.
19. TJCE, Test Claimants in the FII Group Litigation..., cit.; 24 de maio de 2007, Caso C-157/05 (Holböck v FA Salzburg-Land).
20. ECJ: 24 May 2007, Case C-157/05, *Winfried L. Holböck v. Finanzamt Salzburg-Land,* paras. 23–24.
21. ECJ: C-284/06, Finanzamt Hamburg-Am Tierpark v Burda..cit.; 4 June 2009, Joined Cases C-439/07 and C-499/07, *Belgische Staat v. KBC Bank NV and Beleggen, Risicokapitaal, Beheer NV v. Belgische Staat.*
22. EFTA Court: 9 July 2014, Joined Cases E-03/13 and E-20/13, *Fred. Olsen and Others and Petter Olsen and Others v. the Norwegian State,* paras. 96–97, 125.
23. ECJ: 5 July 2005 in *D.,* C-376/03, EU:C:2005:424, paragraphs 54 and 61 to 62.
24. ECJ: 12 Dec. 2006, Case C-374/04, *Test Claimants in Class IV of the ACT Group Litigation,* para. 37.
25. ECJ: 24 May 2007, Case C-157/05, *Winfried L. Holböck v. Finanzamt Salzburg-Land,* paras. 23–24.
26. ECJ: 12 Dec. 2006, Case C-446/04, *Test Claimants in the Franked Investment Income Group Litigation v. Commissioners of Inland Revenue,* para. 118.
27. ECJ: FII Group Litigation, C-35/11, 13 November 2012.
28. ECJ: C-35/11, 13 November 2012, cit., para. 100.

29. Fred. Olsen and Others and Petter Olsen and Others v the Norwegian State, Joined cases E-3/13 and E-20/13, July 9, 2014, EFTA, paras. 94–95.
30. Commission v UK, C-112/14, November 13, 2014, EU: C: 2014: 2369.
31. Fred. Olsen, cit., para. 95.
32. Comm. v. United Kingdom, para. 20.
33. ECJ: 12 Sept. 2006, Case C-196/04, *Cadbury Schweppes v. Commissioners of Inland Revenue.*, para 32.
34. ECJ: 13 Mar. 2007, Case C-524/04, *Test Claimants in the Thin Cap Group Litigation v. Commissioners of Inland Revenue*, para. 34.
35. Brussels, 28.1.2016 COM(2016) 24 final Communication from the Commission to the European Parliament and the Council on an External Strategy for Effective Taxation, p. 3.
36. Brussels, 28.1.2016 COM(2016) 24 final ANNEXES 1 to 2 ANNEXES to the Communication from the Commission to the European Parliament and the Council on an External Strategy for Effective Taxation, p. 3.
37. 28.1.2016 COM(2016), 24 FINAL, Fn. 2, p. 7.
38. Self, Heather, "The UK's New Diverted Profits Tax: Compliance with EU Law", *Intertax*, 2015, n.° 4, pp. 333 e ss.

References

Cordewener, A., G.W. Kofler, and C.P. Schindler. 2007. Free Movement of Capital and Third Countries: Exploring the Boundaries with Lasertec, A and B and Holboeck, *European Taxation*, August/September.

Dourado, Ana Paula. 1994. Free Movement of Capital and Capital Income Taxation Within the EU. *EC Tax Review* 3: 176–184.

———. 2007. National Report Portugal. In *The EU and Third Countries: Direct Taxation,* ed. Lang et Pistone. Wien: Linde Verlag.

Hemels, S., et al. 2010. Freedom of Establishment or Free Movement of Capital: Is There an Order of Priority? Conflicting Visions of National Courts and the ECJ. *EC Tax Review* 19: 1.

Schoen, Wolfgang. 1997. Europaische Kapitallverkehersfreiheit und nationale Steuerrecht. In *Gedaechtnisschrift fuer Brigitte Knobbe-Keuk*, ed. Schoen. Koeln: Verlag Dr. Otto Schmidt.

Smit, Daniel S. 2007. "The Relationship Between the Free Movement of Capital and the Other EC Treaty Freedoms in Third Country Relationships in the Fields of Direct Taxation: A Question of Exclusivity, Parallelism or Causality?", *EC Tax Review* 16, n. 2: 252.

15

Free Movement of Capital: Could the CJEU Smooth Brexit?

Marco Lamandini and David Ramos Muñoz

15.1 Introduction

In Europe free movement of capital is enshrined in Article 63 TFEU. However, this freedom had a very slow start (Schön 2005);[1] it was recognised as having direct effect only after the CJEU Bordessa judgment.[2] Yet, its erga omnes effect, that is, the fact that it can be horizontally claimed also by non-EU nationals, makes it potentially the most far-reaching of all EU freedoms. Thus, in the current context of Brexit, the construction of its scope and content by the CJEU enjoys special importance, because free movement of capital will continue to apply to companies established in the United Kingdom after Brexit. To be true, European openness to capital movements is not unconditional. The Treaty allows restrictions under

M. Lamandini (✉)
Alma Mater Studiorum University of Bologna, Bologna, Italy

D.R. Muñoz
Alma Mater Studiorum University of Bologna, Bologna, Italy

Universidad Carlos III Madrid, Madrid, Spain

© The Author(s) 2017
N. da Costa Cabral et al. (eds.), *After Brexit*,
https://doi.org/10.1007/978-3-319-66670-9_15

specific conditions, for example, in the field of taxation and prudential supervision of financial institutions and on grounds of public security or of public policy, as well as for 'overriding reasons in the general interest'. Restrictions to non-EU capital movements can be adopted by EU co-legislators by qualified majority under Article 64(2) TFEU. Yet, in the past, the CJEU has been prepared to expand the scope of the freedom and interpret the exceptions restrictively (e.g. when assessing golden shares).

15.2 Freedom of Capital in a Post-Brexit Scenario

15.2.1 The Current Approach of the CJEU Based on the 'Center of Gravity'

In a post-Brexit scenario, the TFEU freedom of establishment and freedom to provide services will cease to be legitimate entitlements of UK companies. Thus, a fundamental question will be which activities and transactions crossing the Channel will enjoy freedom of capital, and what kind of freedom they will enjoy. This, in turn, will depend (i) on the degree of capital movement that those activities and transactions entail and (ii) on which of the competing forces underpinning the case law of the CJEU prevails. The last point is important. Although the CJEU has adopted a decisive and expansive approach towards free movement of capital, it has so far taken a restrictive stance on the relationship between free movement of capital on the one hand, and freedom of establishment or freedom to provide services, on the other. Pursuant to this approach, free movement of capital does not apply to (equity) investments or to the provision of (financial) services when they are primarily the expression of freedom of establishment and/or freedom to provide services. Thus, a 'centre of gravity' test is required, meaning that if the activity or transaction is deemed to be an exercise of other freedoms, it will be 'attracted' by them and be subject to analysis only by those freedoms. In practice this means that any restriction of activities considered primarily an exercise of freedom of establishment or services, and only incidentally of free movement of capital, will be considered compatible with the Treaties on the sole ground that those freedoms do not apply to non-EU nationals. The fact that the measure incidentally restricts free movement of capital will not result in an additional evaluation of the restriction. In such case, investors from outside the EU who are concerned, for example, by a restriction to acquire control of an EU company, cannot claim protection under primary EU law. This position was originally stated by the CJEU in a series of fiscal cases—starting from Bachmann[3] (point 34)—and eventually extended to the financial sector in Fidium Finanz.[4] There, the Court discussed the scope of free movement of capital with regard to the provision of banking services to a German citizen from Switzerland. In a departure from the Opinion of AG Stix Hackl (Opinion 16 March 2006, in particular points 62–63), the Court concluded (at point 49) that:

> [i]t is apparent that, in the circumstances of the main case, the predominant consideration is freedom to provide services rather than the free movement of capital. Since the rules in dispute impede access to the German financial market for companies established in non-member countries, they affect primarily the freedom to provide services. Given the restrictive effects of those rules on the free movement of capital are merely an inevitable consequence of the restriction imposed on the provision of services, it is not necessary to consider whether the rules are compatible with Article 56 EC et seq.

15.2.2 'Centre of Gravity' and Its Calibration as to Foreign Direct Investment

The CJEU eventually applied the same principle to foreign direct investment and held, in particular, that equity investment must be classified either as (i) portfolio investments, (ii) investments that institute a 'lasting and direct link' but do not grant control or (iii) investments implying control. Only the first two enjoy protection under free movement of capital. This was not always so. The Court in Konle[5] admitted a parallel and cumulative application of the two freedoms as to cross-border real estate investments. On this basis, AG Alber argued in Baars,[6] at points 49–50 of his Opinion, in favour of a cumulative application of both freedoms.[7]

Yet, here the Court began its drift towards the distinction between different degrees of protection for different types of investment by holding that, in the instant case, the acquisition of control was protected by freedom to establish, without more. Then, in Cadbury Schweppes,[8] the Court expressly rejected the cumulative application of both freedoms to the acquisition of control (points 32–33). This principle has been routinely repeated by the Court ever since,[9] unless there remains an ambiguity on the kind of influence (control or less than control) attached to the investment.[10] Only in such ambiguous circumstances has the Court held—first in Holböck[11]—that a national measure restricting foreign direct investment can fall within the scope of both freedoms.

15.2.3   Beyond the 'Centre of Gravity' Approach

The centre of gravity approach adopted so far by the CJEU has been criticised in the literature, noting that it could have fatal consequences for foreign direct investment from outside the EU.[12] In the current, extraordinary, circumstances determined by Brexit, a reconsideration by the Court of this approach could serve Europe and Britain well, by smoothing out at least some of the otherwise harshest consequences of Brexit. Consider just the case of share acquisitions. If viewed from a company law perspective, the tripartite distinction made by the Court, which rests on the degree of intensity of investors' influence over the company, is brittle in theory and intractable in practice. How should one classify joint control? And significant influence or co-influence? Is there a common, uniform, threshold that triggers freedom of establishment? One for all or one to be determined for each specific company depending on its national company law and ownership structure? There are countless scenarios where this slippery distinction could become a breeding ground for litigation and undesired national discretion,[13] which could easily disguise discrimination against non-EU investments and discourage EU-inbound investment, which still constitutes a core European policy and, in today's landscape of global capital flows, a real necessity. Moreover, if the Court rightly considers that a minority investment implies a capital movement, this is even more so with majority investments, which imply a proportionally larger use of capital. Finally, in company law terms, equity investments, especially those aiming to take control, have both organisational and financial implications. Freedom of establishment naturally relates to the former, while free movement of capital relates to the latter. Both are inextricably intertwined.

Although the above reasoning applies to freedom of establishment, a similar argument can also be made in relation to freedom to provide services. Although a case-by-case approach is recommended in many cases, which entail at the same time service provision and capital movements severing the 'service component' from the 'capital' could prove artificial and even arbitrary.

15.3   Conclusions

In the Court experience, a change in jurisprudence, albeit rare, is still possible and has been adopted on quite substantial matters in the past: Keck and Mithouard[14] (point 16) and Metock[15] (point 58) are very illustrative examples. Thus, if the CJEU could reconsider its case law on the 'center of gravity', this, to our mind, would help to make the post-Brexit scenario for financial activities from London to the Continent less black and white; it could nicely accommodate the transitional period. This pragmatic approach would preserve the right for London-based investors to acquire control of EU-based companies, facilitating group strategies that try to address the new scenario through a mixture of London and continental presence. This would at the same time grant the protection of freedom of capital to (some) cross-border financial transactions or activities that also implicate capital movements. The greatest merit of a reconsidered approach, however, would be to reverse the burden of action on many cross-border financial activities currently performed from London. Even if freedom of capital were made fully applicable by the Court, the EU would still retain the right to limit capital movements from Britain, but this would require a positive action, and a regulation adopted by appropriate majorities. This could offer some leeway for a more sensible and proportionate regime than any of the three other available options (Norway-like, Swiss-like and Canada-like) currently discussed as the most likely alternatives for the post-Brexit landscape. Britain's exit may be the biggest revolution in the EU's history. There is no need to accompany the revolution with a guillotine that drastically severs financial arteries, to the detriment of both Britain and Europe.

Notes

1. Compare W. Schön, '*Der Kapitalverkehr mit Drittstaaten und das Internationale Steuerrecht*', *Festschrift für Franz Wassermeyer* (2005), p. 491 (describing this freedom, at the time, as the 'poor cousin' of other fundamental freedoms).
2. CJEU, Judgment of 23 February 1995, joined Cases C-358/93 and C-416/93.
3. CJUE, Judgment of 28 January 1992, Case C-204/90, in particular point 34.
4. CJEU, Judgment of 3 October 2006, Case C-452/04, departing however from the Opinion of Advocate General Stix Hackl (Conclusions 16 March 2006), in particular points 62 and 63).
5. CJEU, Judgment of 1 June 1999, Case C-302/97.
6. CJEU, Judgment of 13 April 2000, Case C-251/98.
7. On freedom to establish in the CJEU case law, compare G. J. Vossestein, *Modernization of European Company Law and Corporate Governance* (Alphen aan den Rijn: Wolters Kluwer, 2010), p. 77.
8. CJEU, Judgment of 12 September 2006, Case C-196/04, in particular points 32–33.
9. Compare, for instance, CJEU, Judgment of 23 October 2007, Case C-112/05 *Commission v. Germany* (*Volkswagen I:* on this G. J. Vossnstein, *Volkswagen:* 'The State of Affairs of Golden Shares, General Company Law and European Free Movement of Capital', in *ECFR*, No. 1 (2008), p. 115); CJEU, of 26 March 2009 Case C-327/07 *Commission v. Italy*; Judgment of 21 October 2010, Case C-81/09, *Idryma Typou*, point 48; Judgment of 28 September 2006, joined Cases C-282/04 and C-283/04, *Commission v. The Netherlands*, points 42–43.
10. More recently CJEU, Grand Chamber, Judgment of 22 October 2013, joined Cases C-105/12 – C-107/12, *Essent,* (in particular point 40); see also CJEU, Judgment of 28 September 2006, joined Cases C-282/04 and C-283/04, *Commission v. The Netherlands*, point 19; CJEU, Judgment of 8 July 2010, Case C-171/08, *Commission v. Portugal*, point 49.

11. CJEU, Judgment of 24 May 2007, Case C-157/05.
12. S. Hindelang, *The Free Movement of Capital and Foreign Direct Investment,*
    p. 108, where additional references.
13. As to Italy, Tar Lazio, Judgment of 18 May 2010 and Consiglio di Stato,
    Judgment of 2 November 2011, *Delta*.
14. CJEU, Judgement of 24 November 1993, Joined Cases C-267/91 and
    C-268/91.
15. CJEU, Judgement of 25 July 2008, Case C-127/08.

16

Policy Uncertainty and Spillovers into International Financial Markets

Ansgar Belke

16.1 Introduction

The British residents have decided that the UK should leave the European Union (EU) in the near future. The leave campaign succeeded, although the result of the referendum was quite close. Apart from the consequences for the UK, this can be seen as a political disaster for the EU, because for the first time ever, a member state will actually leave. Various researchers and institutions as well as politicians have warned of negative economic effects for both the UK and Europe, claiming that Britain's withdrawal will generate a 'lose-lose' situation.[1]

Brexit can be regarded as the most severe political event in the first half of 2016: poll updates and the actual result on 24 June significantly affected international financial markets (European Commission 2016). It is reasonable to expect that Brexit has an impact on international financial

A. Belke (✉)
University of Duisburg-Essen, Essen, North Rhine-Westphalia, Germany

CEPS, Brussels, Belgium

IZA, Bonn, Germany

© The Author(s) 2017
N. da Costa Cabral et al. (eds.), *After Brexit*,
https://doi.org/10.1007/978-3-319-66670-9_16

markets due to the high integration of financial markets in general. Numerous countries apart from the UK might be negatively affected. By studying the impact of Brexit on financial markets, we might gain an insight into market expectations of the size of the economic impact beyond the UK, and which other countries might suffer most.

In our opinion (Belke et al. 2017), this topic is too complex to simply check for trade and financial linkages to determine which countries will be most affected, due to additional dependencies between countries that the euro area and the institutional framework of the EU has generated. According to the dividend discount model (Gordon and Shapiro 1956), stock returns and other financial market variables will be affected by *expectations about future effects* on the real economy generated by Brexit. Therefore, we give a short overview of the possible effects of enduring Brexit uncertainty on the real economy of the UK and other countries, especially the remaining EU states.

We also need to address the debate about whether and why volatility means uncertainty. In the part of this chapter which surveys the empirical evidence, we use actual asset price changes rather than unanticipated ones. We feel legitimised to firmly follow Belke and Gros (2002) and to use historical volatilities (i.e. the standard deviation) or generalised autoregressive conditional heteroscedasticity ((G)ARCH) estimates as measures of uncertainty.

Our interest is the direction of spillovers into policy uncertainty and financial market volatilities in the UK. Our second research question is whether we can expect contagion from the UK to other countries, through the political or institutional channel, especially the EU states. Therefore, we survey empirical studies which check for spillovers of Brexit uncertainty onto a variety of asset classes in international financial markets (Begg 2016).

This chapter introduces the main arguments and empirical results of studies such as Belke et al. (2017) and has the following structure: the next section gives a brief overview of the possible effects of enduring Brexit uncertainty on the UK and other countries. In Sect. 16.2, we examine the effect of Brexit on the UK's financial market volatilities. In Sect. 16.3, we empirically evaluate the impact of Brexit on international financial markets and a variety of asset categories. Section 16.4 concludes.

16.2   Possible Effects of Enduring Brexit Uncertainty on the Real Economy of the UK and Other Countries

Departure from the EU might have huge consequences for the British economy through following channels: trade in goods and services, investment, immigration, productivity and fiscal costs.[2] It is very difficult to estimate the effect of each channel and the impact on the British economy because Brexit is a political novelty. The fact that the British government and the EU will have to completely re-evaluate their political and economic relationship will further increase the uncertainty around those effects. Moreover, the British government will have to make substantial political decisions, for example, regarding prudential and regulatory laws.

Apart from a weaker pound and lower UK interest rates the referendum itself did not cause a persistent impact (Gros 2016). Financial markets tumbled for a few weeks after the referendum, but have recovered already; consumer spending remains stable. More surprisingly, investment has remained relatively constant, in spite of substantial uncertainty about Britain's future trade relationship with the EU. One might argue that '(t)he United Kingdom's vote to 'Brexit' the EU is on course to become the year's biggest non-event' (Gros 2016). But how to explain the current lack of impact? Maybe because Brexit has not yet happened (Begg 2016). Hence, major economic impacts of Brexit can still not be ruled out for the future. Moreover, CEIC Data for July 2016 already shows that business and consumer confidence has fallen by about 4% and 12%, respectively.[3]

Concerning the trade channel, the most important aspect is that the UK will probably *lose its access to the European single market*. The EU is the UK's most important trading partner. Almost half of UK exports in goods and services are delivered into the EU (approx. 13% of UK GDP in 2014). Apart from an absence of tariffs, the single market guarantees the principle of mutual recognition and the so-called single passport—a system that allows services operators legally established in one member state to offer their services in other member states without further authorisation requirements (EC 2016). Besides, the financial sector is a key component of the UK economy, as London is one of the largest financial centres in the world.[4] Financial services generate about 8% of national income (the EU average is approximately 5%), trade in financial services alone was about 3% of the nominal GDP in 2014 (the EU average is approximately 1%), and 40% of total financial service exports are exported to the EU. The financial centre of London would lose out significantly in terms of attractiveness when it could no longer guarantee access to the European single market.[5]

The effects of Brexit will thus crucially depend on the results of negotiations between the UK and EU about their future economic (and political) relationship. The effects via trade might be small[6] when the UK keeps its access to the European single market. Nevertheless, in the worst-case scenario, if no alternative agreement is reached, the trade relationship defers to the WTO framework (Blockmans and Emerson 2016). In that case, trading links between the UK and the EU will diminish probably, generating reductions in UK income from exports.[7] However, the effects are not limited to trade relationships with the EU. First, the UK will not be part of upcoming FTAs (free trade agreements), which are negotiated between the EU and countries like Brazil, China, and the USA presently. Second, the UK will no longer be subject to the FTAs that have been successfully negotiated by the EU and will therefore experience additional restrictions in trading possibilities.[8] It is questionable whether the UK can offset the decrease in trade with the EU and corresponding national income by focusing its trade ambitions on other markets. While it is possible for the UK to negotiate new FTAs, negotiations will probably take longer than its withdrawal from the EU, generating a potential disruption of trade as trade relationships with those states will default on WTO rules.

The UK has been subject to large FDI (foreign direct investment), mainly from EU countries—nearly half of total FDI. As a strong link between EU membership and inward FDI has been observed, it is legitimised to assume that the amount of FDI coming from the EU will be negatively affected (Fournier et al. 2015; Bruno et al. 2016a, b; Dhingra et al. 2015). Additionally, FDI from outside the EU might decrease as well, as the UK can no longer provide access to the single market. According to the Office for National Statistics, the average flow of inward FDI has been about 5% of GDP between 1999 and 2015. As a financial centre, the UK is dependent on inward FDI and financial flows generally. If London loses its status as a global financial centre, FDI will decrease and so will consumption and investment (Belke et al. 2017).

Figure 16.1 represents a survey of studies that try to quantify the long- and short-term effects of Brexit, for 2018. According to the IMF (2016a, b), under their adverse scenario, the UK might experience a sharp fall in GDP in 2017, causing a harsh recession. The majority of studies indicate significant negative short- and long-term effects, whereas some studies even indicate positive (long-term) effects (Minford 2016; OpenEurope 2015; Mansfield 2014).

Regarding the short-run effects, the Brexit decision in June 2016 caused immediately financial turmoil—stock markets slid in response to the vote in an orderly decline and the British pound decreased. It could take two years for the UK to formally leave the EU, and it is uncertain how the country's relationship with the EU will change. This means that markets are expected to stay volatile, at least until it becomes clear what a Brexit scenario means for the UK and the rest of the EU.[9]

Financial market volatility generally increases sharply and spills over into markets during crises and specific political events. Hence, uncertainty about Brexit might not only directly influence shares and exchange markets, but might also increase spillovers across them. Financial instabilities, such as an increase in FX volatilities, pose further potential asymmetric effects for the economy, implying that firms will delay new investments and hiring decisions, benefiting from the so-called option value of waiting (Belke and Gros 2002).

The potential effects of Brexit are obviously not limited to the UK. There is huge potential for spillover through trade and financial links, particularly to the remaining EU countries. Until now the impact is uncertain and will depend on the future political and economic relationship between the UK and the EU. According to a majority of analysts, other countries are likely to lose out economically. According to trade linkages (exports to the UK in percent of own GDP), Ireland (11.2%), the Netherlands (6.7%) and Belgium (7.5%) are primarily exposed. Regarding banking linkages, the Irish, Dutch, Swedish and German banking sectors are highly connected with the British. Based on capital market linkages (FDI and portfolio investment), Ireland, the Netherlands, Luxembourg and France are the most exposed.

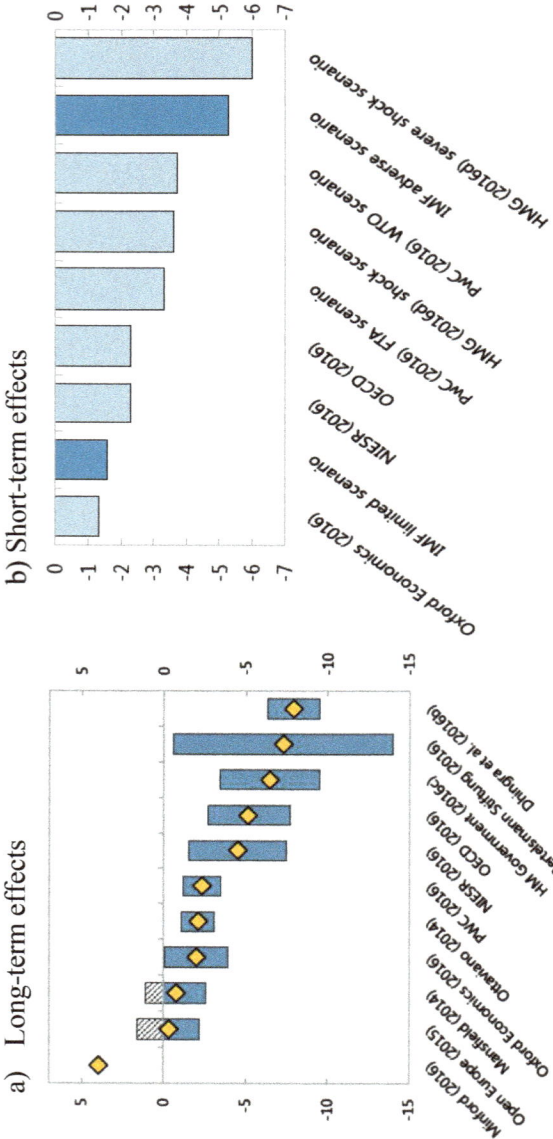

Fig. 16.1 Economic effects of Brexit on the UK GDP. (**a**) Long-term effects (**b**) Short-term effects (*Note:* Deviation from baseline (=UK remains in the EU). (Source: IMF 2016a, b)

The IMF (2016a, b) investigates spillover effects to other (European) countries. Based on financial and trading linkages, Ireland (−0.6% to −2% of GDP), the Netherlands (−0.3% to −0.7% of GDP) and Belgium (−0.25% to −0.65% of GDP) are the most affected countries; other member states are less affected. In the rest of the EU, output falls by 0.2–0.5% below baseline. The European Commission (2016) emphasises that 'the referendum has created an extraordinarily uncertain situation'. According to forecasts, the result of the referendum might put pressure on investment and consumption. Thus, the EC has reduced its GDP growth forecasts for the euro area by 0.1–0.2% for 2016 and 0.2–0.5% for 2017.

Brexit might also generate political and institutional uncertainty about the EU besides direct economic links. The UK will be the first country to actually leave the EU. Moreover, the UK is not the only country where anti-EU movements have won impact. Economic issues, particularly the sovereign debt crisis, have enabled political campaigns especially in France, the Netherlands and Italy to leave the EU. Also, the success of the Brexit movements might generate momentum for similar movements in other countries increasing the probability of more countries leaving the EU. This might damage the reputation of the EU as a sustainable and irreversible institution decreasing its political power, influence, and ability to negotiate new supranational contracts like FTA (Belke et al. 2017).

Political uncertainty may therefore spread across Europe and affect especially countries whose sovereign solvency is closely linked to the existence of the EU and the euro area—namely Spain, Portugal, Italy and Greece. Without the euro area or sufficient contributors, rescue mechanisms like the ESM would cease to exist or be perceived as too small to act as a safeguard if member states are in financial difficulties.

16.3 Brexit and Its Effect on UK Financial Market Volatilities

In this section, we give an overview of estimations the magnitude and the sign of short-run Brexit effects that are related to increased political uncertainty during the time before the referendum and directly after

Brexit vote on UK financial markets. Our focus is on volatilities (second statistical moments) rather than changes of levels (first statistical moment). For the entire estimation procedure, see Belke et al. (2017).

As a measure of uncertainty, (Belke et al. 2017), among others, employ the Economic Policy Uncertainty index (EPU)[10] which draws on newspapers and other written sources and is calculated as scaled counts of articles containing 'uncertain' or 'uncertainty', 'economic' or 'economy', and one or more policy-relevant terms. Policy-driven uncertainty reflects the level of doubt and confusion in the private sector caused by government policies and is shown to increase during political turmoil, elections, or the implementation of major policies and programmes. Regarding its definition, using the EPU Index should be a good proxy for the estimations of Brexit uncertainty and Brexit-vote effects. The other index provided by the same source—the Brexit Uncertainty index—is calculated by multiplying the EPU index by the share of EPU articles that contain 'Brexit', 'EU' or 'European Union'. It is available only until May 2016.

Figure 16.2 shows the EPU index in the UK close to the referendum hovering at its highest point, exceeding previous records. Additional visual inspection of the EPU and Brexit uncertainty reveals a strong but time-varying correlation of both during the period before the referendum. In their empirical estimations, for instance, Belke et al. (2017) use EPU instead of Brexit uncertainty because EPU data is highly correlated with the Brexit uncertainty during the time preceding the referendum but is available for a longer horizon. Moreover, the daily EPU data could be superior to monthly Brexit uncertainty data, since financial markets are very flexible and able to react to news immediately (Belke et al. 2017).

As an example, the model of Belke et al. (2017) includes the following variables:

- Daily stock market volatility[11] calculated as the annualised daily percent standard deviation of daily high and low FTSE 250 prices.
- Daily UK pound sterling volatility calculated as the annualised daily percent standard deviation of intraday high and low exchange rate GBP/USD.
- Daily EPU index constructed by Baker et al. (2015).

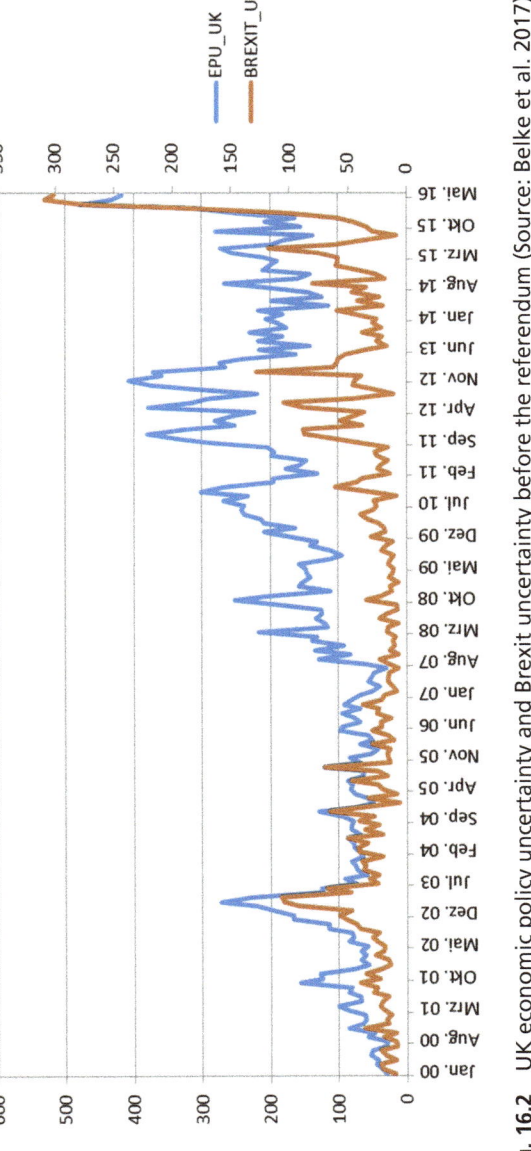

Fig. 16.2 UK economic policy uncertainty and Brexit uncertainty before the referendum (Source: Belke et al. 2017)

In order to distinguish between domestic policy uncertainty and global uncertainty, for instance, Belke et al. (2017) have included the CBOE Volatility Index (VIX Index)[12] as an exogenous variable.

Their sample contains 4105 observations, from 2001:01:01 to 2016:23:09; all variables are taken in logs and plotted in Fig. 16.3. They observe that stock prices and exchange rates went through a major period of volatility during the global financial crisis. Stock prices also experienced increased volatility around August 2011, which could be explained by the effects of the euro crisis (Gros 2011). In addition, there is a sizeable upward spike at the time of the referendum (23 June 2016, marked as a vertical line) for all variables under observation reaching levels similar to previous maxima.

To estimate the impact of policy uncertainty on volatility in financial markets, Belke et al. (2017) use the empirical method proposed by Diebold and Yilmaz (2009, 2012) based on VAR variance decompositions,[13] which allows to assess the fraction of the error variance in forecasting one variable that is due to shocks to another variable.

The *total volatility spillover index* is constructed and measures the contribution of spillovers of shocks across variables under consideration to the total forecast error variance. In order to investigate the direction of spillovers across financial volatilities and policy uncertainty, the *directional spillover* is applied. The *net spillover* from variable i to all other variables j is obtained as the difference between gross shocks transmitted to and gross shocks received from all other markets. The last spillover measure of interest is the *net pairwise spillover index* between variables x_i and x_j which is defined as the difference between gross shocks transmitted from x_i to x_j and gross shocks transmitted from x_i to x_j.

The chosen approach allows to investigate the dynamics of spillovers in the form of rolling regressions, and so the time variations of total, directional, net and net-pairwise spillovers in the periods before and after the Brexit referendum, which are the specific interest of this study.

The generalised impulse responses are significant and display the expected signs.[14] (Fig. 16.4)

According to the Granger causality test, which is presented in Table 16.1a, policy uncertainty 'Granger-causes' stock and exchange rate volatilities. In their study, Belke et al. (2017) perform a causality test

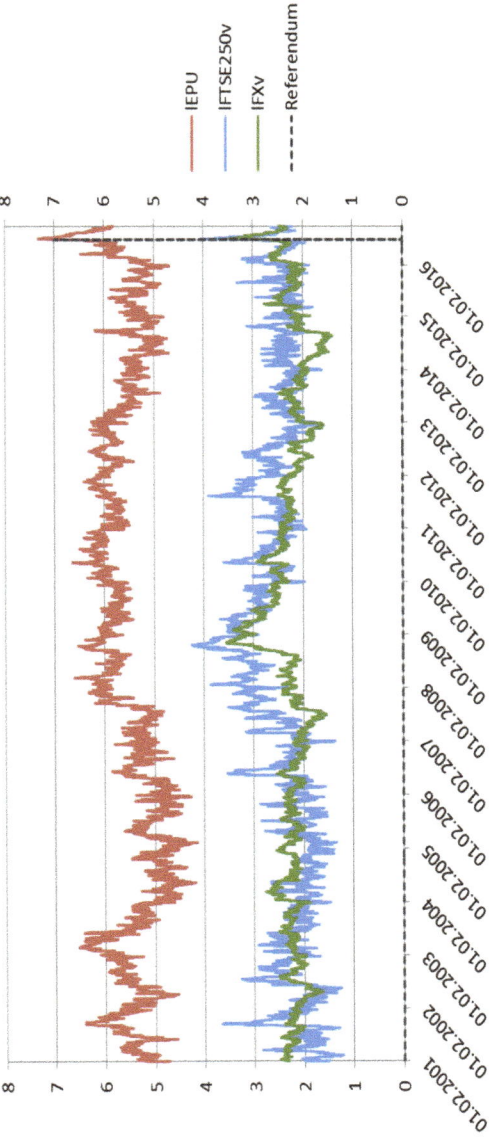

Fig. 16.3 Financial volatilities and EPU index, logs (Source: Belke et al. 2017)

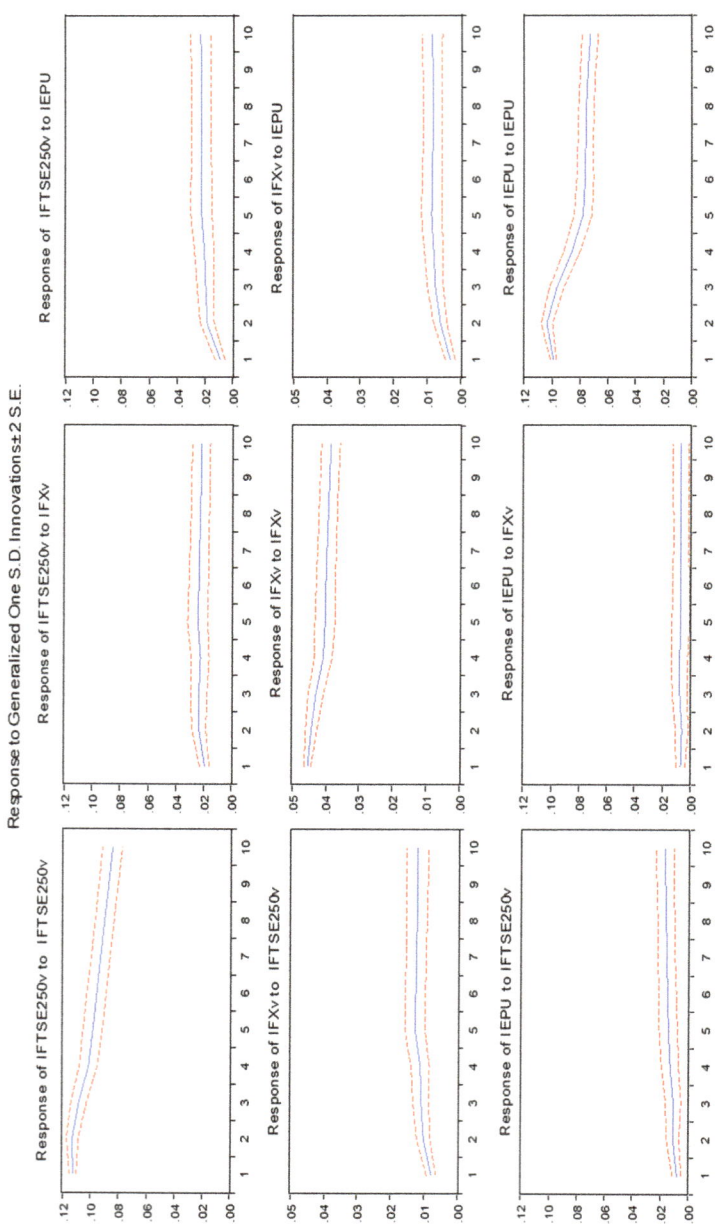

Fig. 16.4 Generalised impulse responses functions, full-sample estimations (Source: Belke et al. 2017)

Table 16.1 Causality tests

(a) VAR Granger Causality/Block Exogeneity Wald Tests

	Dependent variable: IFTSE250v				Dependent variable: IFXv				Dependent variable: IEPU		
Excluded	*Chi-sq*	*df*	*Prob*	*Excluded*	*Chi-sq*	*df*	*Prob*	*Excluded*	*Chi-sq*	*df*	*Prob*
IFXv	8.04	5	0.15	IFTSE250v	19.43	5	0.00	IFTSE250v	16.57	5	0.01
IEPU	37.31	5	0.00	IEPU	22.66	5	0.00	IFXv	3.13	5	0.68
All	47.91	10	0.00	All	48.33	10	0.00	All	20.28	10	0.03

(b) Variance causality test based on Hafner and Herwartz (2008)

MV-GARCH, BEKK—Estimation by BFGS

1. Test for causality of EPU to FTSE250, FX
Chi-Squared(4) = 46.35 or F(4,*) = 11.59 with Significance Level 0.000

2. Test for causality of FTSE250, FX to EPU
Chi-Squared(4) = 86.39 or F(4,*) = 21.60 with Significance Level 0.000

Source: Belke et al. (2017)

based on Quasi Maximum-Likelihood methods proposed by Hafner and Herwartz (2008). The method relies on multivariate GARCH estimations and following Wald testing of appropriate coefficients' set. Their test results (see Table 16.1b) show some evidence of bi-directional causality between policy uncertainty and financial volatilities. This means that not only policy uncertainty affects financial markets but also exaggerated financial volatility adds to uncertainty about policy measures to support the economy and thereby mitigate downside risks.

For the rolling estimations, Belke et al. (2017) have set a rolling window of 500 and a forecast horizon of ten working days.[15]

As described in more detail in Belke et al. (2017), the estimation procedure yields to an input-output decomposition of the total spillover index based on full-sample estimations. Therefore, policy uncertainty shocks contributed 4.1% (third column, first row) and 3.2% (third column, second row) to the variance decompositions of stock market and exchange rate volatilities, respectively. Policy uncertainty itself was mostly affected by stock volatilities (2.63%), while the FX market does not seem to significantly drive policy uncertainty, since its contribution to the forecast error variance is only 0.64%. The total spillover index for all variables is equal to 7.5%. Nevertheless, the estimation was performed employing data for the full sample so this value should be taken with caution. Therefore, the spillover index is only the average measure of spillovers in the period from January 2001 to September 2016. In order to assess the extent and nature of the spillovers variation over time, Belke et al. (2017) carried on with the rolling estimations.

The authors' rolling estimations for total spillovers between stock volatility, FX volatility and policy uncertainty (see Fig. 16.5) display an increase in spillovers during the period from the end of 2008 till the end of 2012, which could be ascribed to the subprime-mortgage crisis, the global financial crisis and the sovereign debt crisis. The subsequent rise of the spillover index directly after the Brexit referendum has topped all historical maxima.

In Fig. 16.6, we are able to recognise that the spike of total spillover index at the end of the sample is actually due to increased spillovers *from policy uncertainty to financial market volatilities*.

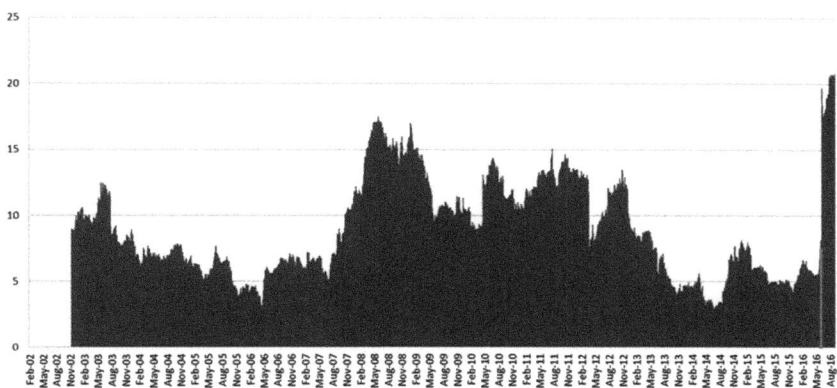

Fig. 16.5 Total spillover index (Source: Belke et al. 2017)

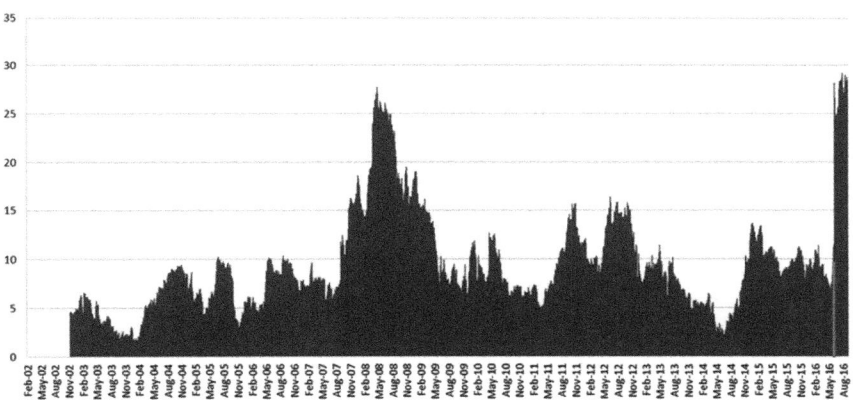

Fig. 16.6 Directional spillovers from EPU to financial volatilities (Source: Belke et al. 2017)

Regarding the results displayed in Fig. 16.7, the index of net spillovers from EPU to financial volatilities has a positive value apart from few exceptions. It follows that policy uncertainty shocks have influenced financial markets to a larger extent than financial market volatility shocks since 2004. Nevertheless, the value of the net spillover index changed dramatically after the Brexit vote and increased from 9% to 26%, staying dominant until the end of the sample.

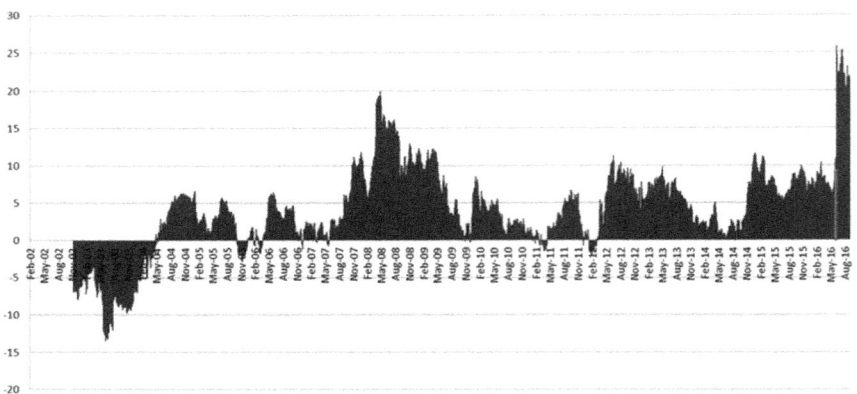

Fig. 16.7 Net spillovers from EPU to financial volatilities (Source: Belke et al. 2017)

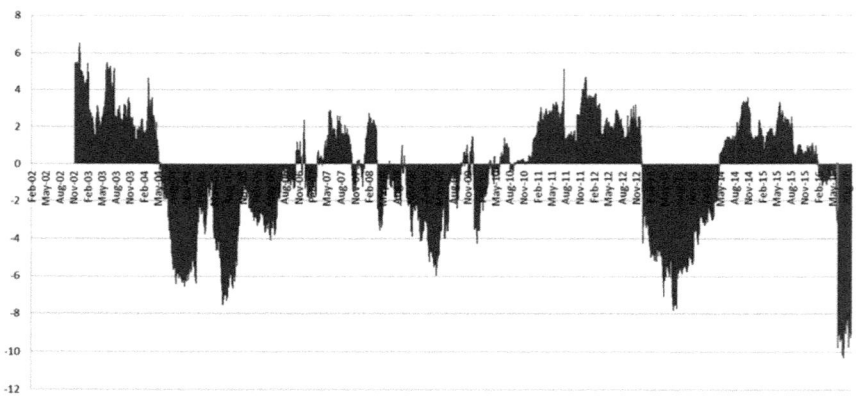

Fig. 16.8 Net pairwise spillovers between stock volatility and EPU (Source: Belke et al. 2017)

The final empirical exercise in this section, again based on Belke et al. (2017), looks at the pairwise net spillovers (Figs. 16.8, 16.9 and 16.10) to expose bilateral relationships between the variables under observation. Regarding Fig. 16.8, stock price volatility was a net receiver of policy uncertainty shocks as from February 2016. Figure 16.9 provides the net spillovers between exchange rate volatility and EPU. Policy uncertainty shocks dominate in net terms beginning in May 2006. The Brexit

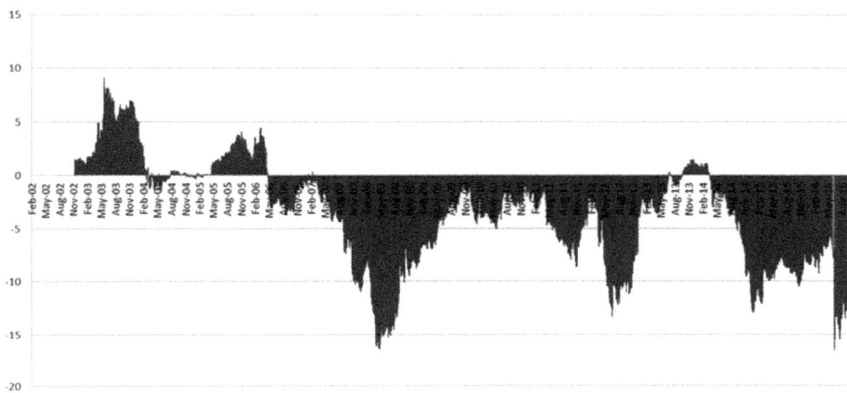

Fig. 16.9 Net pairwise spillovers between FX volatility and EPU (Source: Belke et al. 2017)

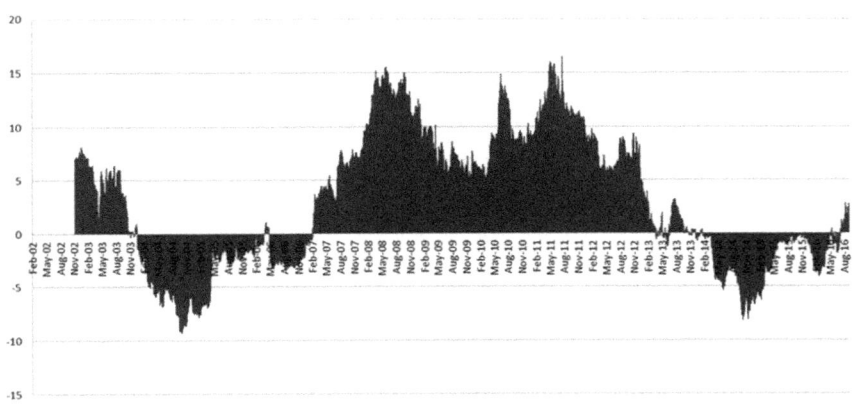

Fig. 16.10 Net pairwise spillovers between stock volatility and FX volatility (Source: Belke et al. 2017)

referendum led to an increase in net spillovers between FX volatility and policy uncertainty like the net spillovers between stock volatility and EPU. From the net spillovers between stock and FX volatilities shown in Fig. 16.10, we see that the FX market was a net recipient of large levels of stock volatility shocks, starting in 2007 up to the end of 2013, and became a net transmitter to the stock market afterward. The time right before and after the Brexit vote does not display extraordinary patterns in the relationship between financial volatilities (Belke et al. 2017).

To conclude, the estimation results displayed so far exposes the considerable role of policy uncertainty on financial market volatilities. Policy uncertainty after 23 June 2016 induced huge spillovers to financial markets and exceeded all previous historical maxima. Interestingly, policy uncertainty spillovers have remained strong since then and are considered not only by Belke et al. (2017) as a proof that policy uncertainty about the development of the relationship between the UK and the EU causes turmoil in financial markets which could further weaken investment and hiring in the UK (and Europe).

16.4   Brexit and Its Effects on International Financial Markets

In this section, we describe how Belke et al. (2017) analyse the effect of Brexit on international financial markets. We now give a survey of estimates of the impact of the increase in the likelihood that citizens of the UK would vote for Brexit on numerous financial variables. The estimates we refer to use daily data between the 1 April and 23 June 2016, thereby examining the critical phase before the EU referendum took place. They are based on data for Austria, Belgium, Canada, Denmark, Finland, France, Germany, Netherlands, Norway, Italy, Japan, Portugal, Spain, Sweden, Switzerland, the UK and the USA.

The measures of daily stock returns are based on the closing prices of the most important stock indexes of the countries under consideration (see Belke et al. 2017 for the exact variables). Additionally, we investigate the effect on ten-year government yields and sovereign Credit Default Swaps (CDS) for ten-year bonds that measure sovereign credit risk. In order to examine the effect of the increase in the probability of Brexit on the external value of the British currency, we use the exchange rate of the British pound vis-à-vis the relevant currencies. The data is obtained from Thomson Reuters Datastream if not stated otherwise.

The most important variables of the study conducted by Belke et al. (2017) are the variables that tracked the probability of Brexit. Because the corresponding coefficients are most relevant to our research question, they use two different measures to check the robustness of our results. Firstly, they use probability data in percentage points based on decimal odds of the online betting exchange 'Betfair'. Secondly, they attempt to measure the probability of Brexit by using survey (poll) data collected by Bloomberg.[16] The variables to track the probability of Brexit are presented in Figs. 16.11 and 16.12.

Both figures show a comparable development about the implied chance of Brexit. Starting around the end of May, the 'leave' campaign gains momentum until mid-June. Although the probability of Brexit

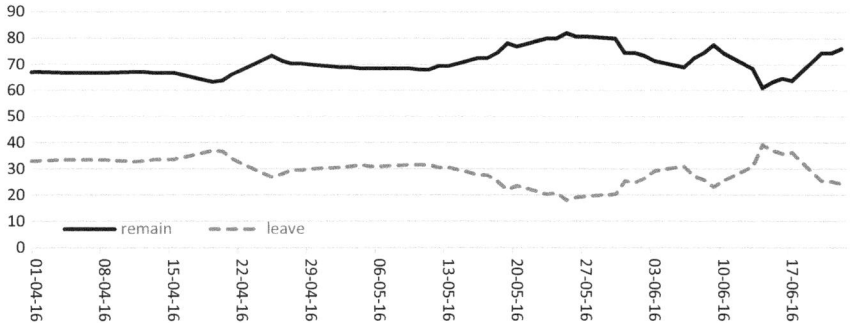

Fig. 16.11 Probability of Brexit before the referendum (in percentage points) (Source: Betfair)

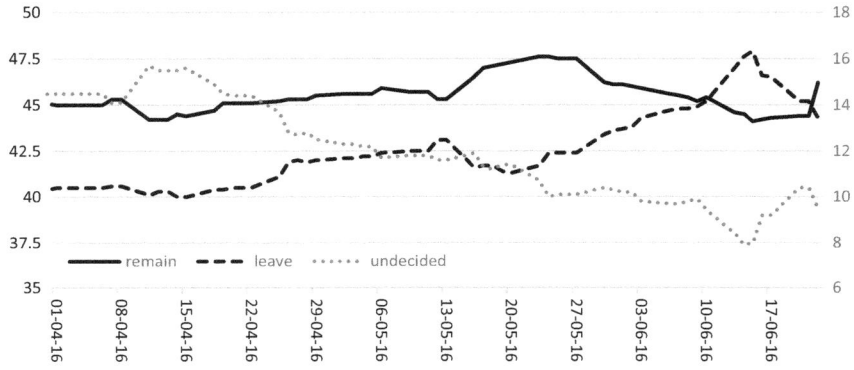

Fig. 16.12 Summary of Brexit polls (Source: Bloomberg)

does not reach 50%, the 'leave' campaign surpassed the 'remain' side in polls in mid-June. Close to the referendum, Belke et al. (2017) identify another period strong growth of support for the 'remain' campaign in both variables.

Although they include both Brexit variables alternatively in their estimations, they focus our analysis mainly on the first one, because the information content of polls and survey data to explain developments of financial variables is respectively low (Gerlach 2016).

While it can be expected that changes in the probability of Brexit should have had an impact on fast information-processing markets, it is legitimate to assume that timing also matters. An increase in the probability three months before the date of the referendum might have had a smaller impact compared to the same increase one day before the vote. Likewise, one may expect that during times of high public attention, the impact on financial markets might be stronger.

To account for these considerations, Belke et al. (2017) use Google Trends data to check for the public interest in Brexit based on Google search requests.[17] The graph displayed in Fig. 16.13 presents a measure of 'public attention' for Brexit in the entire UK and is a ratio compared to the day with the highest attention within the observed time period.

In order to investigate the influence of the Brexit referendum, Belke et al. (2017) use standard econometric procedures. As first step of their analysis, panel estimation is used to obtain first results. Next, they perform

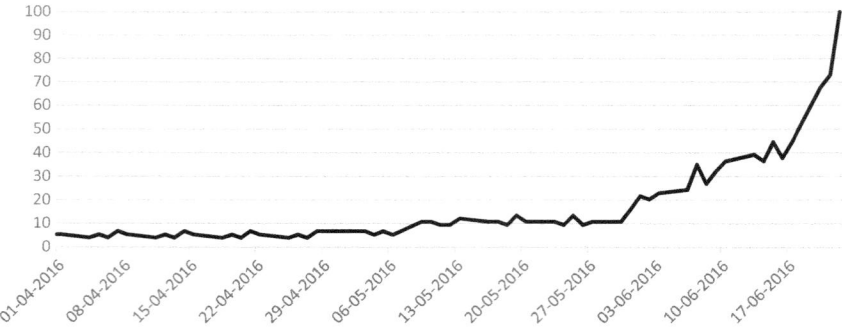

Fig. 16.13 Public attention based on Google search requests (Source: Google Trends)

Seemingly Unrelated Regression (SUR) estimations to obtain country-specific results. The SUR approach consists of several regression equations that are connected by allowing for cross-equation correlations of the error terms. This appears to be an appropriate assumption because financial markets are highly integrated. Furthermore, they estimate specifications in which the observations points are weighed based on Google Trends data to account for the timing of the change in Brexit-vote probability.

Belke et al. (2017) include numerous control variables which can affect financial variables. First, they control for changing expectations concerning monetary policy by including three-month futures of the three-month interest rate. For related reasons, they include the national long-term interest yield as explanatory variable in some specifications. Second, they use the S&P commodity price index which is theoretically an indicator of changing expectations about the performance of the global economy. Table 16.2 gives an overview of our variables.

Their first aim is to investigate the effect of Brexit-vote probability on international stock markets. In their opinion, the effect on stock markets

Table 16.2 Overview of variables used in estimation

Variable	Description	Variable	Description
$Brexit\_Prob_t$	The change in the Brexit probability in t		The percentage change in the CDS in t of country i
$Brexit\_Poll_t$	The change in the support for the leave campaign in t	$Comm_t$	The percent change in commodity prices in t
	The percent change in stock prices in t in country i		The percent change in the British pound against the national currency of country i in t
	The change in the ten-year interest yield in t for country i		The change in the long-term interest rate differential in t.
	The change in the three-month future for the three-month interest rate in t in country (currency area) i		The change in the three-month future of the three-month interest rate differential in t.

Source: Belke et al. (2017)

can be assumed to be generally negative. Nevertheless, there might be differences regarding its extent based on the strength of trade and financial linkages between the UK and the country under consideration.

The dividend discount model assumes that stock prices are not only impacted by the expected level of dividends but also by current and future (short-term) interest rates (see Sect. 16.1). According to announcements by the Bank of England (BOE) and to a lesser extent the European Central Bank, it could be expected that central banks would react in their attempt to offset potential asymmetric effects.[18] Hence, the effect of the likelihood of a Brexit vote on stock markets could be underestimated if a variable quantifying expectations about future monetary policy is not included in the model.

Essential parts of the estimation results gained by Belke et al. (2017) are presented in Tables 16.3 and 16.4. The estimated coefficients of the Brexit variables presented in both tables measure the effects of a one-percentage point increase in the probability of Brexit (*Brexit_Prob*) or Brexit polls (*Brexit_Poll*) on stock prices, in percent. Their panel estimations show strong evidence that an increase in the likelihood of a Brexit vote has strong negative effects on stock prices. For *Brexit_Prob*, they find a decrease in stock prices of around 0.13%. For *Brexit_Poll*, they find a decrease of around 0.42%. Both results seem to be robust to the addition of commodity prices and indicators of future monetary policy.

The SUR estimation results verify the panel results but shed light on country differences. Whereas the largest effects are found for UK stocks when measured in USD, the impact on US and Canadian stock prices turn out to be weaker than the impact on European economies. For both economies, the results become insignificant when we add control variables. Regarding differences, the effects are comparable between European countries. Hence, it is somehow difficult to trace back the results to the degree of trade, banking or capital market linkages. Nevertheless, Belke et al. (2017) notice a tendency that the effects for the GIIPS[19] states are stronger, with the exception of Greece. When they weight the observation by Google Trends data, the effects turn out to be stronger and significant for all countries, indicating that timing does really matter.

Table 16.3 Effect of Brexit-vote likelihood on stock markets; panel estimation

	Random effects							
	(i)	(ii)	(iii)	(iv)	(v)	(vi)	(vii)	(viii)
$Brexit\_Prob_t$	-0.1372	-0.1421	-0.1373	-0.1258				
	(0.000)	(0.000)	(0.000)	(0.000)				
$Brexit\_Poll_t$					-0.4243	-0.4385	-0.4163	-0.4052
					(0.000)	(0.000)	(0.000)	(0.000)
$Future3x6_t^i$		-0.0207				-0.0227		
		(0.1284)				(0.2132)		
$IR10_t^i$			-0.0555				-0.5564	
			(0.000)				(0.000)	
$Comm_t$				0.2691				0.2780
				(0.000)				(0.000)
Pseudo R^2	0.0791	0.0818	0.1348	0.1712	0.0209	0.0219	0.0788	0.1214
Hausman p-value		0.4123	0.9100			0.2876	0.8333	

Source: Belke et al. (2017)

Note: Constants are included. p-values are presented in brackets. The Newey-West estimator is used for the calculation of the covariance matrix. Individual and time effects are included

Table 16.4 Effect of Brexit-vote likelihood on stock markets; SUR estimation

Exo. variables	(1) Brexit_Prob$_t$	(2)[a] Brexit_Prob$_t$ Future3x6$_t^i$	(3) Brexit_Prob$_t$ IR10$_t^i$	(4) Brexit_Prob$_t$ Comm$_t$	(5) Brexit_Prob$_t$ (weighted estimation)	(6) Brexit_Poll$_t$
Austria	−0.1500 (0.004)	−0.1426 (0.012)	−0.1494 (0.005)	−0.1337 (0.001)	−0.2268 (0.000)	−0.5023 (0.062)
Belgium	−0.1503 (0.003)	−0.1473 (0.005)	−0.1524 (0.001)	−0.1395 (0.001)	−0.2292 (0.000)	−0.3684 (0.209)
Canada	−0.0452 (0.067)	−0.0452 (0.066)	−0.0316 (0.205)	−0.0318 (0.053)	−0.0690 (0.000)	−0.2503 (0.003)
Denmark	−0.1709 (0.001)	−0.1492 (0.000)	−0.1627 (0.001)	−0.1624 (0.001)	−0.2269 (0.000)	−0.3508 (0.005)
Finland	−0.0968 (0.182)	−0.0943 (0.203)	−0.1025 (0.150)	−0.0797 (0.193)	−0.2245 (0.000)	−0.4785 (0.000)
France	−0.1818 (0.002)	−0.1771 (0.002)	−0.1823 (0.001)	−0.1689 (0.000)	−0.2750 (0.000)	−0.4979 (0.063)
Germany	−0.1586 (0.006)	−0.1543 (0.008)	−0.1559 (0.008)	−0.1449 (0.002)	−0.2545 (0.000)	−0.5272 (0.040)
Greece	−0.1223 (0.246)	−0.1249 (0.233)	−0.0219 (0.803)	−0.1122 (0.294)	−0.0897 (0.000)	−0.6213 (0.401)
Netherlands	−0.1692 (0.005)	−0.1640 (0.007)	−0.1734 (0.003)	−0.1548 (0.001)	−0.2626 (0.000)	−0.5415 (0.022)
Norway	−0.1225 (0.004)	−0.1220 (0.004)	−0.0938 (0.029)	−0.1053 (0.000)	−0.1935 (0.000)	−0.3352 (0.215)
Ireland	−0.1972 (0.002)	−0.2003 (0.002)	−0.1939 (0.001)	−0.1853 (0.001)	−0.3140 (0.000)	−0.6048 (0.015)
Italy	−0.2132 (0.005)	−0.2081 (0.004)	−0.1784 (0.006)	−0.1869 (0.003)	−0.2574 (0.000)	−0.3305 (0.338)
Japan	−0.1542 (0.002)	−0.1170 (0.025)	−0.1385 (0.012)	−0.1391 (0.002)	−0.1940 (0.000)	−0.5348 (0.243)
Portugal	−0.2003 (0.000)	−0.1999 (0.000)	−0.1768 (0.000)	−0.1852 (0.000)	−0.2823 (0.000)	−0.4811 (0.212)
Spain	−0.2076 (0.000)	−0.2125 (0.000)	−0.1921 (0.000)	−0.1881 (0.000)	−0.2871 (0.000)	−0.4336 (0.181)
Sweden	−0.1405 (0.013)	−0.1386 (0.013)	−0.1362 (0.017)	−0.1247 (0.007)	−0.2476 (0.000)	−0.5170 (0.008)
Switzerland	−0.1218 (0.013)	−0.1213 (0.0149)	−0.1180 (0.014)	−0.1112 (0.008)	−0.2026 (0.000)	−0.5954 (0.002)
UK	−0.1108 (0.074)	−0.1069 (0.063)	−0.1034 (0.092)	−0.0970 (0.068)	−0.2101 (0.000)	−0.4852 (0.007)
UK (in USD)	−0.2336 (0.008)	−0.2163 (0.006)	−0.2163 (0.009)	−0.2116 (0.004)	−0.3872 (0.000)	−0.6823 (0.009)
US	−0.0469 (0.048)	−0.0332 (0.215)	−0.0130 (0.548)	−0.0411 (0.046)	−0.0514 (0.000)	−0.1849 (0.151)
Average R^2	0.1121	0.1514	0.1412	0.2014	0.4152	0.0231

Source: Belke et al. (2017)

Notes: The reported values represent the estimated coefficient of the Brexit variable. The Newey-West estimator is used for the calculation of the covariance matrix

[a]Note that Belke et al. (2017) achieve very similar results for 6×9 und 9×12 Futures.

The effect on long-term interest rate and sovereign credit risk can be assumed to show a larger grade of heterogeneity across countries. In this regard, some countries might profit from increased uncertainty, because their bonds are perceived to be a safe haven in times of market turmoil.

Belke et al. (2017) argue that the countries rated AAA are most likely to profit from reduced bond yields. The panel results for the ten-year interest yield are described in detail in their paper. Due to expected different effects, the sample is split into two groups: the first group includes countries that are considered to be almost 'risk-free' indicated by a rating of AAA and the second group contains countries that have a credit rating of below AA.[20]

Among other results, they find that a one-percentage point increase in the probability of Brexit decreases AAA bonds by about 0.3 basis points, but increases interest rates of riskier countries by about 0.7 basis points. Besides the effects of Brexit probability, they obtain the surprising results that an increase in expected future interest rates increases AAA long-term yields, but has no significant impact on yields of riskier country.

The panel estimation results for CDS are also described in detail in Belke et al. (2017). In general, the results confirm differences between the two groups. When *Brexit_Prob* is used as an indicator, we find no impact on AAA countries. On the contrary, an increase in Brexit likelihood has a significant effect on riskier countries.

According to the SUR estimation results, a strong decrease in long-term interest rates for the UK is observed, amounting to approximately 0.6 basis points. With respect to the other countries, they find the same pattern as shown by their panel estimation results with large increases for 'riskier' countries and decreases for 'risk-free' countries. For the remaining countries which can neither be considered 'risk-free' nor high-risk, they came up with mainly insignificant results, what supports our argument of a safe haven effect.

The results for the sovereign credit risk expose significant positive effects for the GIIPS countries, the UK, Germany and Belgium. Putting these results into perspective, the increases in yields seem to be driven by increases in sovereign credit risk. For the UK, Belke et al. (2017) find the largest increase in CDS spreads indicating that markets assume that Brexit might have an effect on the creditworthiness of the UK (Table 16.5).

Table 16.5 Effects on interest rates and sovereign credit risk; SUR estimation

	Specification						
	10-year interest yield				CDS		
	(1)	(2)	(3)	(4)	(1)	(2)	(3)
	$Brexit\_Prob_t$	$Brexit\_Prob_t$ $Future3x6_t^i$	$Brexit\_Prob_t$ (weighted estimation)	$Brexit\_Poll_t$	$Brexit\_Prob_t$	$Brexit\_Prob_t$ $Comm_t$	$Brexit\_Poll_t$
Austria	−0.0496 (0.583)	−0.0534 (0.568)	−0.0428 (0.002)	0.6360 (0.141)	0.0355 (0.107)	0.0331 (0.114)	0.1091 (0.240)
Belgium	−0.0566 (0.591)	−0.0558 (0.596)	−0.0465 (0.0082)	−0.0036 (0.991)	0.0673 (0.000)	0.0620 (0.000)	0.2258 (0.126)
Canada	−0.5540 (0.0050)	−0.5540 (0.0050)	−0.4596 (0.0000)	−1.2151 (0.009)	0.0001 (0.452)	0.0002 (0.379)	−0.0006 (0.546)
Denmark	−0.3125 (0.0010)	−0.2505 (0.030)	−0.2595 (0.0000)	−0.4096 (0.601)	−0.0114 (0.177)	−0.0143 (0.121)	0.0084 (0.761)
Finland	−0.1609 (0.0731)	−0.1385 (0.120)	−0.0288 (0.0057)	0.3705 (0.368)	−0.0126 (0.093)	−0.0132 (0.097)	0.0938 (0.216)
France	−0.0553 (0.5614)	−0.0588 (0.544)	0.0138 (0.4286)	0.5724 (0.230)	0.0301 (0.541)	0.0245 (0.607)	0.0244 (0.814)
Germany	−0.3151 (0.0002)	−0.3125 (0.0003)	−0.2636 (0.0000)	−0.2350 (0.683)	0.0495 (0.014)	0.0499 (0.012)	0.1547 (0.339)
Greece	2.0558 (0.0427)	2.1477 (0.0480)	1.4181 (0.0000)	2.0897 (0.725)	0.1662 (0.058)	0.1635 (0.059)	0.6272 (0.322)
Netherlands	−0.1500 (0.0758)	−0.1386 (0.132)	−0.1137 (0.0000)	0.2526 (0.573)	0.0142 (0.516)	0.0100 (0.606)	0.1727 (0.474)
Norway	−0.3544 (0.0008)	−0.1647 (0.0247)	−0.3332 (0.0000)	−0.7217 (0.408)	−0.0144 (0.382)	−0.0159 (0.330)	−0.0408 (0.161)
Ireland	0.0955 (0.5931)	0.0346 (0.875)	0.3306 (0.0000)	1.0348 (0.058)	0.0488 (0.014)	0.0408 (0.092)	−0.2553 (0.561)
Italy	0.3450 (0.0851)	0.3324 (0.118)	0.6338 (0.0000)	1.0200 (0.076)	0.1982 (0.009)	0.1832 (0.006)	0.9263 (0.235)
Japan	−0.1334 (0.0722)	−0.2013 (0.0211)	−0.0567 (0.0000)	−0.3063 (0.020)	0.1730 (0.221)	0.1670 (0.235)	0.2501 (0.645)
Portugal	0.8974 (0.0084)	0.8931 (0.011)	1.4330 (0.0000)	2.4518 (0.055)	0.1561 (0.039)	0.1444 (0.046)	0.2880 (0.674)
Spain	0.3989 (0.0261)	0.4053 (0.033)	0.6732 (0.0000)	1.3719 (0.060)	0.1578 (0.000)	0.1489 (0.000)	0.1983 (0.630)
Sweden	−0.3199 (0.0070)	−0.3265 (0.004)	−0.3153 (0.0000)	−0.5805 (0.275)	−0.0028 (0.742)	−0.0049 (0.502)	0.0319 (0.614)
Switzerland	−0.2456 (0.0270)	−0.2458 (0.028)	−0.3398 (0.0000)	−0.8675 (0.200)	−0.0008 (0.339)	−0.0005 (0.475)	−0.0067 (0.146)
UK	−0.6039 (0.0000)	−0.5047 (0.0000)	−0.7194 (0.0000)	−1.5587 (0.067)	0.2109 (0.031)	0.2135 (0.027)	0.9386 (0.060)
United States	−0.4241 (0.001)	−0.2093 (0.0149)	−0.4281 (0.0015)	−1.0500 (0.026)	0.1303 (0.326)	0.1456 (0.300)	0.7226 (0.287)
Average R^2	0.0645	0.2224	0.3521	0.0098	0.014	0.025	0.0253

Source: Belke et al. (2017)

Note: The reported values present the coefficient of the Brexit variable. The Newey-West estimator is used for the calculation of the covariance matrix

An increase in the likelihood of Brexit should cause a depreciation of the British pound because Brexit can be translated into uncertainty and the possibility of an economic deterioration in the UK in the future. This theory is supported by large losses of the pound vis-à-vis other currencies on the day after the referendum.

Nevertheless, the exchange rate of the Pound is also related to interest rate differentials and expectations about (national) monetary policies and not only to expectations about the development of real economic variables and the level of uncertainty.[21] In order to take these aspects into consideration, (Belke et al. 2017) compute the difference between the three-month future of country i and the value for the UK. They follow the same methodology to calculate the (long-term) interest rate differential (Table 16.6).

Conferring to their panel estimation results, a one-percentage point increase of the Brexit probability decreases the value of the pound by about 0.12%. When they concentrate their analysis on poll survey data, the effect is around 0.23%. For their control variables, they empirically corroborate exactly the effect of the interest rate differentials expected from theory.

Table 16.6 Effects on the external value of the British pound; panel estimations

	Random effects					
	(i)	(ii)	(iii)	(iv)	(v)	(ii)
$Brexit\_Prob_t$	−0.1217 (0.000)	−0.1183 (0.000)	−0.1118 (0.000)			
$Brexit\_Poll_t$				−0.2306 (0.000)	−0.2100 (0.000)	−0.2063 (0.000)
$Diff\_$		−0.0557 (0.000)			−0.0551 (0.000)	
$Diff\_$			−0.0331 (0.000)			−0.0342 (0.000)
Pseudo R^2	0.1731	0.1788	0.1862	0.0148	0.0314	0.0517
Hausman-test p-value		0.4998	0.5062		0.7213	0.7009

Source: Belke et al. (2017)

Note: Constants are included. p-values are presented in brackets. The Newey-West estimator is used for the calculation of the covariance matrix. Individual and time effects are included

Concerning the effect on the value of the British pound, they find comparable results across all currencies. When they consider the timing of the probability increase by weighting the observations, we again find larger and highly significant results. For the euro, they find an appreciation of up to 0.14% against the British pound. For the USD, we find an even stronger impact of up to 0.1772%.

In order to verify the robustness of our results, Belke et al. (2017) perform some additional estimations and find nearly identical results.

16.5   Conclusions

In this article, we surveyed empirical studies gauging the impact of Brexit uncertainty on the UK and also on international financial markets. Firstly, we summarised evidence based on estimations of the time-varying interactions between UK policy uncertainty, which can be attributed to a large degree to uncertainty around the Brexit vote, and UK financial market volatilities. Thereby, we identified the considerable role of policy uncertainty for financial market volatilities. The Brexit referendum caused policy uncertainty and resulted in large spillovers to financial markets, with magnitudes that were never observed before. Furthermore, the policy uncertainty spillovers continued to be strong since then, suggesting that political uncertainty regarding the development of the relationship between the UK and the EU causes turbulences on financial markets even three months after the referendum. This can further weaken investment and hiring in the UK (and Europe). Hence, we feel legitimised to confirm the view of the IMF (2016a, b) and others that Brexit-caused policy uncertainty will continue to evoke instability in key financial markets and has the potential to do damage to the British and also other European countries' real economy as well, even in the medium run.

In this vein, Belke and Gros (2017) assess the economic implications of the UK leaving the European Union. The basic data on trade in goods and services and investment between the two parties suggest that cost of 'Brexit' could be substantial. Trade between the UK and the EU27 is large and of a similar order of magnitude as transatlantic trade (between the EU and the US). The precise nature of the (hopefully free) trade agreement UK-EU27 is still being negotiated. But all available studies concur that a significant disruption of trade links will impose economic costs on both sides. However, the EU27 would bear only a disproportionally small share of the total cost—not just because it is about five times larger than the UK in economic terms but also for fundamental reasons such as greater market power of its enterprises. Other studies on different free trade arrangements investigated by Belke and Gros (2017) confirm the general proposition that the smaller party has more to gain from eliminating trade barriers (and to lose from imposing them). This implies that the EU will have the stronger negotiating position.

Secondly, we surveyed results based on empirical models employing two other measures of the perceived probability of a Brexit vote, namely, daily data between 1 April and 23 June 2016 of probabilities released by Betfair as well as (aggregated) results of polls published by Bloomberg. Based on these datasets, we examined the Brexit effect on the levels of stock returns, sovereign CDS, ten-year interest rates in 19 different countries primarily from Europe as well as the British pound and the euro. Here, there is evidence that an increase in the probability of Brexit has particularly strong effects on European stock markets.

Concerning the effect on long-term interest rates and CDS, the surveyed studies reveal a large heterogeneity across countries, which can be attributed to differences in sovereign credit risk. The main reason for this pattern might be linked to an expected decrease in economic activity that might further jeopardise the sustainability of government debt. As Brexit might have unpredictable effects on the stability of the entire EU, the effects may simply be generated by an increase in the still low probability of a breakup of the euro area or the EU. Concerning the effect on the exchange rate, empirical studies show that an increase in the probability of Brexit leads to a depreciation of the British pound. Based on the results obtained from this article, the main losers outside of the UK seem to be the GIIPS economies, which are already struggling with the consequences of the sovereign debt crisis. How, then, should we explain the current lack of an even bigger (real economic) impact? It may just be because Brexit has not happened yet.

Acknowledgements I am grateful for valuable research assistance to Sarah Piwonski.

Notes

1. For a survey of related arguments, see, for instance, London School of Economics (2016). Fears about Brexit are not accidental; they have been indicated by systematic differences in monetary policies on both sides of the Channel. See D'Addona and Musumeci (2011).
2. In the following, we do not discuss the various arguments surrounding immigration and fiscal costs. For a broad survey on the potential economic impacts of Brexit, see IMF (2016a, b).
3. See https://www.ceicdata.com/en/blog/ceic-macro-dashboard-july-2016
4. The UK is the world leader in fixed-income and derivative transactions and far ahead of EU peers in private equity, hedge funds and cross-border bank lending (Bank of England 2015). The UK's insurance industry is the largest in Europe and the third largest in the world.
5. Several asset managing companies (e.g. M&G, Columbia Threadneedle) and several banks have expressed their intentions to move staff out of the UK capital and/or set up fund ranges in neighbouring EU countries for fear of being locked out of European fundraising. This 'escape' from the UK is not limited to the financial sector; Vodafone has already announced that it might move its headquarters if the UK leaves the single market.
6. An alternative might be the Norwegian model (EEA) or Swiss model. See Belke et al. (2017).
7. This view is backed by empirical results underscoring the finding that the reduction in trade barriers due to EU membership has increased UK incomes (Crafts 2016; Campos et al. 2014).
8. For an overview, see Van der Loo and Blockmans (2016).
9. One vision in this respect is the so-called Continental Partnership Proposal delivered by Bruegel (2016), including much free trade and less free movement of labour between the EU and Great Britain. The idea is that free trade substitutes for labour mobility. See also Belke et al. (2017).
10. See http://www.policyuncertainty.com/index.html
11. For more details on the construction of daily volatilities, refer to Alizadeh et al. (2002).
12. Empirical realisations of the VIX index, intraday high and low values of FTSE250 and the GBP/USD exchange rates are obtained from Datastream.
13. Alternatively, Hafner and Herwartz (2006b) proposed a concept of impulse response functions tracing the effects of independent shocks on

volatility and then considered the effect of historical shocks, such as 'Black Wednesday' and an announcement by EC finance ministers on 2 August 1993, on the foreign exchange market. However, we believe that the identification of a 'Brexit shock' is not trivial and should not be restricted to the day of the announcement of the referendum results, but should include the days preceding the referendum.

14. Different Cholesky orderings do not change the signs or the significance of the impulse responses.

15. As a robustness check, Belke et al. (2017) performed estimations with different lag length, rolling windows and forecast horizons—the basic results remain.

16. Further information can be found at: http://www.bloomberg.com/graphics/2016-brexit-watch/

17. The values are based on the search topic: 'United Kingdom European Union membership referendum, 2016' which combines several different research requests corresponding with the Brexit topic. The following additional options are used: Search Category: 'News', Search: 'News-Search'.

18. In August 2016, the BoE decreased the bank rate to 0.25% justifying their decision by potential effects of the Brexit vote on future inflation and growth.

19. The GIIPS states comprise Greece, Ireland, Italy, Portugal and Spain.

20. Ratings are taken from Fitch Ratings. The AAA group contains: Canada, Denmark, Germany, the Netherlands, Norway, Sweden, Switzerland and the USA. The second group contains only the so-called GIIPS states.

21. In case of the euro, Belke et al. (2017) take German 10y yields as a proxy of the 'European' interest rate. However, we do not find different results when Dutch, French or Finnish Yields are used.

References

Alizadeh, S., M.W. Brandt, and F.X. Diebold. 2002. Range-Based Estimation of Stochastic Volatility Models. *Journal of Finance* 57: 1047–1092.

Bank of England. 2015. *EU Membership and the Bank of England*. London: Bank of England, October.

Baker, S., N. Bloom, and S. Davis. 2015. *Measuring Economic Policy Uncertainty.* NBER Working Paper No. 21633, National Bureau of Economic Research, Cambridge, MA, October.

Begg, I. 2016. *European Economic Governance in the Aftermath of Brexit: Integrating or Disintegrating?* Presentation at the Jean Monnet Conference on Economic Prospects for the European Union – Challenges for Economic Policy Until the End of the Decade, Duesseldorf, September 23–24.

Belke, A., and D. Gros. 2002. Designing EU–US Atlantic Monetary Relations: Exchange Rate Variability and Labour Markets on Both Sides of the Atlantic. *The World Economy* 25 (6): 789–813.

———. 2017. The Economic Impact of Brexit: Evidence from Modelling Free Trade Agreements. *Atlantic Economic Journal* 45 (4): 317–331.

Belke, A., I. Dubova, and T. Osowski. 2017. Policy Uncertainty and International Financial Markets: The Case of Brexit. *Applied Economics.*

Blockmans, S., and M. Emerson. 2016. *Brexit's Consequences for the UK – and the EU.* Brussels: CEPS Commentary, Centre for European Policy Studies, June 6.

Bruegel. 2016. *Europe After Brexit: A Proposal for a Continental Partnership.* Brussels: Bruegel, August.

Bruno, R., N. Campos, S. Estrin, and M. Tian. 2016a. *Gravitating Towards Europe: An Econometric Analysis of the FDI Effects of EU Membership.* CEP Technical Paper, Brexit Analysis, No. 3, London.

———. 2016b. *Foreign Direct Investment and the Relationship Between the United Kingdom and the European Union.* CEP Discussion Paper No. 1453, Centre for Economic Performance, London, October.

Campos, N.F., F. Coricelli, and L. Moretti. 2014. *Economic Growth and Political Integration: Estimating the University of Duisburg-Essen Benefits from Membership in the European Union Using the Synthetic Counterfactuals Method.* CEPR Discussion Paper No. 9968, Center for Economic Policy Research, London.

Crafts, N. 2016. *The Growth Effects of EU Membership for the UK: A Review.* Mimeo, University of Warwick, Warwick.

D'Addona, S., and I. Musumeci. 2011. *The British Opt-Out from the European Monetary. Union: Empirical Evidence from Monetary Policy Rules.* CREI

Working Paper No. 6/2011, CREI Centro di Ricerca Interdipartimentale di Economia delle Istituzioni, Universita Romea Tre, Rome.

Dhingra, S., G. Ottaviano, and T. Sampson 2015. *Should We Stay or Should We Go? The Economic Consequences of Leaving the EU*. Paper No. EA022, Centre for Economic Performance, London.

Diebold, F.X., and K. Yilmaz. 2009. Measuring Financial Asset Return and Volatility Spillovers, with Application to Global Equity Markets. *Economic Journal* 119: 158–171.

———. 2012. Better to Give Than to Receive: Predictive Directional Measurement of Volatility Spillovers. *International Journal of Forecasting* 28 (1): 57–66.

European Commission. 2016. *The Economic Outlook after the UK Referendum: A First Assessment for the Euro Area and the EU*. Institutional Paper No. 032, European Economy, Brussels.

Fournier, J.-M., A. Domps, Y. Gorin, X. Guillet, and D. Morchoisne. 2015. *Implicit Regulatory Barriers in the EU Single Market*. OECD Economics Department Working Paper No. 1181, Organisation for Economic Co-operation and Development.

Gerlach, S. 2016. What Brexit Surveys Really Tell Us. *VoxEU*, May 6.

Gordon, M.J., and E. Shapiro. 1956. Capital Equipment Analysis: The Required Rate of Profit. *Management Science* 3 (1): 102–110.

Gros, D. 2011. Euro Crisis Reaches the Core. *VoxEU*, August 11.

———. 2016. *The Economics of Brexit: It's Not About the Internal Market*. CEPS Commentary, Centre for European Policy Studies, Brussels, September 22.

Hafner, C.M., and H. Herwartz. 2006b. Volatility Impulse Responses for Multivariate GARCH Models: An Exchange Rate Illustration. *Journal of International Money and Finance* 25/5: 719–740.

———. 2008. Testing for Causality in Variance Using Multivariate GARCH Models. *Annales d'Économie et de Statistique* 89: 215–241.

International Monetary Fund. 2016a. *Uncertainty in the Aftermath of the U.K. Referendum*. World Economic Outlook Update, International Monetary Fund, Washington, DC, July 19.

———. 2016b. *United Kingdom – Selected Issues*. IMF Country Report No. 16/169, International Monetary Fund, Washington, DC, June.

Mansfield, I. 2014. *A Blueprint for Britain: Openness Not Isolation*. London: Institute of Economic Affairs.

Minford, P. 2016. *The Brexit Consensus Bug*. London: Economists for Brexit. https://economistsforbrexit.squarespace.com/brexit-consensus-bug.

London School of Economics. 2016. *LSE Commission on the Future of Britain in Europe – Overview and Summary of Reports*. London: LSE European Institute.

OpenEurope. 2015. *What If...? The Consequences, Challenges and Opportunities Facing Britain Outside the EU*. London: OpenEurope. http://openeurope.org.uk/intelligence/britain-and-the-eu/what-if-there-were-a-brexit/

Van der Loo, G., and S. Blockmans. 2016. The *Impact of Brexit on the EU's International Agreements*. CEPS Commentary, Centre for European Policy Studies, Brussels, July 15.

17

EU Financial Markets After Brexit

Karel Lannoo

Brexit means Brexit, or out means out—and that includes the UK's exit from the single financial market. With financial services accounting for about 8% of the country's GDP, it is understandable why the UK attaches immense importance to retaining access to the EU's single market. But putting a mutually acceptable regime in place will take years and will allow much less access than UK-licenced firms enjoy today. The 'equivalence' assessment is the basic tool used under current EU financial services legislation to recognise that a third-country legal, regulatory and/or supervisory regime is equivalent to the corresponding EU framework, but it applies only to some measures and to some of the freedoms created by the relevant EU regulations, not across the board.[1] In addition, the equivalence decisions vary, and can be revoked by the European Commission at any time. This framework offers a fairly bleak basis on which the City might continue to thrive as a global financial centre in Europe.

K. Lannoo (✉)
CEPS (Centre for European Policy Studies), Brussels, Belgium

© The Author(s) 2017
N. da Costa Cabral et al. (eds.), *After Brexit*,
https://doi.org/10.1007/978-3-319-66670-9_17

The UK, and the City in particular, is an archetypal example of the functioning of the single market, as envisaged at the end of the 1980s. By harmonising basic rules and providing for mutual recognition, firms could sell goods and provide services freely throughout the EU with a single licence. As a consequence, each EU country or region could specialise in those services and products it was good at. For the UK, this was services, and for the City, it was financial services in particular (Gros 2016). Many financial services providers concentrated their wholesale financial market activities in the City, from which they covered the entire EU. But by stepping out of the EU, the single passport will cease to exist for UK-licenced firms at the moment the withdrawal is complete. The only way in which the UK could continue to have a single licence would be through its accession to the European Economic Area (EEA), but this is not compatible with the referendum outcome to leave the EU.

The single market freedoms for financial services providers are contained in a multiplicity of different EU directives and regulations. They cover basic rules for banking, investment services and insurance, but also investment products and financial infrastructures. Since the start of the single market in 1992, these freedoms have been further elaborated in updates and extensions to the rules.

The financial crisis led to a substantial broadening of the regulatory maze and an extensive deepening, with the consensus reached on a 'single rulebook' and a far-reaching use of secondary legislation. Important elements of the financial system were not regulated at EU level (nor in most cases even at the national level) before the crisis, such as ratings agencies, derivative markets or hedge funds. And many key pieces of legislation, such as those covering banking and investment services, became far more complex. An example of this complexity is MiFID II, which now also regulates the price transparency in bond and commodity markets, as compared to only equity markets before, and introduces tight rules for algorithmic trading and data vendors. In addition, the EU created the Banking Union, which led to an important centralisation of the supervision and resolution functions, but in which the UK does not participate.

17.1   The UK as Bridgehead of a Mighty Financial Centre, the City

London has developed over the last quarter century as the wholesale financial centre for the EU, in the same way that Wall Street functions for the USA, or Hong Kong for China (see Lannoo, 2016). A wholesale financial centre provides for the refinancing of local financial centres, of which there are many in Europe, and financial services for corporations, governments and institutional investors. Back-office functions for these activities are not necessarily all concentrated in London, and have in recent years moved to other cities in the UK as well.

London hosts some 358 banks, many insurance companies and institutional investors, hedge funds and specialised finance providers, and is now also spearheading the growth of Fintech companies. It is home to the largest stock exchange in the EU, the most developed derivative market and related clearing and settlement infrastructures. It also hosts important services for the financial sector. Many law firms have their largest offices for the EU in London. All three rating agencies, each one of US parentage, have their head offices for the EU in London. Data vendors have located their most important operations in London, and so have many large auditing and consulting firms. Hence, the contribution to the UK's GDP will be even larger when these related services are included in the calculations.

The growth of the UK's financial sector owes much to the single market, as noted by IMF (2016). UK trade in financial services as a percentage of GDP has risen much faster than the OECD average, as has its trade in services with EU members. About one-third of the UK's financial and insurance services exports are to the EU, and most of UK banks' investments are in the EU (IMF 2016). The introduction of the single passport for financial services providers was started with the 2nd banking Directive in 1992 and the investment services Directive in 1994. The facilities provided by these directives have been further developed and extended to other financial services in recent years, especially following the G-20's commitment to ensure that all financial services, institutions and markets are responsibly regulated in the wake of the financial crisis.

17.2 The Key Components of the EU's Passport for Financial Services Providers

The single market freedoms created for the various forms of financial services have been embedded in a variety of directives. In most cases, the free provision of services (FPS) or 'passporting', has become extensive. For basic financial services such as banking, investment services or insurance, this has been the result of an extensive and long process of de- and re-regulation at European level. In other cases, for non-core services or products, such as clearing, settlement, financial data and hedge funds, it started much later and/or was largely driven by the experiences and lessons of the financial crisis.

These freedoms also apply in the EEA countries, which implement all these rules, as well as EU regulations, in national law. The EEA has recently concluded an agreement with the EU by which they will also become observers in the European Supervisory Authorities (ESAs) and implement secondary legislation.

The FPS framework is accompanied by additional prudential measures. The financial crisis led to an agreement on common rules for resolving banks in the bank recovery and resolution Directive (BRRD). The UK authorities played an important role in the debate for a resolution framework for banks, drawing on their experience with Northern Rock in September 2007 and other banks following the collapse of Lehman, and adopted their own rules in the 2009 Banking Act. This act requires bank to have recovery plans readily available and set a framework for the resolution of banks, including inter alia the concept of a 'bridge bank'. These concepts were later incorporated in the BRRD. Another part of the resolution framework, the rules for deposit insurance, was also harmonised as a result of the financial crisis, in the deposit guarantee schemes Directive (2014).

Remuneration rules, a particularly sensitive issue for the City, have become standard in most post-crisis updates of EU directives and other new measures (see Table 17.1). They are now part of many of the FPS rules, covering banking, investment and alternative funds and rating agencies, but there are substantial differences across the various measures. The tightest and most widely debated are contained in the capital requirements Directive (CRD IV), which limits a banker's bonus to a

Table 17.1 The various EU financial services and their single passport regime

Financial service	Rule	EU Passport	Start date	Comments	Remuneration rules
Payments and transfers	CRDIV/PSDII/ e-money	Extensive	1992/2007/ 2009	PSD and e-money Directive set rules for wiring services	
Commercial banking	CRDIV	Extensive	1992		Limits on bonuses
Trading	CRDIV/ MiFID II	Extensive	1992/1994	Remote access for brokers to trading platforms	Limits on bonuses
Investment banking	CRDIV/ MiFID II	Extensive	1992/1994	Universal banking was the rule in the EU since 1992	Limits on bonuses
Insurance	Solvency II	Limited	1997	Unlike banking, solvency II does not allow a single capital base	
Pension funds	IORP II	Limited	2002	Labour market and tax rules have limited take-off	
Investment funds	UCITS IV-V	Extensive	1985	First single financial product passport	Remuneration rules
Alternative funds	AIFMD	Extensive	2012	Single licence for hedge funds managers	Remuneration policy to be authorised
Securities and derivative markets	MiFID II	Extensive	1994	Remote access to and collocation of trading servers in financial centres	Remuneration policy to be authorised
Settlement	CSDR	Extensive	2014	Code of conduct before the crisis	
Clearing	EMIR	Extensive	2015	Not regulated before the crisis	
Rating agencies	CRA	Extensive	2012	Not regulated before the crisis	Compensation to be disclosed and not driven by performance
Financial data providers	MiFID II	Extensive	2018	License from 2018 onwards	

Source: Author's elaboration

maximum 1:1 ratio of his/her annual salary. The rules were challenged by the UK government before the Court of Justice of the EU (CJEU), on the ground that these rules would not make the system safer, but the case was withdrawn. The UK's resistance to implementing EU rules was also later reflected in its refusal to apply the European Banking Authority's implementing rules as they did not take proportionality into account.

Among the EU financial services measures of the greatest concern to the City are the following:

- Markets in Financial Instruments Directive (MiFID) is an essential measure for the City, as it provides for a single passport for trading platforms and brokers in the EU. The Directive has just gone through a long process of upgrades and adaptations, which will only come into force in early 2018, because of the depth of the review. It now sets rules for trading of non-equity financial instruments and commodity derivatives, regulates algorithmic trading and data vendors and implements the UK rules of the Retail Distribution Review, which require the unbundling of investment advice from investment services, at the EU level. As an illustration of the importance of this directive, the UK currently hosts 2250 firms using the MiFID passport outbound, as compared to 988 from other EU and EEA countries using the passport in the UK.[2]
- The Alternative Fund Managers Directive (AIFMD) is another core measure for the City as it sets EU-wide rules and a single passport for managers of hedge funds and other alternative funds. The rules were heavily criticised by UK-based firms and organisations when proposed, but the lobbying campaign backfired and remuneration rules were added to the Directive in October 2010, the first EU financial services measure to contain such provisions. EU lawmakers argued that a fund's remuneration rules should promote sound and effective risk management and not encourage risk taking, and need to be authorised by supervisors. The directive requires the full disclosure of remuneration in the annual report, broken down by staff members. There are 212 firms in the UK holding the AIFMD passport, as compared to 45 from other EU and EEA countries.[3]
- Credit rating agencies (CRAs) were not regulated before the crisis, but since 2010, they have been subject to a licence and supervised by

ESMA. The regulation requires CRAs to be independent and to identify and manage conflicts of interest, also in their compensation policies. Supervisors can monitor the methodologies and business model
of rating agents. The three largest ratings agents, which control 94% of
the EU market, have located their head offices for Europe in London
(see Lannoo 2015), but are supervised out of Paris.

- The European Markets Infrastructures Regulation (EMIR) sets rules
  for the obligatory clearing of Over-the-counter (OTC) derivatives and
  for the functioning and governance of central counterparties (CCPs),
  which clear such instruments. The UK is home to a very large part of
  derivatives turnover, OTC and on exchange, in the EU (see, e.g. Miethe
  and Pothier 2016). EMIR establishes that CCPs can offer clearing services throughout the EU. The passporting of CCPs in all the EU member states was the subject of a CJEU case between the UK and the
  ECB, in which the latter argued that euro-denominated clearing could
  only happen within the eurozone. The Court concluded against the
  ECB, finding that clearing services were a single market freedom.

Financial institutions can have several passports under one roof,
depending on the services they provide and the number of EU countries
in which they are active. This fact explains the huge number of passports
that UK-based firms possess, according to the Financial Conduct
Authority, as revealed by the Financial Times (2016).

17.3 Third-Country Access to the Single Market

Leaving the EU means that third-country rules will apply to firms based
in the UK for access to the single market, unless another agreement is
found. The basis is the equivalence assessment, which determines that a
third country's regulatory and supervisory framework should achieve the
same results as the corresponding provisions in EU law, provided that it
is incorporated in relevant rules. Brexit led many groups to argue that this
should not be a problem, as the UK applied the same rules as the EU
until secession. The situation is not that straightforward, however.

The debate on third-country access provisions is as old as the single market. Foreign banks in the City led the charge in the early 1990s, when reciprocity provisions were contained in the 2nd banking Directive. It was argued that market access in the EU should be 'reciprocal' to that given in other jurisdictions, which raised fears that the EU would become a 'fortress'. The provision was never applied, however. Later on, in the measures adopted under the Financial Services Action Plan (FSAP), the term 'reciprocity' was replaced with 'not more favourable treatment', and the EU could start negotiations with third countries seeking to obtain the same treatment as given in EU member states. The financial crisis changed this more lenient regime, as the conviction emerged that much stricter supervision was required, and the post-crisis term became 'equivalence'.

According to the European Commission, equivalence means that 'in certain cases the EU may recognise that a foreign legal, regulatory and/or supervisory regime is equivalent to the corresponding EU framework'.[4] It allows the EU authorities to rely on the compliance of foreign entities with the equivalent foreign framework, stating that 'equivalence decisions may apply to the entire (regulatory) framework of a third country or to some of its authorities only'.[5] Equivalence decisions are taken unilaterally by the Commission, but can be revoked at any time. They are prepared at the advice of the European Supervisory Authorities (ESAs). The recent equivalence decision on CCPs under EMIR, for example, states that a review of the decision can be undertaken at any time and that 'such re-assessment could lead to the repeal of this Decision'.[6]

A comparison of the third-country regime provisions of the different EU FPS measures presents a highly complex puzzle. In certain cases, the regime is quite developed, as in the AIFMD (see de Manuel, 2012), whereas in other cases, it is brief and restricted to certain provisions or is very specific. And in still other cases, it is not provided for at all. Table 17.2 provides an overview of the key items of the third-country regime for banking, investment services, investment funds, trading venues, clearing and rating agents.

What emerges from the enumeration in the table of the main features of third-country regimes is that there is no full access to the single market for third countries. Member states, however, can individually authorise bank branches, investment firms and funds to provide services, but only within their own territory. Access to the EU's single market is governed by

Table 17.2 Main features of the third-country regimes under the most important free provision of financial services measures

Measure	Third-country regime
CRD IV (Basel III)	• Branches of third countries cannot enjoy more favourable treatment than those from EU countries (Art. 27) • EU may conclude agreements with third countries for "analogous" treatment of branches throughout the EU • No free provision of services for third-country branches (Recital 23) • Equivalence assessment of third countries' supervisory and regulatory arrangement (Art. 47), consolidated supervision (Art. 127) and specific measures
MiFID II (brokers and trading venues)	• Commission to adopt equivalence assessment, but this is for investment services limited to eligible counterparties and professional clients • ESMA to register third-country firms (from equivalent jurisdiction) • ESMA to establish cooperation arrangements • Member states can licence third-country service provider, but only within their territory, no Single Market access • Equivalence assessment of third-country markets (Art. 25.4)
UCITS (investment funds)	• No specific third-country regime • Equivalence assessment for third countries' supervisory system of management companies of UCITS (Art. 7.1) (see Art. 14 MiFID) • Delegation of tasks to third country undertaking depends on existence of equivalence agreement and appropriate exchange of information (Art. 13)
AIFMD (managers of non-UCITS funds)	• Until 2018: Non-EEA manager has to be authorised as a manager in the EEA by the EEA regulator in its "member state of reference" • From 2016: EU passport co-exists with national passport • ESMA to propose standards of conditions of equivalence of third countries (Art. 37) and the extension of the passport, annual peer review by ESMA of supervision of third country AIFMs (Art. 38)
EMIR (CCPs)	• Equivalence of third-country supervisory regime, subject to Commission Implementing Act • Third-country CCP can provide clearing services after equivalence assessment by ESMA (Art. 25) • Cooperation arrangements between supervisors
CRA (rating agents)	• Commission to adopt equivalence decision for CRA regime in a third country, ESMA to check whether requirements are 'as stringent as' in the EU • Credit ratings issued in a third country can only be used if they are not of systemic importance to the EU's financial stability (CRA I, Art. 5.1) • A local endorsement of ratings of EU importance produced outside EU is required • Cooperation arrangements between supervisors to be coordinated by ESMA

Source: Author's elaboration

equivalence assessments of the third country's regulatory regime, on which the European Commission carries out an equivalence assessment. For banks, the equivalence assessment is focused on the third country's prudential regime. For third-country investment firms, the access is limited to eligible counterparties and professional clients, and to trading venues.

For UK-based financial institutions, this means that future access to the EU's single market will be very limited compared to what is available today. The UK could start negotiating a trade agreement with the EU as soon as Art. 50 is triggered, but this will certainly not provide for free provision of financial services. In line with international trade conventions, it could provide for most favoured nation (MFN) treatment. In the area of financial services trade, this would, for firms, require a local establishment, but with a 'prudential carve-out', meaning that that access could be denied on prudential grounds. For trading venues and clearing services, an equivalence assessment will be required. In the meantime, the UK will need a transitional agreement, which will provisionally grandfather some existing single market provisions and obtain equivalence, but possibly in a broader manner than what is foreseen under the various rules today.

Either route entails important drawbacks. A trade agreement takes years to conclude, is difficult to sell to public opinion and may have to be ratified by all EU member states. A transitional equivalence agreement should effectively prepare for the best, but may only cover what is foreseen in the different measures governing the single market in financial services. To highlight how political such a decision may become, the remuneration rules could also be part of a future equivalence assessment of the UK's regulatory regime, and that's where it could already get stuck, in the event that the UK regime deviate from the EU rules. The UK could also choose to adopt a lighter touch and more flexibility in financial regulation, which would increase its attractiveness globally, but would reduce the likelihood that such measures would be recognised as equivalent. It is also unlikely that the UK would follow such path in the aftermath of the financial crisis and the monitoring by the Financial Stability Board of the steps taken in compliance with the G-20 commitments.

The UK's withdrawal will also be a setback for continental European financial institutions. EU-authorised exchanges will no longer have access to co-location services for their servers in the City, and traders from the City will have restricted access to exchanges within the EU. The intermediation effects of a large financial centre in foreign direct investment in the EU will decrease. The refinancing of local banks in the EU by large city-based institutions will become more difficult. And finally, the networking and conglomeration effects of acting as a large financial centre will diminish.

17.4   Conclusion

In the area of financial services, the UK has much to lose and little to gain from leaving the EU. Those that will be most severely hit are large integrated financial institutions using multiple passports under one roof, and specialised investment firms and asset managers with a single passport. They will need to disentangle their operations, split up their capital base and create separately capitalised and licenced operations within the EU. There is an urgent need therefore to give careful thought to the content and shape a new deal with the EU might take.

Inspiration could be taken from the relationship that the EU has formed with other trading partners. As with Switzerland in insurance, the UK could strive to negotiate a bilateral agreement for market access with the EU on financial services, pending a more comprehensive trade deal, similar to the arrangements the EU has with many other jurisdictions. The British government, however, will have to overcome the animosity that prevails in the EU towards a special deal with the UK, certainly in the domain of financial services. It will therefore have to start a long and difficult process of persuading the EU of the importance of a global financial centre for the European economy.

Notes

1. This concept is discussed in greater detail below.
2. See Letter from the Chairman of the UK Financial Conduct Authority (FCA) to the Chair of the House of Common's Treasury Committee, 17 August 2016 (http://www.parliament.uk/business/committees/committees-a-z/commons-select/treasury-committee/)

3. Ibid.
4. See Commission website: http://ec.europa.eu/finance/general-policy/global/equivalence/index_en.htm
5. Ibid.
6. Commission Implementing Decision (EU) 2016/377 of 15 March 2016 on the equivalence of the regulatory framework of the USA for CCPs that are authorised and supervised by the CFTC to the requirements of the EMIR Regulation (EU) No 648/2012, Recital 23.

References

De Manuel, Mirzha. 2012. *Third Country Rules for Alternative Investments: Passport Flexibility Comes at a Price*. ECMI Commentary, ECMI, Brussels. www.ceps.eu

Financial Times. 2016. *Banks Fear Chill Wind of 'Passport' Freeze*. September 21.

Gros, Daniel. 2016. *The Economics of Brexit: It's Not About the Internal Market*. CEPS Commentary, September. www.ceps.eu

IMF. 2016. *Macroeconomic Implications of the United Kingdom Leaving the European Union*. Country Report, Washington, DC.

Lannoo, Karel. 2015. *The Great Financial Plumbing: From Northern Rock to Banking Union*. London: Rowman and Littlefield International. October.

———. 2016. *Brexit and the City*. CEPS Commentary, CEPS, Brussels. www.ceps.eu

Miethe, Jakob, and David Pothier. 2016. Brexit: What's at Stake for the Financial Sector. *Economic Bulletin*, DIW, August.

18

How Brexit May Affect Banks' Business Models and the Financial System in the UK and EU: Opportunity to Revitalise the Existing Banking Structures?

Claudio Scardovi and Rabia Deniz Agaoglu

18.1   Introduction and Background

Britain's vote to leave the EU on 23 June 2016 (famously dubbed as "Brexit" vote) has brought significant amount of uncertainty to the UK and the EU, causing ripple effects across the global economies since. Brexit has become the main discussion topic not only for all government officials and public leaders in the UK and the EU political and economic circles but also has been seen as the ultimate danger—a sort of "Sword of Damocles"—that can destroy London's centuries-old financial sector and its long-reigning status as one of the world's leading financial hubs.

C. Scardovi (✉)
Bocconi University, Milan, Italy

Imperial college, London, UK

AlixPartners, London, UK

R.D. Agaoglu
AlixPartners, London, UK

© The Author(s) 2017
N. da Costa Cabral et al. (eds.), *After Brexit*,
https://doi.org/10.1007/978-3-319-66670-9_18

Despite the considerable negative consequences of uncertainty in economies and financial markets, little progress has been made in the first six months since the vote to clarify the terms and conditions of the UK's exit. This was in large part due to the fact that no one in the UK or in the EU really knew how to design and orchestrate such an exit (no member state has ever left the EU since its inception). The principles are going to be defined as negotiations start with the UK trigger of Article 50 of the EU Lisbon Treaty (which took place end of March 2017 upon the Parliament's and peers approval vote in February). It is becoming increasingly apparent that resolution of the situation and UK's actual Exit might take several years (longer than originally considered and as stated in Article 50) and will likely depend on the extent of "Exit" scenario (i.e. "hard exit" vs. "soft exit") agreed on by the UK and EU officials.

However, one thing is certain—the ongoing uncertainty and prolonged negotiations will have significant implications on all UK-based financial institutions using "passport rights" to serve to their European clients (and vice versa[1]), particularly investment banks, asset and wealth managers, payments services and insurance companies. In fact, if passporting into the EU from the UK-based entities is not allowed in the post-Exit phase, transfer of certain activities from the UK to the EU will be inevitable, leading London to lose some business to other European financial centres, and even to locations outside the continent (e.g. New York City) should the international banks choose to move some operations back to their home territories. Many firms in the UK currently use passporting rights to access the EU Single Market. According to the UK's Financial Conduct Authority, the number of UK-based firms granted with the passporting rights under the EU legislations is approximately 5500, as can be seen in the table below (House of Lords EU Committee 2016) (Fig. 18.1).

In this chapter, we discuss the likely impacts of potential Exit scenarios on the UK- and EU-based financial institutions and on the City of London specifically. We present alternative options available especially for banks to ensure a smooth and orderly transition to a post-Brexit world and to use this period as an opportunity to build innovative and more efficient business models to help strengthen the UK and the EU banking systems in the aftermath of the 2008–2009 financial crisis.

	Total	Inbound	Outbound
Number of passports in total	359, 953	23,532	336,421
Number of firms using passporting	13,484	8,008	5,476

Fig. 18.1 Number of inbound and outbound passports issued by the Financial Conduct Authority and Prudential Regulation Authority (An "outbound" passport refers to a passport issued by a UK authority to a UK firm to do business in EU or EEA members states; and an "inbound" passport refers to a passport issued in an EU or EEA member state to a firm from that state, enabling it to do business in the UK (or other member states))

18.2　UK Financial Sector and London's Role as a Leading Financial Hub

UK's, and especially London's, role as a leading global financial centre is indisputable. With its many years of heritage, and first-class ecosystem based on a well-established infrastructure, large, experienced human capital base and strong regulatory framework, London, along with New York City, consistently leads the rankings as the world's global financial capital.

It is estimated that the UK's financial services sector earns £190–205 billion revenues annually, with over 1.1 million people[2] working in the sector across the country. Of the £200 billion revenues, approximately £40–50 billion is estimated to be from international and wholesale businesses related to the EU, that is, from EU client activities in EU-/euro-linked products, and about £25 billion of which is from banking alone (TheCityUK and Oliver Wyman 2016) (Fig. 18.2).

With its central time zone, English language, wide pool of investors and strong support from a world-renowned professional services sector, London has long been established as the main European hub for almost all international banks looking to service clients across the continent. Only one-third of all overseas banks operating in the UK are headquartered in another EU location outside the UK. For instance, US banks including JP Morgan, BAML, Goldman Sachs and Citigroup mainly use their UK-registered entities to access the EU,[3] with thousands of bankers and traders in their City offices performing EU-related transactions.

This relative importance (weight) of the City as the European hub for the global financial services sector is prevalent in the asset management and market infrastructure sub-sectors as well. More than 40% of all EU

UK Financial Services market by origination of earnings (2015, £bn)

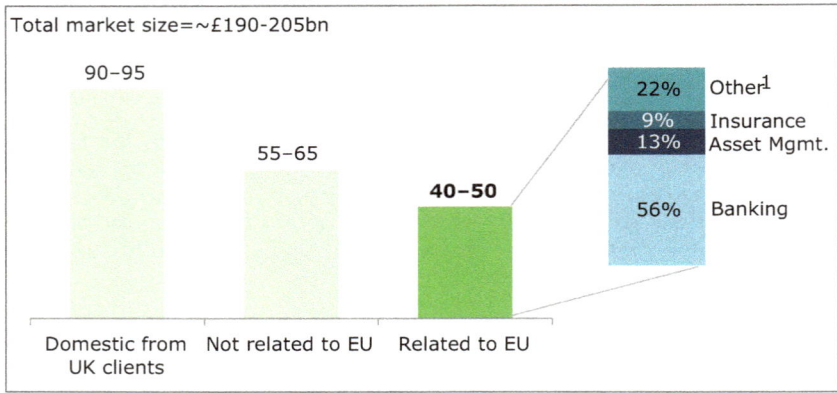

UK-based banking revenues (£bn)

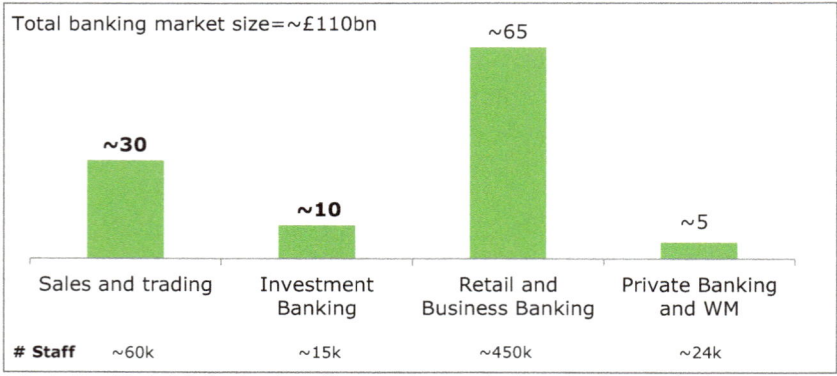

1 Including Market Infrastructure firms such as custodians, trade repositories etc.

Fig. 18.2 UK financial services market by origination of earnings and banking revenues (TheCityUK 2016a, b)

AUM are based in the UK, and 40% of trading in EU27 stock markets are executed on platforms in the UK with few staff based within the EU27. UK also carries out 78% of the EU's FX business and 74% of OTC interest rate derivatives. And 59% of international insurance premiums are written in London (Financial Times 2016).

Although the extent of potential business losses from the UK-based financial services (and particularly banking) sector will depend on the level of access UK will have to the single market at the end of the Exit negotiations, it is estimated that at least 1–10% of the total revenues might be lost due to the UK's exit. Brexit is also likely to impact the level of employment in the sector, with up to 20–25% of UK-based staff at the leading international (especially US) banks potentially at risk to be moved to outside the UK. Some US banks such as JPMorgan and Citigroup have already announced their potential plans to move staff to EU-based entities in the event of UK's exit and loss of access to the Single Market.

Considering all these developments, maintaining London as a leading global financial hub is becoming an even more important task for the UK Government, officials and the financial sector leaders. Given the financial sector's weight on the UK overall GDP (c. 11.8% including the ancillary professional services sector) and its role in driving the economic growth, the sector's requirements such as the continuation of the passporting rights are considered as key agenda items in the government's negotiations with the EU.

Moreover, the sentiment that the loss of business from Brexit could be replaced by other emerging businesses in the City such as the renminbi trading has started to sour in the recent months as it has begun to be seen how Brexit might have spillover effects on such businesses going forward. Although the City of London has recently overtaken Singapore to become the world's second largest offshore renminbi centre behind Hong Kong, the average daily volume of renminbi trading in the City (more than US$40 billion[4]) is still much lower compared to daily euro-based transaction volumes spanning multi-trillion euros: it will therefore not be readily able to replace what is lost from the Brexit fallout.

London's role as the leading global "FinTech" centre might also come into question should young entrepreneurs and start-ups decide to shift their businesses elsewhere in a post-exit scenario—looking at other places such as Berlin, Paris or Amsterdam, further impacting the City's dominance among the financial capitals of the world.

18.3   Potential Exit Scenarios and Implications on UK-Based Financial Institutions

Brexit's extent of implications on UK-based financial services institutions will depend largely on the type and scope of the eventual Exit scenario agreed between the UK and the EU. The UK Prime Minister Theresa

May announced during her speech laying out her Brexit plan that the UK might lose access to the Single Market at the end of the negotiations but that "her aim would be the greatest possible access to EU markets through a comprehensive free trade agreement" (Independent 2017). Given these circumstances, the spectrum of impact level might range from a less probable "high access/low disruption" model to a more likely "low access/ high disruption" one, depending also on the financial firms' existing business models and cost bases (Fig. 18.3).

Best-Case Scenario:

- UK's access to Single Market and EU passport is maintained through full regulatory equivalence although UK is outside the European Economic Area (EEA).
- UK needs to negotiate new arrangements with the EU in a number of legislative areas such as the Capital Requirements Directive (CRD), where no regulatory equivalence currently exists.[5]
- Under this best-case scenario, we expect minimum level of disruption to existing operating models and organisational structures of financial services firms; however, some revenue loss due to worsened economic conditions and additional cost requirements resulting from regulatory adjustments might transpire.

Base-Case Scenario:

- UK becomes a "third country" with no single market access and passporting rights. UK receives equivalence across single market directives and regulations where regulatory equivalence is already established.
- Bilateral agreements are reached with the EU member states to retain access where possible (e.g. in specialty insurance).

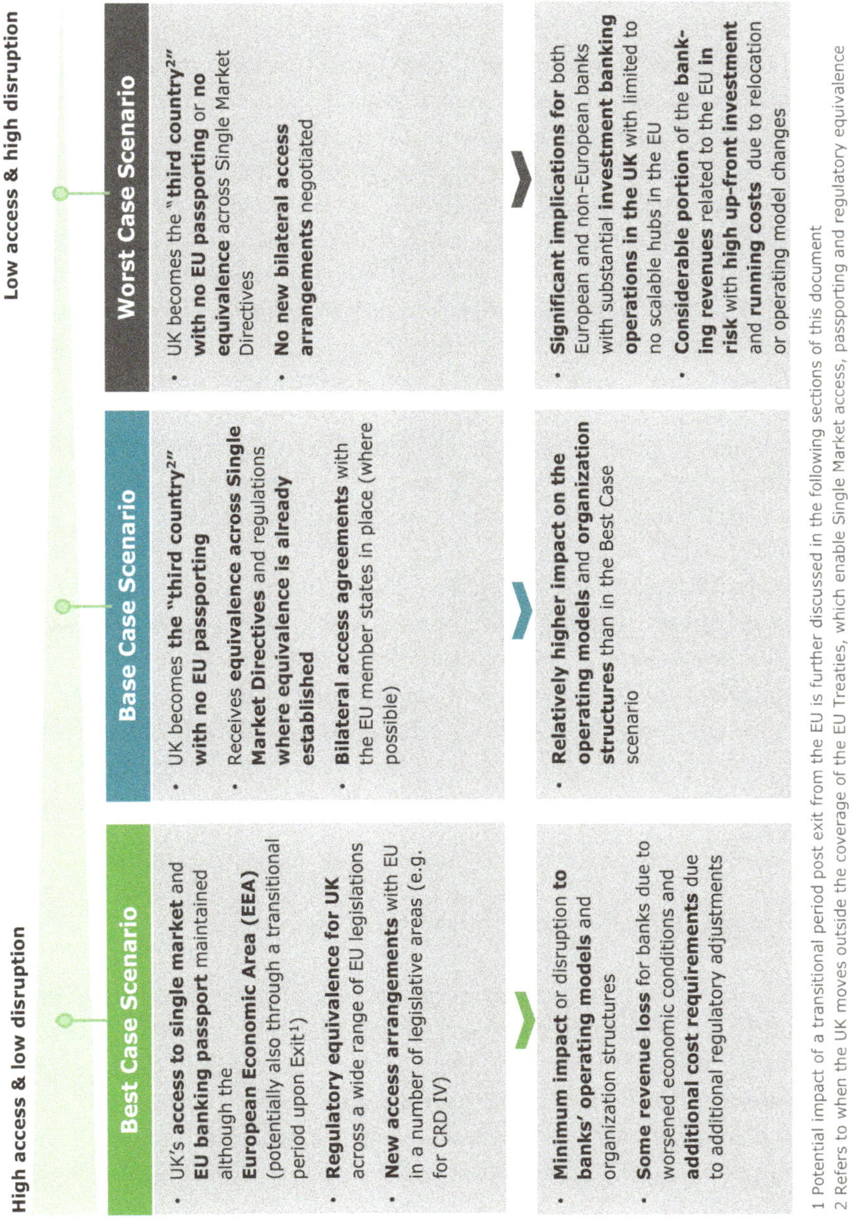

High access & low disruption

Low access & high disruption

Best Case Scenario

- UK's **access to single market and EU banking passport** maintained although the **European Economic Area (EEA)** (potentially also through a transitional period upon Exit[1])
- **Regulatory equivalence for UK** across a wide range of EU legislations
- **New access arrangements** with EU in a number of legislative areas (e.g. for CRD IV)

- **Minimum impact** or disruption **to** banks' operating models and organization structures
- **Some revenue loss** for banks due to worsened economic conditions and **additional cost requirements** due to additional regulatory adjustments

Base Case Scenario

- UK becomes the "**third country**[2]" **with no EU passporting**
- Receives **equivalence across Single Market Directives** and regulations **where equivalence is already established**
- **Bilateral access agreements** with the EU member states in place (where possible)

- **Relatively higher impact on the** operating models and organization structures than in the Best Case scenario

Worst Case Scenario

- UK becomes the "**third country**[2]" **with no EU passporting** or **no equivalence** across Single Market Directives
- **No new bilateral access arrangements** negotiated

- **Significant implications for** both European and non-European banks with substantial **investment banking operations in the UK** with limited to no scalable hubs in the EU
- **Considerable portion of the banking revenues** related to the EU **in risk** with **high up-front investment** and **running costs** due to relocation or operating model changes

1 Potential impact of a transitional period post exit from the EU is further discussed in the following sections of this document
2 Refers to when the UK moves outside the coverage of the EU Treaties, which enable Single Market access, passporting and regulatory equivalence

Fig. 18.3 Spectrum of Brexit implications (Monger et al. 2016)

Worst-Case Scenario:

- UK becomes a "third country" with no EU passporting rights or equivalence across the single market directives, and no new bilateral access arrangements are negotiated or put in place.
- This scenario would bring the highest level of disruption to financial services firms that depend on their UK entities to access the EU market. Should this case transpire, considerable portion of the revenues related to EU businesses are at risk with significant investment costs to be endured due to the relocation needed and the required operating model changes.
- In this scenario, UK-based banks and asset managers would not be able to serve to EU clients from their UK hubs, and unless bilateral agreements are reached with the individual member states, UK insurers and brokers would not be allowed to sell to the EU clients, thus leading such firms to relocate their operations outside of the UK.

Under the aforementioned scenarios, the organisations which would be impacted the most are going to be non-European (universal/investment) banks with no or limited existing hubs (operations) in the EU. On the other hand, for the UK banks serving predominantly UK customers, impacts on their operating models or organisations will likely be minimal.

Below, we present a brief overview of Brexit's potential impacts on different types of financial institutions, starting with universal and/or investment banks.

UK Universal Bank Serving Mainly UK Customers:

- Brexit is likely to have downward pressure impact on both the retail and corporate banking's revenue growth due to worsened economic conditions and consumer confidence in the UK economy (2018 earnings forecasts for the UK banks have already been cut by 12–27% due to lower loan growth and higher loan losses). And corporate banking revenue pools are likely to shrink in line with declining lending and payment volumes.

- Investment banking revenues might also be negatively impacted with ROEs continuing to be under pressure and falling. However, the performance of banks will vary largely based on their business and product mix. For instance, increased volatility might positively affect FX and rate trading, whereas in asset management, potential reduction in AUMs might lead to decrease in related revenues.
- Although we expect a minimum level of impact on this type of organisations by Brexit, certain investment banking operations, especially EU-denominated trading and clearing, might need to be moved to separate entities within the EU.
- In this scenario, banks that do not currently have separate EU-based entities might need to set up such entities and/or subsidiaries in the EU. As a result, transfer of both certain operations and people from the City to the EU-based centres might be required. For instance, one of the leading global UK banks, HSBC, has stated it might consider moving some EU-related operations and approximately 1000 people of its workforce from London to their Paris office.

European or International Investment Bank with Established Operations in the EU:

- UK's exit from the EU will likely have similar macroeconomic consequences and downward growth pressure for these banks due to worsened economic conditions both in the UK and across the EU, with European banks feeling the pain harder than their international counterparts that have less exposure to the European markets.
- The level of impact on these banks will vary depending on the scenario. Specifically, EU-denominated trading and clearing activities might need to be moved out of the UK if passporting rights are lost as a result of the Exit agreement.
- The banks that currently operate through "branches" in the UK might require additional capital for their UK businesses (e.g. Deutsche Bank). Such banks might need to convert their current legal structures from branches to subsidiaries and/or start capitalising their UK operations separately if the UK leaves the Single Market.

- Some banks in this category might even consider to move some or all of their other non-EU-related operations out of the UK should they think that the remaining UK operations would not provide them with enough scale or growth opportunity in the post-exit UK economy.
- Such banks have already started assessing their existing activities and operating models in the UK to decide which parts of the business should be moved under the different Exit scenarios (e.g. Citigroup announced in November 2016 that they had started looking into scenarios of moving some of their staff to Frankfurt.)

Non-European/International Universal Bank with No Existing Operations in the EU:

- In addition to the macroeconomic impacts as described above for the other two categories, potential loss of passporting rights would be one of the highest concerns for these types of banks which solely use their UK entities to serve the EU clients.
- These institutions would need to establish separate, capitalised subsidiaries (or branches) in the EU to access the European market, negatively impacting the banks' cost bases and efficiencies of their capital/liquidity management.
- The impact on the banks' operating models would be high as they would need to decide which activities to be kept in the UK versus to be moved to the newly set-up EU entities, and start making investments to build up the necessary infrastructure, IT systems and support functions in their new EU operations.
- Banks will be likely to move euro-denominated trading, clearing and custody operations to the EU, splitting their sales and trading desks between the UK and the EU and entering into new custody agreements with the EU entities.
- They might also need to move some risk management and back-office/support functions and roles (e.g. roles in balance sheet management, capital management, IT) out to the EU-based entities.
- However, the end operating model of the banks will largely depend on the UK's Exit agreement terms. In case, for instance, the UK is pro-

vided with an equivalence status under the Markets in Financial Instruments Directive (MiFID2) (which is to come into force in early 2018), then the banks might not need separate EU-based entities to serve the institutional clients in the EU, eliminating the need to move such operations outside the UK.

Banks' decisions as to which parts of their UK operations should be moved to which EU location(s) will depend on five main factors directly relevant to their business and operating models:

- Business and product mixes, including asset classes (i.e. weight of corporate vs. investment banking; extent of EU vs. non-EU-related asset transactions in the businesses)
- Locations of clients and their requirements (i.e. weight of UK and international clients vs. European clients in the portfolios)
- Regulatory and legal considerations (i.e. availability of strong regulatory/legal frameworks, financial funding/investors, competition and employment laws, easiness of doing business and data privacy requirements in the selected location)
- Tax regimes (i.e. choosing locations with lower effectives tax rates)
- Businesses' scale opportunities (i.e. potential to quickly build up and expand operations in the selected location)

However, trading and clearing of euro-denominated assets might need to be moved regardless of the banks' current operating models, with euro equity derivatives, euro rates and credit trading most likely to move. Other asset groups, such as FX, which are exempt from cross-border regulations, are more likely to continue to be performed in the UK.

Depending on their target business models and strategies, banks might also consider moving their other non-euro-based asset operations (e.g. Debt Capital Markets or OTC derivatives) to the EU or their home territories to gain from economies of scale.

We present below a high-level view of asset classes that are more likely to move to the EU in the case of Exit from the Single Market, including the potential impact of these assets on banks' revenue pools (Fig. 18.4).

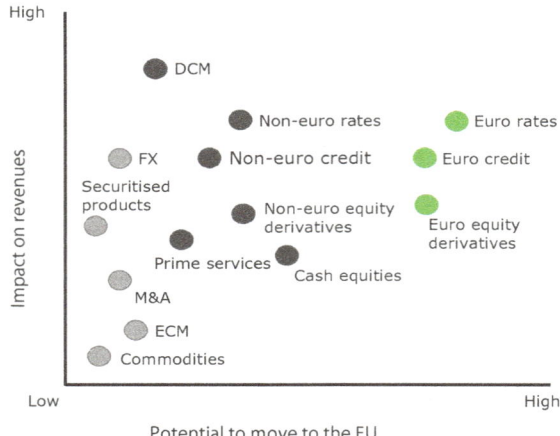

Fig. 18.4 Potential of move to the EU by asset class (Bubble sizes in the chart do not depict revenue sizes. Impact on revenues defined based on global revenue estimates of asset classes)

Brexit will have impacts not only on banks but also on a number of other UK-based financial institutions using passporting rights to access and serve the EU market. In the following section, we briefly summarise Brexit impacts on these organisations.

Asset Managers

Passporting rights will likely be an issue for asset managers. Although the UK might receive "equivalence" status under the Alternative Investment Fund Managers Directive (AIFMD), the UCITS Directive would require UK asset managers to establish an EEA-based gateway hub (i.e. domiciliation of funds in the EEA) in order to be able to serve and distribute to the EU clients.

Approximately €1 trillion of UCITS funds are currently domiciled in the UK, and among the asset managers based in the UK, only 54% are already domiciled in the rest of the EU. Therefore, we could expect some movement from the UK to the EU in this area in the post-exit world.

Impact on asset managers could be extended further as sales and trading (banking) activities migrate from the UK to the EU, causing some companies to start managing larger portions of their assets from their EU bases.

Hedge Funds

London is a leading financial centre for the global hedge funds. According to Preqin (a leading source of data and intelligence for the Alternative Assets industry), out of the 944 EU-based hedge funds it tracks, 590 (62%) are headquartered in the UK, managing a combined $500 billion of assets, compared with just $140 billion managed elsewhere in Europe (Reuters 2016).

Preqin's latest survey results as of November 2016 show that 24% of the UK-based hedge funds are uncertain about their prospects in the UK, and 6% are actively considering moving out of the UK in the event of a Brexit.

Market Infrastructure/Service Providers (e.g. Exchanges and CCPs)

Brexit and loss of passporting rights are likely to have impact on the market infrastructure organisations such as exchanges and clearing houses as well. Central counterparties (CCPs) are crucial for the settlement of securities and derivatives transactions, and thus, euro-denominated clearing houses such as LCH Clearnet might also need to move operations outside the UK (in this case, to Paris) or set up separately capitalised entities in the EU.

As clearing portfolios are more and more split across the UK and the EU, the cost of clearing in the UK might increase leading to inefficiencies and clearing operations moving out of the UK.

Payment Processors

If the UK leaves the Single Market at the end of the EU negotiations, banks in the UK could no longer be direct members of TARGET2 (payments system for the euro area). As a result, they might need to operate through subsidiaries within the EEA.

Corporate and Specialty Insurance

If the UK could not agree on bilateral agreements with the individual EU member states regarding the passporting rights of the insurance sector, the UK insurers and brokers might also need to move operations including underwriting, risk and portfolio management activities to the EU. The greatest impact, in that case, would be on Lloyds' of London.

18.4   Model Options Available for Banks (and Other Financial Institutions)

Given the ongoing uncertainty over the UK Government's Brexit plans and the proceeding Exit process to be followed with the EU states, banks and other financial institutions in the UK have already started assessing their strategic options and business models, considering near- and long-term implications and developing contingency plans. We expect banks to begin taking more concrete actions (i.e. moving certain operations) in case further clarity cannot be established in the near future. (At the time of this chapter being written, the UK Government was yet to present a White Paper outlining its detailed Exit plan strategies.)

In our view, a number of model options are available for banks and financial institutions, in general, in the light of Brexit. The "worst-case" scenario (as described in the earlier sections of this article) would amplify the challenges and risks for banks. However, we also believe that they could use this situation (period) as an opportunity to build more innovative, robust and effective business models that are more competitive in today's financial markets.

Strategic options available for banks will depend on the type of the organisation and will include the following main actions.

18.4.1   Non-European/International Universal Bank with No Existing Operations in the EU

This type of banks is likely to have three key strategic options to choose from, including:

• Setting up an EU-based legal entity (subsidiary) and moving EU-denominated operations to this entity;
• Moving EU-related operations to home countries [jurisdictions] (e.g. USA or Japan in the case of US and Japanese banks); and
• Scaling back the EU-related operations and focusing predominantly on the UK and/or international operations.

In order to set up a separately capitalised legal entity and move operations there, banks would need to deliver a number of activities which would require considerable time, energy and money:

a. **Selecting the new EU jurisdiction to relocate to:** The target jurisdiction will depend on a number of parameters such as the existing legal and regulatory framework, strength of laws, attractiveness of the tax regime, and financial, economic and geopolitical infrastructure present, in all of which London is currently best-in-class.

   However, many of the financial centres in Europe have already started trying to lure banks away from London in the wake of the referendum vote. For instance, it has recently been rumoured in the media that the German government is considering changing the labour laws to make Frankfurt more attractive for the banks looking to move their EU operations from the UK.

b. **Deciding on the legal entity structure:** Banks would need to set up separate legal entities in the EU should the UK lose access to the Single Market and the EU passporting rights. However, banks are likely to face with two different options as they decide on their target legal entity structures in the EU:

 i. Setting up an "Intermediate Holding Company (IHC)" which combines banking and broker—dealer businesses into a single subsidiary (as we see in the USA in the aftermath of the 2008–2009 financial crisis), and

 ii. Establishing a "subsidiary" including upgrading the current booking model and capitalising any existing structures (e.g. branches).

   Whichever option is chosen, implications on the capital, liquidity and compliance requirements will be significant for the banks.

c. **Obtaining regulatory approvals and bank licences in the new host jurisdictions:** As banks look to set up new entities in the EU jurisdictions, they would be required to receive approval for their internal capital and risk models (to calculate capital/liquidity requirements) and apply for a banking license in the chosen jurisdiction.

According to initial estimations, it might take banks two to three months to put a licence application together, and an additional six months to obtain an approval, making the whole process a rather lengthy and costly one.[6]

d. **Setting up the new infrastructure, IT systems, operations and corporate functions:** The new EU subsidiaries/entities would require headcount (both for the front and back office) and infrastructure including new systems and platforms, corporate and support functions including risk management, compliance and finance. All these would mean significant investment (capex) requirements and additional operating/administrative costs for the banks.

According to a recent study by the Boston Consulting Group (BCG), building new operations in the post-Brexit might cause such banks' operating costs to increase by up to 22% (Morel et al. 2016). Costs that banks would need to incur would include compensation and relocation packages for the transferring staff, and/or hiring expenses in the selected locations as well, having significant impacts on the profitability of the banks during the transition period. According to one estimate, it might cost banks about £50,000 per employee to relocate staff to the EU, making the totals banks need to endure just for staff relocation tens of millions of pounds (depending on the size of relocation that would be required).

e. **Hiring and training staff in the new location:** Given the potential high cost of moving staff from the UK to the EU (and risk of losing valuable and experienced human capital), banks might choose to hire for their EU operations directly in the selected jurisdictions/markets. In that case, selection of the location gains more importance as it would be preferable to be set up in a market with access to a strong pool of talent that is relatively cheaper than in the UK.

18.4.2   European or International Universal Bank with Existing Operations in the EU

The main strategic options available for the banks in this category are:

- Moving to EU hubs and scaling up their European operations, and
- Reassessing the whole UK operations to decide either to invest in or to scale back/retreat from the UK.

Banks would likely start with performing a review of their current UK operating models and identifying scope and extent of operations (activities) to be moved to their EU hubs.

One of the key actions these banks would need to take is developing new capital and risk models for their UK and EU entities, and planning for capital increases in both their EU and UK bases.

They would also require strengthening their EU hubs with additional headcount and infrastructure investment to handle the increased capacity and scope of activities in the EU operations. Their preparations would involve moving specific staff from the UK to their European hubs and/or hiring directly for the EU operations.

18.4.3   UK Universal Bank Serving Mainly UK Customers

The strategic options available for the banks in this category would be similar to the ones we describe above for European or International Banks with existing operations in the EU:

a. Setting up an EU legal entity or moving EU-related operations to the existing EU entities
b. Reassessing the UK operations to invest in, transform and/or innovate

Some of the UK banks in this category already have EU-based subsidiaries (or entities). Such banks will largely work on to identify the scope of operations to be moved to these entities and to enhance their existing infrastructure, operations and talent pool in the EU. Those banks that do not own readily established EU-based entities would first need to identify the jurisdiction to relocate to and the entity structure, and then plan in detail to obtain the necessary approvals in the new selected location to set up their EU-based operations.

In either case, a detailed review and restructuring of the UK operations would be crucial to adjust the remaining UK business to lower transaction volumes and lay the strong foundation for future growth (Fig. 18.5).

In spite of all the uncertainties and complexities, Brexit could offer opportunities for all banks (both in the UK and across the EU) to assess their current operating models and fully restructure their organisations to radically reduce costs and uncover previously untapped business potential. Using a "Zero-Based" approach to designing and rebuilding their organisations, banks could achieve much leaner and simpler models with lower cost bases that could better compete with nimbler emerging business models such as FinTechs.

Banks could also look to gain additional efficiencies through innovative models and cross-bank (cross-sector) collaborations, including use of industry utilities or activity pooling/platform sharing initiatives, significantly renewing the face of the European banking sector and making it more competitive against international (US) rivals. Leveraging such outsourced, collaborative models for non-core business processes (e.g. post-trade processing, KYC and client reference data) and duplicative operations could help reduce banks' cost bases significantly.

Brexit process could thus provide the sense of urgency to address such opportunity to build up a simpler, more effective and profitable European banking sector.

18.5   Transition Period to the Post-exit

Considering the complexity of the negotiations period awaiting the UK after the trigger of Article 50, defining the post-exit financial services sector and the specific sectoral regulations is likely to take time. Having a "transitional period" between the UK's formal exit from the EU and the implementation of the new terms and conditions would be crucial to ensure a smooth exit process for the financial services sector and to minimise the negative effects on the UK and the EU markets.

The importance of "transitional arrangements" in the Brexit process has also been announced publicly by Mark Carney, governor of the Bank of England, who "urged the UK Government to seek transitional arrangements with the 27 remaining members of the EU" (Financial Times 2016).

Although a prolonged Exit period (longer than the two years required by Article 50) might meet with some resistance among the "Brexiteers" in the UK, we think a "transitional period" would help banks and other financial institutions properly prepare for the post-Exit world, especially in case of a "low access/high disruption" scenario.

Bank type	Key strategic options	Key consideration points
A **Non-European or International Bank with no operations in the EU**	Set up an EU legal entity (subsidiary) and move EU-denominated operations to this entity Move EU-related operations to home country (e.g. US or Japan) Scale back in the EU and focus on the UK and international operations	• Select the new EU jurisdiction to relocate to • Decide on the legal entity structure (branch, subsidiary or holding) • Obtain regulatory approvals and bank licences in the new host jurisdiction(s) • Obtain approval for new capital and risk models from the regulators • Set up the new infrastructure, IT, operations • Move /hire and train staff in the new location
B **European or International Banks with existing EU hubs/operations**	Move to and scale up the EU operations Reassess the UK operations: Scale back /retreat from or invest in	• Identify scope and extent of operations to be moved to the EU hub • Plan for capital increase and management strategies for the UK and the EU entities • Obtain approval for new risk models • Build up the EU infrastructure and operations • Redefine the UK strategy and business/entity model; transform where needed
C **UK Banks serving EU clients from their UK bases**	Set up an EU legal entity and/or move EU-related operations to any existing EU hub Reassess the UK operations: Invest in, transform and/or innovate	• Select the EU jurisdiction to relocate the EU-related business to or set up a new entity • Decide/review the EU legal entity structure • Obtain regulatory approvals • Enhance the EU-based infrastructure, operations and talent pool • Review the UK business model and deliver cost transformation or growth initiatives

Fig. 18.5 Strategic model options available for banks

As stated by a number of officials and sectoral leaders (including Mr Carney), all new rules and trade deals use some sort of phasing-in to be implemented. For instance, Basel rules have been phased in over an eight-year period and the Vickers reforms over a four to six years period. Therefore, using such a transitional period, even if not as long as six years, but longer than the two years, would be beneficial not only for the UK and the UK-based financial sector, but also for the overall financial stability of the EU.

18.6   Conclusions

As our analysis shows, the impact of the UK's exit from the EU on the financial services companies and the City of London will largely depend on the type of Exit scenario reached between the UK and the EU. The spectrum of impact level will range from a less likely "high market access/low disruption" one where the UK maintains its access to Single Market and EU passporting rights (though, we see this scenario even less likely upon the recent announcements by Theresa May) to a more likely "low access/high disruption" one where the UK becomes a "third country" with no EU passporting rights or "equivalence" status under the single market directives.

A "high-access and low-disruption" scenario accompanied with a sensible transitional period would be the most beneficial option for the financial institutions. However, if the UK loses the passporting rights at the end of the EU negotiations, it might be inevitable that some business will be moved from London to the other emerging European or global financial centres such as Paris, Frankfurt, Amsterdam, Dublin or NY. Although both the UK Government and the City of London expect a modest amount of business loss due to the Brexit, up to £18–20 billion of revenues and 100,000 jobs might be moved out of the City in case of a "hard exit".

Certain single market directives such as MiFID2 could decrease the impact of the Brexit (and loss of business from the City) if the UK is given an equivalence status to the EU under this regulatory regime as this directive could allow non-EU firms to provide services to institutional clients within the EU without the need to have a local presence in the EU.

Given London's indisputable role as one of the world's leading financial capitals, and other European centres' relatively sub-scales and less developed infrastructures and regulatory frameworks, it is hard to see the City losing its reign in the financial services sector altogether. However, it is likely that with the move of some business (especially, euro-denominated trading and clearing) to other financial centres, the UK could lose economies of scale and doing business in the City might get more expensive.

We do not foresee any of the other European financial centres taking the place of London in the aftermath of Brexit, considering their sub-scales and less interconnectedness with the global trade world. Therefore, the consequences of the Brexit should be of concern for the EU banking sector as a whole, and not just the UK.

Considering the higher costs, lower profitability and diversion of management attention Brexit would bring to the sector, we advise financial institutions to carefully assess their strategic options during the process, and be smart to take full advantage of the situation to build innovative, robust and more efficient business models.

Brexit could offer a valuable opportunity for both the UK and EU-based institutions to perform a full restructuring of their organisations including streamlining operations, digitalising end-to-end processes and using industry utilities or cross-bank activity-pooling/platform sharing initiatives to radically transform their businesses, and the European banking system.

Glossary

AIFMD   Alternative Investment Fund Managers Directive
Article 50   Article 50 sets out the procedure by which a Member State can leave the EU
AUM   Assets under management
CCP   Central counter-party, also known as a clearing house
CRD   Capital Requirements Directive
EEA   European Economic Area
EMIR   European Market Infrastructure Regulation
Equivalence   Provisions in certain pieces of EU legislation allow market access to firms from non-EEA countries judged to have an equivalent regulatory and supervisory regime to the EU

EU	European Union
FX	Foreign exchange
KYC	Know Your Customer
MiFID	Markets in Financial Instruments Directive
OTC	Over the Counter. Refers securities traded outside a formal exchange
Passporting	The right for a firm registered in the EEA to do business in any other EEA state without needing further authorisation
ROE	Return on equity
UCITS	Undertakings for the Collective Investment of Transferable Securities

Notes

1. European banks using "passport" services to access the UK market.
2. Increasing to 2.2 million if jobs in supporting/ancillary services are included.
3. Citigroup also has a separately capitalised subsidiary in Dublin.
4. Daily volumes of overall renminbi trading reached US$61.5 billion in 2014, according to the City of London.
5. Investment banks obtain passport under CRDIV and investment firms under MiFID2.
6. The period to get an approval for the banking licence for retail banks might be even longer (circa nine months).

References

Giles, C. 2016. Mark Carney Urges Transitional Brexit Deal. *Financial Times*, November 27.

Irwin, G. 2015. Brexit: The Impact on the UK and the EU. *Global Counsel*, pp. 20–21.

Jenkins, P. 2016. The City of London Faces Up to the Future Beyond Brexit. *Financial Times*, October 4.

Lockett, H. 2016. UK Becomes Second-Largest Rmb Clearing Centre. *Financial Times*, April 28.

Merrick, R. 2017. Theresa May Says Brexit Deal Cannot Mean Membership of Single Market. *Independent*, January 17.

Monger, T., P. Morel, O. Sampieri, Y. Senant, and B. Wade. 2016. *What Brexit Means for Financial Institutions*, The Boston Consulting Group, August.

More British Hedge Funds Say Nay Have to Move After Brexit. *Reuters*, December 9, 2016.

Morel, P., C. Teschner, D. Martin, W. Rhode, and A. Bohn. 2016. *Global Capital Markets 2016: The Value Migration (Part 2) – Assessing the Impact of Brexit*. Bethesda: The Boston Consulting Group.

Sants, H., M. Austen, L. Maylor, P. Hunt, and D. Kelly. 2016. *The Impact of the UK's Exit from the EU on the UK-Based Financial Services Sector*. Oliver Wyman for the CityUK.

The Authority of the House of Lords. 2016. *Brexit: Financial Services*, European Union Committee 9th Report of Session 2016–17.

TheCityUK. 2016a. *Brexit and the Industry*, the CityUK Member Briefing, September.

———. 2016b. *Key Facts About the UK as an International Financial Centre*, November.

Index[1]

[1]Note: Page numbers followed by 'n' refers to note.

© The Author(s) 2017
N. da Costa Cabral et al. (eds.), *After Brexit*,
https://doi.org/10.1007/978-3-319-66670-9

421

Lightning Source UK Ltd.
Milton Keynes UK
UKHW05n1245090318
318984UK00008B/8/P

9 783319 666693